Peace Research

'This is a book by one of Europe's best peace researchers. It spans a distinguished career of theory, empirical research, and practice, showing how social scientists can inform policy, and vice-versa, and all those who hope to reduce violence in this world.'

Professor Bruce Russett, *Yale University, USA*

Comprising essays by Peter Wallensteen, this book presents an overview of the thematic development of peace research, which has become one of the most dynamic and innovative areas of war and conflict studies.

Peace research began in the 1950s, when centres were formed in the USA and Europe, and today there are research institutes and departments on every continent, with teaching and research programmes in most countries, and peace researchers contribute to the development of international studies, development research and security analysis. Professor Wallensteen has been a witness to much of this since forming the Department of Peace and Conflict Research at Uppsala University in the late 1960s, and this book brings together thirteen of his articles with five new essays in one volume.

The book presents articles on such key issues in peace research as the causes of war, conflict data, conflict diplomacy, non-violent sanctions and third-party diplomacy. In this way, it demonstrates how basic research can be conducted in fields often seen as 'unresearchable' and 'too complicated to deal with'. This volume shows that it is a matter of developing definitions, creating valid measures and finding ways of collecting information, recognising that innovations of this kind require supportive research environments. Furthermore, the results are useful not only for the growth of research activity itself, but for finding ways of dealing with actual conflicts. Thus, attention is also paid here to conflict prevention, peace agreements, sanctions and third-party activity for preventing and ending armed conflict, and building a lasting post-war peace.

This book will be of great interest to all students of peace studies, conflict resolution, war and conflict studies, development studies and international relations/security studies in general.

Peter Wallensteen holds the Dag Hammarskjöld Chair of Peace and Conflict Research at Uppsala University, Sweden, and is the Richard G. Starmann Sr. Professor of Peace Studies at the Kroc Institute, University of Notre Dame, USA. He leads the Uppsala Conflict Data Program and a program on sanctions. He is author of many papers and articles, as well as several books, including *Understanding Conflict Resolution* (3rd edn, 2011), a leading textbook.

Routledge Studies in Peace and Conflict Resolution

Series Editors: Tom Woodhouse and Oliver Ramsbotham
University of Bradford

Political Discourse and Conflict Resolution
Debating peace in Northern Ireland
Edited by Katy Hayward and Catherine O'Donnell

Economic Assistance and Conflict Transformation
Peacebuilding in Northern Ireland
Sean Byrne

Liberal Peacebuilding and Global Governance
Beyond the metropolis
David Roberts

A Post-Liberal Peace
Oliver P. Richmond

Peace Research

Theory and practice

Peter Wallensteen

*To my dear friend, Bob,
for many years shared
in the pursuit of making
peace a serious topic for
research and for political change
Kohë Are, Sep 6, 2011
Peter*

Routledge
Taylor & Francis Group

LONDON AND NEW YORK

First published 2011
by Routledge
2 Park Square, Milton Park, Abingdon, Oxon OX14 4RN

Simultaneously published in the USA and Canada
by Routledge
711 Third Avenue, New York, NY 10017

Routledge is an imprint of the Taylor & Francis Group, an informa business

British Library Cataloguing in Publication Data
A catalogue record for this book is available from the British Library

Library of Congress Cataloging-in-Publication Data
Wallensteen, Peter, 1945-
Peace research : theory and practice / Peter Wallensteen.
p. cm.
Includes bibliographical references.
1. Peace–Research. 2. Conflict management–Research. I. Title.
JZ5534.W35 2011
303.6'6--dc22
2011000779

ISBN13: 978-0-415-58088-5 (hbk)
ISBN13: 978-0-415-58089-2 (pbk)
ISBN13: 978-0-203-80896-2 (ebk)

Typeset in Baskerville by Prepress Projects Ltd, Perth, UK

Printed and bound in Great Britain by
TJ International Ltd, Padstow, Cornwall

Dedicated

to

Etta, Aron, Morris, Nina and Tage

Contents

Figures and boxes

Figures

Boxes

Tables

Preface

This book reflects the journey of one peace researcher by presenting themes and issues of significance in peace research. It reproduces thirteen articles and book chapters, some updated through 2010, as well as five new essays adding context and a contemporary perspective. In short, it attempts to portray a researcher's intellectual evolution without being a personal story.

The book emphasizes the importance of the work environment – a milieu conducive to advances in scholarly study. Thus, one section of this volume focuses on the creation of the Department of Peace and Conflict Research at Uppsala University and the role of its education and training programs while another section presents the emergence of the Uppsala Conflict Data Program (UCDP) – now a world-leading provider of conflict data.

Causes of war and efforts to peaceful conflict resolution are central to peace research – and UCDP – hence, these issues take two sections of this volume.

In addition, a section demonstrates ways in which peace research can relate to international policymaking, for instance through sanctions research (the so-called SPITS project). A final section shows the utility of what might be called applied peace research and direct action by peace researchers in the form of mediation and academic diplomacy.

Research is about not only individual ideas and achievements but also creative cooperation. Peace research at Uppsala University clearly demonstrates this. The department would not be where it stands today without contributions by its faculty and staff: Mats Hammarström, Kjell-Åke Nordquist, Erik Noreen, Thomas Ohlson and Anna Norrman, among many others.

Of course international influences and inspiration from prominent researchers and personalities at different, significant junctures have been of utmost importance: Johan Galtung and Bruce Russett (1960s), Ingrid Segerstedt-Wiberg, Alva Myrdal and Maj-Britt Theorin (1970s), J. David Singer and Jimmy Carter (1980s), J. Ann Tickner, Hayward Alker, Ted R. Gurr and I. William Zartman (1990s), Anna Lindh and Jan Eliasson (2000s). The relationship with Nordic colleagues, notably Helge Hveem, Nils Petter Gleditsch, Sverre Lodgaard, Raimo Väyrynen and Håkan Wiberg, has been particularly stimulating, all, wittingly or not, contributing to this book and the journey it portrays.

My wife, Lena has been a judicious advisor, skilful supporter and source of inspiration, and Bill Montross has continually read and improved on the author's use of the English language.

This book is dedicated to my five grandchildren.

Peter Wallensteen

Uppsala and Notre Dame, December 2010

Acknowledgements

The following chapters in this volume reproduce with permission, in whole or in part, the following articles and chapters, by the author, alone or co-authored (as indicated):

Ch. 2: Bengt Gustafsson, Lars Rydén, Gunnar Tibell and Peter Wallensteen, 'The Uppsala Code of Ethics for Scientists', *Journal of Peace Research*, Vol. 21 (4): 311–316, 1984.

Ch. 4 and Ch. 5: 'Incompatibility, Confrontation and War: Four Models and Three Historical Systems, 1816–1976,' *Journal of Peace Research*, Vol. 18 (1): 57–90, 1981.

Ch. 6: 'Universalism vs. Particularism: On the Limits of Major Power Order', *Journal of Peace Research*, Vol. 21 (3): 243–257, 1984.

Ch. 7: 'Global Governance: The UN between P1, G2 and A New Global Society', in Dag Klackenberg (ed.), *En diplomatins hantverkare: Vänbok till Jan Eliasson*, Stockholm: Atlantis, pp. 133–147, 2010.

Ch. 9: 'The Uppsala Conflict Data Program 1978–2003', in Mikael Eriksson (ed.), *States in Armed Conflict, 2002*, Uppsala Publishing House and Uppsala University: Department of Peace and Conflict Research, pp. 11–31, 2004.

Ch. 10: Peter Wallensteen and Frida Möller, *Conflict Prevention: Methodology for Knowing the Unknown*, Uppsala Conflict Data Program, Report No. 7, Uppsala University: Department of Peace and Conflict Research, 2004.

Ch. 11: Lotta Harbom, Stina Högbladh and Peter Wallensteen, 'Armed Conflict and Peace Agreements', *Journal of Peace Research*, Vol. 43 (5): 617–631, 2006.

Ch. 12: 'Dag Hammarskjöld and the Psychology of Conflict Diplomacy', in Tommy Gärling, Gunnel Backenroth-Ohsako and Bo Ekehammar (eds.), *Diplomacy and Psychology: Prevention of Armed Conflict after the Cold War*, Singapore: Marshall Cavendish, pp. 15–42, 2006.

Ch. 14: *A Century of Economic Sanctions: A Field Revisited*, Uppsala Peace Research Papers No. 1, Uppsala University: Department of Peace and Conflict Research, 2000.

Ch. 15: Peter Wallensteen, Mikael Eriksson and Daniel Strandow, *Sanctions for Conflict Prevention and Peacebuilding: Lessons Learned from Côte d'Ivoire and Liberia*, Uppsala University: Department of Peace and Conflict Research, 2006.

Ch. 17: 'The Strengths and Limits of Academic Diplomacy: The Case of Bougainville', in Karin Aggestam and Magnus Jerneck (eds.), *Diplomacy in Theory and Practice*, Malmö, Sweden: Liber, pp. 258–281, 2009.

Ch. 18: 'An Experiment in Academic Diplomacy: The Middle East Seminar', in Jørgen Johansen and John Y. Jones (eds.) *Experiments in Peace: Festschrift for Johan Galtung 80 Years*, Oxford: Fahamu Books and Pambazuka Press, 2010. Revised and translated from 'Seminariet som akademisk diplomati', in Kaj Falkman, Maud Kronberg, Peter Landelius and Lars Vargö (eds.), *Plikten och äventyret: Upplevelse av diplomati*, Stockholm: Carlssons, pp. 247–256, 2008.

Part I

Making peace researchable

1 Making peace researchable

Making peace researchable

The fundamental idea of peace research was to make peace researchable. This would generate lessons from history and provide benchmarks for courses that could lead to peace and away from war. It would give research a voice in the pursuit of peace policies, but on a basis of accumulated knowledge with the use of modern scholarly methods. "Peace," in other words, would become as research-able as was already the case for "health," "economic growth," or "democracy," all relevant goals to be achieved by society. "Peace" was no different from other problems society faced, many initially deemed to be age-old and "normal" until they had been problematized, were open for systematic thinking, and, thus, could be acted on.

However, it was still no small task to attempt to put "peace" on the national and international research agenda. Such studies could easily be seen as political and normative. There were also interested actors and institutions which regarded this field as their exclusive domain. Other would see peace as part of security, defense, and even industrial activity. The topics to be made researchable were, however, more general and not immediately directed toward particular actors or national policies. The story of how peace research emerged following a series of globally experienced traumas – large-scale, unanticipated human-made calami-ties – is a longer one. It is sufficient is to say that World Wars I and II, the atomic bombs on Hiroshima and Nagasaki, the dangers of the Cold War, the destructive Vietnam War, the genocides of the 1990s, and September 11, 2001, all pointed to the importance of developing peace strategies. In particular this would have to be action based on historical realities and with an ambition to lead toward more durable conditions of peace (Wallensteen 2011). This was a broader agenda of research than what was pursued in particular institutes or university disciplines at the time.

Still, there was a clear focus. The first and still primary concern for peace research is to find ways to prevent the onset of war and identify ways to solve disputes peacefully. After World War I it was a matter of preventing another world war. After World War II, the chief interest was in preventing a nuclear war. It could come about from direct crises between the two sides of the Cold

War or through the escalation of wars in the Third World. Since the end of the Cold War, the focus has been on the prevention of internal war, sometimes with regional or global repercussions (civil wars, terrorism, regional wars, genocides and other forms of mass killing). Prevention has to be based on an understanding of the causes of conflict and war. Over the years, the agenda has been enlarged with respect to the core theme of causes of war and conflict resolution. There are now a large number of possible causes and impacts of war, ranging from gender to climate change (Wallensteen 2001, 2011; Pim *et al.* 2010).

The peace research agenda has always been large and this affects the question of how to make peace researchable. The idea that has turned out to be highly productive is to develop a milieu in which the issues of peace are central. A shared concern stimulates thinking, generates ideas, and provides quality control. It would also make peace researchers professional and proud of this profession. Research at leading institutions, notably in Britain and the United States, was then – and still is – highly individualistic. The individual researcher runs his or her projects, interacts with colleagues, but has a focus on his/her career. Remarkably, many leading universities did not have milieus specifically devoted to peace studies, or even security issues, in the 1950s and 1960s. Researchers with a peace concern were found in a diverse set of departments, notably in political science, history, sociology, education, and psychology.

Furthermore, when thinking about the possibility of being relevant for this large problem of "peace" and "war" more concerted action is required. Creating a milieu would not be enough. The research problem has to be *more narrowly focused*. Modern research requires more precision. Methodological developments have made it possible to ask more exact questions. Data collection has provided more advanced resources for locating information. However, focusing the research problems more narrowly also means that not all milieus can deal with all issues. There will be some issues that are not attended to or deliberately left out from a particular institution or milieu. This is necessary to progress toward good-quality work. In fact, it means stimulating a *division of labor*. Some milieus will have to deal with some problems, other milieus with others. For instance, there have always been local agendas for peace research (such as a particular conflict, or a particular national security issue), not only general and global issues. This is logical, as research has to respond also to the concerns of the surrounding society. Such concerns also promote a division of work, but without isolating one milieu from the rest. There is a need for *creating and maintaining networks*, exchanges, and an informal way of jointly guiding research so as to cover the peace agenda as completely as possible. However, strict coordination is not acceptable in peace research, or in any other science.

Another way to say this is that the components of peace have to be disaggregated into researchable elements. Optimistically put, at the time of the beginning of peace research it was thought to mean that a minimum of five or six leading scholars would get together and jointly and deliberately create a milieu with a specific focus. It would be some time before this happened, and this chapter tells the story of the milieu that emerged at Uppsala University, Uppsala, Sweden. It is not primarily an exercise in history but a way to illustrate possibilities and possibly provide some inspiration. It is not the only one that has emerged, of course. There is also the School of Peace Studies at Bradford University in Britain and the Kroc Institute of International Peace Studies at the University of Notre Dame in the USA. Others exist under different headings but with a focus that substantially is "peace" (e.g., at Stanford, George Mason, Yale, Columbia, and New York universities). However, these efforts have been parallel to the Scandinavian story to be told in this chapter.

Making peace research milieus

Peace research came to Sweden in the middle of the 1960s. In 1966 a first seminar was set up in Uppsala, run by the university extension service (Kursverksamheten). It engaged younger PhD candidates and undergraduate students as well as teachers and professors. The first theme of inquiry was into nonviolent means, notably sanctions, an issue we will return to in Part IV of this volume. Whether and how to use sanctions was a central issue in the debate on how a small, neutral country could relate to international concerns, particularly those having to do with developing countries. At the same time similar seminars were formed at Göteborg and Lund universities with their own foci. The inspiration for setting up milieus of peace research was the Peace Research Institute in Oslo (PRIO). It was founded in 1959, and a decade later Johan Galtung's theory weeks – for a number of years run in the cold Nordic month of January – became an attractive "must-attend" event that generated considerable learning and inspiration. A number of young people who later became formative for peace research in the Scandinavian countries were participants as students and junior researchers at these seminars (Nils Petter Gleditsch, Raimo Väyrynen, Håkan Wiberg, Herman Schmid, to name just a few). Many remained in peace research; others took up careers as activists, publicists, or administrators (Wiberg 2010).

The small group from Uppsala returned with ideas of working for something that would be parallel to what it had experienced. PRIO worked as a milieu in line with how peace could be made researchable. The different elements of the institute's agenda – at least in Galtung's presentations – appeared to be closely connected in a coherent framework of relevance for peace.

However, the visits to PRIO also gave rise to the observation that peace research milieus in the early 1970s largely resided outside the universities. Institutions such as PRIO, as well as SIPRI (Stockholm International Peace Research Institute) and TAPRI (Tampere Peace Research Institute, in Finland), were foundations or special units. They had limited connections to regular teaching and, for instance, SIPRI did not directly recruit students or PhD candidates. Only a few academic courses were offered. These institutes also had large shares of their funding from government ministries. They were vulnerable to political fluctuations, as was soon witnessed in Denmark, where one peace research institute was closed down, only to reemerge in a new shape, and again suffering the same fate in the early 2000s. The author of this chapter drew the conclusion that peace research has to reside *within* the universities in order to be more protected from political pressures but also because it would become stronger qualitatively when building directly on young, aspiring researchers. The challenge from research colleagues as well as from students would help to make peace research a solid discipline that could stand up to the demands of specialization. The arguments for this seemed strong; there was considerable receptivity among students and some researchers for this. Still, reaching the goal turned out to be more difficult than expected.

There was also a need in find a particular focus for a new milieu of peace research. As some institutes already existed, why would there be a need for peace research also within the universities? Like peace research activities elsewhere, the efforts in Sweden had to relate to specific Swedish concerns. The government supported the creation of a peace research institute, based in Stockholm, with international recruitment: SIPRI. It began its operations in 1966 and had a strong focus on roads to decommissioning of nuclear and other weapons of mass destruction. The first chair of the board was Ms. Alva Myrdal, Cabinet Minister for Disarmament and deeply involved in the international nuclear disarmament negotiations. Disarmament issues received considerable attention in the 1960s and 1970s. Myrdal was supportive of having peace research at universities. In her view it would be a way to reach younger generations about the urgency to stop the ongoing nuclear arms race. However, that argument would not be enough to convince skeptics within academia of the need for more peace research. SIPRI may have illustrated the utility of such a focused research milieu for public policy, even in the field of international affairs, but was there really a field of inquiry based on theory and methods that could be taught to students?

Making peace research academic

The challenge was to develop a peace research field also from an academic point of view. It required a concern for theoretical development and empirical testing. The department in Uppsala originated as an informal seminar drawing together students, PhD candidates, and faculty members who were concerned about the need for peace and the university's role.[1] In 1971, the national government created three assistant professor positions at Swedish universities (Uppsala, Lund, and Göteborg). This gave some stability to the existing seminars. In Uppsala and Göteborg the focus was not only on research, but also on developing an educational program at undergraduate level. The courses quickly filled up and the students became an active pressure group for more research and teaching on global affairs from a peace perspective. There was a demand for academic teaching. Research projects were developed. In Uppsala, issues of causes of war, connections between disarmament and development, and matters of global militarization drew interest. This showed that there were relevant issues that were not taken up by SIPRI, nor were they part of traditional defense and security studies. It demonstrated that there were researchable issues waiting to be studied.

The most significant breakthrough was the creation of a peace research chair named after Dag Hammarskjöld, the Swedish UN Secretary-General. A bill was passed unanimously in the Parliament in his honor twenty years after his untimely death on a peace mission. That decision, in turn, was based on a national plan for developing peace research at Swedish universities, proposed by the Minister of Education. This proposal stemmed from five different parliamentary motions in 1979, from four different political parties, together having a majority and cutting across political divisions. The fact that active milieus existed and had demonstrated the fertility of the field encouraged the minister and the MPs to move ahead in order to stimulate, as it was phrased, broader research and teaching on security and peace.

At the time, a university chair was normally coupled to a PhD program. Thus, this decision would mean the creation of a new basis for the ambition of developing a peace research milieu. This was the beginning of the development of a professional discipline with a strong standing in the research community and at the same time of practical relevance. The parliament had created something new. The national plan, furthermore, included a second chair, based at Göteborg University. The possibilities seemed many and encouraging.

Making peace research at Uppsala University

A new chair for research and teaching was, of course, always welcome at a university. It meant new resources. However, such opportunities are of interest to many and the peace researchers were a small group. They did not have a department of comparable strength to their support, and, indeed, they were new at the power games that go on within universities. For leading spokespersons of political science, well trained in such business, it would, seemingly, not be difficult to turn the chair into one of political science, rather than allowing a new milieu to emerge. A major battle followed, taking place not only within the university but also in national media, in the parliament, and in government ministries. It was a painful period, but in the end the idea of creating a new research tradition prevailed. The present author was appointed as the first holder of the Dag Hammarskjöld chair in peace and conflict research in January 1985. In a follow-up decision by the Board of the Social Science Faculty, a PhD program in peace and conflict research was to start by January 1986. A vision was beginning to take material form.

This meant having to develop a full department from the bits and pieces that existed. There were negative experiences to learn from at the time. The Department of Social Anthropology was regarded as politically radical, but its critics could not close it on that ground. The ethos of academic freedom would be violated. However, the department did not manage its finances properly. It ran into debt, and decisions by the department's leadership could not salvage the situation. The department's position became vulnerable. There were administrative motives for intervention from higher levels. The existing department was terminated, and new one was created with a different agenda. A similar fate also befell the small department of peace research at Lund University.

From such experiences it was clear that the key to survival and progress for a new unit in the university system were four. They continue to be generally valid:

1 *Protect the basic idea!* It is necessary for a milieu to rule itself as much as possible and use its autonomy to develop the idea of being a place where the study of peace is the central concern, not something on the margin of other activities. This means independence vis-à-vis other departments, but also from the outside world. Integrity is important in all directions. Integrity provides the necessary respect for the milieu. It also means to resist all ideas of amalgamation into larger units, however well argued in terms of benefits of scale they may be. Research thrives where the researchers have control, participate in decisions, and are fully informed on the conditions of their works. The rule of thumb seems to be: the larger the unit, the less influence and empowerment of the researchers.

2 *Achieve the highest standards of competence!* This is necessary for teaching and research. It is the main route for recruiting talented young people. Particularly important is to have an independent PhD program, and to run it in such a way that its output (in the form of articles, dissertations, and post-doctoral works) is methodologically respected. The best ambassadors of any department are its students, but its future growth rests on its PhD candidates and young PhDs. This means, for a department, promoting and protecting competence, by generating innovative research grants and filling tenured positions after open scrutiny. Furthermore, the highest quality of research is likely to result from a cooperative environment, rather than one marked by rivalry and competition.

3 *Keep the department's accounts in order!* Know where the money comes from and where it is going, and make sure it follows established rules. This requires an administrative staff that acts like hawks to avoid debts. It requires a leadership that promotes applications for external funding. It means struggling with higher levels of the university to get the attention and priority a dynamic department is entitled to. Factors 1 and 2 together are likely to attract external funding, but revenue is only one aspect. Expenditures have also to be closely monitored. It is important to make sure that grants are spent in correct ways and are properly reported on, thus providing the safest basis for the long-term development of a milieu.

4 *Gain international recognition!* A good measure of whether or not a particular milieu has achieved necessary focus and quality is its international standing. Thus, developing international relations within the field is important. It strengthens a department's position within the university. It also makes it attractive as a place of scholarship and for resources, thus affecting the other factors.

These are administrative principles, and for the new full-fledged Department of Peace and Conflict Research at Uppsala University they became the cornerstones for what was to follow.[2]

Making peace research synergetic

The first efforts focused on building the PhD program and recruiting interested young researchers.[3] However, it was also important to establish a continuous flow of students at undergraduate and master levels.[4]

Thus, a parallel task was to develop a teaching program from the university entrance level to the level from which strong candidates could apply to the PhD program. For a period of time, the department introduced a new course almost every year. In the early 1990s there was a structure in place making it possible for a competent student to begin in peace and conflict studies on the A level (freshman level, in US parlance) and continue to D level (master), from which an application could be made to the PhD program. By the mid-1990s, the bulk of the PhD program consisted of students recruited from within the department. It meant building a strong foundation, while still allowing for students from other fields and with other backgrounds to enter the program. Thus, competence in teaching as well as in the doctoral research became high. Dissertations became of increasingly higher quality, often benefiting from students having the experience of presenting work at international fora such as the International Studies Association.[5] The Swedish tradition of public dissertation defense made it possible to check the quality by inviting international well-known scholars to be external examiners (opponents) and/or part of the dissertation grading committee (*betygsnämnd*).

This was further manifested by the presence of international scholars in the department, dealing with international conflict issues from a theoretical and empirical perspective. Some were invited to become honorary doctors (Johan Galtung, J. Ann Tickner, Bruce Russett), visiting researchers (Hayward Alker, Ted R. Gurr, Barbara Harff, Daniel Druckman), or participants in particular conferences. As part of making the department known it was possible to organize a series of Executive Seminars during the 1990s, often with high-level external funding and participation of ministers as well as leading scholars. These meetings could also be used to connect PhD candidates to the established international scholars (J. David Singer, I. William Zartman, among many others). This further stimulated research in relevant fields.

The resulting program of activities, thus, became highly focused, in line with factor 1 above. A large part of the department's activities dealt with causes of conflict, conflict dynamics, and conflict resolution. This guided the educational programs, it stimulated international invitations, and it worked in consonance with a research agenda dealing with conflict and conflict developments. The Uppsala Conflict Data Program (UCDP) emerged in parallel with this development, a story that is told in Chapter 9 in this volume.[6] The interaction between UCDP and the other elements of the department is an example of synergetic relations. PhD candidates could work with UCDP for a period of time; master students and young MAs were particularly well suited for collecting data on conflict. By 2010, this had developed into a self-reinforcing system, in which many PhDs actually had spent periods of their academic life in UCDP as assistants or project leaders and then returned to it with new projects, thus keeping UCDP alert to new developments in research and methodology.

In 1988 an annual international program was started on conflict resolution, providing the department with international connections in ways not seen before. It was based on funding from Swedish development assistance.[7] Not only did this allow for inviting promising young scholars from Third World countries, it also gave resources to invite international scholars as teachers in the program. Its focus on conflict resolution, furthermore, helped to sharpen the department's interest in this particular area.

It also attracted international attention to the department as a resource not only in research and teaching but also in practice. One result was the academic diplomacy exemplified in Part V of this book. Another was the development of long-term relations with Swedish diplomats, notably Jan Eliasson, for a period of time also Swedish Minister for Foreign Affairs, starting with his teaching in the international program. He as well as UN Secretary-General Kofi Annan were awarded honorary doctorates by Uppsala University.

International interest in the department emerged in the late 1980s. A first manifestation was the connection to the Carter Center in Atlanta, which for a series of years published the data from UCDP. This resulted in President Carter's participation in a student panel at Uppsala University in 2002, following his visit to Oslo to receive the Nobel Peace Prize. He was one in a series of high-level visitors to Uppsala, many also occurring in the framework of the annual Dag Hammarskjöld lectures that were initiated in the mid-1990s, bringing international political personalities to Uppsala. This demonstrated the department's significance for the university's image in society at large.[8]

There has also emerged a strong interest from others to cooperate with the department. There is a close relationship with PRIO, the Peace Research Institute in Oslo. Many researchers from the department are involved in the boards of leading scholarly journals, notably *Journal of Peace Research* (JPR).[9] There is continuous cooperation with SIPRI. In recent years, agreements have been made with Accord in Durban, South Africa, and with the Kroc Institute, University of Notre Dame, USA. Young researchers have been appointed at Otago University, Dunedin, New Zealand, while keeping ties to Uppsala.[10] This all testifies to an international standing that would have been hard to imagine when the idea of such a milieu was first formulated in the 1970s.

Thus, by 2010 the department was making peace research that drew attention. The four factors interacted in a way to make the milieu highly synergetic. There was a clear purpose for the department to which the researchers could connect, there was documented high quality in its output, its economy rested on external funding but was in balance, and it had a strong international standing. Was it also doing something for peace?

Making peace research for peacemaking

The milieu had become a department, the department had a strong reputation, but what could it do for peace? One more basis for relevance was to be concerned with how to engage in affairs outside the university. The Uppsala Code of Ethics for researchers, reproduced in Chapter 2, was the result of deliberations on such issues within Uppsala University in the early 1980s. It still remains valid. It states that the researchers should be careful in making sure their research does not have a harmful effect on society. This serves as a strong reminder not only on humility but also of dangers. Ethical concerns have to be voiced throughout the research enterprise. If research aims at affecting the world, this is even more important.

The Uppsala experience suggests at least four areas in which its research actually may have a direct impact. They all build on the fact that the research is seen as solid and the milieu exhibits the key factors mentioned above: that it is independent from all interests other than the pursuit of academic interest; has high competence; is run effectively; and is internationally recognized.

On this basis the department became involved in activities that have to do with disarmament issues (particularly in the 1980s, not recently), conflict prevention (as exemplified by the executive seminars mentioned in above, largely an activity of the 1990s), sanctions research (from the early 2000s, elaborated on in Part IV), and academic diplomacy (throughout the period; events since 1990 are described in Part V). The impact can be debated. Certainly, the department has been a meeting place for opposing sides. Its research has helped clarify issues. Direct involvements in political processes are more difficult to evaluate. There is an interest in engaging the researchers, but when and to what extent will vary with developments in politics and society. At certain junctures its research becomes relevant; in many other instances it may be below the political horizon. The public agenda is not set by the researchers. Nor should it be. However, with a strong empirical foundation, peace research is relevant and ready to contribute, when asked to do so.

Notes

1 Bo Wirmark put together the first seminar; Professors Ulf Himmelstrand and Stefan Björklund were the senior scholars on the board.

2 I was the head of department from the inception of the department as a unit (1972) until 1999, operating on these principles with the support of Anna Norrman.

3 The first two PhD candidates in peace and conflict research defended their dissertations in 1992 (Ramses Amer and Kjell-Åke Nordquist).

4 There were several directors of studies involved in this, notably Kjell-Åke Nordquist, Erik Noreen, and the pedagogically talented Mats Hammarström.

5 Mats Hammarström took over from me, becoming the department's first Director of Doctoral Studies in the late 1990s. He instituted a number of innovations that refreshed the program and gave it the academic strength it now has.

6 The starting date is 1979, but the present wide scope of activities emerged in the early 2000s.

7 There has been a series of directors since I initiated the program, originally termed PACS (Peace and Conflict Studies, focusing on Conflict Resolution), later TOPS (Top Level Seminar on Peace and Security). Kjell-Åke Nordquist and Thomas Ohlson have been particularly associated with this. Thomas Ohlson has energetically elaborated on this program and involved a new generation of teachers.

8 Following an international scientific evaluation, Uppsala University in 2008 specified peace, democracy, and human rights as one of its five profile areas.

9 An example is Mats Hammarström, who became Associate Editor of JPR, as has Magnus Öberg.

10   The program with Accord builds on the efforts by Thomas Ohlson, Kristine Höglund, and others; the cooperation with the Kroc Institute partly rests on a grant from the National Science Foundation to Erik Melander; and the Otago connection is pursued by Isak Svensson and Karen Brounéus.

References

Pim, Joám Evans, Herbert C. Kelman, Chadwick F. Alger, Nigel J. Young and Zahid Shahab Ahmed. 2010. 'Peace research', in Nigel Young (ed.), *The Oxford International Encyclopedia of Peace*. Oxford: Oxford University Press.

Wallensteen, Peter. 2001. *The Growing Peace Research Agenda*, Occasional Paper 21, OP 4, Joan B. Kroc Institute for International Peace Studies, University of Notre Dame, Indiana, USA.

Wallensteen, Peter. 2011. 'The origins of contemporary peace research', in Höglund, Kristine and Magnus Öberg (eds.), *Understanding Peace Research*. London: Routledge.

Wiberg, Håkan. 2010. 'Nordic peace research', in Nigel Young (ed.), *The Oxford International Encyclopedia of Peace*. Oxford: Oxford University Press.

2   The Uppsala code of ethics for scientists[1]

Bengt Gustafsson, Lars Rydén, Gunnar Tibell and Peter Wallensteen

Ethical problems in research

What can we do to stop the armament race and promote peace? In particular, what can we scientists do? The obvious risk of nuclear disaster makes it necessary for any scientist to scrutinize his/her own resources, and to try new unconventional ways to contribute to global disarmament and a reasonable future. One of these resources is the scientist's own personal appreciation of right and wrong, that is, our ethics. In the following we shall describe an attempt to mobilize this resource in order to affect the choice of research field and application of research.

At Uppsala University a small group of scientists has met regularly since 1981 to penetrate ethical problems of research. The variety of disciplines represented (natural sciences, medicine, social sciences, technology, law, theology) has greatly contributed to making the meetings fruitful. From an early stage, the seminar has attempted to formulate a code of ethics for scientists. A first proposal for such a code was circulated in late 1982 and, based on the debate that followed, the seminar published a final version of the code in early 1984 (see Box 2.1).

Box 2.1 Code of ethics for scientists

Scientific research is an indispensable activity of great significance to mankind – for our description and understanding of the world, our material conditions, social life, and welfare. Research can contribute to solving the great problems facing humanity, such as the threat of nuclear war, damage to the environment, and the uneven distribution of the Earth's resources. In addition, scientific research is justified and valuable as a pure quest for knowledge, and it should be pursued in a free exchange of methods and findings. Yet research can also, both directly and indirectly, aggravate the problems of mankind.

This code of ethics for scientists has been formulated as a response to a concern about the applications and consequences of scientific research. In particular it appears that the potential hazards deriving from modern technological warfare are so overwhelming that it is doubtful whether it is ethically defensible for scientists to lend any support to weapons development.

The code is intended for the individual scientist; it is primarily he or she who shall assess the consequences of his/her own research. Such an assessment is always difficult to make, and may not infrequently be impossible. Scientists do not as a rule have control over either research results or their application, or even in many cases over the planning of their work. Nevertheless this must not prevent the individual scientist from making a sincere attempt to continually judge the possible consequences of his/her research, to make these judgements known, and to refrain from such research as he/she deems to be unethical.

In this connection the following should particularly be considered:

1 Research shall be so directed that its applications and other consequences do not cause significant ecological damage.
2 Research shall be so directed that its consequences do not render it more difficult for present and future generations to lead a secure existence. Scientific efforts shall therefore not aim at applications or skills for use in war or oppression. Nor shall research be so directed that its consequences conflict with basic human rights as expressed in international agreements on civic, political, economic, social and cultural rights.
3 The scientist has a special responsibility to assess carefully the consequences of his/her research, and to make them public.
4 Scientists who form the judgement that the research which they are conducting or participating in is in conflict with this code, shall discontinue such research, and publicly state the reasons for their judgement. Such judgements shall take into consideration both the probability and the gravity of the negative consequences involved.

It is of urgent importance that the scientific community support colleagues who find themselves forced to discontinue their research for the reasons given in this code.

N.B. The code consists of both the introductory text and the four points. We shall be grateful if, in any publication, the four points are not separated from their context.

Uppsala, Sweden (January 1984)

As scientists involved in this endeavour, we would like to present the code and discuss some questions of principle that have been repeatedly raised in the seminar within Uppsala University, in the media, and in discussions with colleagues internationally (Gustafsson 1984; Tibell 1984).

First, however, let us make clear that, to our knowledge, there exists no similar code of ethics for scientists. Obviously, there are a number of codes or similar statements concerning the ethics of research; they can probably be counted in the hundreds (Rydén 1984). None of them seems to correspond directly to the aims of the Uppsala seminar. The great majority of statements are research guidelines, that is, they refer to the ethics of conducting research, for instance the use of human subjects in medical research. An early example is the Nuremberg Code, prompted by the use of science in Nazi Germany (Mappes and Zembaty 1981). There are also codes of ethics or of conduct within professional associations. Mostly such codes refer to the professional in question and his/her relations to clients, for instance the Hippocratic oath, which deals with the relationship between doctors and patients. In a few cases, a paragraph or a sentence in the preamble concerns the relationship between the professional and society at large. The statements are usually very general, such as 'Members should use their knowledge and skill for the advancement of human welfare' (Chalk *et al.* 1980; see also *Bulletin of Peace Proposals* 1975). Similar statements are found in proposed codes that have been published, for instance, in the general sections of interdisciplinary journals. In the work of the Uppsala seminar such general statements have not been found very useful. A code should give some details about the responsibility of the scientist and some advice on how to act when an ethical dilemma arises.

It is worth noting that we have not found a single code mentioning the ethical aspects of weapons development. The reason might be understood from the experience of one of the working groups of Pugwash, meeting in Varna in 1978. Some members suggested that scientists should, in principle, refuse to work in military research, or even stop working in basic research that might one day have military significance. The proposal was not adopted since some military research was considered necessary for defensive purposes and because in some cases basic research has important peaceful applications (Rotblat 1984). Such remarks give some essentials of the arguments against a code restricting the development of weapons.

The responsibility of scientists

The idea that an individual is responsible for the (long-term) consequences of his/her actions as a basis for moral judgement has gained wide acceptance. However, the Uppsala code of ethics goes beyond that. It rests upon the idea that the scientist is, at least to some extent, responsible for how his/her findings are put to use in society – by others. This view seems to be shared by many scientists (e.g. Hård af Segerstad 1984; Tibell 1984), although others keep to the more classical view that freedom of research is unduly hindered if individual scientists should take the possible consequences of their research into consideration.

An important objection to requiring such a responsibility is the difficulty involved in judging the consequences of research. The situation is different in basic and applied research, but even in the latter case it may often be impossible to foresee the consequences within, say, ten years after the research has been carried out.

Sometimes, however, important practical consequences become apparent quite soon after a discovery has been made in basic research. As an example one could mention the applications of the fission reaction discovered in 1938 by Hahn and

Strassmann and published in *Naturwissenschaften* in early 1939. Only a few months later a French team, led by Frederic Joliot-Curie, found that in the process several neutrons were emitted, thus making a chain reaction possible. In a surprisingly short time these two discoveries led to the construction of the first nuclear reactor, in 1942, by Fermi and his collaborators. In another three years, the first nuclear bombs were made and detonated over Hiroshima and Nagasaki.

It is not likely that Hahn and Strassmann could foresee this development. Even Niels Bohr in 1939 gave 'fifteen weighty reasons why, in his opinion, practical exploitation of the fission process would be improbable' (Jungk 1958). If we go back another twenty to thirty years, Rutherford, the father of nuclear physics, is said to have mentioned that he believed that nothing of practical value would ever come out of his research (Kapitsa in Tibell 1984). One must remember, however, that the military goal would not have been reached in such a short time without the enormous concentration of brains and money in the lavishly supported Manhattan project.

To mention another area, medical research, it is conceivable that a scientist working, for instance, on diagnostic methods can predict that ethical dilemmas will appear for doctors and patients quite soon after a new method has been introduced. Just as was the case in the application of the fission reaction, so in the medical field, once the scientific efforts have reached the applied stage, it may happen that research will go on in parallel with discussions on the moral consequences.

The Uppsala code assumes that scientists have a responsibility and that they should attempt to estimate the practical consequences of their research.

The Uppsala code has a number of additional features that we would like to comment on:

1   The code is intended for the individual scientist.
2   The code specifically addresses questions of ecology and war.
3   The code is largely based on negative formulations of the type 'thou shalt not . . .'
4   The code explicitly specifies actions to be taken in case of ethically doubtful research, notably the duty to inform.

Individual responsibility

There are several reasons for confining the code to use by the individual scientist only. We consider the ethical dilemmas that the code addresses to be personal ones; they are matters of conscience. If the code were adopted by a university or a similar authority, it would fall into the category of laws enforced by governmental bodies. The individual scientist would no longer have the same obligation to take a personal stand. It would all be done *for* him/her, not *by* him/her. We ourselves do not feel competent to judge whether other people are unethical or not. Also, if judgements were to be made in court-like proceedings, details regarding the ethical rules would have to be worked out, which certainly would require considerable efforts. Finally, it would be a complicated process for any organization to adopt a code of ethics of this kind. An interesting example is the discussion at the University of Michigan, where an entire procedure was outlined for the scrutiny of research applications in order to restrict military-related research. The proposal gained considerable support within the university but was ultimately turned down by the Board of Regents (see, inter alia, Report of the Research Policy Committee 1983). The individual researcher is, at least in principle, free to disengage himself/herself from such research at any time.

Ecology and war

It is necessary to spell out some implications for research in two fields of particular importance. First, there are the ecological consequences. It very soon became evident in our discussions that the ethics of ecological consequences is a question of judgement. All research may have at least some ecological consequence for our environment. Which of these effects should be considered ethically acceptable? In most people's opinion it is not immoral per se to endanger the existence of a species, a life form. The extinction of the smallpox virus (which has been accomplished except for some frozen samples) was carried out with the help of science, and is probably beneficial for everyone except the virus. The extinction of the malaria parasite would certainly be considered a great accomplishment, if ever realized. We finally decided to suggest a formulation ('. . . do not cause significant ecological damage') that leaves most of the burden of judgement to the individual.

The most controversial statement in the code concerns research for war preparations. However, this has been at the heart of the seminar's concern from the beginning. We agree with J.D. Bernal's statement that for scientists:

> the application of science to war is the worst prostitution of their profession. More than anything else the question of science and war has made scientists look beyond the field of their own inquiries and discoveries to the social uses to which these discoveries are put.
>
> (Bernal 1967: 186)

However, everyone wants to live in an autonomous or free country and as a consequence most people, whether scientists or not, consider armed defence necessary. If this is a higher value than that of not contributing to war, it may be immoral not to give the national defence the best possibilities and conduct research to achieve that. Our point is that the relative priorities of these two values should be affected by the fact that the world now has come to the brink of a globally destructive war. In the present situation additional armaments seem to enhance insecurity rather than promote security. If so, the situation prompts a discussion on finding solutions to achieve overriding aims (such as human survival) as well as questions of ethics.

Even if most scientists were to accept military research as such, their personal attitude to this activity would probably be ethically balanced. For instance, for ethical reasons, most researchers would abstain from developing chemical and biological weapons, even if these were to be very 'useful' for defending their own country in a war. Likewise many scientists would agree that further addition of nuclear weapons or new space weapons is not in the interest of their country (regardless what country), whereas there was a near-consensus on the necessity of developing the first atom bomb. One way to codify a balanced attitude to military research would be to differentiate between defensive and offensive wars. However, we have not found a simple way of doing this. It is not obvious what constitutes an offensive war or what could become such a war. Nor is it clear what would be a defensive weapon or if such weapons contribute to making our world more secure (Jervis 1978). The recently initiated debate on defensive force structures might, however, also result in new ways of making a distinction between offensive and defensive of relevance for the scientists' dilemma (see *Journal of Peace Research* 1984).

The seminar has chosen to retain in the code a paragraph regarding war, but again leaves the burden of judgement to the individual. Owing to the gravity of the global situation our formulation ('. . . scientific efforts shall not aim at applications or skills for use in war') is rather categorical, but it may suggest that some aggressive intent has to be involved.

Negative or positive code?

A frequent reaction to the code has been that positive rules would be preferable: a code should state what scientists should do rather than what they should not. The seminar has, however, decided against positive formulations for several reasons. The fundamental one is that science is usually not driven by ethical convictions or rules. Rather, it is the autonomous search for knowledge and abilities that motivates research. The major part of research might not have identifiable ethical consequences, such as developing a new theory in mathematics or physics. What is required is a specification of the limits of scientific activity, not proposals to direct it. Furthermore, positive formulations that have been suggested seem to encounter many difficulties. Such is true for Hutton's recent proposal, which, having stated in positive terms what scientists should do, also includes the phrase 'scientists shall boycott the work on developments that seem to have negative consequences for man' (Hutton 1983). It seems more complicated to adhere to a positive code, and certainly such implications as suggested do have far-reaching consequences for all academic activity. A possibility would be to mix positive and negative formulations, as in a proposal from a Pugwash group meeting in Oxford 1972: 'I will not use my scientific training for any purpose which I believe is intended to harm human beings. I shall strive for peace, justice, freedom and the betterment of the human conditions' (Rotblat 1984).[2] The mixture, however, does not solve any of the problems.

Duty to inform

When a scientist finds his/her own work unethical he/she should interrupt it. The Uppsala code, however, also requires that the decision and the reason for it should be made public. Although a considerable fraction of the world's scientists work in situations where their work is secret, it is interesting to note that this requirement of the code has met with almost unanimous approval. Scientists in East and West have stated that they have special responsibilities to inform about research results, make them understandable to a wider public, and also explain their consequences (Hutton 1983; Tibell 1984). An instructive demonstration of how this could work out in practice was provided by the recombinant DNA case. The discovery of the possibility of artificial gene transfer from any organism to bacteria was made in 1972. It was followed by a moratorium of several years on major uses of this technique and a prolonged public debate. A lesson to be learned is that a public debate needs an informed public and that considerable efforts are needed to convey the important facts to the layman. Certainly, this also applies to other areas such as the nuclear arms issues.

Our aim in publishing the code of ethics is twofold. First, of course, we hope that it will be useful to many individual scientists as a guide, stimulating critical appreciation of their own activities, and as a support in case some of these are ethically unacceptable. Second, we hope that it will contribute to the debate on the roles of science and scientists in our world. Perhaps these roles should be changed, as one of many changes that are necessary if we want to create a more satisfactory world.

Notes

1 Several of the studies carried out by the Seminar on Ethics in the Sciences have received support from a grant made available by the Swedish Department of Foreign Affairs in connection with the work of the United Nations Expert Group on Military Research and Development.
2 The first sentence was proposed by Professor Harald Wergeland, Trondheim, as a suggestion for a pledge to be adopted by scientists.

References

Bernal, John D. 1967. *The Social Functions of Science.* Cambridge, MA: The MIT Press.
Bulletin of Peace Proposals 1975, no. 2.
Chalk, R., M. S. Frankl and S. B. Chafer. 1980. *AAAS Professional Ethics Project.* Washington, DC: American Association for the Advancement of Science.
Gustafsson, Bengt. 1984. *The Uppsala Code of Ethics for Scientists: Discussing and Working on the Code of Ethics, 1983–1984.* Seminar on Ethics in the Sciences, Uppsala University.
Hutton, D. R. 1983. 'The Peace Education Role of Scientists and Technologists', paper presented to the Seminar on Peace, Science and Technology, UN University, Tokyo.
Hård af Segerstad, Peder. 1984. *Research and Ethics: An Investigation of Swedish Researcher Attitudes to Issues of Research Ethics.* Seminar on Ethics in the Sciences, Uppsala University.
Jervis, Robert. 1978. 'Cooperation under the Security Dilemma', *World Politics*, 30 (2): 167–214.
Journal of Peace Research 1984, no. 2. Special Issue on Alternative Defense.
Jungk, Robert. 1958. *Brighter than a Thousand Stars.* New York: Harcourt & Brace.
Mappes, T. A. and Zembaty, J. S. (eds.). 1981. *Biomedical Ethics.* New York: McGraw-Hill.
Report of the Research Policy Committee. 1983. *Review of Non-Classified Research.* Ann Arbor: University of Michigan, 9 March.

Rotblat, Joseph. 1984. *Digest of Pugwash Discussions Relating to Working Group 6: Public Opinion and Arms Control*, for the 34th Pugwash Annual Conference, Björkliden, Sweden.

Rydén, Lars. 1984. *Ethical Rules in Basic and Applied Research.* Seminar on Ethics in the Sciences, Uppsala University.

Tibell, Gunnar. 1984. *Ten Interviews with Scientists on Research and Ethics.* Seminar on Ethics in the Sciences, Uppsala University.

Part II

Knowing war – understanding history

3 War in peace research

Knowing war

Understanding causes of war and finding remedies to their seemingly constant recurrence is a central theme in peace research. Central in most definitions of peace is the absence of war. This implies a hope for a world without war. This topic was firmly put on the agenda by the First World War and was further reinforced by the experiences of the Second World War and the dangers of the Cold War. The number of armed conflicts has refused to come close to the zero level. The vision may be widely shared, but the ways to reach the goal remain unclear and without global agreement, whether in politics or in academia. There are organizations in place with this as a major purpose. The United Nations was created to achieve this goal, and it has been used increasingly since the end of the Cold War. But it still is far from dealing with all conflicts, and those on its table often remain elusive to lasting peacemaking. A different approach is to develop relations which are not dominated by the immediate fear of war. This is exemplified by the European Union. Its ambition is to bring countries together through integration, interdependence, shared values and a willingness to acknowledge past suffering. On many scores it may be more successful than the UN, but this experience is limited to those that are within the Union or aspire to enter it.

The purpose of the systematic study of war was to arrive at conclusions for the policies to prevent recurrence, point to routes that should be avoided and possibly suggest constructive actions of peacebuilding. In this research tradition, the Correlates of War (COW) project, originating at the University of Michigan and led by J. David Singer and Melvin Small, was seminal. It initiated a system study of war that hitherto had often been the domain of speculation and opinion, rather than of theory, logics and empirical testing.

The focus of COW was particularly relevant during the Cold War, but this was also a period when there was less receptivity to academic prescriptions that included thinking outside the norms established by global tensions. COW's data collection continues, led by Paul Diehl, John Vasquez and others. It is fundamental, and has now been followed up, in a period in which the concern is not only with inter-state conflict but also with internal wars (Sarkees and Wayman 2010). The COW data can be used for many purposes; the primary one so far has been to establish general patterns – correlates – that could be seen as causes of war. Some may be closer to the original intention of testing different realist theories (Vasquez 2000). Others have used the data for studies that included dimensions other than power and weaponry, such as democracy, interrelationships and international organization (Russett and Oneal 2001). Indeed, the finding that democratic states rarely fight each other in war, the 'democratic peace', has become one of the most quoted results based on COW data.

The focus has remained on war, although no longer on world wars, major power wars or even inter-state wars, but on civil wars and terrorism. This evolution of research interest closely corresponds to the political agenda, of course. This means that research that today may appear 'academic' may again acquire stronger meaning as global conditions change. Still, some discernible constants can be seen in the thinking about wars, whatever their specific type.

The debate on the causes of conflict remains wide-ranging and is often subsumed under very general headings such as 'liberal' versus 'realist'. There are many different ways of making inferences from such labels. In Chapter 4 a contribution is reproduced assembling thinking on the causes of war into four basic categories: *Realpolitik*, *Geopolitik*, *Idealpolitik* and *Kapitalpolitik*. This typology attempts to bring together thoughts about the way major power relations are structured. When organizing thinking in such categories, it is also possible to establish which theories have had the most scholarly attention. For instance, the Correlates of War project was largely concerned with *Realpolitik* thinking (alliances, military expenditures, military capabilities etc.) as a reservoir of hypotheses on war. In that sense, many of the theories that were tested with COW data were close to the political dilemmas in the days of the Cold War: Was NATO useful for the USA and for peace? Should military expenditures be increased, for instance with more nuclear weapons to maintain peace? What were the dangers of arms races?

This means that understandings of geography and territory were mostly on the sidelines, only to forcefully be put on the agenda by Vasquez (1995). He could quickly demonstrate that this perspective was equally valid. Territory may seem invariable, but indeed there were variations in both control and perceptions of its value. Thus there was again room for *Geopolitik* scholarly thinking and perspectives. What came out of the work by Vasquez was probably closer to decision-making discussions in Europe and Asia, which all lived with major powers close to their borders.

However, matters of political systems and ideologies – the matters that belong to the *Idealpolitik* domain – were not originally part of the COW programme. Studies seemed to show that democratic states were as much involved in wars as were non-democratic (Maoz and Abdolali 1989). As we just mentioned, this dimension was energized in the post-Cold War period, captured by the eye-catching phrase of a 'democratic peace'. Russett could demonstrate that it seemed to matter what type of regimes were in conflict with one another, that is, the dyadic element was important; this meant focusing on the relations between states (e.g. one democratic state versus another), not just on their attributes. It was a statistical demonstration that *Idealpolitik* matters, also seen in Maoz and Abdolali (1989). This was a theme already in the present author's PhD dissertation in 1973 (partly done with Bruce Russett at Yale University in 1969). The work of Russett (1993) as well as Maoz (Maoz and Russett 1993) formed the discussion on inter-state conflict. Hegre and colleagues (2001) also took up the issue of the democratic peace in internal armed conflict. This in turn has led to a debate on the importance of democratization, for both inter- and intra-state conflict (Russett 2005). Thus, international affairs are no longer analysed simply in terms of *Realpolitik* considerations.

However, the fourth notion, the one of *Kapitalpolitik*, remained under-studied. In the Cold War period it received almost no attention in mainstream work, apart from theories that discussed capabilities and possible connections to power transitions (Gilpin 1981). It was, however, important in the Marxist literature, although seldom operationalized, in ways that could be tested and thus be potentially refutable. It may never have made a strong impact on leading American scholarship, but was influential in the rest of the world, in spite of poor underpinnings with modern methods. The present author's dissertation (Wallensteen 1973) was an attempt to demonstrate the utility of such approaches, but also their limitations. Galtung, by then, had already published his work on structural violence, which also had an empirical application ('A Structural Theory of Imperialism', 1971, which remains one of his most quoted articles). A grandiose attempt to integrate such perspectives into a new way of writing world history is the world system approach, initiated in the 1970s and primarily championed by Immanuel Wallerstein (1974).

However, since the end of the Cold War – and the demise of official Marxism, remarkably – *Kapitalpolitik* notions have gained more prominence. As just noted, Russett's work included studies on trade. However, the *Kapitalpolitik* approach by Galtung and Marxists was also concerned with who would benefit from the trade, not just the fact that there was trade. The possibility of trade being exploitative was central. This focused on whether interactions were generating more spin-off effects for one than for the other (who might even suffer negative spin-offs). The new idea of 'Capitalist Peace' (Weede 2005; Gartzke 2007), that capital markets are integrated and make cooperation more feasible, is thus intriguing. It seems to have convincing empirical support, even to the point at which one author argues that this is also what drives democratic peace (Gartzke 2007), in other words basic economics underpins *Idealpolitik*. It is, however, a perspective that emphasizes integration more than exploitation.

The idea of capitalist peace is so far only applied to inter-state relations, but there are parallel investigations which point to the role of economic dependencies in intra-state wars as well (Collier 2007, 2009). It comes closer to the idea of unequal gains, particularly as it connects to matters such as governance, corruption, access to arms and availability of exploitable resources. In scholarly discourse it has often been summed up as 'greed'. This concept makes the issue more a matter of personal desire than necessarily is the case. These theories are more structural in their basic assumptions.

This means that today the four schools are getting attention (although few researchers try to cover all of them at the same time) to arrive at some conclusions of their comparative strengths. The various controls in the quantitative studies of inter-state democratic peace attempt to cover alternative explanations, but then have to rely on available indicators, which may or may not cover the original intent of the various schools of thought. Chapter 5 in this volume is an early attempt to carry out the task of applying indicators representing all four types of thinking. The results give a stronger role to *Idealpolitik* than has normally been the case and, perhaps, point towards the democratic peace notion. They also show that *Kapitalpolitik* considerations generate considerable disputes and confrontation, but that they rarely escalate into war. However, they find a role for *Geopolitik* as well as *Realpolitik*. These notions continue to be helpful in organizing ideas and findings, primarily for inter-state relations (see Wallensteen 2002, 2007, 2011).

Reducing the plurality of thinking of war to only four schools appears preposterous today. There are at least four other clusters that deserve the label of paradigms: feminist thinking, ecopolitics, ethnographic perspectives and humanism ('psychologism') would make for new ideas of how to understand relations between societies and humans. In particular, notions such as 'equal peace' are more important, bringing attention to the gender effects of war and peace (Tickner 1992; Caprioli 2005; Olsson 2009). Issues of climate-induced conflict have generated a series of investigations, particularly of low-level conflicts (Nordås and Gleditsch 2007; Salehyan 2008). Ethnopolitical cleavages have also been given attention with the use of statistical analysis (Melander 1999; Fearon and Laitin 2003), whereas psychological factors still remain limited in their use for decision-making in war situations (Winter 2004). This opens up our thinking for many other ways to study the causes of war. It remains to demonstrate these additional perspectives more fully.

Still the thoughts on different schools and issues as important for understanding peace and war laid the ground for the Uppsala Conflict Data Program (UCDP) (see more in Chapter 8). In this programme the particular notion of an incompatibility is central. This refers to a fundamental disagreement as basic for why disputes would escalate to war. The author's work in the early 1980s (Chapters 5 and 6) demonstrated empirically that territory and governance were significant variables. The connections to these schools of thought also made clear that there were strong theoretical reasons for this. Thus, as incompatibilities, they became significant in UCDP. Relating back to the study in Chapter 5, two incompatibilities became part of the definition of an armed conflict: conflicts over government and over territory. Later research (see Part III) shows that this was also important for peace agreements; the pattern of agreements and their durability varies with respect to the incompatibility.

War and historical change

The COW data now cover almost two centuries. This is unique and should stimulate research on trends and causes. The data can also be used to write history in a more systematic way, something that has not yet been attempted. Chapter 4 is not only a way of working on the four theoretical frameworks, it also provides for dividing the world into a series of consecutive systems, based primarily on the number of major powers. Systems thinking was (and is) basic to COW and corresponds also to a practitioner's understanding of why some things are comparable and others are not. The systems emerging from COW definitions as well as published results are identified in Chapter 4 as a Euro-centric system from 1816 to 1895, an interregional system from 1896 to 1944 and a global system since 1945. The basis for the distinction was the number of major powers, as defined by COW. Chapters 5 and 6 apply the distinctions, with some further specifications in Chapter 6, seeing more changes in shorter periods. These chapters were written in the early 1980s, and they require updating. The COW data have been revised since then, for instance, but no such work is done in these chapters for this volume. However, here it can be useful to provide some reflections, building on what has happened in the world as well as within the COW project. This can be related to Chapters 4, 5 and 6.

In the latest iteration, the COW project has introduced two new major powers from 1990 (Sarkees and Wayman 2010: 34–36). These are Germany (reunited in 1990 to again have the full resources and the stature of being a major power, not just a potential major battlefield) and Japan (thanks to its economic growth, but possibly also its increased activity in the United Nations).

There is no doubt a historical turning point at the end of the 1980s. COW's temporal delimitations are built on scholarly consensus. The change may not be captured, however, only by the fact that there were two new major powers. Also, the exact turning point can be discussed and it tells something about the criteria for finding change. It has been convenient to place the change at 1989 with the fall of the Berlin Wall (as a tangible result of a policy shift taking place earlier). It would, thus, relate the change to events on German soil. It could as well be dated to 1985 (the year when the Soviet leader Mikhail Gorbachev came into power and had a first summit meeting with US President Ronald Reagan), thus pointing to what became a fundamental shift in the Soviet Union and in US–Soviet relations, including a first, radical nuclear disarmament treaty in 1987. It could also be set at the end of 1991 with the formal dissolution of the Soviet Union, thus reducing the status of this nation as a superpower to one in a category of a regional major power. The endpoint will also say something about the starting point: what was the Cold War actually all about? If it was about the handling of Germany, the country's reunification becomes a logical endpoint. If it was about nuclear weapons and the fears they generated, 1987 becomes a significant break-point. If it was about ideology, then the end of the Soviet Union also becomes the final date, as this meant an ideological shift in one of the poles of the Cold War. Economically, it meant the opening of Russia for international investment and a new, vast market for exports.

Such delimitations have an effect, of course, on the way one looks at wars. In concrete terms it would determine whether the US intervention in Panama in December 1989 (too small for COW to include as war, nevertheless an armed conflict by UCDP standards, opposed by the Soviet Union at that) or the Gulf Crisis of August 1990–March 1991 (demonstrating remarkable US–Soviet cooperation) should be seen as part of the 'old order' or the beginning of a new one. It may be convenient to make the cut-off at 1 January 1990, it being obvious by that time that Germany was likely to be reunited (which it was in October the same year). At that time it was also clear that the Soviet understanding of its role as a global power was changing, notably with agreed withdrawals of its own or allied troops from Angola, Afghanistan and Cambodia.

Thus, the post-Cold War period began, with more major powers than had been the case previously (now seven in all), but at the same time with one pre-eminent beyond all the others (even taken together, US military expenditures would be higher; SIPRI 2009). Possibly one could call this a period of *Pax Americana*. In reality it may have been the closest we are likely to be in the decades to come to a unipolar world. The United States no doubt had a unique position, perhaps comparable only to the stature it had immediately after the Second World War. In the 1990s the American preferred diplomacy was to exert influence with occasional use of air power (Yugoslavia in 1995, Sudan and Afghanistan in 1998, Kosovo in 1999) rather than engaging ground forces (as was done in Somalia in 1993, and thus avoided in Rwanda the following year). The USA was the undisputed leader, the most prominent of the five permanent members of the UN Security Council, in the UN referred to as the P5. One could be termed P1 (see Chapter 7 for more on this).[1]

In the 2000s, force had again become prominent in America's conduct of international relations against Afghanistan and Iraq, as well as in Somalia, Yemen, Pakistan and other places where semi-clandestine operations could take place against (alleged) terrorist groups. Even if the military force was overwhelming, the sheer fact that it had to be used may be an indication of changing times. The USA was challenged, and not only by non-state organizations. Following 11 September 2001 the relationships changed between the United States and all other actors. The world saw an assertive major power, demanding and taking a pre-eminent role and expecting the others to cooperate (some did, for instance in the war on Iraq in 2003; most others did not).

The Obama administration was elected in 2008 by an electorate that wanted a different approach. It wanted the USA to withdraw from armed conflicts and focus on its own domestic agenda. Again, the USA has to look for allies to do a job it cannot and does not want to do alone. There are many options. The choice remains to be seen, notably China (in a group of two, a so-called G2 configuration), Russia (Euro-Atlantic cooperation), G20 (involving Brazil, India, Indonesia, South Africa, South Korea and others) or other constellations. These questions have to be asked as there were shifts occurring suggesting a gradual move to a more multilateral world for how states could operate. This was not all; there was also a more complex world with non-governmental actors as well as non-state actors dealing with global issues according to their own agendas.[2] These issues are important to explore and a beginning is made to that in Chapter 7, which, by necessity, is more speculative and forward-looking.

Table 3.1 uses the data from the COW project, dividing the era since 1816 into the four periods we have just seen to be important. It thus complements the arguments from Chapter 5, which builds on the information that was available in

Table 3.1 Historical systems and wars: Correlates of War data, 1816–2007

System	Time	Length of period (years)	Number of inter-state wars	Number of intra-state wars	Intra-state wars as percentage of all wars
Euro-centric	1816–1895	80	27	103	79.2
Inter-regional	1896–1944	49	30	59	66.3
Global	1945–1989	45	29	111	79.3
Post-Cold War	1990–2007	18	9	61	87.1

Source: Sarkees and Wayman (2010).
Note
The column to the right includes all intra-state wars as a percentage of all intra- and inter-state wars for each period.

the early 1980s. In particular, Table 3.1 shows that intra-state conflict has always been the most common, comprising at least two-thirds of all conflicts throughout the period. Thus, the fact that such conflicts have been so neglected is testimony to the prevalence of strategic and perhaps *Realpolitik* thinking. Inter-state relations have been seen as the ones determining the future of the state. However, for most local residents the much more frequent experience of intra-state conflict is likely to be more of a problem.

There are important variations among these four consecutive inter-state systems. For instance, between 1896 and 1944 intra-state conflicts were at their lowest and in the following historical periods they have become as common as they were in the 1800s. This period, of course, includes the two world wars, and they can legitimately be said to have coloured thinking in peace research as well as world politics in general. Still, this makes it clear that today's prevalence of intra-state conflict is nothing new. The novelty may be that, in a more integrated world, the domestic conditions of countries are as important as their international relationships.

This also suggests that there may be rather different instruments needed to deal with these challenges to humankind. Inter-state relations may more readily be affected by overall major power relations, whereas the same may not be true for intra-state conditions. In Chapter 6 this is approached by defining the quality of major power relationships in terms of particularist and universalist relations. This has turned out be a reasonable way to understand the onset of inter-state war (Schahczenski 1991; Valeriano with Theo 2009). It is likely to be affected by overall major power relations. In periods of universalist approaches, this means a preference for cooperation and, thus, a will from major powers to contain such conflicts, as they may have a potential to affect international relations in general. In particularist periods, however, the attitude would be different: such conflicts can be exploited for major power purposes and thus be used against the adversary. Further arguments on this are found in Chapter 6.

For the 192 years the COW project identifies 421 inter-state wars and intra-state conflicts. In addition it also documents more than 200 extra-state conflicts

Table 3.2 Universalist and particularist approaches in inter- and intra-state wars: Correlates of War data, 1816–2007

Period	Inter-state wars per year (and total number)	Intra-state wars per year (and total number)
Particularist	0.59 (53)	1.46 (131)
Universalist	0.41 (42)	2.00 (203)

(largely colonial wars) and non-state wars. Table 3.2 emerges from the first two categories. It demonstrates that, both in absolute number and in relation to the length of the two types of periods, there is a difference between the frequencies of inter-state wars and intra-state wars: universalist times have fewer of the former, but more of the latter. This seems to be in line with a relaxed approach to intra-state conflicts: they are not part of power rivalries and can be allowed to go on. Inter-state conflicts, however, have to be contained. In the particularist periods, the result is the reverse: it is more important to gain advantage over the opposing side, thus inter-state conflicts are not contained. Intra-state conflicts may be fewer, as the focus is on inter-state relations, but military interventions may also be more likely, which could affect the onset of such conflicts.

The relationship between wars and the quality of major power relations, however, should not be exaggerated. It can shift more quickly than structural relationships. The approach taken depends to a large degree on the internal conditions of major powers. Thus, the détente of the 1970s ended rather abruptly – intentionally or not on the part of the Soviet leadership – with the Soviet decision to invade Afghanistan in 1979. The period, which had included engagement across the Cold War divide since Presidents Nixon and Ford, was initially continued by President Carter, but he had to shift his position. Thus, the approach to international affairs is affected by events in global relations. This is not unusual and can go in both directions. Carter's successor, President Reagan, won the 1980 election on a platform of hostile policy to the adversaries (at that time not only the Soviet Union but also Iran), but in 1985 he embarked on a very constructive policy of universalism. This policy, remarkably, survived the shifts both in the USA and in the Soviet Union, including into the Russian Federation. Only after 11 September 2001 did the United States take a more typical particularist approach. Thus, we can see that international relations are affected by such internal changes of policy, which in turn can be triggered by a domestic interpretation of preceding international events. It is, however, likely that major power approaches to intra-state conditions do not follow the same logic so easily.

With this in mind, it is now time for the reader to confront the following chapters.

Notes

1   In retrospect, 1996 may have been the peak year for US global standing. It had successfully helped end the war in Bosnia and was not fighting anywhere else; and its economy

was doing very well, having paid off debts and brought balance to its budget following the Reagan years. Russia was still weak and China, India and Brazil had only begun to lay the groundwork for the remarkable period of growth that was to follow in the early 2000s.

2   This was dramatically illustrated in 2010 with the Wikileaks publishing of hundreds of thousands of documents from the US Defense and State Departments on the Internet.

References

Caprioli, M. 2005. 'Primed for Violence: The Role of Gender Inequality in Predicting Internal War', *International Studies Quarterly*, 49: 161–178.

Collier, Paul. 2007. *The Bottom Billion*. Oxford: Oxford University Press

Collier, Paul. 2009. *Wars, Guns and Votes: Democracy in Dangerous Places*. New York: Harper Perennial.

Fearon, James D. and David D. Laitin. 2003. 'Ethnicity, Insurgency, and Civil War', *American Political Science Review*, 97 (1): 75–90.

Galtung, Johan. 1971. 'A Structural Theory of Imperialism', *Journal of Peace Research*, 8: 81–117.

Gartzke, Erik. 2007. 'The Capitalist Peace', *American Journal of Political Science*, 51 (1): 166–191.

Gilpin, Robert. 1981. *War and Change in World Politics*. Cambridge: Cambridge University Press.

Hegre, Haavard, Scott Gates, Nils Petter Gleditsch and Tanja Ellingsen. 2001. 'Toward a Democratic Civil Peace? Democracy, Political Change and Civil War 1816–1992', *American Political Science Review*, 95: 33–48.

Maoz, Zeev and Nasrin Abdolali. 1989. 'Regime Types and International Conflict, 1816–1976', *Journal of Conflict Resolution*, 33: 3–35.

Maoz, Zeev and Bruce Russett. 1993. 'Normative and Structural Causes of Democratic Peace, 1946–1986', *American Political Science Review*, 87 (3): 624–638.

Melander, Erik. 1999. *Anarchy Within: The Security Dilemma between Ethnic Groups in Emerging Anarchy*. Uppsala: Department of Peace and Conflict Research, Uppsala University.

Olsson, Louise. 2009. *Gender Equality and United Nations Peace Operations in Timor Leste*. Leiden, Netherlands: Martinus Nijhoff.

Nordås, R. and N. P. Gleditsch. 2007. 'Climate Change and Conflict', *Political Geography*, 26: 627–638.

Russett, Bruce M. 1993. *Grasping the Democratic Peace: Principles for a Post-Cold War World*. Princeton, NJ: Princeton University Press.

Russett, Bruce M. 2005. 'Bushwhacking the Democratic Peace', *International Studies Perspectives*, 6 (4): 395–408.

Russett, Bruce M. and John Oneal. 2001. *Triangulating Peace: Democracy, Interdependence and International Organizations*. New York: W.W. Norton.

Salehyan, I. 2008. 'From Climate Change to Conflict? No Consensus Yet', *Journal of Peace Research*, 45: 315–326.

Sarkees, Meredith Reid and Frank Wayman. 2010. *The Resort to War*. Washington, DC: CQ Press.

Schahczenski, Jeffery. 1991. 'Explaining Relative Peace: Major Power Order, 1816–1976', *Journal of Peace Research*, 28 (3): 295–309.

SIPRI (Stockholm International Peace Research Institute). 2009. *SIPRI Yearbook: Armaments, Disarmament and International Security 2009*. Oxford: Oxford University Press.

Tickner, J. Ann. 1992. *Gender in International Relations.* Cambridge: Cambridge University Press.

Valeriano, Brandon with Kwang Theo. 2009. 'The Tragedy of Offensive Realism: Testing Aggressive Power Politics Models', *International Interactions*, 35: 179–206.

Vasquez, John A. 1995. 'Why Do Neighbors Fight? Territoriality, Proximity, or Interactions', *Journal of Peace Research*, 3: 277–293.

Vasquez, John A. (ed.). 2000. *What Do We Know about War?* Lanham, MD: Rowman & Littlefield.

Wallensteen, Peter. 1973. *Structure and War: On International Relations 1920–1968.* Stockholm: Rabén & Sjögren.

Wallensteen, Peter. 2002, 2007, 2011. *Understanding Conflict Resolution.* London: Sage (different editions).

Wallerstein, Immanuel. 1974. *The Modern World-System, vol. I: Capitalist Agriculture and the Origins of the European World-Economy in the Sixteenth Century.* New York: Academic Press.

Weede, Erich. 2005. *Balance of Power, Globalization and the Capitalist Peace.* Potsdam: Liberal Verlag.

Winter, David G. 2004. 'Motivation and the Escalation of Conflict: Case Studies of Individual Leaders', *Peace and Change: Journal of Peace Psychology*, 10 (4): 381–398.

4   Four models of major power politics

Geopolitik, Realpolitik, Idealpolitik and *Kapitalpolitik*[1]

The system of states

Traditionally, the study of conflict between states has had two main foci: the state and the individual. There are good reasons for both, and research may progress most by concentrating on the interaction between the two. Although there are strong arguments for synthesis, there is also a need for the elements to be clear enough to coalesce. The study of the system of states has still not reached the maturity required for a process of amalgamation.

'Conflict' is indeed a loose word, referring to the abstract incompatibility between two parties as well as to actual destructive behaviour. The most pertinent question, then, is: which types of incompatibilities are the most important for giving rise to conflict behaviour between two parties? To this, the following study is devoted, with the states as the actors to be scrutinized. The formulation of the object of study also suggests that conflict, that is, the incompatibility, can best be understood by examining the relationship between parties. Together, such relationships make a system. The system of states, then, is the starting point for the following investigation: which incompatibilities, it is asked, are most likely to give rise to conflict behaviour (i.e. war and military confrontations) between which members of a given system?

The system of states (or the state system; these notions will be used interchangeably in the following) has some unique features as a social system. Other social systems, such as the system of competing business enterprises or the system of rivalling parties, have some elements in common with the system of states. The totality of the state system is, however, unique. This can be seen when analysing the defining characteristics of the state. In political science, the state is defined as the only authority having legitimate use of physical violence.[2] This means, first, that the state system is composed of *independent* actors. Certainly sovereignty between actors could also be found in other social systems, for instance between parties competing for power or companies competing for profit. Thus, the independence of the actors is not unique in itself. The uniqueness arises from a combination of sovereignty with other properties of this very system. Independence, however, is often seen as *the* mark of the international system even to the point at which scholars would describe this system as 'anarchical'.[3] Such a description is hardly

a valid one, since the concept of 'anarchical' carries with it non-analytical connotations of chaos. The system is much more organized than is conveyed by the
choice of word. Anarchy would mean that the system is 'without rulers', but it is
more precise to say that the system *has too many rulers*. If Greek should be used for
describing this system, *polyarchical* would be a more fitting term.[4]

The second attribute of the system of states is the one of *territorial* control.
Other systems of independent actors have a different way of relating to territory:
companies may close down their plants or move their headquarters, parties may
gain or lose support in a given area, humans may move from one community
to another, or even from one state to another. The state, however, is stuck to the
territory it is controlling. Certainly, the territory can be enlarged or reduced, but,
if territorial control vanishes, the state vanishes. Exile governments may exist for
some time, but only with support of other states. Territoriality, then, is a special
characteristic of the state. The inter-state system is organized to the extent borders
are clearly defined between different states. This system, in other words, becomes
concerned with territorial extension, borders and defence, in a way no other social
system does.

The third attribute of the state system is its legitimate control of *physical violence*.
This is the focal point of the political science definition of the state, and certainly
distinguishes the state from all other actors. It has a profound impact on inter-
state relations. This can be appreciated if we make the theoretical experiment
of equipping competitors with arms: peaceful competition between companies
rapidly becomes transformed into 'wars', and, as a matter of fact, situations with
political parties fighting one another with weapons are normally termed 'civil
wars'. Supposedly the latter are 'civil' because they are less professional than 'military' wars, and also because they challenge the supreme (military) authority of the
state. The state, in other words, is a military actor. Its monopoly control of arms
is the 'normal' state of affairs, and refusal to accept this will be resisted. States will
oppose other actors becoming armed, that is to say, the fight against terrorism,
gangsterism and homicide is crucial. The maintenance of monopoly control of
arms internally arises from two different considerations, one being the citizens'
demand for 'law and order' (the right of not being robbed), the other the state's
own desire to maintain its monopoly.

A fourth attribute of the state system is its *economic authority*, the state (or its
various subdivisions) being the sole legitimate collector of money from the inhabitants (taxes) and from the goods moving across its borders (tariffs). The economic
authority historically is not unrelated to the attributes just mentioned. It is costly
to hold an army to guard a given territory. Thus, the state has never been 'outside'
economics, as some writing on neoclassical economic theory would like to have it.
Its military functions have more frequently been integrated into economic theory
as a 'collective good'. Historically, the state has been a very important investor
(not only in the military field), controller of monetary flows and regulator of
foreign trade.[5] The relatively low state participation in, for instance, the early
economic development of the United States is exceptional rather than typical.
Also other actors have economic functions, but political parties rely on voluntary

contributions, and companies rely on their ability to sell. Only the state has the authority to demand money from inhabitants. No doubt, its control of physical means simplifies this task.

Finally, states – being equipped with the authority to arrest, subjugate, tax and even kill people – are in need of *legitimacy*. If the operations of the state were illegitimate, the state would appear to the inhabitants as just another 'terrorist'. Indeed, even terrorists try to justify their actions with general principles. In order to exert authority and to make people carry out orders (which could be destructive to other human beings) it needs convincing justification. This is not a property unique to the state. All human beings try to give their actions some purpose. The legitimacy of the state, then, becomes exceptional only in combination with the above-mentioned traits.

Together these five attributes make the state unique as an actor and the system of states becomes a system without parallel. This does not mean the system cannot be studied, however. There are, as already indicated, *partial* similarities with other systems, which can provide fertile ground for comparison and evaluation.[6] Furthermore, the system can be compared over time, as the system continuously changes. The basic, defining characteristics of the system take different values at different time. Such an *historical comparative approach* is the one to be attempted here.

One assumption and four models

Looking more closely at the five attributes, one differs from the others in an important way: the independence of the state. A given piece of territory can be divided between different states, be annexed to another state or constitute a state of its own. States thus emerge through interaction with other states. A large number of the presently existing states are the results of separation, amalgamation, or annexation. Once a given grouping is accepted as a state by other states, it will continuously be moulded by its relations to the others. This process forms its territorial extension and its military and economic strength as well as its legitimacy. The self-preservation of the state, then, appears not only as a requirement to be an actor but also as a goal for the state itself: *to preserve the organization as an organization*. Actors tend to prefer to remain actors.

The overriding concern of the state to remain an actor may contradict other interests favouring, for instance, integration into another state, acceptance of a global economic community or the joining of a military pact. Different and contradictory forces will come into play, shape the state or even lead to its cessation: history, indeed, witnesses the demise of entire civilizations. The feeling that no state is eternal might explain the state's very obsession with its own survival. The perception of threats and dangers, and its interpretation of the unknown as being of shady colour, are thus part of the milieu of the state. Primitive fear may be driven away by the hope of attaining security, the concept most frequently used to describe the ultimate aim of the state.[7]

In the following, the independence of states will be taken for granted, thus focusing the analysis on the other four characteristics outlined. This means excluding the highly important problem of dependence. This can be empirically justified only by concentrating on states that are regarded as highly independent from one another: the major powers in the system. It could be debated how independent these states in fact are. Nevertheless, it appears correct to say that they are the most independent actors in the inter-state system. This means that the question of independence has to be kept in mind when dealing with any of the other relations in the inter-state system. Certainly, interaction between big powers and smaller ones will have dependence as a major concern, at least on the part of the smaller ones. Also, relationships between smaller nations are strongly affected by their links to greater powers in the system.[8]

A more precise analysis of the four traits is required. It is appropriate to do this by regarding them as the basis for four different analytical models. These models are labelled and presented in Table 4.1. Two labels suggest themselves: *Geopolitik* and *Realpolitik*. The former concept was introduced by the Swedish scholar Rudolf Kjellén in 1916, and gained adherence particularly in Germany. It explicitly assumed independence as the basis for the state's policy vis-à-vis other states, and it was in particular concerned with geographically natural boundaries. Certainly, such considerations had been made before and had even been formalized, but the label remains with Kjellén.[9]

Realpolitik is also connected with Germany, or, to be more precise, Prussia. It was coined by a German journalist, August Ludwig von Rochau, in a book published in 1848 laying down the foundations of power politics. The concept was introduced in order to separate real politics from philosophical speculation. The strong, according to von Rochau, could not accept to be ruled by the weak. Certainly, this idea was not new, but again the label was.[10]

Both the mentioned authors were mixing analysis and normative statements, aiming not merely at telling the 'truth' but at influencing the course of events in certain directions. Both authors, incidentally, were favouring the rise of German power and both scored some success. *Geopolitik* was undoubtedly an element in Hitler's thinking on inter-state relations, and Bismarck became more connected to the term *Realpolitik* than its inventor. Also, one might add, both policies in a long-term perspective ended with disaster, and not only for Germany.[11]

Geopolitik, then, is the politics of territory, resources and size of the state. Here, *Geopolitik* will be restricted to the concern with territory, borders and neighbours. This may dilute some meaning of the concept, but serves to make the analysis more precise.

Realpolitik particularly devotes itself to the question of military power. Victory and defeat, uses of military might, alliance patterns and arms technology are among its key variables. The state is of primary interest because of its control of military might.

This leaves two models, which, as of now, lack labels. In order to follow the Germanic language already introduced and indeed linking the thinking to a great German scholar, the concern with economic conditions could be termed *Kapitalpolitik*. In this analysis, it will orient our work to the development of industry and international commerce.[12]

Table 4.1 Four models of inter-state relations. Basic assumption: preservation of state (security)

	Geopolitik	Realpolitik	Idealpolitik	Kapitalpolitik
Ordering concept	Territorial extension	Military capability	Legitimizing principle	Economic advancement
Ranking				
1 Concepts	Core–periphery	Major–minor power	Legitimate–non-legitimate	Advanced–backward
2 Criteria for ranking	Size Location	Number of arms Quality of arms	Number of believers Closeness to origin	Amounts Inventiveness
Conflict expected				
1 Locus	Intersection of core areas	Declining majors	Emerging principles (revolution)	Emerging technologies
2 Dyads	Core–core	Major–major	Old–new	Old, advanced–new, advancing
Historical turning points (criteria for)				
1 Redistribution	Territorial change between core states in core areas	Victory/ defeat between majors	Old principle gaining over other old principle	Stagnation of advanced
2 Creation	Formation of new sizeable states	Emergence of new armed states	Emergence of new principle over old one	New technologies, rapid advancement
3 Disintegration	Break-up of sizeable core area states	Defeat, disarmament of a major	Competing claims to original closeness	Overdevelopment, crisis, underdevelopment

Furthermore, the concept of *Realpolitik* was, by its very inventor, considered the counterpoint to the concept of morals. Above it was argued that legitimacy is needed for the state to operate smoothly. It might even be more important than *Realpolitik* itself. The principles of legitimacy used for the state, then, are its *Idealpolitik*. The contradictory nature of *Idealpolitik* is not only that it can be used by the state, but also that it affects the state, as holders of power are shaped by the principles of legitimacy themselves. Indeed, *Realpolitik* analysts constantly expose the contradictory phenomenon of power-holders refusing to accept the simple dynamics of *Realpolitik* alone.[13]

It should be repeated that Table 4.1 uses the state as point of departure. There is little difficulty in isolating other models which would involve the state, but departing from other elements in the social system. Thus, we could think of, or even normatively prefer, models of *Humanpolitik*, seeing the human being as the measure of all, rather than the state, or *Ekopolitik*, departing from a concern of global environment rather than a given state. However, such global perspectives will still have to come to grips with states that refuse to wither away.

Table 4.1 presents systemic aspects of the four models, that is, the approaches they would take to understanding the world, if brought down to their basics. Thus, we assume *Geopolitik* to be concerned purely with territory, *Realpolitik* only with military victory, etc. In this 'pure' form, each model has to find its own criteria for important decisions such as ranking of states in the system, location of incompatibilities and dyads of conflicts as well as ways of finding historical turning-points. As the models all deal with the same inter-state system, ranking, conflict and change have to be accounted for.

In Table 4.1, concepts have been used in order to polarize the models as much as possible. Certainly, some adherents of one given school would object to some concepts used: geopolitical analysts, for instance, using 'big power' as frequently as *Realpolitik* writers. However, this would tend to obscure significant differences. Our object here is instead to clarify the 'world' as seen from the basic ordering concept. Thus, the words used for each model are designed to convey different world perspectives.

Each of the dimensions presented in Table 4.1 can be operationalized. To determine the size of the territory of a given state provides relatively little difficulty (although, at certain occasions, the actual control over claimed areas might be disputed). Size is a quantitative criterion, and such criteria are found for other models as well.

The second criterion for ranking is of a more qualitative nature and, hence, more difficult to grasp. 'Location' refers to the *Geopolitik* theories dividing the world into 'Heartland' and 'Rimland', thus departing from a notion of an 'objective' centre from which the rest of the world can be controlled. Such notions rest on the observation that the world's fragmented geography makes certain spots more important than others, for instance for transportation. *Geopolitik* analysts, then, work from a notion of what is central and what is not. An empirical treatment of the question would, for instance, look at patterns of communication.

Quality in military matters poses the question of military software: military might consists not only of numbers but also of organization, strategy and relative sophistication of weapons. In the nuclear age, vulnerability has become one indicator of 'weakness', but earlier ages may have had similar notions, related to other types of weapons.

To try to rank states with respect to *Idealpolitik* might surprise at the outset, but nevertheless constitutes an important concern for many writers. As each state has to consider its legitimacy, it will also have arguments for its particular legitimacy vis-à-vis states building on the same principle (e.g. monarchical rule resting on lineage, Communist rule on closeness to Marx), as well as states building on contradictory principles (e.g. monarchies given by God versus rule by the people, or Communist rule being superior to other types because it expresses the unfolding development of the modes of production).

Finally, *Kapitalpolitik* provides simple measures for inventiveness, for instance resources channelled into research and development or share of GDP devoted to productive investments.

The four models, however, are not restricted to a procedure of ranking. Our chief concern is their conflict prediction. This leads to the next dimension presented in Table 4.1. The models will all devote themselves to the questions of *where* and *between whom* incompatibilities will exist. The answer to these questions will, furthermore, reveal something of the theoretical underpinnings, the *why?* of the model.

The *Geopolitik* analyst is particularly concerned with intersections, for instance between Heartland and Rimland. In particular, this leads to a concern for core states in core areas. Borders are either solutions or causes of conflict. Conflicts are seen as the results of 'outward pushes' whereby states try to move their border. This 'push' thus becomes a crucial driving force, which, incidentally, is often left unanalysed. It is simply taken for granted, or enhanced by reasoning not necessarily derived from *Geopolitik* considerations. Core states 'pushing' outwards are expected to 'meet' other core states, and friction will be the result. The argument points to the 'risks' for peripheral states of being neighbours to core states, and, in particular, to the 'necessity' for neighbouring core states to be in constant conflict with one another. The more core states based in one and the same region of the world, the more conflict can be expected.[14]

The *Realpolitik* model emphasizes military might and primarily expects well-armed states to be concerned with one another: threats to the security of one come from the weapons of the other. To 'lag' behind other majors is, then, highly 'dangerous' for a given actor. Such 'declining' majors could easily become targets for other majors, who might 'rush in' to take their spoils or prevent others from taking too big a share. Major powers, following this line of thought, are in conflict because they are afraid, and, thus, need to react and guard themselves. The driving force is 'fear' leading to expansionism to eliminate the perceived threat. At one point or another, the drive to rid oneself of fear becomes a drive for global dominance. Thus, the major powers would be governed by paranoid tendencies, nervously reacting to the moves of others, and interpreting them in the worst possible light.[15] Basically, the powers fear defeat. Earlier experience of victory and defeat, then, would have a significant impact on major powers and their behaviour.

Idealpolitik reasoning also rests on 'fear', but in this case the principle of legitimacy is the means of alleviation. Ideology gives persuasive arguments to the leaders as well as to the led, justifying why some belong to one category and others do not. The just cause gives strength and makes it possible to endure hardship. The 'fear' underlying *Idealpolitik* analysis is the fear of having one principle replaced by another: revolution (also termed counter-revolution, when history is read in a linear fashion, giving room for only one revolution) is the nightmare. Fundamental revolutions change the patterns of perception, bring new leaders to the forefront, and are seldom restricted to the country where the revolution takes place. The continuous existence of several leading principles contesting and contradicting each other would thus constitute a major incompatibility, and lead to conflicts in dyads of states supporting contradictory principles.[16]

Finally, the conflict expectations in the *Kapitalpolitik* model emphasized technological change; new technologies will replace old ones. This means that new actors emerge, although through a less dramatic process than in *Idealpolitik* revolutions. The most advanced state, the model suggests, will be conscious in keeping its leadership, simultaneously trying to prevent the competitor from overtaking. Thus, incompatibility exists between old corporations and new ones, between old professions and new ones, and, consequently, between states advancing on new technologies over states relying on old. Again the driving force could be fear, but more likely a fear linked to profits or benefits in monetary terms rather than the simple zero-sum game of *Realpolitik*.[17]

Taken together, the four models point to *change* as the most important factor in conflict. Rising states are expected to contradict leading ones; advanced ones are expected to exploit the declining ones. Strength comes from different sources, being the vast territory in the case of *Geopolitik* (but, the sceptic could wonder, would not vast territory lead to satisfaction, rather than a 'push outward'?), the fear of becoming vulnerable to defeat for *Realpolitik* (but, the same opponent might ask, the more invulnerable one actor is, the greater the other's fear?), the danger of being replaced by an illegitimate order for *Idealpolitik* (but perhaps all orders are equally legitimate or illegitimate?), and the possible loss of leadership in the case of *Kapitalpolitik* (whatever the cost/benefit calculus of leading is?). Change and dynamics, looking ahead rather than looking back, direct the course of the system.

The models, consequently, should be suitable for describing change, and this is what Table 4.1 captures in its third dimension. Change takes primarily three forms for the high-ranked states in the system: redistribution (or reallocations) between them, creation of new high-ranked states and disintegration of older ones. The system, then, is thought to change when the relationships between the high-ranked states change. The four models suggest highly different criteria for observing such change, ranging from territorial redistribution by military victory to revolution or economic crisis. These criteria primarily locate disruption, rather than 'stability' between points in time. Thus, change creates new conditions on which policies have to be formed, but the actual description of a new situation is not readily given by the models. 'Stability', from this perspective, is nothing but non-change. This very 'stability' is what is here termed the structural characteristics of the system. We have also argued that different structural conditions give rise to different policies. In this chapter, however, we concentrate on structure rather than policy.

Three state systems in 160 years

The Correlates of War (COW) project at the University of Michigan provides information on inter-state relations since 1816. As this chapter uses the project's data as its basis, some reflections on the 160 years up to 1976 are necessary. The project has mostly treated the entire period as one temporal unit, or as one global system of states. It could be argued, however, departing from the four models, that this span of time actually exhibits some dramatic changes not easily accounted for in such an analysis. Concentrating on the leading states in the system, the system would change when these states change in some important respect. But this then presupposes a definition of 'leading state', which in turn can only be determined after we have defined the extent of the system, temporally as well as socially. Thus, all tasks become interrelated.

COW has solved this problem by resorting to scholarly consensus. This results in the listing of nine 'major powers' (COW's terminology) for the entire period.[18] Only three of these are majors for the whole period (England, France and Russia/ USSR, although with short breaks for the last two), whereas two appear in 1816 but later drop out (Austria-Hungary, Prussia/Germany), two enter after 1816 but leave well before 1976 (Italy, Japan), and two enter late and remain in 1976 (United States, China). Thus, there is considerable temporal variation of major powers.

The scholarly consensus reported by COW provides a fruitful point of departure in discussing state systems since 1816. Such a discussion can be pursued in the categories provided by the four models of Table 4.1.

First, in order to define a state as a major, it needs to qualify as an actor: that is, have a certain internal stability and international recognition as an actor. This, one could assume, is the reason why the project includes China only from 1949, when the victory of the Communist Party provided unity to the country and, thus, could make it an actor in inter-state relations. Similarly, the unification of Italy in 1861 makes that country an actor. Second, however, there is a need for additional criteria in order to separate 'normal' actors from 'leading' ones. This is where the criteria for ranking become important, and also where fruitful discrepancies emerge between scholarly consensus and empirical indicators. For instance, it is generally agreed that the USA should be included as a major power from 1898. However, by the *Geopolitik* criterion of territory, the USA by 1816 was already larger than many of the majors. Also, by a *Realpolitik* indicator, such as arms expenditure, the USA passes other majors for a good part of the period before 1898. Furthermore, *idealpolitically* the perception of 'freedom' in America had a strong appeal in European countries throughout the nineteenth century, and America was, by many European regimes, regarded as the most revolutionary of all states. Finally, by the *Kapitalpolitik* measure of iron production, the United States out-distanced Austria and Prussia already by 1816, and during the 1800s overtook the other majors one by one, finally even the United Kingdom by 1890.

Does this mean, then, that the scholars have missed such an important phenomenon as the USA? Probably not. Rather, they would argue that USA was of no significance in the whole state system but held a regional role. Thus, the USA could act as a strong state in the Western hemisphere and in the Pacific, but this would not involve it in contradictions with Europe-based leading countries. In some ways, the USA was outside the dominant system.

This is to propose that the entire state system of the 1800s consisted of several *regionally confined systems* only loosely tied together.[19] One is the European region, from a global perspective a small one, highly populated, and divided into a large number of states. Europe, furthermore, is the centre of a network reaching not only Northern Africa and the Middle East, but Southern Asia as well. A second region is the Americas, less populated, more spacious and with a colonial heritage built on the destruction of all indigenous state organization. Eastern Asia could be seen as a third region, including China, Indochina and adjacent islands (Japan and Taiwan). Finally, at the outset of the period of investigation (1816) most of Africa is a system on its own. As can be seen, these delimitations are not geographical, but account for social links and could be more closely determined by the use of the four models.

The leading region during the nineteenth century is undoubtedly the first one, the only one reaching out of its own geographical confines. The 1800s witness the continuous expansion of the Euro-centric region into the others, notably Africa, but also Eastern Asia. Challenges against Europe do not emerge until the end of the century, when Japan and the United States gradually emerge as rivals in *Real-* as well as *Kapitalpolitik* terms. The historical evaluation points to a change in the system by the 1890s: the United States and Japan both begin to build empires in much the same way as the Europeans, bringing themselves into interaction with these very European nations. The inter-state system thus gradually transforms itself from a *Euro-dominated world to an inter-regional one*, where geographical territory is disputed between countries not necessarily European.

If this holds true, it means that we would expect less discrepancy between the historian's rank order and those of the objective criteria for the period following 1920. The countries with the largest iron and steel production in the 1920s and the 1930s are the United States, Germany, the United Kingdom, France, the Soviet Union, Italy, and Japan – all appearing on the scholarly list as major powers. These same countries are those spending most on armaments, thus indicating that our reasoning is correct.

New discrepancies emerge, however, following 1945. The scholarly consensus reported by the COW project gives five major powers, but three of these are outdistanced by non-majors on at least one measure: both Japan and West Germany have by 1970 a greater iron and steel production than the United Kingdom, France and China. Further, West Germany has, at times, greater military expenditures than France and the United Kingdom. On most measures of *Geo-*, *Kapital-*, and *Realpolitik* origin, however, the United States and the Soviet Union appear in a category of their own. Thus, these two powers, also leading in *Idealpolitik* for parts of the world, undoubtedly qualify as dominant states. The others, however, are either more regionally significant (for instance, the UK, France and China) or more sectorally significant (for instance, Japan and West Germany, with respect to *Kapitalpolitik*). These five states, in other words, appear on a lower level than the two first mentioned. Taking this together, however, the post-1945 period could best be described as *a global system*: the two leading states could operate globally, their influence not being confined to clear geographical regions or to certain sectors.

This means that, using changes in composition and relative weight among major states as the criteria, the epoch stretching from 1816 to 1976 could be conceived of as *three consecutive state systems:*

1 *The Euro-centric system* lasting from 1816 to 1895 with the regions of the world separated, although one region being more important.

2 *The inter-regional system*, witnessing increased interaction between the regions, but still with discernible differences between arenas of military action. This period covers the years 1896–1944.

3 *The global period*, with two global powers and a set of regionally significant ones: 1945 to present.

As this study encompasses the entire epoch of 1816–1976 we have four time-points which are regarded as major shifts. These are the years 1816, 1895/1896, 1944/1945 and 1976. The first as well as the last of these appear less important than the other two, and they are justified on other grounds than our four models. 1976 is a date of convenience. In retrospect, it might turn out as a date of significance, although not reshaping the entire system, at least marking a change in relations between global powers. The year of 1816 could perhaps be replaced by an earlier date, for instance 1789 or even 1648, if the study were to encompass the entire history of the system of states. However, the relative stability achieved in 1816 included traits of the four models, thus making that year a significant enough turning-point, and leaving a time-span sufficiently long for an analysis of the Euro-centric state system.

The turning-point 1895/1896 is arrived at through the following considerations: *geopolitically*, it meant the introduction of new arenas of contention among the majors (e.g. East Asia), *realpolitically*, the emergence of two new major powers and, *idealpolitically*, the rise of anti-European nationalism (Japan). Finally, around 1895 there were significant *Kapitalpolitik* changes, notably the USA overtaking the United Kingdom as the most important producer of iron and steel, and the high degree of industrialization achieved among most of the majors.[20]

The years 1944/1945 mark a turning-point for reasons parallel to those of 1895/1896. *Geopolitically*, the outcome of the Second World War meant the end of Europe as an independent region, *realpolitically*, the emergence of two major contenders with new formidable weapons, *idealpolitically*, the rise of a combined universalist–nationalist contradiction, and, *kapitalpolitically*, industrialization reaching new heights, at least among the already industrialized major powers.

The purpose of dividing the epoch 1816–1976 into three distinct periods is to achieve comparability. The way the distinctions have been made suggests that patterns of conflict, confrontation and war would be different between the three periods. This is what is then discussed in Chapter 5 of this book.

Notes

1 Sections of this chapter were presented at the First World Peace Science Congress, Harvard, June 1980; at the Nordic Theory Week, Oslo, August 1980; and at seminars at the Mental Health Research Institute, Ann Arbor, and the Department of Peace and Conflict Research, Uppsala. Important comments from these presentations have been incorporated. I am also grateful to Klaus Jurgen Gantzel, Bjorn Hettne, Miroslav Nincic and J. David Singer for valuable suggestions. The original article is divided in

two, one part constituting this Chapter 4, immediately followed by the second part, here reproduced as Chapter 5.

2   The exact formulations may vary and so do the emphases of different authors, but the heart of the matter is similar enough to state that there is a political science consensus on the definition. See, for instance, Lasswell, H.D. and A. Kaplan, *Power and Society: A Framework for Political Inquiry*, New Haven, CT: Yale University Press, 1950, pp. 181–185.

3   See, for instance, Waltz, Kenneth N., *Man, the State and War: A Theoretical Analysis*, New York: Columbia University Press, 1959, ch. VI.

4   Wallensteen, P., 'Anarki, konflikt och krig', *Tiden*, 1979, 8.

5   Many political science definitions seem to miss the economic importance of the state. In an evolutionary perspective this becomes an important aspect. See, for instance, Tilly, C. (ed.), *The Formation of National States in Western Europe*, Princeton, NJ: Princeton University Press, 1975.

6   For instance, it is possible to compare the various subsystems of a given system by isolating subsystems on grounds of geographic proximity (regions) or military capability (small states). The question of independence, however, enters strongly into this type of comparisons.

7   On the concept of structure, see Wallensteen, Peter, *Structure and War: On International Relations, 1920–1968*, Stockholm: Rabén & Sjögren, 1973, p. 32.

8   The question of dependence and war constituted the central theme in Wallensteen, *op. cit.*

9   Kjellén, R., *Staten som lifsform*, Stockholm: Hugo Gebers förlag, 1916, p. 43. See also Whittlesey, D., *German Strategy of World Conquest*, New York: Farar & Rinehart, 1942, ch. 5 in general, and p. 71 in particular, and Cohen, S. B., *Geography and Politics in a World Divided*, New York: Oxford University Press, 1973, p. 44.

10 von Rochau, A. L., *Grundsatze der Realpolitik*, 1857 (2nd edn), cited in Pflantze, O., *Bismarck and the Development of Germany*, Princeton, NJ: Princeton University Press, 1963, p. 48.

11 Hitler's links to *Geopolitik* served to discredit the entire field of political geography, something Whittlesey sought to undo, *op. cit.*

12 *Das Kapital* contained little on inter-state relations, but, of course, underlined the significance of industrialization for inter-class relations.

13 This prompts a leading *Realpolitik* scholar such as Hans J. Morgenthau to ask for a 'pathology' of international politics in order to understand the American policy in Vietnam, without seeing that this undermines the whole idea of power politics as rooted in objective laws of human nature; see *Politics among nations*, New York: Knopf, 1973 (5th edn), p. 7. Following a similar line of argument, John C. Stoessinger deplores the *Idealpolitik* of a series of American presidents: 'unfortunately the moralist mentality is embedded very deeply in America and seems to come in cycles', *Crusaders and Pragmatists*, New York: Norton, 1979, p. 289.

14 Often, *Geopolitik* writers refer to lofty drives of a sort similar to many other writers, but representing different models. Cohen talks about 'man's need for large space', *op. cit.*, p. 40, and Morgenthau states that the 'drives to live, to propagate and to dominate are common to all men', *op. cit.*, p. 34, pointing out that zoologists have found the drive to dominate 'even in animals', *loc. cit.*, note 5.

15 The obsession with 'threat' certainly differentiates the military world from the civilian one. Also, the more power possessed by a given actor, the more threats there appear to be. Thus, both the USA and the Soviet Union eagerly watch the moves of the other party, constantly fearing the worst. Thus, the most powerful are the fearful. Such *Realpolitik* paranoia can be reinforced by *Idealpolitik* considerations: Stalin, being the most powerful man in the Soviet Union, appears to have lived in constant fear of intrigues stimulated by his own interpretation of Marxism as well as his power position.

16 Interesting contradictions can emerge between a universalist ideology and an actor having less than universal influence: either ideologies have to adapt to the actors to which they apply (notably, the formulation of 'Socialism in One State' when no further Revolutions occurred after 1917) or the contradiction can be 'solved' by expansionism, aiming at making the message universally applicable. The latter certainly was in the minds of personalities as diverse as Mohammed and Napoleon.

17 It could, of course, be debated whether well-paid top executives in corporations or ministries actually strive to maximize their monetary returns. Perhaps they should be regarded as 'barons' rather than 'robbers' as E. J. Hobsbawm suggests when describing early American capitalists: they were maximizing power and building empires. The discussion would apply equally well to the Soviet Union and Eastern Europe, where, nominally, the 'robbers' have been abolished. See Hobsbawm, *The Age of Capital*, New York: New American Library, 1979, p. 157.

18 Singer, J. D. and M. Small, *The Wages of War: A Statistical Handbook*, New York: John Wiley & Sons, 1972, p. 23.

19 The conception of 'world systems' which do not cover the entire geographical 'world' was introduced by Wallerstein, I., *The Modern World-System*, New York: Academic Press, 1974, and the view of 'regions' as not confined to continents by Russett, B. M., *International Regions and the International System*, Chicago: Rand McNally, 1967.

20 Also historians have emphasized this change, notably Barraclough, G., *An Introduction to Contemporary History*, Harmondsworth: Pelican, 1979, who, however, sees no significant shift around 1945.

5 Major powers, confrontation and war, 1816–1976[1]

The major powers

The four models on international relations and war in Chapter 4 expect 'conflict' to arise in certain relationships between certain states. Put differently, they suggest that certain incompatibilities, arrived at through careful theoretical reasoning, are more likely to lead to conflict behaviour than others. Thus, each model would argue – at least in an extreme version – that it captures the more 'basic' operations of a given system better than other models. The task is now to make a comparative analysis of the strength of the four models. Given that the 1816–1976 epoch involved *three consecutive systems*, it must be determined whether a given incompatibility appears generally to result in conflict behaviour, that is, applies to all three systems, or is true for a certain type of system (i.e. for one or two of the three) or bears no relation at all to conflict behaviour.

The four models have been interpreted to suggest that certain dyads of states are those most likely to experience incompatibility and conflict behaviour. This, of course, starts from the old notion that it takes two to make a conflict. It means that this study will look at *pairs of states* in order to locate incompatibilities. As we work with three systems, the basic unit of analysis becomes *system pairs*. For each of the three systems, the pairs of actors are specified. Thus, in cases where the same two actors appear in all three systems, they appear as three different system pairs. This is necessary to account for the changes of the state systems seen during the 1816–1976 epoch. Furthermore, in this chapter, the number of actors is restricted to the leading ones, which are termed the majors in the Correlates of War (COW) language. This delimitation is done on the assumption that independence is the supreme value for state decisions. In a system of states, no state is completely independent, but the majors are relatively more independent than others. Thus, when analysing major–major pairs, dependency problems can be neglected more easily than when studying major–minor relations.

This leaves us with the problem of determining whether a given incompatibility exists or not. In doing this, one can resort to statements to this fact either by competent observers or by the parties. The latter method is, however, not applicable, as the models address themselves to underlying cleavages not necessarily obvious to the parties, and indeed the models may have the function of clarifying to the parties what they actually are fighting about. Thus, the judgement of the competent observer provides the basis for the model. This means that it is here assumed that a statement by an observer that there exists an incompatibility between two actors means that there *is* such an incompatibility. As it is possible for anybody, whether competent or not, to suggest incompatibilities, the interesting problem is not the existence of incompatibilities in themselves, but, rather, their link to actual conflict behaviour. Thus, the important incompatibilities searched for are those that also correlate highly with war-type behaviour. This means that the pairs of states in the three systems can be characterized with respect to suggested incompatibilities and then be correlated with actually measurable conflict behaviour. Furthermore, the pairs can be divided into those having the suggested incompatibility and those not exhibiting this feature as well as into pairs of conflict behaviour and those without.

In order to make the analysis somewhat more penetrating, conflict behaviour is measured with two variables: *wars* and *military confrontations*. The definitions and the data are those of the COW project.[2] Wars between major states are rare, whereas military confrontations are more frequent. The military confrontations, which include lower levels of warfare as well as threats to use force, would thus come closer to measuring the suggested incompatibilities, as many of them occasionally are expected to reveal themselves in 'friction' or 'tension' rather than all-out war. Table 5.1 summarizes the concepts and gives the data on which the article is building. The concepts in Table 5.1 need some explanation. First, pairs with wars between majors will be termed *war relations*. A given war, involving two opposing majors, is thus one war relation. A war with two majors against a third enters as two war relations, one for each major–major pair involved. Whether or not minor powers participated in the war effort is disregarded here. Furthermore, we are only registering whether a war occurred or not in a given system pair. The phenomenon of repeated warfare in the same pair in the same period is very rare.

The second operational concept is *confrontation relation*, which is measured in the same way as war relations, but includes military confrontations as well as wars. As the intensity in this case is more interesting and more measurable, the number of confrontations has been calculated for each system pair, the *added confrontation relations*. For instance, the British–Russian pair during the first system is coded as a war relation (the Crimean War), as a confrontation relation and as an added confrontation relation with nine confrontations in this period. Having arrived at the total number of added confrontation relations, which gives information on how many confrontations there were in all pairs of major states, the pairs can be divided into those of *high* and *low* frequency of confrontations using the average as cutting point. The British–Russian pair in the 1816–1895 system was one of high confrontation, the average number for all pairs in this system being 2.4.

Among the measures in Table 5.1, items 12, 13 and 14 capture the systems, when allowance is made for their differing number of majors as well as varying lengths of time. Together these figures reveal some distinct differences. The second system scores highest on war relations (two world wars!), whereas the third one is highest in military confrontations. On all measures, the first system emerges

Table 5.1 Systems and majors, war and confrontation relations, 1816–1976 (absolute numbers)

Variable	System		
	Euro-centric (1816–1895)	Inter-regional (1896–1944)	Global (1945–1976)
1 Major states	5–6	7–8	2–5
2 Major–major pairs	15	28	10
3 Major–major wars	5	4	1
4 Major–major war relations	6	20	3
5 Major–major war relations/pair	0.4	0.7	0.3
6 Major–major confrontations	22	31	20
7 Major–major confrontation relations	13	25	7
8 Major–major confrontation relation/pair	0.9	0.9	0.7
9 Added major–major confrontation relations, total	36	63	33
10 Added major–major confrontation relations/pair (i.e. average)	2.4	2.3	3.3
11 Above average pairs	5	8	3
12 War relations/pair/length of period × 100	0.5	1.5	0.9
13 Confrontation relations/pair/ length of period ×100	1.1	1.9	2.2
14 Average confrontation relations/ length of period × 100	3	4.8	10.3

as the most tranquil one. There is, furthermore, one discernible trend, a general increase in average confrontation relations when accounting for time (measure 14), the second system being considerably higher than the first, while the third, in turn, exhibits a remarkably higher level than the second.

Does the number matter?

The four models have one assumption in common: the number of actors is larger than one. None of them has, however, anything to say about how large the number is or should be. Theoretically, it could vary from two to twenty or more, depending on the number of members of the system. Obviously, the whole notion of 'major' assumes that systems tend to have some very few, dominating actors. There is greater difficulty in isolating 'dominating' actors if the assets are evenly distributed. A pessimistic view would hold that equal distribution on one dimension will be offset by unequal distribution on another, as human beings will always try to find reasons for ranking themselves. Even if this were used against equalization on any dimension, it could also be an argument for seeing the achievement of equality as a continuous struggle, with, at best, a series of inconclusive victories.

No matter how we view the general question of equality, the consensus among the historians suggests that there are some distinct features of dominance in the inter-state system. Table 5.1 points to some such elements. The inter-regional system has the highest number of major powers, indicating it was more equalitarian in power distribution than the other two. It was also the period with the highest number of war relations and confrontation relations per pair. Certainly the global system is higher on confrontation indicators, but lower on war measures, when considering its shorter duration. This might suggest that the fewer the majors, the less likely is war, that is, it might support arguments of concentration of power in the state system. This needs some elaboration.

First, we have to ask what difference the number of majors could be expected to make. The main argument is one of *predictability*. The fewer the actors, the greater the knowledge among the actors about the other actors, the more experience in handling conflicts and, hence, the less likely miscalculation. Confrontations in general, and war in particular, would, from this perspective, be a result of miscalculation. It could, of course, also be maintained that decreased predictability would induce caution, whereas increased predictability would lead to offensive action. On the whole, however, assuming the actors to be on high, if not entirely equal, levels of capability, the first argument seems more plausible. A different line of argument suggests that in a system of a large number of actors, *interaction* would be more diversified. This would result in differing allegiances, which would reduce the likelihood of sudden changes in the system. Increased interaction opportunities would reduce the frequency of war.[3]

Table 5.1 shows that the Euro-centric and the global systems deviate from the inter-regional one in much the same way: on eleven out of fourteen measures they both show lower values, for instance with respect to the number of actors and war relations. There is one striking difference between the Euro-centric and the global systems, however: the number of confrontations in the latter period is more than double that of the inter-regional and triple that of the Euro-centric system, when accounting for the length of the periods (variable 14 in Table 5.1). This means that in a very short time the global system has witnessed almost as many military confrontations as the much longer Euro-centric system did.

This difference need not contradict the argument of predictability, but undoubtedly leads to a reformulation of it. If we calculate the share of those major–major relations with a high number of confrontations out of all relations, we find that this exclusive group in the Euro-centric system is involved in 69 per cent, in the inter-regional 61 per cent and in the global 73 per cent of military confrontations. Furthermore, the group itself is much smaller in the global system than in any other. This illustrates that the global system has the highest concentration of conflict behaviour. The inter-regional system shows the lowest concentration of all. Thus, in both the Euro-centric and the global systems one pair is far more involved in confrontations than any other (Britain–Russia in the former and United States–Soviet Union in the latter). The inter-regional system, however, lacks such a leading pair. Taking the evidence and the arguments together, we can propose that a high number of majors tends to decrease predictability and thus increase the likelihood of confrontations and war. The difference between the Euro-centric and the global systems suggests, however, that the relationship between number and confrontation is not linear. The high concentration of confrontations to one pair in the global system indicates that an inter-state system with too few majors might experience a relatively higher frequency of confrontations. A system of, say, five equal majors would then result in a lower frequency, whereas a system of seven or eight would again be higher.

This investigation cannot take us further, and indeed the conclusion is based on somewhat shaky ground, as the number of systems compared is limited to three. We are, however, not prevented from speculation. The question raised initially requires an answer. Would a system of ten or more majors have fewer wars and confrontations than in the Euro-centric systems, which, after all, included five major wars? History may deprive us of a conclusive answer as it prefers not to provide any acceptable examples. Studies of regional, multi-actor systems, such as early Italy, China or Greece, might provide one way out. It seems, given a long enough time-span, that such studies point to a tendency of the number of actors to decrease, the smaller ones being eliminated by the bigger ones.[4] This corresponds to an often-cited tendency of the market system to gradually concentrate around a few major actors. This tendency, we might assume, is inbuilt in most competitive systems. It also means that history will not allow us to know whether a system of many majors is more peaceful than one with very few, as the former tend to transform into the latter. However, history might also suggest the opposite process: the break-up of major empires (Pax Romana) seems as frequent as the elimination of multi-actor systems. Neither system, then, would have the stability to maintain non-war conditions for longer periods of time.

Given that history can be seen as a continuous dialogue between concentrated and dispersed systems of dominance, can *changes* between systems occur without war? The transformations seen in the limited epoch we are dealing with indicate that the process of dispersion (from a Euro-centric to an inter-regional system) was somewhat less violent than the process of concentration (the global system requiring the physical elimination of a set of actors). Furthermore, given the very high concentration of the global system, a process of dispersion appears the most probable development for the near future. However, given its high concentration (i.e. two dominant actors with superior weapons), the chances of a successful, non-violent transformation might not be too bright. The capacity of the present majors to prevent their position from being eroded appears definitely greater than was the case for the then-majors at the end of the nineteenth century.

Geopolitik: contiguity leads to caution or conflict?

The *Geopolitik* model aims at predicting which territorial features are more prone than others to give rise to conflict, tension and war. In particular, it focuses geographical contiguity, simply predicting that major powers being close to one another will also watch one another, and tend to react to anything which seems either threatening to its own territory or promising for its expansion. However, expansion could not easily take place at the expense of another major's core area. Rather, it would be more likely in peripheral areas. In effect, this gives rise to two contradictory hypotheses. Contiguity is expected at the same time to (a) induce tension and (b) lead to tension-reducing caution. This does not mean that the lack of contiguity would not mean tension, only that other factors are operating. Thus, countries separated by buffer zones could well either agree on or compete for the conquest of the separating piece of territory.

The question of contiguity is one of the most researched ones, and several studies point to a general association between contiguity and various forms of conflict behaviour. Also, some differences have been observed between the nineteenth and twentieth centuries, correlations being generally higher for the former than for the latter.[5] With the distinction of different systems applied here, Table 5.2 gives additional evidence. Table 5.2 shows war and confrontation involvements of contiguous major–major pairs for the three systems.

Table 5.2 shows that the number of contiguous majors is very small and decreasing over time. This suggests that the hypothesis of relating geography to war/non-war has an increasingly limited explanatory value at least among major powers. The change over time is also in conformity with our expectation as the periods have been designed to capture the continuous expansion of the inter-state system. With increased expansion follows increased distances and decreased contiguity.

However, the third and following columns are of greater interest. They show that, given contiguity between major powers, such majors tend to have confrontations. The number of confrontations is not necessarily high, but tension is still obvious. Furthermore, in a high number of these pairs, war has occurred. Some of the most publicized and most disastrous confrontations and wars of the epoch make up the historical essence of Table 5.2: France–Germany, Prussia–Austria/Hungary, Germany–Russia, Russia–Japan, and the Soviet Union–China. Certainly, this list would satisfy the *Geopolitik*-minded scientist. These major powers lie like tightly placed boulders along the Euro-Asian continent from the Atlantic to the Pacific. The *Geopolitik* scholar might even argue that these conflicts are more

Table 5.2 Major–major relations, contiguity, and confrontation patterns in three systems

System	No. of contiguous pairs	Share of contiguous pairs of all pairs (%)	No. of contiguous pairs with military confrontations	No. of contiguous pairs with 'high' military confrontations	No. of contiguous pairs with war	Share of all contiguous pairs with war (%)
Euro-centric	6	40	6	2	3	50
Inter-regional	7	25	6	3	6	86
Global	1	10	1	0	0	0

basic than others as, for instance, one line of thought emphasizes the control over the Euro-Asian landmass to be critical for world domination. Indeed, some of the wars between non-contiguous states could appear less 'basic' as they are often the result of alliance configurations. Thus, the war in 1914 between Britain and France, on the one side, and Austria/Hungary, on the other, the *Geopolitik* analyst might reduce to an alliance-induced offspring of German–Russian rivalry. Similarly, the wars between Britain and France on the one side and China on the other in 1950 could be excluded, the former being brought into the Korean War by way of their alliance with the United States. However, such a distinction between 'basic' and 'superficial' becomes increasingly difficult as we move down the list. Possibly, England was drawn into the war with Germany in 1914 by its alliance membership, but then why would England pursue an alliance policy contradicting its *Geopolitik* interests? Equally difficult becomes the exclusion of the United States–China, United States–Japan or United States–Germany wars. These relations appear as 'basic' as any other, although they can hardly be described as being contiguous, unless that very concept is watered down to meaninglessness.

A final note needs to be made on Table 5.2. The first two systems stand out as highly different from the third one. Contiguity, confrontation and war are more common in the former. In the global system, there is only one contiguous pair among the majors, the Soviet–China one. As of 1976 there have been a few confrontations in this pair, but still not as many as in the non-contiguous pairs of this system. Thus, we can conclude that the relationship between the global powers, the USA and USSR, is less determined by considerations that plagued earlier inter-state systems. This does not mean that territorial questions have no salience, only that conflicts do not rise out of friction over smaller pieces of territory as was earlier the case. As noted, there are no territorial demands raised by either of the two superpowers against the other.

If we speculate in the *Geopolitik* tradition, however, we could note an interesting difference between the two superpowers with respect to territorial questions. The geographical position of the Soviet Union is very different from that of the United States, as it is surrounded by majors or former majors from which territorial transfers have taken place in recent history (notably China, Japan and Germany). Thus, territorial questions could pose more immediate considerations to the Soviet leadership than to the American. After all, the United States has always been secluded from the Eurasian continent and never experienced contiguity with other majors. The closest parallel we could think of is the Soviet ally, Cuba. American reactions to this experience appear not qualitatively different from those seen by Eurasian states. Still, this experience is a recent one, and may not have turned American policies into *Geopolitik*. This, then, points to a discrepancy in perception of international affairs between the leading states in the global system. The United States might not see the world in narrow territorial terms to the same extent as might, for instance, the Soviet Union and China, particularly when they watch each other.

Realpolitik: learning from experience?

The *Realpolitik* model deals with victory and defeat. Arms and alliances are means for achieving desired results, but rivalries are formed from the outcome of previous wars. The structural determinant, it is suggested, is the experience of war and the experience of repeated confrontations. Although the variable 'previous war experience' has been operationalized, the research results have not been rewarding. The relationship between war experiences in terms of destruction of life seems to have little bearing on future war involvement of a given state.[6] By focusing on defeat, however, the war experience is set in a sharper political context. How, we will ask, does the experience of defeat affect a given state's relations to another state, in particular the victorious one?

Consider the following two contradictory hypotheses. The defeated state could *accept* the defeat, redefining its position as no longer being a leading major. This could lead to reduced war involvement in general and non-repetition of its previous war relations in particular. The opposite hypothesis would rather expect continued hostility, *revanchism* gaining ground, resulting in increased conflict involvement or renewed confrontation in a given pair.

The number of majors defeated by majors in the epoch studied is small. Also, when looking at the three systems, one is without defeat (the global system, in which the Korean War most appropriately is seen as a draw),[7] whereas the Euro-centric system has to be seen in the context of the preceding, not analysed, system, as it follows from the defeat of France in 1815. Still, these are the same few experiences that provide the basis for much *Realpolitik* analysis, which justifies a more systematic discussion.

The period of analysis commences in 1816, after a 'resounding' victory over France, including the removal of the revolutionary empire and the restoration of the previous dynasty. Did France accept its defeat and define itself as a 'normal' power among the others, or did it develop into a revanchist and revolutionary one? It does not take much imagination to see that the coming to power of a new Napoleon thirty-three years after the fall of the first one would have an impact on inter-state relations. The war pattern during the neo-Napoleonic times, as a matter of fact, involved three wars between France and its former adversaries, none of them achieving much glory for France, and one of them leading to the fall of the regime. Although Napoleon III lacked the success of his uncle, and the style of the new empire was hardly revolutionary, it is the closest we come to a defeat being avenged in this system. This shows that military defeat does not necessarily lead to the elimination of the major power as a major.

The pattern of maintaining major states as majors even following defeat was obviously prevalent during the Euro-centric system, not only with respect to France. Seven of the fifteen major–major pairs in this system were winner/loser pairs. Three of these saw new wars in the period (all with France as one party and with Napoleon III as ruler). Two experienced war in the following system. As a matter of fact, the Franco-German pair is highly exceptional with its repeated war experience in these two systems. Two other war relations in the mid-nineteenth century were France–Russia and Prussia–Austria. It is obvious who the victors were. Still these two pairs show a realignment, making these previous warring states the core of opposite alliances set into operation in 1914. This then indicates that even an experience of defeat in a major–major war is less formative for future conflict patterns than might be expected.

The inter-regional system, of course, exhibits many more pairs of victor/ loser relations. Out of twenty-eight pairs, twenty involved at least one war, but only four saw a repetition of war during the time of this system or the next one. Again these are well-known: the Western powers and Germany (three pairs) and the Russo-Japanese pair. Between the Euro-centric and the inter-regional system there are links in terms of previous experience of defeat. The global system is, however, markedly different. None of its leading powers has suffered a defeat from any other in the immediately preceding period. The only case of direct warfare between the Western powers and Russia occurred in the wake of the October Revolution. The fighting was comparatively limited, however, and is not, by the COW project, classified as a war. Similarly, the United States aided the anti-Communist side in China immediately after the Second World War, but without direct American troop involvement. If the Second World War marked the end of Europe as a leading region, it also ended some of the recurrent con-flicts that had plagued this continent and the world at least since Napoleonic times. That 1945 constitutes a dramatic breaking-point can be seen when we analyse the defeat experiences of all majors for the entire epoch. In all, there are eleven such defeats. If we categorize them as acceptance, revanchism or cycles of change between these two poles, we find the following: six of the majors display a pattern of acceptance (Austria 1859, 1866, and 1918 as well as the three losers of 1943–1945), two are more ambiguous (Russia 1855 and 1905) and three follow a cycle of initial acceptance and later rejection (France 1815, 1871, Germany 1918). If we, furthermore, look at the different defeats more closely, those that are light (involving little loss of territory or prestige, such as Austria's first two defeats) and those that are very heavy (dismembering the major and inflicting a high degree of destruction, such as Austria's third defeat and the three losers' almost unconditional surrender in 1943–1945) are those that are accepted. Defeats found in between these extremes, seem, however, to result in patterns of recurrent conflict.

Again these cycles are relevant up to 1945. The defeat of France in 1816 brought to power a new Napoleon within thirty-three years, the new defeat in 1871 led to an anti-German alliance within twenty-three years and the defeat of Germany in 1918 led to a revanchist regime in less than fifteen years. After the Second World War, however, a longer period elapsed without signs of the same type. The defeats in 1945 appear more fundamental than any of the previous ones. Not only did they involve change of regimes in the losing countries (so did the defeats in 1815, 1871, and 1918) and the dismembering of the losers (something that also happened in 1815), but possibly these defeats avoided the humiliation of a symbolic defeat as no peace conference was convened (whereas the Congress of Vienna as well as the peace ceremonies in Versailles in 1871 and 1919 were highly humiliating). Perhaps even more striking, the defeats of 1945 were more 'resounding' than any other seen in this epoch. The discrepancy between victor and vanquished was far greater than after earlier wars. New weapons created a new era. This also means that the variable 'previous war experience' or 'defeat' which had importance in the pre-1945 period has less significance in major–major relations in the post-1945 time.[8]

Let us now address the question of *Realpolitik* learning in a different manner. The confrontation data include wars as well as use of force on lower levels of hostility. This makes possible an investigation into the question of whether states appear to learn from confrontation, that is, whether confrontations can or cannot be repeated without resulting in war. This proposition makes little sense for pairs with few confrontations, as learning requires repetition. Furthermore, this assumes that learning is not carried from one relationship to another. Indeed, the learning problem is more complicated than this. A repeated occurrence of military confrontations could well set in motion forces not under the control of the leadership. The 'learning', in other words, is not necessarily one of confidence in the predictability of the adversary, but might be the reverse, mistrust. The full picture emerges when studying pairs with above-average frequency of confrontations. As can be seen from Table 5.1, these relations are few, and, when dividing them into war/no-war experiences, the number of cases in each category becomes very limited.

In the Euro-centric system there are five high-frequency pairs, of which four were also war relations. In the inter-regional system, seven out of eight high-frequency pairs also saw a war, and, in the global system, one out of three. This means that there are sixteen pairs with high numbers of military confrontations. Of these, twelve, or 75 per cent, also saw a war. Examples are, for the first period, Britain–Russia and France–Prussia; for the second, Britain–Germany, France–Germany and Russia–Japan; and for the third period, the United States–China. As these examples make clear, a major–major war does not necessarily put an end to conflicts between the adversaries. Military confrontation has frequently occurred both preceding and succeeding major wars. Thus, the British–Russian relationship contained the highest number of confrontations in the Euro-centric system. One of these resulted in a major war, the Crimean War, the others did not. These two countries fought the First World War on the same side, but after that war reverted to a pattern of frequent confrontations. The same is true for the Second World War (allies) and the post-1945 period (high level of confrontation).

Still, the general lesson seems quite clear. High frequency of confrontation in a given pair tends also to mean that there is a war in that relation. A war, it seems, seldom 'solves' the incompatibilities between the parties. This is difficult to substantiate with our data, as a number of the states in the inter-regional system were not counted as majors in the preceding or succeeding systems. However, it can be illustrated, for instance, by the Russo-Japanese pair. This pair saw three wars during the inter-regional system, and it continued to be a pair of high tension also in the global system, some of the issues from the Second World War being unsettled thirty-five years after the termination of fighting.

Interestingly, there are two high-confrontation pairs that later turned into ones of low frequency or no confrontation. The first is the British–French pair, the second the Franco-German one. The first changed in the wake of the Fashoda confrontation of 1898. The second change is connected with the defeat of Germany in the Second World War and the non-dominant major power position achieved by France at that time. Both these changes occurred at points in time which are major shifts in the entire inter-state system. Out of many possible interpretations, undoubtedly one is that major powers do not reduce their conflict patterns unless the entire set-up of the system compels them to.

Bringing the findings of this section together, we find that in general a high number of confrontations between majors is associated with war, that war defeats tend to be accepted only if they are light or very severe, and that neither confrontations nor wars are likely to reduce the incompatibilities between the states. This would suggest that the *Realpolitik* game can continue without reaching lasting solutions to the problem of war in the inter-state system. Other findings point out, however, that acceptance of defeat is possible and that high frequencies of confrontations can be brought down to lower levels, but these phenomena take place only in conjunction with major changes in the entire system. Furthermore, we find that the global system is different from the others, having a high frequency of confrontations in one pair, but still only one major–major war (Korea) at the time of writing.

Idealpolitik: contradictions between old and new?

In theory, the state can use whatever principle it likes to justify its control over a given territory or a given people. History provides a record of inventiveness. Among the more common notions appealed to are God, Tradition, Family or mystique. The Enlightenment and the French Revolution challenged all these and suggested some new ones. The Napoleonic Wars meant a rapid dissemination of new principles of legitimacy to the rest of Europe. The epoch we are analysing, then, is one when new principles of legitimacy confront the old ones, and, as events unfold, on the whole replace them.

The state needs a principle of legitimacy, we have argued, because it retains the territorial monopoly of lethal violence. In order to gain acceptance, it has to justify its actions to the population within its boundaries, as well as to sustain its identity vis-à-vis states on the other side of the border. Legitimacy, then, is a two-way affair, having both an internal and an external component. A given principle, say the idea that authority is given by God, can be challenged internally in one country (revolutionary sentiments on the rise) or by another country applying another principle (a revolutionary state). As ideas are more easily transported than many other values, influences readily disseminate across borders. A revolution in one major power, consequently, will concern not only the losers in that state but also the regimes in the other majors (as well as minors) based on the challenged principle.

The French Revolution and the Napoleonic Wars resulted primarily in two new principles of legitimacy: *popular control* and *nationalism*. This meant a challenge to other powers building on monarchical power (ordained by family, tradition or God) as well as non-nationalism (e.g. multi-linguality, multi-ethnicity). The problem created by contradicting principles of legitimacy arises, in a conflict theory perspective, from the absence of a common rule on how to decide which principle should be applied to government in a given state at a given time. Contradictions *within* a given principle usually have some rules of conflict resolution. For instance, a monarchical society has a set of regulations on how to choose the successor (the eldest son, the first-born child, etc.). Undoubtedly, history provides a series of cases when such rules have not been easy to interpret, and, as a matter of fact, the 1700s were full of wars originating in this very ambiguity. This might very well have been a major stimulant for the search of new principles. A parliamentary system also has rules for solving such disputes (the biggest party, the biggest coalition, the least opposed alternative, etc.). Neither the monarchical nor the parliamentary (nor any other principle) system is invulnerable to conflict based on contradictory interpretations of the governing rules. Such conflicts, furthermore, often result in substantial changes of the rules. Still, this state of affairs contrasts sharply with the difficulty of handling contradictions *between* principles. A legitimate order building on the principle that God gave the rules cannot suddenly say that a popular referendum can determine whether the divine rule applies or not. There is a need for a *meta*-principle for solving such conflicts, but the only one so far in common use is force, whether violent or non-violent. New principles, in other words, often emerge through clashes with the old ones.

The contradiction between monarchical and popular rule (i.e. a conflict over form of government) is a legacy of the French Revolution. The simple dichotomy of the 1800s, between states governed by monarchs and states governed by people, during the 1900s took the form of a conflict between democracy and dictatorship, where the dictator governed no longer in the name of God but in the name of The People. Just like God, however, The People was given no voice of its own. The *Idealpolitik* contradiction between monarchical (dictatorial) and popular (democratic) states can be related to the question of war and military confrontation, as Table 5.3 shows.

Table 5.3 Contradiction of monarchical and popular forms of government. Pair of major powers, three systems, contradictions at outset of system or time of inclusion as major

System	Total no. of pairs with contradiction	Number (percentage) of contradicting pairs with		Percentage of contradicting pairs of all	
		Wars	High military confrontations	Wars	High military confrontations
Euro-centric	9	5 (56)	3 (33)	83	60
Inter-regional	16	12 (75)	5 (31)	60	3
Global	6	3 (50)	3 (50)	100	100

The numbers in Table 5.3 are small, but still clearly suggest that the contradictions over government legitimacy (in one form or the other) have been an element in many war and confrontation relations. Of thirty-one pairs with contradictions, twenty also included a war, that is, 65 per cent. In each system the percentage is high.

The contradictions coded in Table 5.3 are defined at the outset of each period, which leads to the question of *change during the system*. Interestingly, we then find that the Euro-centric and global systems witnessed less of *Idealpolitik* change than the inter-regional one. The contradicting pairs at the beginning of the Euro-centric system remained the same at the end of the period. The country with *Idealpolitik* change during the nineteenth century was, of course, France. However, already at the outset, the monarchical countries, such as Prussia and Austria, retained a high degree of suspicion of France. The monarchy installed in 1815 was weak. France, even between the revolutions, appeared to them as a liberal country. The return of the Empire in 1851 did not mean a return to monarchical rule as the Emperor was elected and based his power on popular referendum. Thus, although the different nineteenth-century French revolutions in themselves injected fear, brought down governments and disseminated democratic ideas, the monarchical powers throughout the period saw themselves in contradiction to France. In the global system, the most notable change is the one of China. It is, however, not included as a major until the end of the Civil War in 1949, which means that the change from Kuo Min-Tang rule to Communist control is not included.

The relative *Idealpolitik* stability of the Euro-centric and global systems stands in sharp contrast to the turmoil of the inter-regional one. Three of the majors experienced dramatic changes of government: Russia (but in this context exchanging one authoritarian system for another), Germany (having a brief spell of popular control between two authoritarian regimes) and Italy (turning into a more dictatorial regime). In these cases, the change did not simply mean the exchange of one government for another. It also meant the replacement of one principle of legitimacy with another. The *Idealpolitik* pattern of the Euro-centric systems was reversed. The states that in the first period had been the 'revolutionary' ones (Britain and France) now faced revolutions against their own principles. To the new revolutionaries, the old ones appeared reactionary.

The difference between the systems can be expressed in quantitative terms. In the inter-regional system, 39 per cent of all major–major pairs experienced *Idealpolitik* change, compared with no change in the two others. Of the eleven pairs with such change, ten experienced war, whereas the ten pairs without change saw only four wars in the period (Austria has been excluded from this count, as it was a major for only half the time of the inter-regional system). From this it can be concluded that *Idealpolitik* changes in one major tend to be related to conflict with other majors. Furthermore, even stable *Idealpolitik* contradictions are related to major–major conflicts. However, stable contradictions may, to a higher degree, be predictable and, thus, manageable. The inter-regional system appears as an exceptionally traumatic and unstable system of *Idealpolitik* change.

The French Revolution also set in motion another set of *Idealpolitik* contradictions:

nationalism. Nationalist *Idealpolitik* obviously has a different impact from the principles of forms of government just analysed. Whereas the latter principles may be set in a global, general language and may thus theoretically be applicable to all states, nationalist policies do exactly the opposite. They single out the unique feature of a given culture. The question of form of government is potentially revolutionary anywhere in the world, whereas nationalism rests on a parochial appeal. The entire epoch since 1816 is one of rising nationalism, yet it is very hard to measure and differentiate between states with varying degrees of nationalism. Here we will approach the question by differentiating between countries that had *some* non-nationalist appeal and those that had an entirely nationalist one.

Nationalism in its original form was tied to radicalism. The introduction of conscription by the French revolutionaries was an act of amassing popular support in an onslaught on the old regimes of Europe. Also in the earlier parts of the 1800s nationalist causes were tied to liberal ones. National liberal parties existed in many countries. Popular control meant at the same time national control, and together these forces were expected to bring down the monarchies. The remarkable development, then, was the gradual turning of nationalism into a pro-monarchical force by the mid-nineteenth century. Perhaps it was the policies of Bismarck that served to bring this about.[9] The unification of Germany meant at the same time the identification of the nationalist cause with the monarchy and the retrogression of the liberal groupings.[10] However, identifying the monarchy with nationalism runs into considerable problems in multi-ethnic states. The outstanding example is Austria, a highly multi-national state extremely vulnerable to nationalist causes. This state was, in fact, constructed solely around the monarchical family ('Happy Austria, Marry'). Among such non-nationality states we might also include Russia. Although controlled by Russian monarchs, a sizeable proportion of the population remained non- or even anti-Russian. The expansion of the empire during the 1800s served to emphasize this. Perhaps Russia could be described as a multi-national state ruled by a nationalist elite. In any case, this would create an ambiguity for the state in dealing with nationalist causes. For a while, the regime tried to portray itself as 'pan-Slavic' in an obvious attempt to solve this internal inconsistency. From this, we can conclude that all majors of the Euro-centric system became increasingly nationalist, whether combined with popular or monarchical forms of government. Austria is the clear exception and Russia is found in a more ambiguous position. The inter-regional system is the heyday of nationalism. The new actors, Japan and the United States, displayed a nationalist fever similar to that of the majors of the Old World. The countries of great *Idealpolitik* change in this period all surfaced with nationalist doctrines. This is evident in the cases of Italy and Germany. The Soviet doctrine of socialism in one state follows the same pattern.

How, then, would we regard the global system? There are two actors that have to be discussed more closely in this respect, the United States and the Soviet Union. The other three, France, Britain and China, all show distinct traits of being nationalist. The United States and the Soviet Union are both multi-national societies, although the American is definitely more integrated than the Soviet one, having one language spoken all over the country. Both, however, bring forward a non-nationalist appeal even in their names, not identifying the state with any national group. Furthermore, they both use an internationalist jargon pleading for new, universally applicable forms of government. In practice, however, we see that the Soviet Union is governed by Russians, while the leadership in the United States is less clearly composed of one single national group. Their universalist appeal, furthermore, could more be a function of their global power position requiring global *Idealpolitik*. This position, however, could also build on their relative detachment from the nationalist policies of Western Europe. Their revolutions might be thought to absolve them from earlier misfortunes and give them legitimacy as carriers of new societies.

If we conclude that there are some non-nationalist elements in the legitimacy sought by the United States and the Soviet Union, this does not mean that there is no *Idealpolitik* contradiction between the two. Rather, the conflict reverts to one regarding form of government in the following way. The non-nationalist legitimacy of the Soviet Union rests on its contradiction with the previous order. Without its ambition to replace the capitalist system with a socialist one, the entire October Revolution becomes meaningless. The fact that the United States participated in a limited intervention against the Bolsheviks seemingly confirms an expectation of 'inevitable' conflict with capitalism.

For the United States, also in search of a non-nationalist legitimacy, the Soviet Union appears as nothing but a continuation of old policies with new means. The new Russian regime, from this perspective, started as a disguised German operation, continued by slaughtering citizens and party members alike, signed a pact with Hitler and took control over Eastern Europe. In this light, the Soviet regime could not be different from the previous authoritarian, Russian ones. Thus, the non-nationalist legitimacy sought by both gives a similar picture for the two countries, both seeing themselves as the new, liberating state facing an old-fashioned, repressive adversary. The contradiction is different in complexity from that of the earlier system, but it is obvious.

If we now venture into the problem of the effect of nationalist *Idealpolitik* on patterns of war and confrontations, what do we find? First, let us consider pairs of nationalist states. As the idea of nationalism is one of exclusion rather than messianism, it could be expected to result in withdrawal rather than expansion, or non-war rather than war. The most stable inter-state relations, a proponent of nationalism could suggest, arrive if each state consists of all the nationals that belong to it.[11] Certainly, it takes some rearrangement of the map, but that could be regarded as part of the cost to achieve a lasting beneficial situation. However, exclusion may in itself give rise to feelings of superiority, which can justify expansion and control over other nationalities. Throughout the epoch under scrutiny, wars have been waged both to redraw maps to fit nationality borders (nationalist states, however, are curiously reluctant to give up control over territory populated by non-nationals: Prussia under Bismarck aimed at the same time to further German unification and prevent Polish separatism) and to place the state in a 'deserved' place in the sun.

A different set of pairs emerges if we consider non-nationalist–nationalist major–major relations. The prime example is Austria's relationship to the other major powers. The very non-nationalism of this country seems to have involved it in repeated wars with majors (France, Italy, Prussia and Russia) as well as with neighbouring minors. This pairing, of which we do not have many examples, thus seems as war-inducing as the nationalist–nationalist one. As a matter of fact, during Austria's time as a major (1816–1918) it was at war with all the other majors. This is a 'record' matched only by its neighbour, Germany.

Finally, we have to consider the relationship between non-nationalist majors. Again, we lack examples. The only pair resembling this is the American–Soviet one in the global system, which, indeed, has a 'record' of high confrontation. Thus, on the bilateral level, we have difficulties in establishing any clear pattern with regard to nationalism–non-nationalism. There is, however, an interesting difference between the three systems. The Euro-centric and the global systems have a greater room for non-nationalist issues than was the case for the second system. The inter-regional system appears the most nationalist one, all majors displaying nationalist sentiments. This means that for this period the variable of nationalism has little explanatory value as it cannot discriminate between different pairs. Thus, it appears more appropriate to conclude that nationalism should be regarded as a general system variable, conditioning perceptions of the actors, rather than having a direct link to the onset of war between pairs. The Euro-centric and the global systems, then, become more interesting as we find contradictions between states basing themselves on nationalist and non-nationalist appeals. There is an historical parallel between Austria, in the first system, and the United States in the third one. Both were advocating special forms of government, both running into constant contradiction with more nationalist-inclined states, and both had other considerations than the general principle in itself. Both, furthermore, found Russia as an opponent, a country we earlier defined as ambiguous with respect to nationalism in the first system and exhibiting much of the same ambiguity in the third one. This very ambiguity could easily result in unpredictability. By the end of the first system, Russia suddenly changed its policy away from monarchically based collaboration with Germany and Austria to a nationalist-based opposition to these two powers. This unpredictability, indeed, was one element in the inter-regional system as well. A sudden shift, but this time in the opposite direction, preceded the war in 1939.

The main purpose of *Idealpolitik* is to provide autonomy of action for the rulers of the state. The notion of national interest, which is an *Idealpolitik* rather than a *Realpolitik* concept, is a most appropriate tool for this purpose. The very vagueness of the concept provides it with its political usefulness. In many respects it is much more useful than, say, democracy or human rights, as the latter concepts have a practical applicability the former lacks. Rulers equipped with two different sets of legitimizing principles would, however, be infinitely more autonomous than those with only one. It is, however, not necessarily true that more autonomy reduces the likelihood of war. It might well do exactly the opposite by decreasing predictability. *Idealpolitik* is thus a necessary but insufficient condition for political action. It can provide some consistency in the same way as individuals justify their actions. As every social situation contains contradictory elements, different sets of *Idealpolitik* can provide different pictures. *Idealpolitik*, in other words, might not be the cause of conflict, but it is the ultimate requirement for perceiving conflict.

Kapitalpolitik: competition or cooperation?

In the capitalist business system, competition is regarded as creative and healthy. Competition in the inter-state system is often seen as either unavoidable or potentially destructive. Merging these two systems, one could argue that a capitalist inter-state system would be more competitive than any other social system, and that it would be most conflictful. Can it then be demonstrated that capitalist industrialization creates new conflicts between states or that it, at least, intensifies old rivalries to the point of war? Also, to what extent is integration possible in such a system and would it affect the emergence of war?

Competition between industrial or industrializing states is often seen as a form of inter-state conflict. It is obvious, however, that, as long as we concentrate on capitalist states, competition exists between corporations rather than between states. Thus, the hypothesis should be more immediately applicable to a state-controlled economy than a privately run one. Lenin, in his work on imperialism, never faced this question properly but instead assumed coordination between state and capital.[12] This assumption seems hazardous, as most states in the Capitalist system prefer to stay out of production, leaving even state-owned corporations to make their decisions on commercial grounds.

Let us, however, for the sake of argument, assume complete coordination. How, then, would industrial competition result in conflict and war? One way of reasoning is to regard rank as the most important variable. Thus, a given state would be anxious to preserve its own leading position and resent the emergence of others, which in turn would be eager to overtake the leading one. Conflict behaviour erupts as a means of keeping advancing states down, or for advancing states to get ahead. As the argument is roughly parallel to security thinking it might have a bearing on perception of conflict. It would be particularly valid in an early phase of industrialization, when the measurement of rank is still simple and only few dimensions count. Later phases of industrialization with great diversity lead rather to repeated experiences of being overtaken but at the same time provide other sectors on which to claim a more advanced ranking. Thus, the competition argument would make sense, in particular, in the Euro-centric system. That was, of course, also the time during which the argument was advanced in its original Leninist form.[13] Using statistics on iron production (1816–1899) and iron and steel production after 1900 as measures of industrial growth, we find that the phenomenon of 'catching up' has occurred in eleven major–major pairs during the whole epoch. As the total number of pairs is fifty-three, 'catching up' took place in 21 per cent of the pairs.[14] The differences between the systems are small: four, six and one change respectively. This means that the stability in rank of industrial production is markedly high. This, in turn, would increase the likelihood that changes actually would catch the attention of the decision-makers. Some of the changes are noteworthy, moreover, particularly in the Franco-Prussian pair, Prussia producing more iron than France, for the first time, in 1870. Some changes are more temporary, for instance France in 1930 having a bigger iron and steel production than the United Kingdom.

Still, this yields little evidence of a close relation between industrial competition and war. In the eleven pairs, war took place within a ten-year time span (before and after the passing) only three times. Two of these might correspond to the theory, namely the Franco-Prussian war in 1870 and the Prusso-Austrian war in 1866. The third one seems highly unrelated, China in 1960 producing more iron and steel than France, and the two countries being adversaries in the Korean War ten years earlier. Also the estimate of China's iron production is dubious. This leaves us with only two serious candidates for the situation we have been seeking. Historical accounts do not support the idea that either of these two wars emerged from industrial competition. It seems more plausible to say that industrial capacity stimulated an already existing ambition on the part of Prussia to gain control over Germany.

Furthermore, some of the shifts in industrial production that bear no relationship at all to war still changed economic power in the system. The United States passed the United Kingdom in 1890, thereby not only enhancing its military capacity, but also actually deposing the leading industrial nation of its leadership. Certainly, this is the type of situation the competition hypothesis would particularly expect to lead to conflict. Later, the United Kingdom was also overtaken by Germany and, although some confrontations occurred, and the states were at war with one another some fifteen years later, it seems far-fetched to impute this to the overtaking itself.

A third noteworthy example is the Franco-Russian pair. By the end of the 1890s, Russia's iron and steel production surpassed France's. During most of the nineteenth century these countries had been in conflict with one another. Consequently, one would expect this change between the countries to result in intensified confrontation. Instead, an alliance between the two was forged some years before the surpassing, and stood the test in the years following it. Rather, this relationship seems to point in a different direction: the alliance was preceded by increased cooperation in the economic field between these two industrializing countries. Industrialization, in other words, need not necessarily result in conflict, but could lead to interaction and even opportunities for cooperation.

This makes the question of economic transactions between major industrial states important. It appears, as a general rule, that major states tend not to be dependent on other majors.[15] This is partly because of the size of their interaction, as widespread interaction is often part of being a top dog in a system, and partly attributable to deliberate policy. Economic interaction can be measured in direct trade between the majors. Although world trade grew at a dramatic speed during the period of industrialization, it did not create dependence between the major industrializing states. Industrial interconnection is a more recent phenomenon. The trade patterns of the 1800s are more an exchange of complementary goods than integration of production and markets. Thus, for the second half of the century, the major import goods for Britain, the leading trade partner, is food followed by raw materials for its textile industry. The major export is manufactured goods. The exchange pattern, then, was clearly one of trading unprocessed goods for processed ones, an exchange which, at least among industrializing nations, could be seen as complementary: it made it possible, for instance, for Russia to buy machinery required for its industrialization from Britain in exchange for wheat from the Ukraine.[16]

With more countries industrializing, however, the competition for markets could be expected to increase, and the likelihood of government interference to protect indigenous industry to rise. The later part of the 1800s is coloured by the attempts of industrializing states to curtail imports from Britain: protective tariffs were installed by the United States, Germany, France, Russia, Austria and Japan. Such measures did not necessarily lead to military conflicts with Britain, however. Rather, the 'tariff wars' that followed were waged between the countries introducing the tariffs. Most notable is the tariff war between Germany and Russia, but similar conflicts emerged between France and Italy, and between majors and minors.[17] None of these conflicts escalated into military hostilities or wars, and their lasting effect may rather have been one of reinforcing existing prejudices about the adversary than either creating or modifying them. It is not even obvious that the tariff conflict between Germany and Russia had an effect on the trade between the two countries. During the early 1900s Russian industrialization was increasingly relying on machinery imported from Germany. Germany's share of Russia's total import in 1913 is estimated to be 52.7 per cent while Germany's share of Russia's export was 31.7 per cent.[18] Possibly this pair of majors was one of the most closely intertwined ones, but this is also the relationship through which the July crisis of 1914 was turned into a world war.

Some other major–major relations might have been fairly close at the turn of the century. Britain and the United States would be such a case, Britain during the late 1800s being a major source of capital for American railroad building. Also, Germany and Austria-Hungary might have been interlinked as complementary markets for industrial and agricultural products. Finally, France and Russia both tried to cement their relations with the help of industrial projects and capital transactions. As a matter of fact, this may have been the most lasting political effect of the German–Russian tariff war, which reduced Russia's financial reliance on the German stock market. Russian dependence on German goods was not ended, however.[19]

The lack of reliable data for the 1800s makes it difficult to pursue the interaction analysis further. The scarce evidence available seems to suggest, however, that there is very little correspondence between economic interaction and military conflict among the majors in this period. For the post-First World War period, data are more readily at hand. A previous study shows clearly that the frequency of economic interaction between the majors has little correlation with war relations. The high intensity of commercial exchange between the United States and Japan had little effect in preventing a war between the two in 1941. The low interaction between the United States and the Soviet Union following the Second World War did not reduce conflict between the two.[20] These investigations show that major–major wars and confrontations tend not to arise from economic interaction.

Summarizing this section, we would say that neither direct competition nor bilateral cooperation between industrializing major states has a strong relationship to confrontations and wars. This finding requires comment. First of all, all majors are on a comparatively high level of industrialization. This means that they may be more sensitive to more minor changes than those we have been investigating, for instance monetary flows or exchange of particularly important goods. Second, our conclusion does not rule out the existence of competition or conflict. Rather, it says that such competition tends not to spill over into a military treatment of the conflict. It appears more likely that economic conflicts are treated with economic means and that military means are more often used in conflicts with a more direct military connection. Third, the majors tend not to be dependent on each other. As many economic conflicts could arise from dependence, this origin of conflict tends not to be applicable to major–major pairs. This does not exclude the possibility that economic reasons are more basic in major–minor conflicts. Fourth, the industrial capacity of particular importance in major–major relations is the one actually or potentially tied to military production. The epoch investigated was one of rapid industrialization, which also meant industrialization of warfare. Arms production was transformed from handicraft to industry during the later part of the 1800s. Actually this suggests some interesting differences, not between pairs of majors, but between the three systems. The Euro-centric system is one of limited industrial arms production, apart from improvements of guns and cannons. The inter-regional system emerged at a time when large-scale military industrial projects were launched for the first time. The big battleships thus mark not only a new naval strategy but also the beginning of industrial manufacture of weapons. In the inter-regional system industrial gains made with the civilian market as a main target found military uses as well. The global system differs from the earlier ones by having a much higher degree of specifically military-related industrial production in peace time, by devoting a larger share of research resources to military development than ever before, and thus by having a phenomenon not seen earlier: a military–industrial complex. We leave this observation as a plausible path for further exploration on the level of pairs of majors. One indication of the importance of this avenue is the very high correlation found between pairs of rapidly arming countries and the escalation of confrontations into war.[21]

Evaluation of four models

The previous four sections have confronted some of the most prevalent conflict models with data from pairs of major states in the three inter-state systems of 1816–1976. This gives us a basis for judging the explanatory power of these models, assuming that the various measures are appropriate. A cautionary remark is needed here, as the measures are simple and there are considerable data problems. Thus, there is room for improvement.

The four models can be evaluated in two different respects. First, we can ask, *given* a pair of major states with a *certain incompatibility*, what is the historical record of confrontation and war in that type of a pair? This, in a sense, is the test proponents of each of the four models would prefer: the models would have some predictive value; if they point to an incompatibility as 'dangerous', a positive result would strengthen the fruitfulness of the model and intensify research along the lines of the model.

Second, we can ask, given a recurrent phenomenon of war and confrontation, to what extent can a given model explain *the entire phenomenon* of such conflict behaviour? This is a more all-encompassing task and it leads to an evaluation of the range of explanatory power of a given model. Perhaps a model can capture a certain type of incompatibility, but this may only cover a small fraction of the entire conflict problem. Table 5.4 brings together the findings presented in the last four sections for the three systems. The various incompatibilities are presented as 'incompatibility relations' in column (1). Columns (2) and (3) contain information

Table 5.4 Types of incompatibility, confrontation and war relations, 1816–1976 (system pairs, percentages)

(1) Type of incompatibility relation	(2) Share of all incompatibility relations having military confrontation	(3) Share of all incompatibility relations having war relation	(4) Share of all system pairs having given incompatibility (n = 53)	(5) Share of all confrontation relations having given incompatibility (n = 45)	(6) Share of all war relations having given incompatibility (n = 29)
Contiguity (*n* = 16)	93	64	26	29	31
Experience of defeat in previous system (*n* = 10)	90	60	19	20	21
Repeated confrontations (*n* = 16)	–	75	30	36	41
Idealpolitik contradiction (*n* = 31)	94	65	58	64	69
Idealpolitik change (*n* = 11)	91	91	21	22	34
National– non-national contradiction (*n* = 16)	81	63	30	29	34
Catch-up relation (*n* = 11)	91	27	21	22	10

needed for answering the first question, whereas columns (4), (5) and (6) are relevant for the second one.

Let us now address the first question. The numbers in columns (2) and (3) are quite high. However, they have to be compared with what we would expect to be 'normal' in the system. Thus, the figures of column (2) should be compared with the fact that the share of all system pairs having military confrontation is 85 per cent, in other words the vast majority of all major–major relations include some confrontation during the period 1816–1976. Only in situations where a given incompatibility has a higher number than 'normal' could we say that it has more to tell us than would result from sheer randomness. Table 5.4 thus shows that, for all types of incompatibilities, military confrontations are more frequent than would be expected, with the exception of contradictions over non-nationality.

Similarly, column (3) data should be compared with the share of all system pairs having wars, that is 55 per cent. All column (3) figures are well above this, with the exception of the *Kapitalpolitik* indicator of 'Catch-up'. Most notable is the measure of '*Idealpolitik* change': in major–major pairs with change of legitimacy in one of the majors, there is a high frequency of war.

Internal revolutions in major states are related to external conflicts, in one way or the other. This suggests that at least three of the four models have struck at important factors in the inter-state system. In a way, the models would not have been constructed did they not have some real-world examples to rest on. The dynamics suggested by the *Geo-, Real-* and *Idealpolitik* models consequently need to be taken into account in inter-state analysis. The *Kapitalpolitik* model, the way it has been interpreted here, seems also to suggest some important aspects, but rather with respect to confrontations in general, not to war in particular. Now, let us address the second question: to what extent can the models say something about the entire phenomenon of confrontation and war between major states? In this case column (4) gives the 'normal' distribution, with which to compare the frequencies of columns (5) and (6). Column (4) clearly illustrates that the various incompatibilities suggested by the models have a very limited applicability to the entire population of system pairs: they do not, with one exception, cover more than 20–30 per cent of all pairs in the system.

The exception is '*Idealpolitik* contradiction', which is found at almost double the frequency of all the other incompatibilities. In a way, this suggests that the ideological questions have had the greatest distribution of all in the period, perhaps even proposing that the period of 1816–1976 is an era of ideology, more than anything else: the incompatibilities around which major states have preferred to group themselves have concerned such issues as forms of government: monarchy and republic, dictatorship and democracy, etc. Turning to column (5), a comparison with column (4) reveals to what extent a given incompatibility is 'overrepresented' among all confrontation relations of the epoch. The general picture is one of such an overrepresentation for all incompatibilities, but the degree of overrepresentation is particularly high for 'repeated confrontation' and '*Idealpolitik* contradiction'. The values of all others tend to lie within the range of ± 3 percentage points.

Finally, column (6) gives the figures for war relations. Again, the numbers move upward for all variables, with the exception of the *Kapitalpolitik* indicator. The same variables that exhibit much confrontation are also important for war, with the addition of the '*Idealpolitik* change' variable. These three variables are over-represented in column (6) compared with column (4), by 11–13 percentage points. This, we would argue, makes them very important elements in any explanation of the phenomenon of conflict behaviour in the inter-state system. Still, none of these three alone accounts for the entire phenomenon of conflict behaviour, but '*Idealpolitik* contradiction' has an unusual magnitude: close to 70 per cent of all war relations also involved an incompatibility over legitimizing principles of government.

'*Idealpolitik* contradiction' comes out as quite exceptional, both in its presence in a great number of pairs and in its high link to military confrontation and war. In a way, this is not surprising: ideological questions are often invoked when explaining why a certain conflict exists and why a given war is necessary. Although a number of wars have not officially been described, at the time, in the light of a certain '*Idealpolitik* contradiction', such a view may still have been the underlying one. However, the spread of *Idealpolitik* contradictions to a great number of major states also appears to reflect a diffusion of certain forms of government: the contradictions emerge to some extent because the number of forms becomes restricted. Thus, the epoch witnesses the emergence of one major contradiction: popular versus non-popular forms of government. As this contradiction is formulated in a general language, it transcends borders of territory and nationality more easily than many of the others. As it also relates to social systems, it is a contradiction which can emerge and disappear: it has a high degree of changeability, compared with, for instance, contiguity. Thus, *Idealpolitik*, being changeable, stimulates conflict behaviour, and, as we also have seen in Table 5.4, '*Idealpolitik* change', although not as frequent in major–major pairs, has the highest degree of conflict behaviour, and it is the incompatibility relation that is the most 'overrepresented' among war relations.

Regarding the other incompatibility relations present in Table 5.4, we can see their limited applicability from column (4), and indeed many of them are very specific: applicable to certain typical pairs. This we have exemplified in the preceding sections, and it also illustrates that the four models have been constructed with certain examples in mind, notably the Franco-German or the Americo-Soviet ones. When we scrutinize such examples, we find that they exhibit not only the incompatibility suggested by one model, but also those of another. The Franco-German pair in the Euro-centric system, for instance, contained incompatibilities suggested by most models. In this respect, this very major–major pair remains rather exceptional. It also means that it is very difficult to use this example as an illustration of any one of the four models. Rather, it suggests that various combinations of incompatibilities would be the most fruitful way of pursuing analysis. One could, for instance, suggest that the more incompatibilities exhibited in one and the same pair, the more frequent would confrontation and war appear in that pair. Carrying out such an analysis does not improve our understanding, however.

Thus, in the Euro-centric system, there is one pair, the Austro-Russian one, with a considerable number of incompatibilities but nevertheless no war at all during the period. There is, in fact, no clearer correlation between what we could term 'accumulated incompatibility relations' and war or confrontation relations for the entire period than we have found, when pursuing a one-model test. Still, there might well be certain combinations between, for instance, *Idealpolitik* contradictions and one or another incompatibility which would yield more obvious results. This analysis remains to be carried out.

State systems and incompatibilities

A premise of this study has been the existence of systems of states, and that conflict and war most fruitfully can be understood from an analysis of the state and the system in which the state finds itself. This means that the analysis has concentrated on different incompatibilities thought to exist between states, and on a comparison of three consecutive state systems of the last 160 years. Thus, we have not addressed the question of incompatibilities internal to the state, or empirically compared the state system to other social systems. Thus, we can suggest neither that the state system would do better if the states in some sense were 'better' nor that the world would fare better without states. We can suggest, however, that state systems vary considerably and that certain state characteristics are more likely to lead to conflict than others.

When isolating basic cleavages, or incompatibilities, we have taken a structural approach to the problem of conflict and war: certain lasting properties have been investigated whether or not they are associated with conflict behaviour. The cleavages sought have been those closely associated with the exclusive properties of the state, and they have all been of a highly 'objective' nature: fairly easy to observe by independent observers. Thus, the test carried out not only sheds light on the very incompatibilities investigated, but also has something to contribute to the entire discussion on whether 'objective' contradictions have a strongly determining impact on inter-state relations or not. Furthermore, the study has concentrated on those actors in the inter-state system thought to be the most independent ones: the major powers. In this way, some highly pertinent questions with respect to dependence have been avoided. It is likely, and not contradictory to this investigation, however, that relations between major and minor states, as well as those between minor states, are highly conditioned by the existence of dependencies in the system.

Many of our results are negative, when we search for incompatibilities that would, individually, account for a large proportion of the general phenomenon of inter-state war. Most of the suggested incompatibilities have limited explanatory power: they have been found to appear in approximately 30–40 per cent of all war relations, against an expected level of 20–30 per cent. The only incompatibility with a higher share is '*Idealpolitik* contradiction', that is incompatible forms of legitimate government, which are found in almost 70 per cent of all war relations. This is, however, an incompatibility which is less stable than many others:

revolutions, although not frequent, do occur and have a profound effect on the relationship between major powers. *Idealpolitik* change in a given pair exhibits a markedly high association with war in that relation. This might suggest that stable incompatibilities, in general, are accepted as part of the game, and that decision-makers react more to changes in that game than to the foundations of the game itself. Also, it suggests that legitimacy, which we regard as one of the five defining characteristics of the state, is of concern not only to the major state which has a certain form, but also to its surroundings. Revolutions, in other words, not only mean a change in a given relationship, but could lead to diffusion of alternative ways of thought that affect also the other pair in that relation.

The importance allotted to *Idealpolitik* contradiction compared with other forms of incompatibilities is at first surprising. Certainly, anyone preferring any of the other models suggested could minimize this contradiction and reduce it to a derivative of other, more 'basic' incompatibilities. However, legitimacy is closely linked to identity. The moral right of a given state to be a state and command its inhabitants even to go to war requires very strong ideological commitments. In a period when popular influence has been on the rise, ideological motives become increasingly important. This, furthermore, leads to an emphasis on ideological consistency in policy: with too many detours in international affairs, the internal legitimacy of the state might be endangered. Such a requirement of consistency, in other words, would reduce the autonomy of decision-making. This in many ways would contribute to a reduced risk of warfare, as decision-makers would be more careful not to manoeuvre themselves into blind alleys. It would, however, make the situation of *Idealpolitik* change more tempting for intervention or confrontational behaviour, and, in that special circumstance, increase the likelihood of war. This study suggests that a highly pressing problem for continued research is *Idealpolitik* contradictions and their settlement or containment in other forms than war between states: coexistence is just one possibility, dialogue another, but so are compromise social formations.

The other incompatibilities investigated in this study also have high correlations with confrontation and war, but, as these contradictions are less frequent in the inter-state system, they cover less of the entire phenomenon of conflict behaviour. They are either system-specific (applicable to one or two of the systems we have investigated, but not all of them) or pair-specific (applicable to only some few of the pairs). Typical of the first is the *Realpolitik* variable 'previous defeat', which is important in the Euro-centric and inter-regional system, but not in the global one, or the *Idealpolitik* variable 'national–non-national contradiction', which is significant for understanding Austria's relations with the other majors, but less important for all other pairs.

Interestingly enough, we find that *Kapitalpolitik* indicators show a different pattern: they are associated with confrontations but not with wars. This would mean that economic disagreements can lead to friction, but that major powers would not in general go to war with one another for predominantly economic reasons. This does not exclude them waging war against minor states for that reason. It does not mean that *Kapitalpolitik* is not linked to conflicts, but suggests less of an escalating effect. Economic disagreements, we would then suppose, are more easily resolved than those which involve, for instance, ideology: after all, a bag of money can more easily be divided than can the legitimacy of a given state.

Together, these four models, derived from the unique properties of the state, provide a convenient analytical tool for investigating individual pairs of states. Cross-sectional or cross-temporal comparison on a dyadic level is simplified. It is also fruitful to look for incompatibilities: there is no case of a war relation in a pair in which there has not been any incompatibility at all. However, there are many different types of incompatibilities, and pairs, thus, will differ. Also, there is not much of a cumulative effect: the more contradictions of different types, certainly the more problem there is to manage, but that in itself does not make war more likely. One cleavage is enough to make a war; many cleavages may in fact caution decision-makers.

Finally, the study has shown some of the benefits of making comparison across systems. The three inter-state systems delineated in the 1816–1976 epoch have different characteristics, and they make sense out of a mass of information. Certainly, they are all systems of states, but the systems are highly different. The distinctions were drawn with respect to the inclusion and exclusion of major states. The three systems differ with respect to number of majors, as well as to the frequency of confrontations and wars, and to the four models. The Euro-centric and the global systems, for instance, were similar in '*Idealpolitik* contradictions', the contradictions remaining the same throughout the system. The inter-regional system appeared as a more chaotic period, with a higher number of majors, much *Idealpolitik* change, nationalist policies, and previous defeats. It comes forward not only as an inter-regional system, but as an inter-system system: a period of turmoil between two more structured and ordered systems.

History provides its own logic. The inter-state systems from 1816 to 1976 thus mark a logical evolution from one type of order, the Euro-dominated world, to another type: the superpower global order. The inter-regional period is one of challenge against the Euro-dominated world: new, non-European powers enter, new non-classical ideologies appear. The European (or, largely, British–French–Russian) dominance meets at its very high-point (symbolized, for instance, by Queen Victoria's Silver Jubilee in 1897) its own contradiction. With Bismarck fired, Germany enters a policy of German chauvinism. Japan and the United States expand: a non-formalized coalition of challengers against the classical form of settling inter-state conflicts emerges. There is a straight line from Kaiser Wilhelm to Adolf Hitler, as well as from Woodrow Wilson to Leon Trotsky, from Japan to Italy: a process where another order is searched for, and where the different challengers have conflicting views of what the new order should look like. The first result is the breakdown of one order, without finding a replacement. The next result is the resurrection of a global system, where two of the challengers fundamentally destroy the old order as well as all other challengers, and arrive at an order which none had wished. The global system, then, is a system whose dominant actors have no confidence in each other, and, consequently, an order which has no appeal to anybody else. It is an order where conflicts are settled by confrontation and brinkmanship. It is a result of historical logic, the climax of an evolution of the inter-state system. For the two main contenders, the remaining step is a logical one: global peace will come, if only the opponent can be eliminated. The agonizing problem is that the same historical logic still has not produced a path to another system except through another inter-system period: without such a path, the global system might end with the elimination not only of the main contenders but of all systems of the globe.

Notes

1 Sections of this chapter were presented at the First World Peace Science Congress, Harvard, June 1980; at the Nordic Theory Week, Oslo, August 1980; and at seminars at the Mental Health Research Institute, Ann Arbor, and the Department of Peace and Conflict Research, Uppsala. Important comments from these presentations have been incorporated. I am also grateful to Klaus Jürgen Gantzel, Björn Hettne, Miroslav Nincic and J. David Singer for valuable suggestions.

2 The definition of war is found in Singer, J. D. and M. Small, *The Wages of War: A Statistical Handbook*, New York: John Wiley & Sons, 1972, and of military confrontation in Militarized Dispute Coding Rules, available at the Correlates of War project, Mental Health Research Institute, University of Michigan, Ann Arbor, Michigan. Here four wars which did not involve a prior military confrontation have been included among the military confrontations, making the total 229. This includes all military confrontations between major states and between major and minor states, 1816–1976, as found by the project, spring 1980.

3 See Kaplan, M., *System and Process in International Politics*, New York: John Wiley, 1957, ch. 6–8; Singer, J. D. and K. W. Deutsch, 'Multipolar Power Systems and International Stability', *World Politics*, 1964, 16 (3): 390–406. Also Wallace, M., 'Alliance Polarization, Crosscutting and International War, 1815–1964', *Journal of Conflict Resolution*, 1973, 17 (4): 575–604, discusses the possibility of a curvilinear model.

4 Franke and Chi throw some light on this question with Italian and Chinese examples in Kaplan, M. (ed.), *New Approaches to International Relations*, New York: St. Martin's Press, 1968, pp. 405–458.

5 Studies building on COW data reaching this conclusion are Mihalka, M. D., *Interstate Conflict in the European State System, 1816–1970*, dissertation, University of Michigan, 1976, and Gochman, C. S., *Status, Conflict and War: The Major Powers, 1820 1970*, dissertation, University of Michigan, 1975. Gochman finds that 30 per cent of all confrontations between neighbours end in war compared with 18 per cent for non-contiguous states during the nineteenth century, whereas the same numbers for the twentieth century are 24 per cent for each category. Also Russett, B. M., *International Regions and the International System*, Chicago: Rand McNally, 1967, finds proximity to be important, as does Richardson, L. F., *Statistics of Deadly Quarrels*, Chicago: Quadrangle Books, 1960, p. 297.

6 See Gochman, *op. cit.*, pp. 60–61, 163 and 204, who applies a 'fifteen year decay function' and finds no relations. This is too mechanistic a treatment of this variable.

7 See Singer and Small, *op. cit.*, pp. 348–349.

8 As the theme of 'German revanchism' has been emphasized since 1945, this requires some comment. Obviously, there has been very little sign of the type of revanchism witnessed before 1945 in Germany or in France. Also, there is little likelihood of Germany again emerging as a power on the level of superpowers. West Germany's reluctance to accept the changed map of Europe thus served to maintain some grain of credibility in the theme. It is probably more correct to describe the Cold War as a conflict between the Soviet Union and the United States with Germany as one of its objects but not as a subject.

9   The literature on this topic is extensive; see, for instance, Eyck, E., *Bismarck and the German Empire*, London: Unwin, 1968 (3rd edn), and Pflanze, *op. cit.*

10   The identification of monarchy with nationalism may well have saved the monarchies in a number of countries dominated by non-nationalist liberals: in Britain and Scandinavia the monarchies became national symbols, rather than symbols of authoritarianism.

11   See Herz, J. H., 'The territorial state revisited', in Rosenau, J. W. (ed.), *International Politics and Foreign Policy*, New York: Free Press, 1969, pp. 88–89.

12   Lenin, V. I., *Imperialism: The Highest Stage of Capitalism*, Broadway, NSW: Resistance Books, 1999 (first published 1917).

13   Cf. Organski, A. F. K., *World politics*, New York: Knopf, 1968 (2nd edn), ch. 5. Organski argues both that the dominant will not accept being bypassed and that the 'challenger' will grow increasingly confident as the 'gap' to the leaders narrows. He is, however, unclear as to *when* (before or after), *by whom* and even *why* overtaking will lead to war. There will be a fight, he asserts, but also discusses exceptions, notably the US–UK relationship, pp. 356–357, 363.

14   In this test, five-year periods are used rather than annual data in order to capture more lasting changes. Data are taken from the Correlates of War project, using iron production for 1816–1895 and iron and steel production for 1900–1970. In this count, changes between systems which are the result of war have not been considered, notably Germany, Italy and Japan being overtaken in 1945.

15   See Wallensteen, Peter, *Structure and War: On International Relations, 1920–1968*, Stockholm: Rabén & Sjögren, 1973, pp. 90 93, 162.

16   Sartorius von Waltershausen, A., *Die Entstehung der Weltwirtschaft*, Jena: G. Fischer, 1931, pp. 323, 357.

17   Ibid. pp. 492, 515–523. Cf. Nicholson, M., 'Tariff Wars and a Model of Conflict', *Journal of Peace Research*, 1967, 1: 26–38.

18   Storanovich, T., 'Russian Domination in the Balkans', in Hunczak, T. (ed.), *Russian Imperialism from Ivan the Great to the Revolution*, New Brunswick, NJ: Rutgers University Press, 1974, pp. 228–229.

19   Germany's policy has been heatedly debated; see, for instance, Eyck, *op. cit.*, p. 294, and Seton-Watson, H., *The Decline of Imperial Russia*, London: Methuen, 1952, pp. 177–178.

20   Wallensteen, *op. cit.*, pp. 163–167.

21   Wallace, M., 'Old nails in new coffins', *Journal of Peace Research*, 1981, 1: 91–95.

6 Universalism versus particularism

On the limits of major power order[1]

Universalism versus particularism

Autonomy has been a most cherished value for major powers throughout history. It has been a motivating force for smaller powers to free themselves from the influence of others. Liberation has been the ambition of revolutionaries. Still, at no time has autonomy been more restrained than today, even for the major powers. Nuclear threats and strategic doctrines link even the most powerful to one another and restrict the space for independent action. In spite of nuclear vulnerability, major powers can pursue policies to further their particularist interest, as witnessed in Eastern Europe, West Asia or Central America. Also, they may pursue policies of universalist application, taking into account legitimate interests of others as witnessed during the period of détente. In this sense, nothing is new. Similar options have always been available to major powers, and, at some period in time, universalism has been preferred to particularism. This chapter analyses experiences of major power universalism as opposed to particularism: what has historically been the difference, what has been the result, why have policies shifted and which lessons can be drawn?

Universalist policies are understood to be concerted efforts among major powers to organize relations between themselves to work out acceptable rules of behaviour (general standards). Particularist policies, in contrast, are understood to be policies which emphasize the special interest of a given power, even at the price of disrupting existing organizations or power relationship.[2] In the first case, the aim is order, but this is not to say that order is the result or that disorder necessarily follows from the other. On the contrary, some would argue that the pursuit of self-interest is creating more order than is altruism, as it redirects imbalances in power distribution and makes possible the voicing of grievances. Thus, it is for the historical record to decide whether universalism or particularism results in war.

This formulation of the problem is hardly novel or original, but still there have been few efforts to systematically compare the outcome of the different set of policies. Under the concept of world order fruitful incursions into the area have been made by the Institute for World Order, as well as by scholars such as Stanley Hoffmann.[3] The conceptions might be different, but mostly they point in a similar direction: world order policies aim at including more than the particularistic interest of a given actor as the actor's goals. There is, in other words, a more universalistic ambition. Apart from preserving the actor itself as an actor, there is also an understanding of the demands and worries of the opponent. Obviously, the structural frameworks in which such globalistic policies are carried out differ; the Institute for World Order in general wants to go beyond the nation-state, and develop policies more fitting for local ('smaller') actors, whereas the Hoffmann conception clearly focuses on the role of the major powers. Here it suffices to note that the structure of the global system makes it necessary to point to the significance of the major powers and their mutual relations. It is also evident that mutual relations between these powers tend to undergo dramatic shifts and changes, swinging between more universalistic and more particularistic emphases. Thus, major powers pursuing universalistic policies would, for some, be world order policies. For others, this might still be unsatisfactory if the basic question is policies *by whom?* It is self-evident that there are limits to universalism of the major powers. Their status as major is not to be threatened. On the contrary it constitutes the postulate of their policies. Thus, at some point, the divergent definitions of world order also become incompatible, boiling down to the question of whether, in the long run, major powers are to remain majors or not.

Individual actors can have individual orders of preference and priorities can change over time. However, we are interested in the collectivity of major powers. General standards are general only to the extent they have support from many actors. Major powers are significant in setting such standards and in achieving adherence to them. Thus, if a collectivity of major powers, tacitly or openly, sets up certain rules of behaviour and applies them consistently over time, this will have an effect beyond the collectivity. If, on the contrary, there are no such agreed rules, particularism is likely to become a predominant pattern.

Here the focus is on comparing periods of collective major power universalism, and on contrasting them to periods of predominant particularism. Historical experiences of universalism can give insight into useful methods, but also into the limits of such efforts. The study of particularism might yield knowledge of legitimate dissatisfaction with existing arrangements. If a given – formal or informal – collective arrangement constantly works to the advantage of some and to the disadvantage of others, the arrangement itself becomes questioned.

Identifying universalism and particularism

Since the Napoleonic era, there have been several serious attempts at creating universalist relations among major powers. These attempts, initiated by major powers, have built on the consent of all or most major powers. They have sometimes been constructed around particular organizations (such as the League of Nations) or around more informal arrangements (such as the Concert of Europe). Common to them is the ambition to develop general rules of behaviour among the major powers, and attempts to reconcile differences so as to maintain the consensus among the involved powers. Thus, what historians refer to as periods of concerts, orders or détente are what we here label universalism. Such periods are delimited on two grounds. First, there has to be a certain consistency and continuity in the policies pursued by the major powers within the particular period. Second, there has to be a marked difference (qualitative break) between these policies and those in the following period. The analysis, in other words, has a double task: to find the consistent elements within a given period and to find the important factors contributing to the qualitative change in relations.

Table 6.1 reproduces eight periods of universalist and particularist policies among major powers since the Napoleonic age. The periodization is drawn from customary historical writing. The organizing principle is that of policy. The periods are separated with respect to the existence or non-existence of a consistent effort among the major powers to pursue universalist ambitions. These periods are our units of analysis in the following.[4]

Table 6.1 gives some characteristics of each of the periods, at the same time explaining the various delimitations. However, some comments are necessary. The European Concert of 1816–1848 is recognized by historians as a period of its own, centred on the activities of the Austrian Chancellor Metternich, but involving all the major European powers. The revolutions of 1848, rather than those of 1830, are considered to mark the ending of this period. The subsequent period was one exhibiting many of the marks of particularism, as we have defined it. Several countries were, in this period, pursuing more limited ambitions (notably unification and aggrandizement). Thus, in the writings of historians, this period also stands out clearly. The next two periods are more difficult to separate. Bismarck's policy had a universalist colouring, in which the definition of Germany's interest was equated not with the expansion of the Reich, but rather with the establishment of a workable relationship, cementing what had already been gained. Germany, then, was a central force in this attempt at universalist construction. Following the downfall of Bismarck, and the rise of a more daring political leadership in

Table 6.1 Universalism and particularism, 1816–1976: periodization of relations among major powers

Analytical classification	Historical labelling	Time period	No. of years	No. of majors
Universalist	Concert of Europe	1816–1848	33	5–6
Particularist		1849–1870	22	5–6
Universalist	Bismarck's order	1871–1895	25	6
Particularist		1896–1918	23	8
Universalist	League of Nations	1919–1932	14	7
Particularist		1933–1944	12	7
Particularist	Cold War	1945–1962	18	5
Universalist	Détente/peaceful coexistence	1963–1976	14	5

Note
Major power definitions follow the usual Correlates of War practice. (See Small and Singer 1982, pp. 44–45.)

Germany, the situation changed during the 1890s. The exact dating might be hard to pinpoint, but the difference is there. Here it has been set as 1895, but that is an approximation. It should be noted that other, non-European, countries also at this time began to pursue particularistic interests (the United States and Japan). The organization created after the First World War was a more conscious attempt to work out constructive relations among the majors, this time centring on France and Britain. However, the universalism was incomplete, a great number of countries were not involved or supportive of these attempts, and, with Hitler's taking of power in 1933, the arrangement rapidly fell apart. Finally, following the Second World War, the alliance between the victors, containing a potential for universalist relations, was quickly changed into a severe confrontation. Not until after the Cuban missile crisis did a period of more constructive relations emerge.

This means that our analysis will concentrate on eight periods, four of each type. It is interesting to note, from Table 6.1, that there is more consensus among historians on the labelling of periods of universalism. The particularist periods are not dominated by one overarching ambition, and consequently the naming becomes problematic. There is, however, one exception to that, the period 1945–1962. The bipolarization of the confrontation between the United States and the Soviet Union has given it one customary label. Universalism in this bipolar world has, however, attracted two different conceptions, suggesting that there might, at this time, be more agreement about conflict than about collaboration.

The facts that the periods in general appear to become shorter, and that the universalist periods are smaller relative to the particularist ones, might be indicative of a general rise in confrontation among major powers. The development of conflict behaviour in the different periods can be seen more closely in Table 6.2.

Table 6.2 shows a different pattern for the two sets of policies. There are no major–major wars reported in the periods of universalism, whereas all the major–major wars are to be found in periods of particularism. This observation should be treated cautiously, however, as it could be affected by the labelling. Historians

Table 6.2 Wars and military confrontations involving major powers, in universalist and particularist periods, 1816–1976

	Universalist periods	*Particularist periods*
Major–major wars	0	10
Major–minor wars	10	16
Major–major confrontations	24	49
Major–minor confrontations	72	84
Length (years)	86	74
Average no. of wars and confrontations per year	1.2	2.1
Wars to confrontations, ratio	1:9.6	1:5.1

Sources: Wars: Small and Singer (1982). Military confrontations: data from the Correlates of War project, 1980.

might be quicker to find an orderly pattern in periods without major power wars, and thus we would face a tautology. It might, however, also suggest that universalist policies are successful, at least with respect to major power relations. As the ambition is to develop constructive relations, and as a dominant group among the majors agree on this, major power war could be avoided. An indication is that no periods of universalism end with the outbreak of a major power war. Rather, such wars come some way into a period of particularism.[5]

Furthermore, it could be noted in Table 6.2 that there is some conflict behaviour recorded in all other categories. One-third of all major power confrontations have taken place in periods of universalism. This might mean that such periods have witnessed a somewhat greater ability to cope with confrontation than have periods of particularism: none escalated into a major war. With respect to major–minor confrontations, fewer escalated into war in periods of universalism than in periods of particularism. The ratio of wars to confrontation (a rough measure of escalation) for all categories shows a lower frequency of war per confrontation in periods of universalism. This reinforces, although it does not prove, the thesis that major power policies have a significant bearing on the chances of war. If such relations are couched in a cooperative, constructive fashion, the danger of war might decrease.

Many of the typical structural traits that often are pointed to in order to explain differences will not help in discriminating between these periods; often the same countries found themselves involved in both. The five states making up the Concert of Europe are also those involved in the susequent, more tumultuous period. Similarly, the countries setting up the League in 1919 are also those confronted with German challenges in the 1930s. The actors of the global competition after the Second World War, from 1963 onward, attempted to work out an orderly relationship. Thus, it appears more promising to relate such changes to short-term variations rather than to lasting properties of the global system.

Let us only note that as none of the four periods of universalism has lasted, but all have been transformed into periods of particularism, the inadequacies of the policies pursued need to be specified. The shifts and changes obviously give food for thought to the pessimist as well as to the optimist: no period of universalism has lasted, but neither has a period of particularism.

Universalism and particularism in practice

The strongly different outcomes of periods of universalism and particularism make a closer scrutiny important. Thus, we ask what the differences in policy consist of. The eight periods of major power relations differ from one another in many ways. The economic conditions, the reach of weapons, the speed of communication and the ideological framework have greatly changed over time. Thus, the periods are comparable in some respects but not in others. A comparison over time becomes less comprehensive the longer the time-span applied. In this case, it means that considerable detail is lost in the search for general phenomena. Still, a general observation, such as the shifts in the predominant pattern of policy, could be expected to be associated with a general explanation. In this light we attempt to search for discriminating patterns of policies in some admittedly limited but still crucial areas.

First, Table 6.2 suggests a difference in symmetric and asymmetric relations: major powers might approach one another differently from how they approach non-majors at the same time. Thus, we will compare the experiences of universalism and particularism in both these relationships. Second, the analysis employs a framework of four sets of policy, introduced in a previous chapter: *Geopolitik*, *Realpolitik*, *Idealpolitik* and *Kapitalpolitik*.[6] *Geopolitik* is, in particular, concerned with the geographical conditions: contiguity and ways to handle contiguity, as well as control over distant (from the point of view of core countries) territories. *Realpolitik* emphasizes military capability, arms build-up of particular countries and the formation of alliances. *Idealpolitik* concerns the handling of nationalistic or ideological disputes, ranging from messianism to neutrality with respect to such issues, whereas *Kapitalpolitik* refers to the economic capabilities and interactions among states.

The difference between the two patterns in *Geopolitik* terms can be seen in the different policies pursued in the 'core' areas, in territories particularly close or militarily significant to the major powers. During several periods of universalism, conscious attempts were made to separate the parties geographically, thus attempting to reduce the fear of attack or the danger of provocation. The creation of buffer zones was a particularly pronounced effort, for instance, in relation to France after 1814 or Germany after 1918. In times of particularism, policies were reversed: the buffer zones were perceived as dangerous areas of 'vacuum', making majors compete for control. Examples are the Prussian expansion into Central Europe in the 1850s and the 1860s and Germany's invasion of demilitarized zones or neighbouring countries during the 1930s. Also, following the Second World War, the United States as well as the Soviet Union tried to secure as much territory as possible before and after the German and Japanese capitulations. Indeed, in the 1945–1962 period, 'free' territory was equally disliked on both sides, neither being willing to accept neutrality or neutralism, for instance. In the periods 1870–1895 and 1963–1975 such basic arrangements were left intact, keeping the parties in close geographical confrontation, but at the same time other measures were instituted to somewhat reduce the fear of attack from the opponent (e.g. confidence-building measures in the latter period). Compared with earlier experiences of universalism, these periods saw fewer such attempts, however.[7]

Looking at the major–minor relations, the patterns are less clear-cut. Although the expectation might be for 'softer' attitudes during periods of universalism, this appears not to be borne out. Rather, during periods of universalism, major powers tried to establish or extend control, as in periods of particularism. Perhaps there is a discernible trend of greater major power collaboration during the former than during the latter. Thus, the colonization of Africa took place largely during a period of universalism, and partly this process was mutually agreed on by the major powers themselves (notably at the Berlin Congress in 1884–1885). Similarly, British and French controls were extended into Arab countries during such periods, during the 1880s as well as in the 1920s. It is, furthermore, interesting to observe that the decolonization process was initiated during a period of confrontation between the major powers. The peak year of African independence, 1960, coincided with particularly tense times in American–Soviet relations (e.g. the aborted Paris summit meeting and the U-2 affair).

Realpolitik concerns itself with military power and alliance patterns. In periods of universalism, we would expect less emphasis to be put on military armaments, while greater efforts would go into diplomatic means to work out major power relations. Studying the four periods, this is clearly true for three, but not for the fourth one (1963–1976). Conversely, the periods of particularist policies would exhibit a more rapid arms build-up among the majors. Again, this is true for three out of four periods, the exception being the 1849–1870 period. Partly, this might reflect an important inter-century difference: during the nineteenth century, the institutionalized pressures for arms build-up did not exist to the same degree as has been true for the twentieth century. With respect to the nuclear age, the patterns are somewhat surprising. In terms of military expenditures, the increase seems less striking during the 1950s than during the 1960s or 1970s, for the United States and the Soviet Union. In terms of the amassing of nuclear arsenals, however, there is a continuous increase for both sides.[8] Again, the 1963–1976 period does not follow the pattern of previous universalist periods.

Most periods of universalism seem associated with a loose alliance system. The exception is the 1963–1976 period, but also in this period there are some elements of a loosening-up of the system (notably the withdrawal of France from military cooperation in NATO, and Romania taking a special position within the Warsaw Pact). However, particularism could also go well with a loose alliance pattern, as alliances might restrain rather than give freedom to a given actor. Three periods of particularism showed fairly tight alliance patterns, but in one of these (1933–1945) not all powers were involved in the alliance configurations. In one, the 1849–1870 period, loose alliances served the particularist ambitions well.

There is an interesting trade-off between alliance patterns and arms build-up. In a sense, one reason for entering into an alliance is to reduce the need for armaments. In this way, a major power can increase its military strength at a lower cost and at a faster rate than otherwise would have been possible. This, then, favours the emergence of loose alliance patterns, and thus makes it plausible that universalism as well as particularism might be associated with such a pattern. On the other hand, if the alliances are closely knit, and the option of withdrawing or switching is not available, the only way to increase the strength for a given actor and for the alliance as a whole is through arms build-ups. Thus, in bipolarized situations with 'permanent' alliances, arms races become a more likely outcome. The few examples available of such situations indeed suggest this to be the case (1895–1918, 1933–1945 and the post-1945 period).

Armaments and alliance patterns largely concern the relations between major powers. We would expect *Realpolitik* policies in major–minor relations to be less different for the two patterns. Thus, it is noteworthy that, in Table 6.2, universalist periods have also been periods of extensive major power involvement in major–minor disputes. If we take into account the length of the periods and the number of majors, we find that the majors, in fact, during such periods are heavily concerned with minors.

With respect to *Idealpolitik*, universalist policies would be less chauvinistic and less messianic among majors than particularism. Earlier it has been demonstrated that *Idealpolitik* contradictions correlate with wars and confrontations among major powers for the entire epoch (Wallensteen 1981), but we now expect a pattern of shifting periods. It is probably enough to have one major displaying messianism in a given period to upset all relations. This expectation is well borne out: the four universalist periods show very little of either of these types of *Idealpolitik*, whereas, in each of the four particularist periods, there was at least one major power pursuing such a policy. Chauvinism certainly was part of the German unification policy during Bismarck's rule, as was French renaissance during the rule of Napoleon III, both appearing in the same 1849–1870 period. The policies of Wilhelm II and of Hitler are typical examples. In the 1945–1962 period too there was a strong element of messianism, for very different reasons than previous ones, in Soviet as well as American postures.

In their relations to minor powers, the majors have often been less constrained, even in times of universalism. Thus, in the Concert of Europe period, majors did not hesitate to intervene against changes in minor countries going against the convictions held by the major. In the 1870–1895 period, this might have been less marked, as this to a large degree was a period of parallel nationalism, as well as in the period of the League of Nations. In the détente period, however, the reluctance among the majors to accept dissent within areas of their domination resulted in increasing tension, including among the majors. Thus, the Soviet invasion of Czechoslovakia significantly affected the formulation of détente policies. The American war in Vietnam seems to have slowed down the pace of collaboration between the two superpowers. A policy of coexistence between the majors also might require the acceptance of coexistence between different social forms in major–minor relations.

As to *Kapitalpolitik* patterns, there are some interesting divergences, necessitating a lengthier discussion. Universalism would here refer to a policy that attempts to be more inclusive, such as setting up of a joint international regime for economic affairs, or extending trade, investment or capital flows in an equitable way among the major powers. Particularist policies, in contrast, would be those that aim at self-reliance, autarchy or exclusion from ties with other countries. Taken in this way, there seems to be little relationship between the universalist policies described previously and economic relations. Thus, in the period of the European Concert, introvert policies or policies of exclusion seem to have been the predominant pattern. Free trade actually cannot be dated until the very end of this period, with the repeal of the Corn Laws in Britain in 1846. The subsequent period, then, is one of a more ambitious attempt at spreading international trade, pressing for free trade. An important breakthrough was the Anglo-French Treaty of 1860, during a period which, in terms of other affairs, is most appropriately described as a particularist one. Prussia and the German Customs Union followed in this period, to return to high tariff policies only in the next period, in 1879. This universalist period is characterized by a retreat from free trade, rather than the reverse (Kindleberger 1978).

In the period of particularism leading to the First World War, the growth of international trade was strong, but it appears that it also to a larger degree took place within the colonial empires (Kindleberger 1964). Thus, in this period, there might have been a closer correspondence with particularism. The same is true for the post-First World War periods, the universalist period being one of increasing international interdependence, followed after the Great Depression by increasing attempts at withdrawing from the international economic exchanges.

Also, in the post-1945 periods, there is a correspondence between the economic policies and other policies. Thus, for the first particularist period, the West clearly expanded free trade within its area, but consciously tried to exclude the Soviet bloc from trade (e.g. the strategic embargo). Such policies were partially reversed with the onset of détente, symbolized by the first major grain deal between the United States and the Soviet Union in 1963. In US–Soviet as well as in West European–East European relations, the development of economic relations was strongly favoured by the political leadership.[9]

Thus, we find that in several of the periods there has been a close correspondence between increasing economic interaction and universalism, but that this is perhaps more pronounced for the periods after 1895 than before. In periods of particularism, however, policies of economic bloc-building or economic autarchy have been preferred. The closer correspondence between these sets of policies in the twentieth century might suggest closer coordination of international interaction than previously was the case. Political-strategic conditions seem increasingly to have coloured economic relationship.

Table 6.3 shows that the policies pursued in different areas have been designed to support one another and, on the whole, few contradictions or inconsistencies are

Table 6.3 Typical policies in periods of universalism and particularism, 1816–1976

	Universalism	*Particularism*
Geopolitik	Buffer zones (not 1871–1895, 1963–1976)	Elimination of vacuum
Realpolitik	Caution in vital areas Loose alliances (not 1963–1976?)	Boldness in vital areas Solid alliances (not 1849–1870)
Idealpolitik	Slow arms build-up (not 1963–1976) Coexistence among majors	Rapid arms build-up (not 1849–1870) Messianism also among majors
Kapitalpolitik	Extension of relations among majors (not 1816–1848, 1871–1895)	Seclusion for majors or major blocs (not 1849–1870)

Periods are the unit of analysis. In parenthesis: periods departing from the overall pattern. Few systematic differences concern direct major–minor relations.

to be reported. Thus, periods of universalism have generally involved attempts at separation of majors through buffer zone arrangements or self-imposed restraint in vital areas. Predominantly a pattern of slow arms build-ups and loose alliances has been pursued. Ideologically, a policy of coexistence has prevailed and, economically, trade has been extended among the dominant countries. Taken together, this means that the concept of 'universalism' summarizes consistent efforts among many major powers, working in the same direction of building constructive and multi-dimensional relations. We have already observed, in Table 6.2, that in such periods the incidence of war and confrontation among major powers is lower.

The patterns displayed in periods of particularism are in sharp contrast. Buffer zone arrangements have been overturned, less restraint has been exhibited in vital areas, rapid arms build-ups have occurred and solid, internationally binding alliances have been formed. Among at least some of the majors, messianism/chauvinism has been prevalent, and trade has been used as an instrument for coercion or exclusion. Again this is a pattern of internally consistent policies, all reinforcing the underlying conflict between major powers. Indeed, as we have already noted, periods of particularism are also periods with major power wars and military confrontations.

However, there are some notable inconsistencies in these patterns. Most exceptional is the 1849–1870 period; in several ways it had traits also typical of the periods immediately preceding or succeeding: loose alliance structures and little arms build-up, apart from the time immediately before a major war. Thus, in these respects, there is considerable intra-nineteenth-century similarity. Also, with respect to economic relations, this period was one of free trade becoming more acceptable as a general policy, and countries, in most other respects aiming at their own self-aggrandizement, embraced the concept. This, then, is in contrast to the other nineteenth-century periods, which both were, for a considerable extent of time, markedly self- or intra-bloc-oriented.

For the twentieth century the inconsistencies are few but still obvious. First, the 1933–1944 period showed less solidification of opposing blocs than could be expected. Second, the period 1963–1976 saw a notable absence of the loosening of blocs that previously had been associated with universalist patterns and, most markedly, a failure to curtail the arms build-up and accept internal dissent.

Looking over the entire period, most of these inconsistencies refer to the *Realpolitik* domain; the alliances and the armaments do not correspond with the message from other policies. In *Geopolitik* terms, the consistency is fairly complete (with some exceptions as to buffer zone policies), as is also the case for *Idealpolitik* and *Kapitalpolitik* (with the nineteenth-century exceptions pointed to). In one period the *Realpolitik* divergence goes in a universalist direction, perhaps influencing the major wars of the period to become shorter (1849–1870). In another period the outcome might well have been the reverse, meaning the abandoning of universalist policies altogether (1963–1976).

Consistency would, in particular, have the effect of reducing uncertainty among the major powers. Given that these powers have a fairly uniform understanding of the dimensions involved, consistency would reinforce a given message. Thus, at times some inconsistency might have been less important, notably the lack of correspondence of *Kapitalpolitik* policies with other elements in the nineteenth century. In the twentieth century, however, *Kapitalpolitik* might have been more important. With such an understanding it becomes clear that all universalist periods are highly internally consistent, with one exception, 1963–1976. Also, on the whole, all the twentieth-century particularist periods are highly consistent, with two of them ending in world war, and one in a crisis that might well have resulted in the third one.

Inconsistency could give rise to a demand for change, consistency being a more preferable condition. Thus, a given period could change into its opposite. However, change would also have other roots, and to these we now turn.

From universalism to particularism, and vice versa

Although the universalist policies have largely been consistent and not resulted in major war, they were all abandoned. Obviously, the policies pursued were not satisfactory to all involved. This means that they were built on a foundation that was solid enough for a certain period of time, but not solid enough to handle particular changes.

Also the conditions that brought about the universalist periods in the first place should be considered, as this might suggest the outer limits of the policies. Thus, there are two particular points of change that need to be scrutinized: the change from universalism to particularism and changes in the opposite direction.

Such changes could be sought in three particular areas:

1 Changes among the majors: the composition of their relationships, relative capabilities, but also inconsistency in policy.
2 Changes involving the minors: their direct relations to the majors, degree of independence, etc.
3 Internal changes in the different actors, notably in the majors: revolutions, change of perspectives.

Altogether, there are six shifts to consider, three in each direction. In all cases, the years of change have been identified and factors mentioned by historians as influential have been collected. Some typical variables are presented in Table 6.4. Although Table 6.4 indicates dates for changes, such dates of course are but symbolic; changes are always the result of long-term trends. Some of the changes, consequently, are harder to locate exactly in time. However, dates are important for understanding charge; their symbolic value is highly educational.

First, the transformation from *universalism to particularism* is comparatively non-violent; there are some wars recorded, but no sharp change is evident in the power relationships between the leading actors. The wars at the time were those of major powers solidifying their position by attacking minors (e.g. Prussia on Denmark, Japan on China, the United States on Spain), but such wars are hardly novel or directly related to the shifts. More interesting, and more frequently emphasized

Table 6.4 Factors affecting change in policy patterns, 1816–1976

	From universalism to particularism	From particularism to universalism
Identified time-points of change	1848/1849, 1895/1896, 1932/1933	1870/1871, 1918/1919, 1962/1963
Geopolitik	End of expansionism in 1895/1896	Territorial redistribution 1870/1871, 1918/1919
Realpolitik	Entrance of new actors in 1895/1896	Defeat in war 1870/1871, 1918/1919
Idealpolitik	Internal revolutions 1848/1849, 1932/1933	Revolutions 1870/1871, 1918/1919
Kapitalpolitik	Economic crisis 1932/1933	Economic turmoil following war 1918/1919

by historians, are the internal changes within major powers. The revolutions in France, Austria and Germany are related to the breakdown of the existing order. In the first two cases, revolution brought back a Napoleon and brought down a Metternich; in the third case it overthrew the Weimar Republic and created the Third Reich. These changes were not ordinary domestic shifts of power, as the internal orders were integral parts of the entire international arrangement at the time. Consequently, these revolutions were challenges as much to predominant universalism as to the internal order. With Louis Philippe and the Weimar Republic removed, not only were symbols of the previous order replaced, but something more fundamental had changed; the roles of these countries as majors were redefined. The shifts in 1848/1849 and 1932/1933 could both be seen this way.

The third change away from universalism is more difficult to analyse. The shifts around the turn of the century resulting in the confrontation patterns leading to the First World War were more gradual. There is no particular revolution to point to. Instead factors such as the removal of Bismarck from power in Germany, the realignment among European powers, the decreasing number of territories available to territory-seeking European countries and the emergence of non-European major states seem important.

However, the parallel between the changes in 1848/1849 and those of 1932/1933 might still permit a more general conclusion: the revolutionary changes were related to economic crisis, uneven development of industry, unemployment and, thus, protest and radicalism ('leftist' as well as 'rightist', and in both situations 'rightists' coming out on the top). The regimes that were overthrown were closely identified with the previous 'world order' either in a personal capacity or in (close to) legal terms. This close association between the internal and international arrangement led to the downfall of both.

Possibly, we can specify a chain of events that is potentially very destabilizing for a given international arrangement: economic mismanagement and reduced popular support for a regime whose role is highly significant for universalist policies will not only endanger these regimes but, very likely, also upset the entire policy. In other words, a weakness of these universalist policies might have been their excessive reliance on the maintenance of a particular order in particular countries. The policies were, in a sense, not adaptive enough to handle the internal changes of leading and crucial states. Indeed, the policies of appeasement, pursued during the 1930s, rested on the assumption that adaptation was possible, and that, at a given moment, Germany's ambitions could be satisfied, preserving most of the League arrangement.

The challenge to the entire Versailles construction was understood only at a very late moment. Such a policy of adaptation is, in other words, not likely to be successful if/when the entire international arrangement is the matter of dispute. The only alternative might be a policy of 'pre-emptive' adaptation to defuse tensions when they are still latent. However, to change an already existing arrangement before it has become an issue will mostly not have sufficient political support. Politics seems to require much more concrete signals of warnings.

The changes in the mid-1890s followed a slightly different logic. There were no internal revolutions, but the interaction between inter-state relations and internal politics was still there. The removal of Bismarck suggested that Germany's role in the world could be seen in a different light by Germany as well as by others, notably Russia. The rapid colonization meant that there were fewer distant territories to struggle for. Together these factors might have contributed to making Germany take a stronger, less compromising, stand.[10]

Turning to the transformation from *particularism to universalism*, we find more violent change, and among the majors themselves at that. Two of the shifts are multi-dimensional, and relate to two major wars: 1870/1871 and 1918/1919. These changes are, however, not ordinary major power defeats; the eras investigated saw a number of such defeats (e.g. Russia in the Crimean War and in the Russo-Japanese War). In addition, they involved considerable internal changes. New regimes and new constitutions were developed in France and Germany. The new orders created were not simply rearrangements of inter-state relations. Rather, the three universalist periods following a major war (including, for the sake of the argument, 1814, as well as 1871 and 1919) are parallel; they aimed not only at containing a given major power but also at reducing the perceived threat of certain types of internal policies. Thus, universalism became linked to particular regimes. In post-Napoleonic France, as well as in the Weimar Republic, these new regimes became identified with the defeat. This seems, however, not to have been the case for the post-1871 Third Republic.

As was the case with transformations away from universalism, there is one case which is less clear-cut. It is comparable to the 1895/1896 shift but the direction is the opposite one: 1962/1963. There can be no doubt that the policy of détente, introduced in the immediate aftermath of the 1962 nuclear confrontation between the United States and the Soviet Union, reflected a fear of a nuclear war between the two. Also, at this time, increased attention was given to Third World problems (the United States becoming increasingly involved in the Vietnam War, the Soviet Union extending support to liberation movements throughout the Third World).

The process of decolonization created a new area for the leading majors, the year 1960 and the Congo crisis being symbolic. Thus, the universalism introduced and pursued until the end of the 1970s seems to have had a double origin: fear of nuclear war and focus on Third World activities.

This means that the policy of détente had a different origin from the other universalist policies encountered in this analysis: it was a matter not of victors setting up a system to be preserved against others, but rather of the competitors trying to preserve themselves against a possible catastrophe. Nuclear weapons, in other words, changed the dynamics of relations between the major powers. In one sense, this was a profound change; it meant that anticipation of devastation was brought into the calculations before devastation actually took place. In another sense, it was less profound; the consensus among the majors was less developed than was the case in earlier universalist periods. An argument could still be made in favour of confrontation, brinkmanship, in order to continue the battle between the majors. Unlike the other situations, there was no reordering of priorities; rather a policy of caution succeeded a policy of boldness. In this vein, the shift in 1962/1963 is comparable to the one of 1895/1896: no change in basic goals or basic perception of incompatibility, but a change in the means to be used. Wilhelm II grasped for vigour, Kennedy/Khrushchev for caution; Wilhelm was in a hurry to arrive at final victory, Kennedy/Khrushchev settled down to wait for the ultimate collapse of the other, either from internal contradictions or from changes in global relationships.

In 1895/1896 the lack of 'empty' territory meant that the conflict had to be pursued in more vital (to the majors) areas; in 1962/1963 the 'opening up' of new territory through decolonization meant that the same conflict could be pursued in less vital areas. Either way, the armament build-up received new stimuli.

This, in other words, suggests a possible link between 'central' and 'peripheral' areas, the one replacing the other as a forum for continued confrontation between major powers having defined themselves in incompatibility with one another. In general terms, such incompatibilities can end in major wars (as indeed has been the outcome for two periods of particularism, as shown above) or internal revolutions (as indeed has been the outcome for two periods of universalism), or in a continuous shift between 'arenas' of competition, as long as such arenas exist (as happened in the two remaining transformations). In the last case, this means that 'peripheral' areas are 'outlets' for major powers, striving to gain leverage on the other, but hoping to manage this without a direct onslaught.

A final note: 1976 is here, as a matter of convenience and availability of data, regarded as the ending of one universalist period. In retrospect, it appears correct to suggest that détente gradually thinned out beginning at approximately this time, culminating with the Soviet invasion of Afghanistan in 1979 and the election of Ronald Reagan in 1980. Seen in this light, it is interesting to relate some of our previous findings to this development. In terms of neither *Idealpolitik* nor *Kapitalpolitik* are there any important changes among or within the major powers. In *Realpolitik* terms there are some changes: a new actor, China, entering more actively during these years of transition, forming new relations with the West.

Also, there is a set of new challenges emerging from the Third World: the oil crisis and rising Islamic fundamentalism, the latter resulting in confrontation with both superpowers (in Iran and Afghanistan, respectively). A criterion for success for détente might have been the ability of the United States and the Soviet Union to win Third World support, but these developments were setbacks for both. Thus, there is a parallel between this transition and the one in 1895/1896. Failure in promoting success in distant areas (from the point of view of the major powers) tends to result in increasing tension in the central arena. To this, then, should be added the obvious inconsistencies in the policies of détente, pointed to in the previous section, primarily the failure to control the arms race.

Limits of major power universalism

Major powers have continuously tried to work out constructive relations among themselves. Such attempts have, in some periods, lasted for a considerable period of time. The record suggests that the pursuit of such universalist policies is associated with fewer wars and confrontations in general and among the major powers in particular. Such policies have served at the same time to maintain the independence of the majors and reduce the dangers of war among them. Invariably, however, they have been superseded by periods of particularism, when one or several of the majors have embarked on policies advancing the particular interest, rather than the joint interest of all. Such periods are associated with higher levels of war and confrontations among the majors. In several instances they have resulted in the dismemberment or defeat of one or several of the majors. Invariably, such periods have been followed by universalist policies.

Looking at the four concerted attempts at universalism in the 1816–1976 period, they display some discernible common traits.

First, they have been arrangements worked out among *major powers, normally the victors* in a previous war: the Concert of Europe, Bismarck's order and the League of Nations all followed immediately on major wars. Thus, they represented attempts by the victors to handle their victory, to avoid the re-emergence of threat from the losers. The détente period differs, but in some respect it could be seen as a belated attempt among the victors to agree on a set of relations, in particular for Europe. More directly, however, it attempted to stabilize the relations between the majors themselves in the face of a mutual nuclear threat. The first three examples of universalist policies, consequently, built on a much more developed common interest than did the period of détente. In the former situations, the victors had a clear actor to worry about; in the latter case, the fear came primarily from the other party or from the general threat of nuclear war. There was, consequently, less of an incentive to solve conflict in the latter case. The focus was more on avoiding escalation than on conflict settlement.

Second, all these arrangements have been *conservative* as they have tried to stabilize the status quo: maintaining the major powers as majors, keeping the existing power relationships among them and upholding the distance to non-majors. In the face of challenges, the policy has been one of adaptation, trying to make the challenges fit within the existing framework, rather than substantially alter the framework itself. The duration of some of the periods of universalism indicates that this sometimes has been possible: confrontations among majors have been resolved without escalation to war. However, the conservative nature obviously has some shortcomings, as there are many challenges which are less easily accommodated.

Third, the *consistency across several dimensions* of policy has been marked for most of the periods, except most notably for the détente period. This internal consistency might well have contributed to reducing uncertainty and thus to make actions and reactions more predictable. Such more predictable relations, it could be argued, would reduce the emergence of conflict in the first place. An indication of this is that the number of wars and confrontations with major powers involved per year is much lower for the periods of consistent universalism than for the period of détente.[11]

Fourth, all universalist periods witnessed a shift in focus away from direct major–major confrontations in central areas to a *preoccupation with major–minor relations*. Most markedly this is true for the Concert of Europe, Bismarckian and détente periods. This diversion of attention could deflect some of the tension in the central areas and point to common interests in other areas. Inevitably, however, it means that the universalist policies become dependent on the degree of success in that field, resulting in interventionism. For both the Bismarckian and détente period, frustrations in these respects seem to have made the powers turn to the central area again. If that is where the origin of conflict is, this can be seen as logic within this framework. In both these cases it resulted in an intensification of arms build-ups and increasingly unpredictable major power relations.

Fifth, the universalist policies have not simply been an arrangement built among states. There has also been a *significant internal component* to them. In the cases where victors worked out an order for the post-war period, new regimes have been installed in the defeated countries. These regimes have been the ultimate guarantors of the new order, meaning that the orders become vulnerable to the efficacy of these regimes. Internal change in such countries becomes directly relevant to international relations. Thus, the French regime in 1815 and the German Weimar Republic had to carry a double burden of confirming the defeat and reconstructing their countries. In the end neither succeeded. Most notable, however, is the fact that the Third Republic was not, in the same way, identified with the war defeat. In somewhat the same way, the new German governments after 1949 have been absolved of the misdeeds of their predecessors.[12]

Major power universalism has been highly constrained. Most markedly this appears true for the most recent attempt, the period of détente. It could not build on the power of united victors, it failed to be consistent across significant dimensions and ultimately internal inconsistencies brought it down. The question, then, arises if there is an alternative to such universalist policies.

This analysis suggest some principles for an alternative form of universalism, making it possible to break out of some of the historically observed constraints:

- a greater involvement of non-major powers in questions of world peace and security;
- a greater openness, on the part of the major powers, to change in non-major countries and in relations among states;
- a greater consistency in major power relations, particularly in the fields of disengagement, disarmament and dissent;
- a greater restraint on permissible behaviour of major powers in Third World conflicts;
- a greater domestic accountability for the foreign policies of major powers; and, breaking out of the framework,
- a greater reliance on non-governmental organizations.

These principles would serve to make universalism truly universal, not simply the universalism of major powers.

Notes

1 This work is part of an ongoing project on Armed Conflicts and Durable Conflict Resolution, at the Department of Peace and Conflict Research, Uppsala University. Valuable comments have been made by many readers of an earlier draft, notably Nils Petter Gleditsch, Miroslav Nincic, Melvin Small and Raimo Väyrynen, as well as by students in my seminar on War and World Politics, University of Michigan, winter 1984.
2 The definition of universalism and particularism by Parsons focuses on norms rather than actions. Still the concepts are useful as they point to the general rather than the specific as the centre of attention. (See Parsons and Shils 1951, p. 82.)
3 Most definitions of world order are multidimensional. Falk and Mendlovitz find world order to be the answer to questions of worldwide economic welfare, social justice and ecological stability as well as to reduction of international violence. (See Falk and Mendlovitz 1973, p. 6.) A broad and most stimulating contribution is Falk (1975). Hoffmann (1980, p. 188) also gives a very broad definition of the concept of world order, as a state in which violence and economic disruptions have been 'tamed', 'moderation' has emerged, economies progress and collective institutions act. The concept of Common Security, introduced in the so-called Palme Commission, involved a conception similar to that of Hoffmann. (See *Common Security* 1982.)
4 Thus we attempt to describe dominant traits in the major power relations during these periods. A most interesting contribution in the same direction is Rosecrance (1963). Recently, the interest in long waves has resulted in similar generalizations for particular periods, mostly focusing on economic variables. A contribution pertinent to the present discussion is Väyrynen (1983).
5 Such wars have come at earliest in the sixth year of particularist policy: the Crimean War in 1854, the Russo-Japanese War in 1938 (Changkufeng War) and the Korean War in 1950, all within this range, the Russo-Japanese War of 1904 being somewhat later. This list, furthermore, suggests that such first major–major wars occur in areas fairly distant from the main major power area of contention (at all these times this being Europe). For data, see Small and Singer (1982).
6 This distinction, built on the basic arguments in different schools of thinking, is elaborated in Wallensteen (1981), i.e. Chapters 4 and 5 in this volume.
7 The lack of disengagement in German–French relations following the war of 1871 is often pointed to by historians. The annexation of Alsace-Lorraine became a humiliating experience for the French, although the military value of the area to either party

could be disputed. Thus, no buffers were created between the two, making the relations tense. A result of this was the War Scare of 1875. See Kennan (1979, pp. 11–23). For a general discussion, see Patem (1983).

8 For an overview of the development of arms expenditure for these periods, see Nincic (1982). For an overview of the nuclear arsenals, drawn from several sources, see Botnen (1982) and SIPRI (1983). The total nuclear arsenals are estimated at 1,000 in 1952, 23,500 in 1960, 35,500 in 1970 and 48,800 in 1975.

9 Reporting to the US Congress on his visit to Moscow in 1972 Nixon summarized this policy as one of 'creating a momentum of achievement in which progress in one area could contribute to progress in others', and 'when the two largest economies in the world start trading with each other on a much larger scale, living standards in both nations will rise, and the stake which both have in peace will increase'. Cooperation in space exploration was also part of this, resulting in a joint orbital mission in 1975. See 'Address by President Nixon to a Joint Session of the Congress', June 1, 1972, in Stebbins and Adams (1976, pp. 80–81). The resulting space mission was in 1975 hailed by *Le Canard Enchaine:* Vive La Coexistence Espacifique!

10 Such links form some of the conclusions in Choucri and North (1975, ch. 16). On the significance of Bismarck's departure, see Kennan, *op. cit.*

11 The average annual major power involvement in war or confrontation is, 1.0 for 1816–1848, 0.9 for 1871–1895, 1.7 for 1919–1932 and 2.2 for 1963–1976. The last figure actually puts the détente period parallel to some of the particularist periods, notably the 1896–1918 period with 2.3 and 1933–1944 with 2.2.

12 The significance of the German question is given an extensive and interesting treatment in DePorte (1979).

References

Botnen, Ingvar (ed.). 1982. *Fakta om Krig og Fred.* Oslo: Pax.

Choucri, Nazli and Robert C. North. 1975. *Nations in Conflict: National Growth and International Violence.* Cambridge, MA: MIT.

Common Security: A Programme for Disarmament. 1982. Report of the Independent Commission on Disarmament and Security. London: Pan.

DePorte, A.W. 1979. *Europe between the Superpowers.* New Haven, CT: Yale University Press.

Falk, Richard and Saul Mendlovitz. 1973. *Regional Politics and World Order.* San Francisco: Freeman.

Falk, Richard. 1975. *A Study of Future Worlds.* New York: Free Press.

Hoffmann, Stanley. 1980. *Primacy or World Order: American Foreign Policy since the Cold War.* New York: McGraw Hill.

Kennan, George. 1979. *The Decline of Bismarck's European Order.* Princeton, NJ: Princeton University Press.

Kindleberger, Charles P. 1964. *Economic Growth in France and Britain, 1851–1950.* Cambridge, MA: Harvard University Press.

Kindleberger, Charles P. 1978. *Economic Response: Comparative Studies in Trade, Finance and Growth.* Cambridge, MA: Harvard University Press.

Nincic, Miroslav. 1982. *The Arms Race.* New York: Praeger.

Parsons, Talcott and Edward A. Shils (eds.). 1951. *Towards a General Theory of Action.* Cambridge, MA: Harvard University Press.

Patem, Michael. 1983. 'The Buffer System in International Relations', *Journal of Conflict Resolution*, 27 (1): 3–26.

Rosecrance, Richard N. 1963. *Action and Reaction in World Politics.* Boston: Little, Brown.

SIPRI. 1983. *World Armaments and Disarmament.* London: Taylor & Francis.

Small, Melvin and J. David Singer. 1982. *Resort to Arms*. Beverly Hills, CA: Sage.

Stebbins, R.P. and E.P. Adams (eds.). 1976. *American Foreign Relations 1972: A Documentary Record*. New York: New York University Press.

Väyrynen, Raimo. 1983. 'Economic Cycles, Power Transitions, Political Management and Wars between Major Powers', *International Studies Quarterly*, 27 (4): 389–418.

Wallensteen, Peter. 1981. 'Incompatibility, Confrontation and War: Four Models and Three Historical Systems, 1816–1976', *Journal of Peace Research*, 18 (1): 57–90.

7 Global governance in a new age

The UN between P1, G2, and a new global society

Challenges to global governance

On August 2, 1990, the role of the United Nations (UN) Security Council changed. Iraq's invasion of Kuwait faced an unusually negative and united international community. The UN Security Council met within hours. The former Cold War adversaries, the United States and the Soviet Union, both reacted against Iraq's unprovoked action and demanded Iraq's withdrawal. It marked the beginning of a new world of cooperation between the leading major powers. "Global governance" became a new term of considerable significance and with a more positive ring to it than "world government," as Thomas Weiss has pointed out (Weiss 2009). It set a precedent for the following decade of international affairs. The UN was to be used for dealing cooperatively with international crises. Indeed, there were many conflicts to follow. The Uppsala Conflict Data Program records 128 armed conflicts between 1989 and 2008 (Harbom and Sundberg 2009).

Figure 7.1 illustrates this activation of the UN. During the Cold War, the UN was not a center of decision-making for international affairs. The Security Council passed a few resolutions a month; as the graph shows, rarely more than two. Furthermore, most of these resolutions were recommendations, that is, under Chapter VI of the UN Charter. The number of no-votes ('vetoes') on draft resolutions was high, as shown by a lower curve in the graph. However, since 1990 the situation has been different. There are decisions more than once a week, vetoes are rare, and more decisions are binding for the member-states (Chapter VII resolutions). The UN has been activated and it has come to play the role envisioned when the organization was created. The organization has also had considerable impact on the course of conflicts, often through the use of peacekeeping operations; support for peace processes through mediation and similar efforts; and the use of sanctions. The UN is no longer just a "mirror" of world affairs, as Torsten Örn (1969) once wrote; it is a lens, through which energy is focused on world events.

Twenty years later, it is time to look at the new challenges to the UN. There are always competitors and the UN has seen many during the past decades. Some of these are likely to remain. Three stand out. A first challenge is the temptation of the preeminent actor, the United States, to take a casual approach to the UN: the P1 temptation. A second is the oligopolistic tendency: leading states preferring

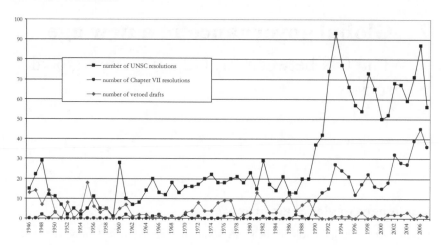

Figure 7.1 UN Security Council resolutions 1946–2008. From Johansson (2009) with
permission.

to work matters out between themselves: the attraction of oligopoly. A third one
is the effects of the globalized and open societies around the world, a new global
society that is difficult to reconcile with the state-centric construction of the UN:
the irrepressible global society.

The P1 temptation

The bipolar world quickly became unipolar in 1991, and the unipolar moment is
still with us, twenty years later, but now exposed to severe pressures, from competitors and from a more democratic and global society.

The Gulf War in 1991 was a UN-authorized operation, building on agreement between the P5, the Permanent Five members of the Security Council. At
the time, two members were more important than the others: the USA and the
USSR. The dissolution of the Soviet Union meant that only one remained in the
group, what we could call P1, the preeminent one, that is, the USA. However, the
approach of resorting to the UN was still prevalent during the Bush Sr. and Clinton
administrations. There was a preference for not involving US forces around the
world and instead working with the globalized world that quickly unfolded following the opening up of Eastern Europe, China, and India. The approach, in
a sense, was universalistic: the interests of all major actors and many small ones
were integrated into the policies (Wallensteen 1984). Collective organizations were
useful for that, mostly being the UN, sometimes NATO (as in Kosovo 1999).

With the attack on the USA on September 11, 2001, the new Bush administration changed the American focus: It was no longer the UN framework that
mattered, but the fact that there was one preeminent actor. It was the United
States and its interests that counted. Being the victim of the attack, furthermore, it
had the moral right to set the agenda for international security. There was a shift
to a particularistic approach. In this mode, the security of the strongest actors was

also the interest of all the others. The strongest one had might as well as right to set the tune. Thus, the United States cooperated with those it wanted, sometimes being the UN and other permanent members (as in Afghanistan 2001), sometimes with the European Union (EU) (as in the Balkans), sometimes with a coalition of the willing (as in Iraq 2003). It was a particularistic US policy, bent on fighting wars and armed conflicts in the search for the chief enemy, Al Qaeda, or its supporters. The war on terror was global in reach, it had support from the UN, but it was orchestrated from one decision-making center.

There were reasons for the United States to take a leading role. It was, throughout the period, the largest military power. Stockholm International Peace Research Institute estimated the US share of world military expenditure to be 42 percent in 2008 (*SIPRI Yearbook* 2009). The country closest to this was China with an estimated 5.8 percent. No other country was above 5 percent of world military expenditure. Certainly, the USA had for long been the largest spender, but the efforts during the first decade of the 2000s saw a strong, not to say dramatic, rise in military expenditure. In 2000 the share of national defense in the US gross domestic product was 3.0 percent; in 2009 it was estimated at 4.5 percent.

The combination of resources, the feeling of injustice, the September 11 trauma, and civilian victimization triggered a desire to act alone. This is, however, also a general temptation of any P1. It will easily take the view that power is what ultimately determines outcomes and is thus the way to go. It is not only a matter of global leadership; it is also a question of shaping the world. Many in the Bush administration held such ideas already in the 1990s. For the Bush Jr. administration this became a theme: undoing potential threats against the United States required global action, largely on US terms.

However, these policies run into severe setbacks, following the initial quick removal of the Taliban regime in Afghanistan in 2001. The Iraq War in 2003 did not generate the same international support, sympathy, and solidarity. Many actors were not convinced of the need for a war. For one, there was already a process to check for weapons and capacity to produce weapons of mass destruction in Iraq, led by former Director-General of the International Atomic Energy Authority (IAEA) Hans Blix. The attempts by the United States, the UK, and other allies to garner support for a new resolution on Iraq in February and March 2003 failed. Consequently, the US coalition decided to act outside the UN. This was new, in a world that had learned to appreciate the uses of the UN for legitimacy and common interest. The Cold War, certainly, had seen many actions outside the UN. However, a new norm had already been established. It was now prudent, not to say required, to involve the UN in most major decisions or at least have a sizeable collective support for any armed action.

Whereas the Gulf War had generated strength for the UN, the 2003 Iraq War led to a crisis for the organization, and ultimately also for the United States. It demonstrated to the UN that the USA had to be part of its activities otherwise there would be limited impact of UN decisions. It showed to the USA that international support actually translated into international resources, legitimacy, and – in fact – power. The United States had to face the post-war troubles in Iraq largely on its own. However, the UN had to find a way to reach back to the USA.

Secretary-General Kofi Annan's initiative to create his High Level Panel for Threats, Challenges and Changes was a way to search for a global compromise. Its report in late 2004 was a crucial input into the UN General Assembly 60th session, led by Ambassador Jan Eliasson in 2005–2006 (*A more secure world* 2004). The reform agenda was significant for the UN itself; the ambition to reach out to the Bush administration may have been less successful. For instance, the United States did not want to participate in the new Human Rights Council when it was created in 2006. Actually, the voting pattern in the General Assembly often saw a polarization between the United States on the one hand and a majority constituted by the Third World members on the other. It was P1 versus G77, the group that included around 130 of all UN members. The EU, the General Assembly Presidency, and the Secretary-General had to operate as bridge builders.

US preeminence remains a fact but, with the Obama administration, there has been a return to more universalistic policies, appreciated not least by the Nobel Peace Prize Committee. The UN is again taking a significant role in the formulation of US foreign policy. However, it remains, from the P1 perspective, only one of its options, others being, for instance, NATO. The challenge remains for the UN in finding ways to link the United States more closely to the UN framework on significant security issues.

The attraction of oligopoly

Global governance can also be operated in another way. As some countries are more important than others, it is possible to argue that if the powerful get together that can be an effective way of governance. There is an attraction in finding small groups that determine what is necessary and can bring the decisions to those affected and to the outside. Indeed, the Security Council itself, although a global organization, has this set up. The P5 have special rights and the five remain globally important. By 2008 the five states still were the countries with the highest military expenditure, together accounting for 60 percent of world outlays for defense purposes. Still, other groupings emerged.

This was so as some issues had to do with security in a broader sense. Since the end of the Cold War also a financial grouping, initially G7, later G8, had arisen as a forum for economic discussion, but also with international security concerns on its agenda. Although lacking a formal structure, a permanent secretariat or even proper archives, it continued to function as a meeting place of major powers. It was seen as an effective forum for frank talk and for developing shared understandings. Predictably, it created frustrations among those not included. Russia gradually managed to get a seat, but China has not yet, for instance. The same applies to other financially strong actors. Although G8 had tried to include other countries on an ad hoc basis and at accompanying meetings, this has hardly been satisfactory. It still leaves many out, and there is no legitimate procedure for representation. Indeed, the meetings of the G8 had attracted the wrath of civil society organizations as well. The G8 came to be seen as a self-selected and exclusive group. Its combined economic clout was impressive, the informal way for leaders to talk was valuable, but its legitimacy was low and it remains to be studied whether its decisions are actually implemented. There seems to be little self-evaluation of its earlier decisions, for instance.

The financial crisis that became fully visible in the autumn of 2008, as well as the climate issue that was central in the following years, added new realities, although pointing in different directions. The economic crisis stimulated summit meetings within the G20 group, departing from the previous practice of only being for finance ministers. It included the G8 members but added booming economies such as China, India, Brazil, Indonesia, Australia, South Africa, Turkey, and South Korea, as well as the EU as such. Like the G8 it remains an informal set-up, but may have generated stronger international support by involving a larger number of countries. The different reform proposals for the UN Security Council, for instance, often anticipate a Council of twenty-one to twenty-four members, thus coming close to the regional composition of the G20 and in reality likely to consist of many of the same countries.

The financial crisis, with the USA as a major debtor and China as its leading creditor, has created a discussion on yet another grouping, G2. The contours of a G2 relationship emerged in 2009, and the two seemingly demonstrated a shared interest at the climate summit meeting in Copenhagen in December 2009. G2 may not be more than a media creation but it points to another attraction of oligopoly. There are only a few countries that pollute the planet to such an extent that it threatens the global climate. Thus, if these countries agreed on significant restrictions, implemented them, and monitored each other that might be the most effective way of dealing with the climate threat. It would be parallel to the reduction of nuclear weapons that was agreed on by the major weapon states. They did not want to involve others in their security issues. Whether the global accord reached at Copenhagen in fact is the beginning of such a group for climate change, a Climate G7 or Climate G8, remains to be seen.

The oligopolistic tendencies may turn into a new form of exclusion. It may be preferable to the unipolar particularism of the early 2000s or the bipolarization of the Cold War, but it still reduces other actors to marginal positions. These developments constitute real challenges to existing collective organizations. If the top leaders choose to act in more informal, even ad hoc, constellations, this shifts power and attention away from the formal institutions. However, sooner or later decisions have to be formalized and the collective organizations still have a role. It is only through them that one can make binding decisions for all countries. Even if the original decisions have been worked out in informal settings, the process of making them formalized also means involving other actors in the decision-making. Even so it means that collective organizations need to reform themselves in order to enhance their capacity and their utility. They may need to scrutinize their mandates, their operations, and their competence to have a professional impact.

The irrepressible global society

As if this were not enough, there are additional challenges effectively constraining the role of the state and thus the status of intergovernmental organizations. There is a new global society emerging, questioning the textbook world of independent national states. There are two in particular: *the rise of a vibrant international civil society* (expressed in civil society organizations, CSOs) and *the rise of the big multinational corporations* (MNCs). Both these phenomena are beneficiaries of the increased ability of communication across the world. This is what makes them truly global as well as very local at the same time. Inputs can be transmitted through their networks in seconds; decision-making may differ, but in global reach they are comparable.

First, the number of nongovernmental organizations has increased dramatically, not the least since the end of the Cold War. Their way of reaching out to ordinary citizens is unsurpassed by most states. Many of these organizations are highly democratic in their set-up, building on large memberships. Even if they are not, they build on and project democratic values of human rights, freedom of movement, cross-border solidarity, etc. This civil society consists of a mixed bag of organizations. Some are faith-based and missionary in their approach; some express particular values such as humanitarian concerns; some are highly practical self-help organizations for ethnic kin spread around the globe; some might be front organizations for businesses, political interests, or organized crime. At this point, however, it is enough to observe the rise of such organizations in numbers, resources, memberships, and their ability to reach out to segments of the general public, in developed and developing nations alike. They do so in combination with the new technologies of communication and mass transportation.

This is a phenomenon that operates on a global arena provided by international meetings and organizations, *and* at the level of the national state. Effective CSOs, in other words, are those that gather support from some states, use that to impact global agendas, and then bring global decisions, recommendations, or statements back to the local arena. These connections make CSOs politically important actors nationally as well as globally. They can act as pressure groups in particular states as well as on international organizations. As most of them do have fairly focused agendas of their own, they will be able to bring pressure on specific items, thus not necessarily competing with the power of political parties or trade unions that espouse more general interests in economic policies. CSOs build on their competence in particular fields and their ability to mobilize opinion, outside established institutions. They can make campaigns effective when involving a large number of CSOs, as witnessed in the global struggle in favor of a land mine convention in the mid-1990s. The network approach and large-scale coalition-making are traits of many CSOs. This makes democratic leaders sensitive to their proposals, and even interested in using them for their own purposes.

CSOs have become agents for much development assistance and humanitarian aid, thus, delivering support actually funded by taxpayers. This has been a pattern since the end of the Cold War. Prior to this, development cooperation was part of Cold War policies, and, thus, often regarded as a security matter, closer to traditional state interests.

This suggests that an intricate, and not necessarily transparent, interplay takes place between states and CSO interests. This is, of course, not novel in a national context. Many of today's political parties have been formed by such civil society organizations (e.g., the modern story of the formation of Christian democratic, socialist, and environmentalist parties). They may also be important inside political parties (e.g., the Christian right in the Republican Party in the United States). However, CSOs as significant actors on global issues have emerged more strongly since the end of the Cold War. It appears contradictory, but maybe it is not: CSOs can benefit from state support as well as from international organizations, and the reverse may also be true. Still, CSOs are likely to pursue their own interests and have, over the past twenty years, become particularly skillful at new forms of international diplomacy and are often highly media savvy. They constitute an independent category of actors with increasing power of its own.

The UN has had an open approach, particularly in conjunction with the big international conferences of the 1990s. There has been a willingness to incorporate ideas and dynamics of this global society. At the climate conference in Copenhagen in 2009, however, there were visible tensions between the official representations and the CSOs. It is a challenge for the future of finding fora and connections, perhaps even representation of this diverse but energetic mobilization of opinions and insights.

An often overlooked, but crucial, element of globalization is the rise of the MNCs. They are often the agents behind trade liberalization measures, and are those that can quickly take advantage of policy changes in this sphere. They build on an economic interest in the most profitable production and are driven by the competition of the market. There is a tendency for companies gradually to become bigger, but the innovative nature of capitalism and market conditions seems to also allow for the demise of companies and their replacement with others. Companies that were big and dominant twenty or thirty years ago may no longer exist, such as the Pan Am airline, or be replaced by others building on new techniques, notably IBM being superseded by Microsoft, which in turn is challenged by Google. Competition is the rule, but it does not exclude mergers, take-overs, break-ups, reconfigurations, and shifts in activity, performance, and geographical location.

If there is an important distinction of value in this context it has do with the relations to the consumers. Companies that are far removed from direct contact with large numbers of public consumers may act differently from those that are entirely dependent on a positive image with millions of individual customers. The latter, be they McDonald's, Coca-Cola, H&M, IKEA, Zara, Nike, the diamond industry, or others, are in sharp competition and may fear that adverse publicity will immediately affect sales. This group of MNCs will be more likely to listen to CSOs, opinion-makers, and parliamentarians. Others that pursue production that goes unnoticed to most customers may still have to consider their impact on localities, not the least on the environment (forest and mining companies, for instance). Many others are even further detached and are likely to be even less sensitive (e.g., financial companies, arms dealers). Indeed, much clandestine activity also takes place in the form of companies, but without much access for national authorities, media, and the public. These variations in the category of corporate actors are important to keep in mind.

Overall, we may conclude that corporate decision-making is likely to have many similarities with the way state leaders have to act, in order to preserve their power and sovereignty. Corporate leaders (CEOs) aim at preserving their company's independence, profitability, and "edge."

CSOs push governments into action through open activities – demonstrations, direct actions – as well as through competence and debate. MNCs are not visible in the same way. They are demonstration-shy but back-channel sharp. Money, lobbyists, and PR agents provide avenues to powerholders. Thus, the impact of one over the other is difficult to establish except for particular cases. Still, most observers would give both a strong role in the way global governance is actually done today.

The need for a new reform process

Legitimate global governance is challenged from the top – key actors are not happy with the organizations – and from below – increasingly powerful actors have resources of their own and operate in independent configurations, only reluctantly subjecting themselves to the controls of the state and intergovernmental decisions.

Thus, reforms are needed, but they are not easy to define and even more difficult to implement. At times the UN has been subject to such scrutiny. In the 1990s it was a task of the Commission on Global Governance (1995); in the 2000s the High Level Panel took up the relay baton (*A more secure world* 2004). The Commission resulted in limited changes; the Panel was, as we have seen, coupled to the specific crisis of the UN and to the 60th UN General Assembly in 2005–2006, which was devoted to reform initiatives.

There is time for a new stocktaking of the UN in view of the challenges we have just seen. Furthermore, there is a need to incorporate as many of the new actors as possible into a process of forming global governance. This is not an easy process, but it can be done, if conceived in a broad-minded way and given time. It needs to involve practitioners, academics, diplomacy, and the media, as well as nongovernmental actors. The goal could be to present a globally acceptable report in time for the evaluation of the Millennium Development Goals in 2015, as the record of achievement is likely to generate a discussion on the weaknesses and strengths of global governance.

Fortunately, there is no lack of ideas that such a process could work from.

For instance, there are the UN-focused views, which emphasize increased mandates for the UN in the economic and climate fields. Others suggest that the Trusteeship Council should be given a new role, for climate change. There is a Peacebuilding Commission that has an uncertain role, but may be enhanced to deal effectively with failing states. The UN Security Council needs enlargement under conditions that still provide for effective decision-making (EU counting rules may be an inspiration). Human rights need effective enforcement.

There are also other reform suggestions. Some argue for stronger regional organizations, following the lead of the EU. Others see a functional division of labor, in which some organizations focus on economics, others on the environment, still others on human rights, security, etc., but all with strong mandates and means of monitoring implementation.

Some pursue a reverse set of ideas: less organization, more freedom of action. Market forces are seen as capable of dealing with almost all issues, outside the security and human rights field. Even such market solutions, however, require legal procedures. It remains true that any reasonably free market needs a reasonable legal framework. The balance between freedom and responsibility applies to global governance as well.

And finally there are the people-based thoughts, building structures from the bottom up, incorporating recent advances in communication, for instance. In a world espousing democracy, democratic forms of global governance also have to be entertained.

The ideas abound, the challenges are pressing, and there is a need for political interest in common change.

References

Commission on Global Governance. 1995. *Our Global Neighbourhood*. Oxford: Oxford University Press.

Harbom, Lotta and Ralph Sundberg. 2009. *States in Armed Conflict 2008*. Uppsala: Department for Peace and Conflict Research.

Johansson, Patrik. 2009. 'The Humdrum Use of Ultimate Authority: Defining and Analysing Chapter VII Resolutions', *Nordic Journal of International Law*, 78 (3): 309–342.

A More Secure World: Our Shared Responsibility. 2004. The Secretary-General's High-Level Panel Report on Threats, Challenges and Change. New York: United Nations.

Örn, Torsten. 1969. *FN – Världspolitikens spegel* [The UN – Mirror of World Politics]. Stockholm: Norstedts.

SIPRI Yearbook 2009: Armaments, Disarmament and International Security. 2009. Oxford, UK: Oxford University Press.

Wallensteen, Peter. 1984. 'Universalism vs. Particularism: On the Limits of Major Power Order', *Journal of Peace Research*, 21 (3): 243–257 (reprinted as Chapter 6 in this volume).

Weiss, Thomas G. 2009. 'What Happened to the Idea of World Government', *International Studies Quarterly*, 53: 253–271.

Part III

Towards conflict resolution analysis

8 Widening the researchable

Conflict, resolution and prevention

From Correlates of War to conflict data

Understanding the major wars is fundamental for peace research. For much of the twentieth century there was concern about a new world war. After the Second World War the fear of nuclear war drove much of peace research. Thus, the data collected by the Correlates of War project (COW, as explained in Chapter 3) were approaching a fundamental question of war and peace: under what conditions was another major war between leading states likely; and, thus, by implication, what was needed to prevent such an event? The solution was largely seen to be in structural changes of the inter-state system, that is, new power configuration and increased authority to an international body. Many conventional prescriptions, such as balance of power and alliances, were found to generate new perils. The ideas of giving emphasis to the strategies the powers were using against each other (e.g. universalism, détente and confidence-building approaches) were often seen as temporary and too 'soft' to result in structural changes. However, the Cold War ended largely through such measures. The détente between the USA and USSR created the conditions under which reform was possible in the Soviet Union, even to the point where it resulted in the demise of the union as such. Similarly, the Chinese leaders of the early twenty-first century emphasized 'harmonious' relations with the world conducive for its own growth. The effects of universalist policies may, in fact, be more difficult to predict than the typical polarization and the increased risks that follow on particularism.

The twenty-first century has seen a different agenda of armed conflict. In the 1990s it was the civil wars and breakdown of societies that became the priority, and in the early 2000s the terrorist wars between Western countries and non-state actors, often basing themselves in the very states that were 'collapsing' during the previous decade. Thus, how to deal with these conflicts – and far from all of them were related to terrorism, but many exhibited considerable one-sided violence – became the research agenda. In comparison with inter-state conflicts and world wars, these challenges may have appeared limited. Indeed, the technologies involved were often simple, relying for instance on small arms, guerrilla tactics, sexual violence or cheap ways of producing bomb belts, improvised explosive devices (IEDs) and recruitment of suicide bombers in ways reminiscent of human trafficking. The effects still could be devastating in bringing down entire societies, not least health systems, and generating population movements that led to epidemics and early deaths.

Thus, the conflicts that had to be attended to were of a different quality from previously. This is why the Uppsala Conflict Data Program (UCDP) became more useful. It had deliberately aimed at collecting information on smaller armed conflicts. The history of the project is told in Chapter 9. The information, furthermore, would make it possible to direct attention to conflicts at an early stage, giving space for early conflict prevention. Chapter 10 shows that the topic had not been dealt with in methodologically proper ways and suggests new ways forward.

Although intellectually building on COW, UCDP also included from the beginning the issues, disagreements or incompatibilities, as an important aspect of a conflict. This was not part of the COW definition of inter-state war. It was even dismissed as an unimportant aspect. 'This is like motives, and the stated motives are never the true driving forces', Professor J. David Singer explained to this author when we discussed this in Michigan in the spring of 1980. He may have been right that the underlying ambitions would often be matters of personal or collective power, that is, the *Realpolitik* aspirations typical of inter-state relations. However, it could be argued that, if 'we' were going to help to 'solve' conflicts in ways other than wars, the actual disagreements would be significant. To the present author it was obvious that COW was not about conflict resolution, nor should it be. It was about understanding the origins of war. The rationale was that 'if we only know these causes or correlates, then the real issues could be dealt with'. Given that this is a long-term scholarly and (not least) political agenda there could of course be a need for talks, agreements and mediation, so to say, in the meantime. Our conversations covered other issues as well, notably that the conflicts had to be observed also when they were smaller. One day, however, Singer amicably ended the discussion: 'If you don't like what I am doing, do your own thing!' Sound advice, and UCDP emerged as a project, taking shape in the decade that followed.

From a fragile project to a stable programme

UCDP has become a major data provider for systematic research on peace and conflict issues. It is based at Uppsala University, Uppsala, Sweden (www.ucdp. uu.se). It is now funded by the university and stands firmly on its own. It cooperates with other institutions such as the Peace Research Institute, Oslo, Norway (PRIO), SIPRI (Stockholm International Peace Research Institute), Stockholm, Sweden, and the Kroc Institute for International Peace Studies at the University of Notre Dame, Indiana, USA. However, the conflict data originate from Uppsala and a recommendation is that data always should be retrieved from this original source (they are free!) in order to ensure that the latest version is used. An integral part is the Uppsala Conflict Database, which contains detailed descriptions of conflicts that, in turn, constitute the 'raw materials' for the datasets.

The basic Uppsala definition is that 'an armed conflict is a contested incompatibility that concerns government and/or territory where the use of armed force between two parties, of which at least one is the government of a state, results in at least twenty-five battle-related deaths in one calendar year'. The reasoning behind this definition is presented in Chapter 9, where the further development of this project is also presented. UCDP's central role of course has led to questions and responses (e.g. Sollenberg and Wallensteen 2008).

Being researchers who listen, UCDP has gradually tried to meet the objections to which its basic definition has given rise. It has inspired UCDP to collect data in addition to armed conflict information. Its data on armed conflict continue to be the longest time series and contain the widest information. In addition, the UCDP website now also holds information on conflicts between non-state actors (i.e. relaxing the requirement that the government has to be a central actor) and on one-sided violence, that is, situations of violence against a non-organized party (that is, ordinary civilians) either by governments or by non-state actors.

The criterion of twenty-five battle-related deaths has been kept, as it is assessed to be the most reasonable measure of ongoing, organized activity. Below this threshold, the analyst is likely to encounter other types of violence, for instance, political assassinations (also a dataset under development at UCDP) or random individual actions or massacres. These are deplorable acts as well, of course, but are more likely to be the result of particular personalities or personal relationships, rather than the societal conflict that it is the ultimate purpose of conflict studies to understand. Nevertheless, the availability of arms for the occurrence of homicide might be a worthy study.

The annual articles in *Journal of Peace Research* have been significant in making the UCDP data well known. They were the result of close cooperation with its editor, Nils Petter Gleditsch. The author of this volume has cooperated with several associates to bring these articles about, initially with Karin Axell, then for many years with Margareta Sollenberg and in recent years Lotta Harbom (now Lotta Themnér). The co-authors not only have been writing these articles, but in particular have been responsible for the collection of the data that go into them. Thus, their responsibility has been vast and indispensable for the project.

There are of course several other projects dealing with conflict data. Most of these academic projects were represented at a major conference in Uppsala, Sweden, in 2001 (Granberg *et al.* 2002), which provided for an important stock-taking of the international efforts. It also illustrated the difficulties of keeping projects going over the years. This was not only a funding issue. Researchers' interests tend to shift over time. To provide consistency there is a need for continuity both in staffing and in understanding what a project does. The conference led to strenuous efforts by the UCDP team to identify such a stable arrangement for UCDP. There were many attempts to get major funding agencies to take primary responsibility, proposals to create funding consortia, or attempts to locate government sources (e.g. Sida, the Swedish development aid organization). However, in the end, the best solution was found in 2009 and is now in operation: a permanent budgetary allocation from Uppsala University to the Department of Peace and Conflict Research with the explicit directive to fund UCDP. It will provide a stability that few data-collecting efforts enjoy.

From causes of conflict to conflict management

The incompatibility component in the definition of armed conflict directs the researchers towards the study of peace agreements and peace processes. How are these incompatibilities handled when the parties want to change from a violent to a more constructive relationship? In the analysis of conflict resolution, UCDP has a role. In the present author's work, *Understanding Conflict Resolution*, this is the chief concern, building directly on the work of UCDP. The first publication of UCDP peace agreement data is here reproduced in Chapter 11. My co-author, Ms Stina Högbladh, played the key role in developing this information.

COW's strong advantage is the longer time period, going back to 1816. One of UCDP's strengths, however, is the lower threshold of inclusion, which gives more data points – albeit for a shorter period – but also captures the dynamics of whether internal conflicts escalate to war or not. Thus, it partly complements COW's data on militarized disputes for inter-state relations. It is also noteworthy that many researchers regard the period since 1946 as more relevant and the end of the Second World War as a major disjuncture in history. That, however, was the theme of Chapter 3 in this volume.

The possibility of studying smaller intra-state conflicts and their propensity to escalate is a field that acquired particular importance in the 1990s. The many difficulties in dealing with a rapidly emerging set of new conflicts that followed after the end of the Cold War was a challenge to decision-makers. Conflict prevention became a central concern. A major project was initiated by the Carnegie Corporation (with a final report in 1997) and international conferences were convened on this, including in Uppsala (e.g. Wallensteen 1998; Wallensteen *et al.* 2001). However, many of the studies built on anecdotal evidence and it was difficult to show that preventive action had an impact on the course of events. To answer the counterfactual questions of what would have happened without a particular intervention is almost impossible in the individual case. However, the questions are well suited for statistical analysis, by which the probabilities can be estimated. It requires access to data on which such studies can be performed. In Chapter 11, the present author together with Ms Frida Möller demonstrated that this was necessary for the field to advance, and an approach was suggested. It led to a search for available sources. One was the Minorities at Risk project (University of Maryland) and a study was conducted (Öberg *et al.* 2009).

Parallel to this a successful grant application gave the possibility of collecting new information, based on UCDP criteria. Some first results have now been produced, in a dataset labelled MILC (Mellbourn and Wallensteen 2008; Melander *et al.* 2009). Further work is continuing along these lines, and developments can be followed on the UCDP website. Remarkably, these efforts seem to be quite alone and few similar activities have yet been published. The work that comes closest is done by Jacob Bercovitch at the University of Canterbury, Christchurch, New Zealand, and by Karl deRouen at the University of Alabama, USA. Studies of mediation and peace agreements come close as seen in recent articles applying a global approach (deRouen *et al.* 2009) and a regional focus (Wallensteen *et al.* 2009).

The prevention activities that are in focus are those of third parties and there is an increasing interest in mediators and their achievements. The UN Secretary-General plays a particular role in this respect. Thus, Chapter 12 presents a study of Dag Hammarskjöld's work, based largely on the thorough biography by Sir Brian Urquhart (1972). This study aimed at stimulating research from a psychological perspective, as leadership studies have gained interest (Winter 2004). Other Swedes playing a role in international negotiations have been studied, notably Alva Myrdal in disarmament negotiations (Wallensteen 2003) and Ambassador Jan Eliasson as a third party in armed conflicts (Svensson and Wallensteen 2010). The field of mediation was exposed to thorough scrutiny in a conference in Uppsala in June 2010, pointing to new fields of inquiry (Lindgren *et al.* 2010).

Thus, conflict analysis takes place on a number of levels. The field of peace research has been dramatically enlarged. One level is the systematic study of global conditions, which is the basic rationale for UCDP research on conflict and peace (Chapters 9 and 10). However, the role of third parties is also important, as seen in the development of the study of prevention (Chapter 11). This, in turn, makes it necessary to systematically study the way particular third parties act, for instance, by comparing their operations over time and in varying situations (Chapter 12).

In this way the basic underpinnings of international peace research become applicable in a number of new areas of research. This widening scope of peace research can be garnered from the contributions in Part III. Parts IV and V are, then, devoted to research specifically aimed at policy-making and diplomacy.

References

Reports of recent conflict trends as documented by UCDP have appeared annually in *Journal of Peace Research* since 1993. Since 2004 Lotta Harbom (now Themnér) has been the first name on this publication, being the programme leader for the UCDP armed conflict data collection. The UCDP series *States in Armed Conflict*, also published annually, gives further information in printed form of the project. See also www.ucdp.uu.se.

Carnegie Commission on Preventing Deadly Conflict. 1997. *Final Report*. Washington, DC: Carnegie Corporation of New York.

Granberg, Kristina, Kristine Eck and Peter Wallensteen. 2002. *Identifying Wars: Systematic Conflict Research and Its Utility in Conflict Resolution and Prevention: Executive Summary*. Uppsala: Department of Peace and Conflict Research, Uppsala University.

Lindgren, Mathilda, Peter Wallensteen and Helena Grusell. 2010. *Meeting the New Challenges to International Mediation*. Report from an international symposium. Uppsala Conflict Data Program Paper No. 6. Uppsala: Department of Peace and Conflict Research, Uppsala University.

Melander, Erik, Frida Möller and Magnus Öberg. 2009. 'Managing Intrastate Low-Intensity Armed Conflict 1993–2004: A New Dataset', *International Interactions*, 35 (2): 1–28.

Mellbourn, Anders and Peter Wallensteen (eds.). 2008. *Third Parties and Conflict Prevention*. Hedemora: Gidlunds.

Öberg, Magnus, Frida Möller and Peter Wallensteen. 2009. 'Early Conflict Prevention in Ethnic Crises, 1990–98: A New Dataset', *Conflict Management and Peace Science*, 26 (1): 67–91.

deRouen Jr, Karl, Jenna Lea and Peter Wallensteen. 2009. 'The Duration of Civil War Peace Agreements', *Conflict Management and Peace Science*, 26 (4): 367–387.

Sollenberg, Margareta and Peter Wallensteen. 2008. 'How to Identify Conflict Trends: A Reply to Øyvind Østerud', *Conflict, Security & Development*, 8 (3): 375–382.

Svensson, Isak and Peter Wallensteen. 2010. *The Go-Between: Jan Eliasson and the Styles of Mediation*. Washington, DC: US Institute of Peace Press.

Urquhart, Brian. 1972. *Hammarskjold*, reprinted 1994. New York: W. W. Norton.

Wallensteen, Peter (ed.). 1998. *Preventing Violent Conflicts: Past record and Future Challenges*. Report. Uppsala: Department of Peace and Conflict Research, Uppsala University.

Wallensteen, Peter (ed.). 2003. *Alva Myrdal in International Affairs*. Uppsala: Uppsala Publishing House.

Wallensteen, Peter, Birger Heldt, Mary B. Anderson, Steven J. Stedman and Leonard Wantchekon. 2001. *Conflict Prevention and Development Co-operation*. Uppsala: Department of Peace and Conflict Research, Uppsala University.

Wallensteen, Peter, Karl DeRouen, Jr., Jacob Bercovitch and Frida Möller. 2009. 'Democracy and Mediation in Territorial Civil Wars in Southeast Asia and the South Pacific', *Asia Europe Journal*, 7 (2): 241–264.

Winter, David G. 2004. 'Motivation and the Escalation of Conflict: Case Studies of Individual Leaders', *Peace and Change: Journal of Peace Psychology*, 10 (4): 381–398.

9   The Uppsala Conflict Data Program, 1978–2010

The story, the rationale and the programme[1]

Data search beyond a tape recorder

The conversation in the autumn of 1978 went like this:

> So, Ken, you are listening to BBC World Service at midnight every night?
>
> Yes, that is how I know what goes on in the world.
>
> And you have noticed that much of what is presented at midnight is never found in ordinary newspapers the following day?
>
> Yes, ordinary media only give their choice of what goes on in the world.
>
> So, why don't you record what is presented? That would give us a better picture of world conflicts!

After this discussion between me and my research associate Ken Wilson the recording of ongoing violent conflicts began at the Department of Peace and Conflict Research. A small datasheet was constructed, called *Radio Data*. Ken had a tape-recorder that switched on every night at the right time – automatically, as he well needed his sleep. The next morning he filled out the data form. The data collection began on 1 January 1979 and had from the beginning *global* coverage. In principle, it still keeps going. The data were soon supplemented with additional materials, including clippings from newspapers that were acquired from the Uppsala Town Library. We had discovered that the library simply threw them away when they were one month old. This way we got them for free. Later, our Research Associate Adele Aranki became responsible for the archive of clippings that resulted. These sources provided what then was seen as a remarkable range of information. It went further than, for instance, the project on 'local wars' initiated by the Hungarian historian Istvan Kende, who mostly relied on *The New York Times*.[2]

In the early 1980s an innovation was discovered and used: the *BBC Recorder*, an information archive of BBC news available for free, some days after the news had been broadcast. It illustrates what has been a hallmark of the conflict data project: using the *most modern search methods* for finding global information on conflicts around the world, and thereby avoiding as much as possible the biases inflicted by the skewed world information order. Also, there was always a strong *cost-consciousness consideration*, as the department was poor and peace research was used to living on marginal resources. It was indicative that in the 1990s our Research Associate Margareta Sollenberg was instrumental in developing an economical use of Reuters information at the Dag Hammarskjöld Library. She also helped establish contacts with leading developers of new forms of data collection, not least Dr Doug Bond, who paid frequent visits to Uppsala to discuss automatic search engines in the late 1990s and early 2000s. With the use of Bond's methodology the project now has access to specified data globally.

Indeed, the distance from Ken's nightly recording of international broadcasts to the well-designed mechanical systems of Doug Bond is vast. So is the amount of sources. The original BBC broadcasts have been replaced with *Factiva* relying on, in 2010, 28,000 publicly available sources, many of them highly local in coverage.

In retrospect, the Uppsala data project began at a time which now appears like the stone age of information technology and it has been transformed by the large quantities of information today available through Internet or direct telephone connections. No doubt, the amount of information on local conflicts has increased. It might imply that each piece of information often is thinner, and that earlier sparse reporting was more penetrating. However, it means that information on today's conditions is not easily comparable with situations forty or fifty years ago. Even with the opening of archives, the extent of lost information is considerable. The confidence we can have in global reporting, particularly in terms of geographical validity, is much higher today. This said, we must not forget the need for a careful evaluation also of that large flow of information.

As this also makes clear, the conflict data project relied on *open* sources, not secret information. The main sources are media accounts but, in addition, research publications; public reports from governmental and non-governmental organizations and academics around the world are continuously approached to validate information. It has been the experience that these sources are sufficient for the purpose of the project. It appears that little is to be gained from using unconventional and clandestine information collection. Using such sources would result in considerable drawbacks in terms of credibility, integrity and autonomy. The project idea from the beginning was to have an *updated reporting system*. It was 'ongoing' violence that would be part of the undertaking. This derived from an impression that media reporting was not comprehensive enough while at the same time existing projects were either late by many years(!) in reporting or secret as they were housed within intelligence agencies, for instance. The public and the researchers needed other sources of information. Thus, the format of an annual record was important and also that it should be made available as soon as possible after each New Year. This approach was not only a service to the public, but also an appropriate way of developing a register that could easily capture trends over time, almost in 'real time'. It would provide a more comprehensive presentation as well as comparisons with the recent past. However, there was no ambition of going back in history, but rather to grasp current violence. The project researchers strove to be updated on the present world situation.

There was one more important aspect to this approach, something which has been with the programme ever since: there should be *maximum comparability*. The events that are recorded should both be similar and equally represented. There are a number of projections made, then as now, on how the world is developing, but many times they are based on information that cannot be compared. Events that are difficult to match are still compared, and thus the reader is uncertain whether they are actually equally well recorded around the world. These were two important biases that the project wanted to remedy. This ambition required considerable work on the theoretical as well as operative definition of what is a small or large war, what the project defined as an 'armed conflict'. Thus, the methodology interacts with the definition, which in turn is related to the theoretical considerations behind the project.

An integrated definition of armed conflict

Although the possibility of collecting information systematically was the spark that ignited the project, the idea had been there for long. The mother of all war data efforts was the Correlates of War (COW) project at the University of Michigan in Ann Arbor, Michigan, initiated with characteristic innovation, energy and boldness by the political scientist J. David Singer.[3] The project has been described in Chapters 3 and 8 in this volume.[4] It was courageous as the idea of quantitative studies of war was still novel and controversial. Singer and his associates relied on the behavioural revolution in social science: war was a form of social behaviour that could be explained as a repetitive pattern originating in basic and observable social conditions; in other words, each event was not entirely unique. Singer had no secure funding but had to rely on an 'ice-hopping' strategy, trying to constantly redefine the data collection efforts according to the latest trends in the research funding community. Without his persistence, this would not have worked.

There were several challenges. The first one was that COW was based on the idea of an inter-state system, and that this system was a key variable in explaining why wars took place. States related to each other as they were connected through a pattern of interactions and dependencies. To be a member of the system was an important feature. It meant also that thinking as well as the empirical work had a heavy focus on inter-state wars and conflicts. National attributes such as form of government, economic growth and so on were less significant.[5]

However, the global picture of conflicts did not match this assumption. On the contrary, there have always been many internal wars. COW added this to its data search, but the definition of civil war was derived from the inter-state perspective and did not precisely fit with the characteristics of such wars. For instance, the project recorded internal wars in the system member states and the non-government side had to be able to put up some form of sustained military combat for the conflict to be included. It meant that the project was intuitively searching for state-like entities that were confronting each other also inside states. Furthermore, civil wars were kept as a separate category with somewhat different coding rules, notably with respect to battle-related deaths.[6]

In this respect the historian Istvan Kende's work in Budapest was different as it departed from local conflicts and their conditions, the leading term being 'local war'. They were also seen to be the result of a system, but an entirely different one: capitalism and imperialism. This system, through its global way of operating, resulted in interventions, dictatorships and, as a reaction, popular rebellion against incumbent regimes, that is, local wars. In fact, the project described inter-state wars as 'frontier wars', further marking that the focus was on internal conflicts (Kende 1971: 11). Thus, there was one definition of war, not separate ones.

Much energy was spent on understanding if there were more conflicts over time and if this then reflected rising contradictions within that system. As the war numbers reported by Kende declined for the late 1960s and early 1970s, he argued that this could be related to the détente period and the 'new international arrangements' which had 'caused the retreat of certain belligerent forces' (Kende 1978: 230). When the project was taken over by Klaus Jurgen Gantzel and received its present name, AKUF (Arbeitsgemeinschaft Kriegsursachenforschung, the Working Group for Research on the Causes of War, based at the University of Hamburg), this was accompanied by a change in focus. The project became strongly empirical. Today, if there is an overarching concern it might be that there is a penetration of the global system into societies, affecting (even destroying) their local capacity for conflict resolution (Jung *et al.* 1996). However, the capitalist system is sometimes part of the analysis, as can be seen, for instance, in the observation that wars have shifted from the centres of the capitalist society to its periphery (commenting on the patterns for 1945–1992, Gantzel and Schwinghammer 2000: 94).

Thus, there was a need to develop a definition that focused on political violence as such, at the heart of what is a conflict of concern to international peace research. It would, ideally, mean thinking primarily not about the actors or parties to the conflict or the systems that they were part of, but about their violent actions against each other. It would, furthermore, be the same no matter who the parties were (i.e. whether the conflict were between states or within states). In this way it would ensure strict comparability between inter-state wars and intra-state wars. Thus, already the first definition of the Uppsala project laid considerable emphasis on finding such general criteria. It started with delimiting violent actions. One result was: 'armed conflict behavior is the instrumental application, for the purpose of causing death, injury or destruction, of any means other than those of basic corporal strength and/or psychological power' (Wallensteen and Wilson 1984). Such a definition would include everything above fistfights, it now seems. Clearly, definitions also of goals and parties were important to narrow the field. The ambition still was obvious: there could not be different definitions of armed conflict depending on the actors. There was a search for an *integrated definition* of armed conflict that covered both inter-state and intra-state conflicts, and possibly other forms of organized political violence as well.

Sticking to the issue of armed behaviour, what would be the bottom line for inclusion? What kind of activity was there which constituted such violence and was it likely that it could be recorded globally in a systematic and reliable way?

The definition that was used by the late 1980s, for instance, when Karin Lindgren was leading the operative work of the project, defined armed conflict as 'sustained combat'. It drew on ideas from Kende.[7] Also in COW there was an implicit such criterion, most obvious in the definition of internal wars, which had to accumulate more than 1,000 deaths in a year, including civilians, to be recorded. Applying the criterion of 'sustained combat' meant that for one year, 1988, there was a record of 111 armed conflicts (Lindgren 1989). This figure was internationally well received (Alker 1989). Somehow it seems to have stayed on in the minds of many people.[8]

A second challenge was that COW did not specify what the conflict was all about. The focus was on action and behaviour. The definitions used were wide and could well have included criminal activities (the state in the form of the police having gunfights with organized criminal gangs; in one year there could be more than 1,000 casualties from such fights in the USA, for instance). This was not the main objection, however. It was instead the idea that conflicts may have different dynamics depending on what the parties were striving for. That would also mean that matters of conflict resolution came to the fore. In COW as well as in the AKUF tradition the initial focus was on the origins of war, but not its ending and resolution. Of course, if one knows the origins and can remedy that, there will in the future be no need for settlement, as there will be no serious conflicts to settle. However, before that is possible any settlement process would have to handle the issues that the parties were motivated by. In conflict theory, there was already a concept for that: incompatibility.

Thus, in the Uppsala project much effort was spent in the early 1980s on thinking about how to formulate the term 'incompatibility' in a coherent and succinct way. Kjell-Åke Nordquist contributed to this, particularly with his study on the Palestinian conflict (Nordquist 1985). Already in the first lists covering the year 1979 it was observed that conflicts dealt with territorial issues, such as ethnically dominated or contested regions of a country. Territorial issues have continued to be central in the project, but there was also a need to define those that did not strictly concern such matters as borders and control over particular regions. For this reason a second category was added, defined independently of the first one: control over government. In doing this, the work of Kende was helpful in its focus on 'anti-regime wars'. Thus, conflicts that dealt with either control over territory or government became central in the Uppsala project. It turned out empirically that it was difficult to find armed conflicts that did not deal with one or the other of these two incompatibilities.

By giving a key role to incompatibility the Uppsala project found an identity of its own. It was different from the rather vague notions of 'interest', which was the underlying concept of the other projects, for example national interest or material interests. Conflict theory made clear that contest, rivalry and resulting behaviour are related to incompatibility, which thus takes a central role in conflict dynamics and conflict resolution. The real change in this approach came to the Uppsala project when Birger Heldt defined armed conflicts as dealing with 'contested incompatibilities', rather than actors and actions (Heldt 1993: 2–7). This provided a strong point of departure. By doing this, it became easier to define and distinguish one conflict from another. A first job was to see whether it was a contest over the same or different issues. Thus, the internal affairs of a country could have several struggles over separate territorial issues as well as over governmental issues. In addition, it became clear how different actors related to one another, by following which incompatibility they were part of.

With this in mind, Heldt set out to challenge the earlier list and arrived at seventy-five contested incompatibilities for 1989 (Heldt 1993: 2). The revisions resulted in heavy debates in the project group. These debates and resulting modifications have, however, left a legacy of the project being *open to revision* of codings in view of new information a well as of interpretation of data. This means also, today, that only the latest version of the data is the one that should be used. Data are continuously revised.

A third challenge of the COW definition was the one that always strikes readers and writers as the most arbitrary: the use of number of deaths as thresholds. The Uppsala project did not have such a threshold, nor did the Budapest project, even when it moved to Hamburg and was considerably strengthened by Klaus Jurgen Gantzel and his associate (Gantzel 1981; Gantzel and Meyer-Stamer 1986). There were valid objections to such thresholds (Gantzel and Schwinghammer 2000: 14–15). Attempts at solving the challenge resulted in other problems, however. What would then be the lowest denominator for inclusion? What is 'sustained combat' or, as reformulated, an 'active' conflict? Furthermore, are situations comparable when one is a protracted war and the other a coup that is over in a couple of hours? Indeed, some conflicts were active entirely with non-lethal weapons, such as the conflict between the UK and SOG (the Sons of Glendower, a Welsh independence movement). These examples of conflicts that were included were provided by Heldt (1993: 1). The problem was how to set logical criteria for the lowest level. The issue was forced in a different way: by the research publication editors.

By 1987 the project had agreed with Stockholm International Peace Research Institute (SIPRI) to supply information on major armed conflicts for the *SIPRI Yearbook*. For the Uppsala group this was a way to make its work known to a larger audience. Somewhat surprisingly, the Uppsala data sometimes became known as 'SIPRI's data', although it was clear in the yearbooks that this was not the case. In this context, the important matter is that SIPRI Director Walter Stutzle was only interested in publishing information on *major* armed conflict.

This is where the 1,000 threshold came in handy. Through the COW project this was an established notion to use battle-related deaths as a way to separate large-scale events ('wars') from other occurrences. Singer has claimed that it was actually derived not from the ease with which it can be identified, but from the fact that this was the number of deaths that one single machine gun could produce, thus changing warfare in the late nineteenth century. Some COW students have also stated that there is a qualitative shift around 1,000. A number of conflicts end at a few hundreds killed or alternatively several thousands. It would be an empirically appropriate place to draw a line, in other words. In the Uppsala experience there is less support for such a claim, but it is obvious that it takes more sustained combat (planning, training, resources, will) to pursue actions that will result in such a large number of deaths. The most convincing argument, however, was that such large-scale events were more likely to be reported world-wide, even if one goes back to 1816. Thus, in the context of publishing for SIPRI, major armed conflicts were defined as those with more than 1,000 battle-related deaths during the course of the conflict.

With this in mind, given the new information technologies, it would be possible also to report on lower levels of activity in a reliable and comparable way. This was not of interest to SIPRI, however, although the Uppsala project made suggestions on this ground. Instead, the project was discussed with Nils Petter Gleditsch, editor of the *Journal of Peace Research* (JPR). He had noticed that much information from the Uppsala project was not presented in the SIPRI yearbooks and also that the project included information that was highly pertinent for researchers interested, for instance, in the escalation of conflicts. Such studies required access to conflicts at lower levels. Gleditsch suggested to the Uppsala project that it should have an annual special feature in JPR on conflict data. An agreement was easily negotiated. It required, however, a decision on the lower threshold.

The Uppsala team discussed various levels. Ideal might have been forms of militia combat (use of particular military equipment such as tanks, aeroplanes, particular types of military actions, offensives, etc.), but this turned out be difficult to define at a uniform and comparable level. In the end, the use of a deaths threshold was the only valid indicator for which one could be reasonably sure of sufficient media attention so as to be able to record all (or nearly all) such events. Hence, *twenty-five battle-related dead in one year* was set as the lowest threshold for inclusion. It was easier to understand than, say forty, and more reliable than, for instance, ten.

The data were introduced in JPR in 1993 (Wallensteen and Axell 1993; Axell 1993) and have been used ever since, also in the conflict database. It meant that for the year 1989 the total number of armed conflicts was revised to forty-six, less than half of what Lindgren had reported and less than two-thirds of what Heldt had found. Still, it is a number that the project is confident about: it does reflect what goes on at the global level in a comparable way.[9] It means also that there is a substantial amount of conflict activity going on below the threshold of twenty-five, but much of it likely to be of a non-violent character. It remains for another project to record these events too. For the conflict data project it has turned out to be a reasonable way of making a cut in the information flow, given the resources available for data collection (money, time, researchers) and the theoretical ambitions of the project.[10]

The theoretical basis

As this overview makes clear, the project works from concepts developed in conflict theory. Much of its origin can be traced to the wok of Johan Galtung in the late 1960s and only much later summarized by him (Galtung 1996). His early writings and lectures were well known throughout the peace research community, however, and thus widely in use (Wiberg 1976; Mitchell 1981). It had a focus on the conflict as (1) an incompatibility and provided ways in which such incompatibilities could be analysed. This term was, as has been seen, picked up in the conflict data project. In addition, his conflict theory included (2) attitudes, which were matters of hostility, perceptions and attitudes in general and (3) behaviour, the actions that were undertaken. Then he indicated that there was interplay between these three elements. This resulted in a dynamic perspective between the three corners of what Galtung termed the conflict triangle. This was useful pedagogically as well as theoretically. It did not, however, fully work with the conflict data. In particular, it was not convincing to see attitudes as an equally strong and independent driving force. Rather, attitudes could be the result of conflict actions as well as of deliberate efforts of mobilization by parties. Furthermore, parties and their formation were not elements in the scheme. Drawing this together it emerged that conflicts could be seen as interplay between three strong forces: *actors* (which has a history, a self-understanding and resources), *incompatibility* (a serious disagreement over a scarce, attractive resource such as control over government or territory) and *actions* (which could be armed or non-armed, destructive or constructive) (Wallensteen 1994, 2002). With this scheme in mind, it was possible to clarify why the project would focus on particular actors, incompatibilities and actions.

It required that actors were organized. They would have a history, a set of goals to enhance, and a chance of mobilizing resources. In the project this led to a focus on states and governments as at least one of the actors. This was strengthened by observing the special status of the state as the only actor which has a legitimate monopoly on coercion, taxation and territorial control in a society. There is, however, no assumption that states are part of a system nor that this is what drives them towards conflict. As the data make clear, because most armed conflicts are fought within states, rather than between them, there are other conflict-enhancing factors that have to be focused. On this score the Uppsala effort is different from its two predecessors.

The same then, is true for the focus on incompatibilities, which is derived from the idea that conflicts can be and often are settled through negotiations. The settlement process, however, requires that the parties are precise about their goals, make clear priorities and take part in negotiations, no matter how they originally may have viewed each other (i.e. what their attitudes were). So is the focus on armed action that has caused an annual total of more than twenty-five battle-related deaths. It means that the Uppsala project starts from the notion of a conscious conflict: there are at least two actors knowingly confronting each other, striving to acquire the same valuables (scarcities) at the same moment in time and having defined for themselves that they have the legitimacy to use violence to pursue these goals. These are, in fact, small or large wars, but many of them are highly asymmetric in power (e.g. a powerful state intervening in a smaller country, a powerful government attacking a small opposition movement). By including smaller events, there is a possibility of studying the dynamics of escalation as well as the possibilities of prevention.

Some of these differences can be explored a bit further. The two preceding projects, COW and Kende's work, both had system theory in mind. COW partly wanted to challenge the established *Realpolitik* notions that were used to explain the onset of major wars, such as world wars and forms of great power rivalry. There was also a methodological concern: to demonstrate that quantitative studies and statistics could bring forward our understanding of the origins of wars. These notions were turned into hypotheses that could be scrutinized for logical coherence and for empirical evidence. It meant, however, that much COW work assumed that the states, be they major powers or not, were interconnected through an inter-state system, thus making it necessary to define which were members and which were not. At the same time the linkages in these systems were less constraining. There was an 'anarchical system', in which the capabilities and resources of the states were the 'final' determinants. This connected well with ideas of system analysis that were popular in social science at the time. Much of human interactions could be understood in the same light.[11] Obviously, the inter-state system was less integrated than internal systems or other comparable systems. Concentrations of power could be compared, for instance. Thus, *Realpolitik* notions could be challenged but some could also be confirmed. Perhaps most central to COW was the methodological challenge: *Realpolitik* was not supported by solid empirical research. Possibly this was true also of other common ways of explaining wars. There have been many additions to the original COW, making this now into a family of projects. Some are reactions to the challenges also identified in Uppsala. For the Uppsala programme, however, it was the original COW that was the beginning.

Kende and AKUF researchers have used a system approach, but in this case one which was seen to be more integrated and coherent: the global capitalist system that increasingly reaches across the world. It stems from the operation of the world economy, it is driven by the internal logic of that economy and it is in need of constant expansion. In Kende's time this was connected to the Cold War and the socialist system was regarded as a barrier against this force. The break-up of that system and the many conflicts among 'socialist' states may have made that scenario less credible. Still, the ambition was to see conflict as relating to this grand development of the world economy. The framework is similar to the one today found among many of the critics of globalization. In a way Kende hoped to confirm some *Kapitalpolitik* notions: how material conditions determine global politics, also violence and war. For this, he needed to specifically address the local wars with a novel methodology.

Over the years, both COW and AKUF have become increasingly empirical. This is also the way the Uppsala conflict data approach world realities. The theoretical notions are not tied to large-scale system theories and there is a deliberate avoidance of either *Realpolitik* or *Kapitalpolitik* terminology. It is expected that the data are useful for testing propositions of either kind (as well as other propositions that can be derived from *Geopolitik, Idealpolitik*, gender approaches, environmentalism or elsewhere). This means that the information can be used both for the fairly static hypotheses of *Realpolitik* (seeing the system as moved by the same state-centred rivalries today as 200 years ago) as well as for the more dynamic ones of *Kapitalpolitik* (seeing the system as constantly evolving and expecting phases and shifts). However, even so there are some constraints in the usage, emerging from the use of the state as one actor (as is done in the other projects), the requirements of an explicit incompatibility and the threshold for inclusion. In this way, the Uppsala data become useful for many of the purposes that a researcher would want.

The future of the Uppsala Conflict Data Program, observed in 2011

During these projects many empirical observations have been made. Early on the observation that there are more internal conflicts than others struck many as important and innovative. As we have seen, it may challenge some notions about the inter-state system as the driving force for much violence. Maybe this system is responsible for one form of violence: the world wars could be derived from inter-state rivalry. In absolute numbers this may mean fewer wars but risk the lives of more people. In terms of the daily experience of the world, however, other origins of conflict may be more important. Still, inter-state relations are important, not least to study the experiences of a skewed distribution of power in the world, as expressed in a possibly emerging Pax Americana. Will it lead to fewer wars or only mean that wars are replaced with interventions?

Democracy has increasingly been documented to be important for inter-state peaceful relations. For internal affairs the situation may be more complicated. Already in 1979 Ken Wilson observed a considerable amount of electoral violence in many countries. This observation might still be important. Democratic procedures are introduced to replace violence, as we can observe in peace agreements ending internal wars.

They may also stimulate competition, rivalry, fraud and manipulation, thus turning into new forms of violence. The issue seems to require close attention, particularly in view of the observation that 'semi-democracies' are more prone to internal violent conflict (Hegre *et al.* 2001). For instance, deliberate export of democracy may affect its long-term legitimacy in the recipient societies.

Democracy also has difficulties in managing highly ethnically divided societies, either those with a strong polarization between two or three sizeable competing groups or those with considerable fragmentation, where coalition-making may be difficult. Democracy may need some refinement and development to be a durable solution, and not become a new cause for war.

The issues accumulate and some of them require a reliable data source. The Uppsala project has tried to supply that, in all humility and without much fanfare. It has simply been known as the 'conflict data project' with little consideration of what it actually should be called. Modern requirements, not least in the form of grant applications and presentations on the Internet, necessitated a change. Thus, in 2003 the project took a formal name and turned itself into a programme: the *Uppsala Conflict Data Program* (UCDP). It is far from the catchy Correlates of War and its abbreviation, COW, a resource to milk for information, or the stricter AKUF. The programme has concentrated on being a resource for the research community. The definitions that have been developed should make the data useful for many different purposes, and thus not contain a built-in bias towards a particular understanding of the causes of war as well as peace. However, the definitions themselves do constrain some of the uses, and in that sense limit the search. Thus, the programme has undertaken deliberate work to break loose from some of those constraints. Here are some recent examples.

Since 2005 data are available on a freely accessible database. Originally this was made possible by a grant from Sida, the Swedish International Development Cooperation Agency; now it receives core funding from Uppsala University.

Data are continuously updated. The increasing complexity of the mass of data makes this an important task. The utility of UCDP for the research community rests on the possibilities of maintaining and constantly revising the database and the dataset in view of new information on historical events as well as on updating the published data on a yearly basis.[12]

Conflict data go into recent history. With a grant from the World Bank and in cooperation with PRIO a first backdating has been made of all armed conflicts in every year since 1946.[13] The 'raw material' for the dataset is the information contained in the database of conflicts, and it now contains detailed data for all armed conflict back to 1975. There are also ongoing backdating efforts for other data as well.

Other conflicts than 'wars' are covered. Initially, and in line with the tradition from COW and AKUF, the focus was on conflict in which the state/government was a central actor. In cooperation with the Human Security Research Group at Simon Fraser University in Vancouver, Canada, additional categories of violence conflict have now been included. This includes violence by state actors against non-organized civilians (e.g. massacres, genocides), as well as non-state actors' use of violence against other non-state actors (e.g. communal violence). Part of this work was also to have closer information on battle-related deaths.[14]

There are data also on peace. Peace agreements have been added to the conflict data, as have the ways in which armed conflicts have ended. A first presentation is seen in Chapter 11. This is also available in the database and as datasets for statistical analysis.[15]

There are data on diplomacy to prevent conflict. With several grants UCDP has now collected systematic data on conflict prevention measures carried out by third-party actors. This work is continuously refined.[16] A report based on data available in UCDP could demonstrate that the European Union does not use its full potential as a peacemaking actor.[17]

There are data on the geographical location of conflict. Does it matter where the conflicts take place? One of UCDP's largest new undertakings is to geo-code all data; that means specifying the places where the myriad of events constituting the basis for the identification of particular conflicts actually take place. A first series of data was published in papers at the International Studies Association in 2010 and further data are presented in the coming years. It is strongly believed that this information will have considerable impact on the pursuit of conflict analysis in the coming years.[18]

Certainly there are many additional challenges to a programme such as this. The spin-off effects are in themselves remarkable. In the coming years there will be studies on causes of conflict that have hitherto not been possible or neglected, taking into account factors of geography, climate and quality of government. Also the social and political impact of conflict will be approached, notably its effects on development ambitions and its consequences for humanitarian assistance. There is also work on the role of mediation and third-party action, during as well as after active conflict. Issues of reconciliation and integration after conflict are being addressed. This is to name only a few of the ongoing activities in which the systematic approach to conflict will demonstrate its fruitfulness and thus assist in increasing our insights into the dynamics of war and peace.

Notes

1   This is a first attempt to write a history of a project that has gradually evolved from a limited idea to a full programme. This text has benefited from insightful comments by Mikael Eriksson, Nils Petter Gleditsch, Birger Heldt and Karin Lindgren. The author remains solely responsible for the contents.

2   I had the opportunity to visit an ageing Professor Kende in his home in Budapest. His house was riddled with bullet holes now filled with cement. They stemmed from the 'counter-revolutionary' activities in 1956, he explained. Although close to twenty-five years had passed, the house had not been properly repainted. We discussed that Hungarian crisis in his recording of 'local war'. He said that, according to the official Hungarian position, this was not a conflict. This was also his own position as having experienced this event. It was only a matter of sporadic fighting and thus did not have the 'coherence' of a local war. Thus, he should not include it. However, he said, his chief sources of information for all the recorded local conflicts in the world was the international press (particularly, *The New York Times*). The activities of 1956 according to this capitalist medium were of such a size that they were recorded in its news, so he had to accept them as a conflict as well, no matter what his own position was on this. In this way, he claimed he maintained his objectivity. I had to agree. If the Hungarian revolt had not been part of his data, his work would have lost its credibility (for Kende's own account see 1971: 5–6 and 1978). It still remains a mystery that the Soviet Union was not regarded as an interventionist power in Kende's work, however, although the Hungarian conflict was defined as an 'internal anti-regime war with foreign participation'.

3   COW's founder J. David Singer would of course also have pointed to the work of Pitirim Sorokin, Lewis F. Richardson and Quincy Wright. It remains remarkable that the University of Michigan never expressed its appreciation of Singer's efforts.

4   The list of publications resulting from COW is impressive. Publications with an impact on the start of the Uppsala effort were Singer (1972), Singer and Small (1972), Singer (1979) and Small and Singer (1982). A most comprehensive presentation of the project is Vasquez (2000).

5   Singer (1981: 1–14) succinctly summarizes findings and arguments. As to COW's focus at the time, it is typical that the bibliography in Small and Singer (1982) had no title referring to 'civil war' or similar concepts. In COW vocabulary 'war' largely refers to inter-state wars, e.g. the seminal works of Vasquez (2000), 'What Do We Know about *War*', and Geller and Singer (1998), 'Nations at *war*' (italics added here). In UCDP, 'war' refers to all armed conflicts of a particular magnitude.

6   A first list appeared in Small and Singer (1982: 214–215) including internal wars in system member states and covering the 1816–1980 period. Both civilian and military deaths were included in the data for civil wars.

7   Kende used the term 'continuity' and was clear on excluding 'spontaneous uprisings and riots' as well as incidents (1971: 5–6). That is also part of the AKUF definition (Gantzel and Schwinghammer 2000: 11–14).

8   The figure was used by President Jimmy Carter and the Carter Center. When visiting Uppsala in December 2002 after receiving the Nobel Peace Prize, Carter asked me if there were still 100 conflicts in the world, as I had informed him in 1989. It was true

for the post-1989 period, not one year. With the categories of non-state violence and one-sides, the yearly account may again approach 100.

9 The number of 1989 in the latest UCDP article in JPR is given as forty-three, not very far from the number given in 1993, although the revisions and re-readings and re-codings have been many (Harbom and Wallensteen 2010: Table I).

10 This cooperation with JPR and PRIO has been followed by several other projects, notably one financed by the Ford Foundation and one on 'backdating' of armed conflicts to 1946, which thus also has the joint name of the UCDP/PRIO dataset. The updating of this dataset is done entirely at UCDP. This was initially financed by grants from the EU, the World Bank and the Swedish government.

11 COW was for many years housed in the Mental Health Research Institute at the University of Michigan, where international violence was seen as parallel to other forms of violence, thus an effect of a 'system' that could potentially be compared with other pathologies.

12 This work is led by Lotta Themnér and Stina Högbladh (as of 2011).

13 This work was led by Margareta Sollenberg and Mikael Eriksson, a first version being published in Gleditsch *et al.* (2002). The continuous updates are done by UCDP and the data can be found on its website, www.ucdp.uu.se.

14 UCDP involved innovative researchers for this, notably Kristine Eck, Joakim Kreutz and Ralph Sundberg. The work is now being pursued by Therese Pettersson and involves a number of research assistants. The data are available through the UCDP website and are also presented in the annual volumes from UCDP, *States in Armed Conflict*, and in articles such as Eck and Hultman (2007).

15 This work has been conduced by Joakim Kreutz (most recent is Kreutz 2010) and Stina Högbladh (see Chapter 10 in this volume).

16 The origins are described in Chapter 11 in this volume. Frida Möller was the originator of the first dataset and the work is now being pursued by Nina von Uexkull. Erik Melander has led the efforts.

17 Emma Johansson and Joakim Kreutz led this work; see Johansson *et al.* (2010).

18 The best way to keep abreast of what is coming from UCDP is to subscribe to its news alerts. This can be done on the UCDP website.

References

Alker, Hayward R. 1989. 'Uppsala Fireworks: Data-Based Thoughts on the Origins and Possible Obsolescence of the European State System', in Peter Wallensteen (ed.), *States in Armed Conflict 1988*. Uppsala: Department of Peace and Conflict Research.

Axell, Karin (ed.). 1993. *States in Armed Conflict 1992*. Uppsala: Department of Peace and Conflict Research.

Eck, Kristine and Lisa Hultman. 2007. 'One-Sided Violence against Civilians in War: Insights from New Fatality Data', *Journal of Peace Research*, 44 (2): 233–246.

Galtung, Johan. 1996. *Peace by Peaceful Means*. London: Sage.

Gantzel, Klaus Jurgen. 1981. 'Another Approach to a Theory on the Causes of International War', *Journal of Peace Research*, 18: 39–55.

Gantzel, Klaus Jurgen and Jurgen Meyer-Stamer (eds.). 1986. *Die Kriege nach den Zweiten Weltkrieg bis 1984: Daten und Analysen* [The Wars since the Second World War to 1984: Data and Analyses]. Munich: Weltforum.

Gantzel, Klaus Jurgen and Torsten Schwinghammer. 2000. *Warfare since the Second World War*. New York: Transaction.

Geller, Daniel S. and J. David Singer. 1998. *Nations at War*. Cambridge: Cambridge University Press.

Gleditsch, Nils Petter, Peter Wallensteen, Mikael Eriksson, Margareta Sollenberg and Håvard Strand. 2002. 'Armed Conflict 1946–2001: A New Dataset', *Journal of Peace Research*, 39 (5): 615–637.

Harbom, Lotta and Peter Wallensteen. 2010. 'Armed Conflicts, 1946–2009', *Journal of Peace Research*, 47: 501–509.

Heldt, Birger (ed.). 1993. *States in Armed Conflict 1990–91*, second edition. Uppsala: Department of Peace and Conflict Research.

Johansson, Emma, Joakim Kreutz, Peter Wallensteen, Christian Altpeter, Sara Lindberg, Mathilda Lindgren and Ausra Padskocimaite. 2010. *A New Start for EU Peacemaking? Past Record and Future Potential*. UCDP Paper No. 7. Uppsala University, Department of Peace and Conflict Research.

Jung, Dietrich, Klaus Schlichte and Jens Siegelberg. 1996. 'Ongoing Wars and Their Explanation', in Luc van de Goor, Kumar Rupesinghe and Paul Sciarone (eds.), *Between Development and Destruction: An Enquiry into the Causes of Conflict the Post-Colonial States*. London: Macmillan.

Kende, Istvan. 1971. 'Twenty-Five Years of Local Wars', *Journal of Peace Research*, 8: 5–22.

Kende, Istvan. 1978. 'Wars of Ten Years (1978)', *Journal of Peace Research*, 15: 227–242.

Kreutz, Joakim. 2010. 'How and When Armed Conflicts End: Introducing the UCDP Conflict Termination Dataset', *Journal of Peace Research*, 47 (2): 243–250.

Lindgren, Karin (ed.). 1989. *States in Armed Conflict 1988*. Uppsala: Department of Peace and Conflict Research.

Mitchell, Christopher R. 1981. *The Structure of International Conflict*. New York: St. Martin's.

Nordquist, Kjell-Åke. 1985. 'Conflicting Peace Proposals: Four Peace Proposals in the Palestine Conflict Appraised', *Journal of Peace Research*, 22: 159–173.

Singer, J. David. 1972. 'The "Correlates of War" Project: Interim Report and Rationale', *World Politics*, 24: 243–270.

Singer, J. David (ed.). 1979. *The Correlates of War, vol. 1: Research Origins and Rationale*. New York: Free Press.

Singer, J. David. 1981. 'Accounting for International War: The State of the Discipline', *Journal of Peace Research*, 18: 1–18.

Singer, J. David and Melvin Small. 1972. *The Wages of War, 1816–1965: A Statistical Handbook*. New York: Wiley.

Small, Melvin and J. David Singer. 1982. *Resort to Arms: International and Civil Wars*. Beverly Hills, CA: Sage.

Vasquez, John (ed.). 2000. *What Do We Know about War?* Lanham, MD: Rowman & Littlefield.

Wallensteen, Peter. 1994. *Från krig till fred* [From War to Peace]. Stockholm: Liber.

Wallensteen, Peter. 2002. *Understanding Conflict Resolution*. London: Sage. Second edition 2007, third edition 2011.

Wallensteen, Peter and Karin Axell. 1993. 'Armed Conflicts at the End of the Cold War, 1989–1992', *Journal of Peace Research*, 30: 331–346.

Wallensteen, Peter and G. Kenneth Wilson. 1984. *Reference List: Organized Armed Conflicts since 1979* (unpublished).

Wiberg, Håkan. 1976. *Konfliktteori och fredsforskning* [Conflict theory and peace research]. Stockholm: Esselte. Second edition 1990.

10 Conflict prevention

Methodology for knowing the unknown[1]

with Frida Möller

Introduction

The prevention of violent conflicts became important early after the end of the Cold War. Cases such as the genocides in Rwanda, ethnic wars in Bosnia-Herzegovina, and state failure in Somalia pointed to the necessity of finding means to avert conflicts from escalating into war, human disasters, and regional instability. The purpose of international action to deal with such situation was to curtail the spread of violence and find a solution at an early stage. It is these ambitions that oftentimes are described as conflict prevention (Lund 2002; Wallensteen 2002, 2007, 2011). Experiences have shown that it is not enough merely to take *any* preventive action and get *some* response. It is now time to be more nuanced and ask which actions by whom are more likely to get an effective response. A problem is that we cannot know how a particular conflict would have developed without such a response, the preventive measures, in the event that there were some actions. This is unknown, but necessary to know if we can say that prevention actually succeeds. This chapter is devoted to find possible solutions to this quandary.

The discussion focused on efforts to resolve conflicts before violence had escalated too far, as experience suggests that taking early action is of great importance. Furthermore, the debate claimed that acting in a full-blown war is the costliest and most dangerous way of intervening and also the one least likely to succeed (Annan 1996: 188). If the potential for conflict prevention is to be improved, the sources of its successes and failures must be better understood.

The purpose of this chapter is twofold. First, the methodology of scholars focusing on preventive measures is reviewed. As will be apparent, the literature is not as extensive as the debate would suggest. Second, based on this review, three proposals of how a systematic study on preventive measures can be designed will be presented. An evaluation of the strengths and weaknesses of these approaches is done in order to proceed with a research project in the field.

The overarching purpose is to determine if preventive measures have an impact, keeping disputes from escalating to major armed conflict, or preventing ongoing conflicts from escalating further or spreading across a larger region. To begin with, the first problem (escalation to major armed conflict) is our focus and the suggested project.

The concept of conflict prevention

The term *conflict prevention* suggests different things to different people and there is no agreed-upon meaning among scholars. Here are some examples:

- *Munuera (1994: 3):* "the application of nonconstraining measures (those that are not coercive and depend on the goodwill of the parties involved), primarily diplomatic in nature."
- *Lund (1996: 37):* Preventive diplomacy is "actions taken in vulnerable places and times to avoid the threat or use of armed force and related forms of coercion by states or groups to settle the political disputes that can arise from destabilizing effects of economic, social, political, and international change."
- *Boutros-Ghali (1996: 18):* "Preventive diplomacy is the use of diplomatic techniques to prevent disputes arising, prevent them from escalating into armed conflict [. . .] and prevent the armed conflict from spreading."
- *Carnegie Commission (1997: xviii):* The aim of preventive action is to prevent the emergence of violent conflict, prevent ongoing conflicts from spreading, and prevent the re-emergence of violence.
- *Wallensteen (1998: 11):* constructive actions undertaken to avoid the likely threat, use, or diffusion of armed force by parties in a political dispute.
- *Miall, Ramsbotham, and Woodhouse (1999: 96):* actions which prevent armed conflicts or mass violence from breaking out.
- *Lund (2002: 117, fn 6):* "any structural or intersectory means to keep intra-state or inter-state tensions and disputes from escalating into significant violence and the use of armed force, to strengthen the capabilities of parties to possible violent conflicts for resolving their disputes peacefully, and to progressively reduce the underlying problems that produce those tensions and disputes."
- *Carment and Schnabel (2003: 11):* "a medium and long-term proactive operational or structural strategy undertaken by a variety of actors, intended to identify and create the enabling conditions for a stable and more predictable international security environment."

Carment and Schnabel argue that the definition of conflict prevention should be "broad in meaning and malleable as a policy." Furthermore, they claim that this broad approach has empirical validity because it is applicable across a variety of cases and phases of conflict (2003: 2). However, we argue that most definitions are used very loosely, which makes them too broad to be researchable and, thus, useful. Many do serve a policy purpose, rather than delimiting a field of inquiry into conflict prevention. It is not surprising that they are weak on operationalization. A more precise definition is therefore needed if the research community is to develop the prevention agenda. Also, Lund argues that a more rigorous definition should distinguish conflict prevention from other closely related concepts such as preventive diplomacy, foreign policy, and intervention. It should be applicable to different contexts and yet specified enough to be possible to operationalize (Lund 1996: 32).

Long and short-term prevention

There are two ways of understanding conflict prevention. One concerns the *direct* preventive actions: a crisis is judged to be in a dangerous phase of military escalation, intensification, or diffusion. Thus, there is a need to act to prevent increasing dangers. The actor is a third party whose interests are less immediate and not directly linked to the incompatibility between the primary parties. A second concern is the *structural* prevention, where the idea is to create such conditions that conflicts and disputes hardly arise or do not threaten to escalate into militarized action. Here a third party could be involved in furnishing assistance for such conditions to develop, for instance. These two types of prevention are called light, direct, or operational prevention on the one hand and deep or structural on the other hand, depending on the scholar (Miall *et al.* 1999: 97; Wallensteen 2002: 271; Sriram 2003: 364). Let us here look at the situations of direct conflict prevention, without losing the wider perspective. In many ways this is more challenging than the structural dimension, as the latter could probably be studied with ordinary methodology (observing fewer wars between democratic states, for instance, suggesting that consolidated democracy works as a structural preventive measure). The recent advances in duration analysis may here be helpful when studying long-term effects of structural prevention. Generally, these types of time analyses model hazard rates, that is, "the risk of having the event at time t, given that the event did not occur before time t" (Yamagushi 1991: 9). Such risk analysis is at the heart of prevention thinking.

The dependent variable ("success" and "failure")

The field lacks a shared concept of what constitutes conflict prevention as a dependent variable. The inability to determine what is successful conflict prevention may be partially due to the degree of conceptual ambiguity. As the term *conflict prevention* suggests different things to different scholars, success or failure depends in large part on how prevention is defined in the first place. It is then easy to point to major failures of conflict prevention but also to claim undue success. How should success be defined and operationalized? Some clues can be gained from the literature.

Sriram and Wermester take a case-by-case approach and do not define success as preventing conflict per se. They argue that the success must be very context-sensitive and take history, risks, goals, and so on into consideration (Sriram and Wermester 2003: 29). Väyrynen agrees that the success depends largely on the political context and the ability to read it correctly. Furthermore, he argues that the outcomes vary between the stages of the conflict cycle: pre-war, escalation, and post-war prevention (Väyrynen 2003: 48).

The method of defining success does to some extent depend on the availability of comparable indicators. At present, there exist no precise indicators to determine the outcome, and therefore each case must be interpreted separately. This technique does, however, require deep examination of cases and is, at least, a highly time-consuming method. Comparability is possibly lost and thus the ability to make broad generalizations for research and for policy. A useful definition must be applicable to a large numbers of cases in order to make systematic studies. Also, to make contributions that are useful in future cases they have to be based on a broad generalization that is not too context-sensitive. Miall and colleagues take a cruder measure of success in direct prevention: "the conjunction of a de-escalation of political tensions and steps towards addressing and transforming the issue in the conflict" (Miall *et al.* 1999: 119).

Let us now present an overview of what the dependent variable could be for direct as well as structural conflict prevention (Table 10.1).

Rothchild argues that, rather than viewing successful prevention as "either . . . or," partial and limited success should also be considered (Rothchild 2003: 36). This gives us a more nuanced understanding of what is achieved and is in line with Talentino, who argues that it is not constructive to view success in either the short or the long term. Instead conflict prevention can only be considered successful when it prevents or ends conflict in the short term *and* undertakes efforts to alter the underlying causes of violence (Talentino 2003: 72). As Talentino points out, there is a tendency to view the absence of a speedy solution as a failure. Talentino is the first scholar to our knowledge who tries to systematize the evaluation of preventive success and failure by posing four questions. These are presented in Box 10.1.

Goertz and Regan, in their work on conflict management in enduring rivalries, reason in a similar way when they argue that one can define success of prevention in three ways: (1) short-term success, (2) medium-term effects, and (3) conflict termination. The authors claim that the outcome of conflict management efforts is predominantly seen in short-term consequences, which is conflict management, not conflict resolution. Their preference is the medium-term effects, for instance turning a rivalry into a détente-type of relationship that lasts for a longer period ("more than a couple of years," Goertz and Regan 1997: 323). However, the rivalry is not terminated. This points to an interest in the reduction of the basic hostility level between the actors, not just the solution to a particular crisis (Goertz and Regan 1997: 325–327).

This is a way to see that the change in hostility is not temporary, but that the preventive measures were effective in preventing a long-term escalation. Obviously, the study of enduring rivalries gives a possibility of developing a measure of the "basic rivalry level" (BRL). From this a set of dependent variables can be derived.

Goertz and Regan advocate a medium- or long-term time horizon. In doing this, they examine the patterns of dispute severity instead of using the level of

Table 10.1 Success and failure in conflict prevention

	Success	*Failure*
Light measures	Armed conflict averted	Armed conflict
Deep measures	Peaceful change	Conflict-prone situation

Source: Miall *et al.* (1999: 127).

Box 10.1 Success evaluation questions in conflict prevention

Short-term success

- Have the adversaries engaged in negotiations, truce talks, or any head-to-head meetings?
- Has an effort been made to reduce violence and prevent its re-escalation?

Long-term success

- Have conflict-generating structures been identified and is there a plan to alter conflict dynamics?
- Has the salience of group identity been decreased in the political and economic realms?

Source: Talentino (2003: 73).

severity of the next dispute, which would be another alternative dependent variable (next dispute severity). They construct six different patterns, four of which indicate successful conflict management. They argue that taking a medium-term approach in defining the dependent variable can contribute to our understanding of how conflicts are managed (Goertz and Regan 1997: 326–329). This line of thought can easily be translated into the field of prevention.

A further source to search for dependent variables would be to review the deterrence literature. This approach stems from a policy perspective: an armed attack, it is sometimes claimed, has been deterred by a strong counter-force move, the formation of a new alliance, etc. The fact that there is no attack then testifies to the significance of the strong posture. Here the same methodological problem is encountered: was the attack likely, in which period would we expect it, what about the possibility that the attack was only postponed or deflected, and what if it was not even contemplated? This literature remains to be reviewed.

Still the discussion so far suggests that the effects of preventive measures have to be seen as a continuum of several levels of success and, furthermore, effects have to be seen in at least a medium-term perspective. Only to stop a particular situation from escalating is a form of conflict management or even conflict avoidance, rather than conflict prevention. It is the lowest level of success, but needs to be complemented with other elements. The fact that the dispute erupts again some months later is not satisfactory as a record of success. It may well be the same conflict, it may be something new, but the relationship is still in a volatile stage. Instead we would look for effects that are lasting, in other words that no further crisis is recorded in this relationship. This means watching the situation over a longer period of time. It does not mean, however, that it is a matter of solving the conflict. That is still something else, involving a considerable amount of negotiation, in fact, a peace process. The conflict prevention activities, however, could be a way of laying the foundation for such a process. Thus, the following would be a good candidate as the dependent variable: immediate avoidance of escalation to major armed conflict (minimum success) and no additional serious dispute among the parties (for at least five years, as a way of operationalizing this), that is, a measure of the change in frequency and severity of the following disputes. The initiation of a peace process would be the maximum criterion of success. This provides us with a continuum of varying degrees of success.

However, these types of reasoning cannot capture the variability over time as an event is coded as "either . . . or": something has occurred or not (peace or no peace/war or no war; Box-Steffensmeier and Jones 1997: 1423). A way to circumvent this is to conceptualize the dependent variable as the probability of war: How close to war is the situation? Did the probability of war go down or not after the preventive measures?

Toward a prevention theory?

Sriram and Wermester argue that because of the difficulties with causation it is important to provide a reasoned hypothesis as to why and how certain actions could have prevented or did prevent conflict. The researcher would then have to use counterfactual argument, be specific, and offer causal logic but also offer alternative explanations (Sriram and Wermester 2003: 30). The literature is still not so strong on hypothesis development, however, and nothing close to a prevention theory can be distilled. There are some elements to build on, such as type of preventive action, phases of conflict, including the matter of timing, as well as some insights drawn from the study of the causes of war that can be used.

The literature has spent considerable energy on developing categories for different types of preventive actions. Here it is sufficient to mention two, drawn from rather different backgrounds. One is the work by Michael Lund, who has provided an elaborate toolbox of preventive instruments (Lund 1996). The main categories of the toolbox are reproduced in Box 10.2. Lund tries to synthesize a set of observations on what is actually done in particular conflict situations, and thus arrive at this typology. There is little to say, though, which of these are the most effective or how they can relate to one another.

A different approach is taken by a practitioner, Jan Eliasson, a diplomat and the first Under-Secretary-General for the UN Department of Humanitarian Affairs. He has suggested a ladder of increasingly coercive actions that could be undertaken by the international community to prevent a local situation from getting out of hand. This is reproduced in Box 10.3, building on Eliasson's repeated lectures at Uppsala University.

For each step the reactions of the primary parties would have to be surmised. For instance, Steven J. Stedman has repeatedly emphasized the need for "fact-facing" as a phase that could follow between steps 2 and 3 on the Eliasson ladder.

It is our impression that there is a sufficient understanding in the literature as well as in the public sphere of what preventive actions do include. The difficulty is, perhaps, to differentiate some of these from "normal" diplomacy or "national"

Box 10.2 Lund's preventive diplomacy toolbox

I. Military approaches

A Restraints on the use of armed force
B Threat or use of armed force

II. Nonmilitary approaches

A Coercive diplomatic measures (without the use of armed force)
B Noncoercive diplomatic measures (without armed force or coercion)

III. Development and governance approaches

A Policies to promote national economic and social development
B Promulgation and enforcement of human rights and democratic and
   other standards
C National governing structures to promote peaceful conflict resolution

Source: Lund (1996: 203–205).

Box 10.3 The Eliasson ladder of conflict prevention

7 Actual use of military force, on the basis of UN chapter VII
6 Threaten to use military force, on the basis of UN chapter VII
5 Use chapter VII peaceful coercive measures such as sanctions,
   not the least targeted sanctions
4 Use the new generation of peacekeeping operations, including
   preventive deployment
3 Stimulate the parties to use the eight measures of chapter VI,
   Article 33
2 Fact-finding missions, by UN, by regional organizations
1 Early warning, react to early signs

policies. If the actions are taken by international organizations that start not from
a particular interest, but from the combined concern of the member-states, that
may be one way of differentiating different types of diplomacy from each other.

Phases of conflict prevention are important to many writers. That is part of
Lund's scheme as well as the Eliasson ladder, as they both indicate that conflicts
move into phases of different hostility. It needs to be systematized, however, in

order to make possible a comparison between different situations. Rothchild mentions four different phases – potential conflict, gestation, trigger, and escalation – and post-conflict phases of conflict and prevention (Rothchild 2003: 44–56). Wallensteen and colleagues mention three phases: emergence, dynamics, and peace-building (Wallensteen *et al*. 2001: 4). It is highly plausible that the potential to prevent conflict differs in the different phases. The focus on phases should be useful as it makes it possible to analyze what resources are necessary and when they need to be employed. Low-risk situations need fewer resources than high-risk ones that may require greater levels of commitment (Rothchild 2003: 44). The research problem is that there are no sharp lines between the phases and such phases often can be seen "afterwards" but may not be perceived at the time. In other words, there remains a problem in delimiting phases.

Related to this is the issue of *timing:* when preventive measures fail the action is often claimed to be "too little, too late," implicitly saying that the timing is the most important factor. However, Sriram and Wermester argue that what matters is whether the action is tailored to match the emerging situation. Sriram and Wermester give examples of different preventive actions and their efficiency. Efforts may be targeted and coordinated but simply come too late in order to prevent escalation. However, we cannot be sure whether the action failed because it was "too" late or because it failed to address other elements in the challenging situation (Sriram and Wermester 2003: 15). This renders the following question: When is "early" in a conflict and how can we know it when we see it? "Early" may not mean the same thing in different contexts, especially if some conflicts are on a steeper escalation curve than others (Hampson 2002: 144–145).

There is also a frequent statement that conflict prevention must be *context-specific* in order to be effective (Ackerman 2003: 343; Väyrynen 2003: 48; Lund 2002: 104). For one thing, taking the context into consideration when operationalizing does require deep examination of cases, which, as noted, is time-consuming. It also reduces the ability to generalize. To this should be added that the preventive methods often are the same, requiring concepts that bring out similarities in the actual situation, as well. From the policy-maker perspective they may appear more similar than a researcher may think. Ackerman even argues that there is agreement that effective prevention must be country-specific. It is not clear how the author has arrived at this conclusion since there is no method guiding either the evaluation of the character or the impact of the measures taken. The context needs also to be operationalized and made comparable. In fact, it might be argued that existing studies that focus on the success or/and failure of conflict prevention run the risk of being based on a biased selection of cases. Prevention researchers, in other words, run the risk of "selecting on the dependent variable."

Can these different strands of thinking be brought together in a prevention theory? Clearly, it is possible to generate hypotheses about different types of actions and their likely impact. However, the questions need to be related to other possible explanations of why a particular conflict takes a particular course of action. This becomes very clear if a systematic approach is pursued, involving a strict comparative or quantitative approach.

Searching for systematic approaches and independent variables

Clearly the literature consists of case studies. As far as we can see, no systematic study has been conducted. Furthermore, most published work on preventive action concentrates on studies of successful cases in which a typical study starts with outlining the climate and factors contributing to the crisis. Then, the various measures taken by actors are presented in a chronological order to point to how these actions prevented the escalation. This makes it necessary to review other type of studies.

In explaining interethnic cooperation, Fearon and Laitin take an interesting approach in making an estimate of *potential* incidents of communal violence in Africa. To avoid selection bias they compare actual cases per year with indicators of potential cases per year. In constructing the number of potential cases, the researchers used a proxy. First, the potential cases are an estimate of the ethnic dyads in regular interaction. Second, the number of languages is used as a proxy for the number of ethnic dyads (Fearon and Laitin 1996: 717). Through this procedure, Fearon and Laitin estimate that the mean number of actual violent communal events in Africa as a percentage of potential events "hovers around zero." They even write, "communal violence, though horrifying, was extremely rare in Africa" for the twenty years they study (1960–1979; ibid.). When violence appeared/was prevented they attribute this to the absence/existence of networks and the calculations people make (as to punishment etc.). They note, for instance, that the actors will know that the state will intervene only when violence is at a certain, high level (Fearon and Laitin 1996: 731). Thus, there is an incentive for the neighborhoods to keep violence at a lower level. This would suggest that also, in the situations we are concerned with, actors might not expect early action from the outside, and thus contain their disputes. A somewhat disturbing aspect of this is, then, that known external interest in intervening may serve to escalate (rather than prevent) further violence.

The observation that there is less armed violence than many expect is actually supported also by data from the Correlates of War: the number of militarized disputes is vastly higher than the number of wars. It suggests that conflicts do not readily have the potential of escalation. There are containing or inhibiting factors, some of which might be defined as preventive measures. Furthermore, previous experience of war in a relationship is related to renewed occurrence of armed conflict in that relationship, helping us to identify that there might be particular relationships that are more war-prone than others. For instance, Goertz and Regan note that enduring rivalries (a small fraction of the armed conflicts) take up more than 50 percent of the mediation attempts.

These general studies do not provide us with concrete cases of prevention. Despite the difficulty in locating successful cases, there are several situations where researchers and policy-makers argue that the measures taken in all probability prevented escalating violence. These are referred to in the literature. In media and much analysis they are not given the same attention as cases where the international community fails to prevent escalating violence. Examples of claimed successes are Guatemala, Fiji, Macedonia, South Ossetia (Georgia), Moldova, the Baltic area, Hungary versus Slovakia, and Libya versus Chad (Eliasson 1996: 322; Miall *et al.* 1999: 98).

From this scattered literature we can draw the conclusion that typical independent variables would be the following: the type of preventive action (degree of coercion, for instance), characteristics of the preventive actor (third parties being neighbors, major powers, international organizations, NGOs, etc.), timing of the preventive measures ("phases," "early/late," etc.) and expectation of some outside action. Given our knowledge of causes of war, however, this has to be controlled for against a background of factors that are known to result in escalation and war. Such variables could, in fact, be those that explain why a particular situation does not escalate: type of incompatibility, type of primary parties (symmetry, asymmetry), experience of previous war/peace, presence of military escalatory measures, degree of democracy in the relationship, the regional context, etc.

What is needed is an evaluation of how the typical factors that explain the onset of war can be offset by the preventive actions that the prevention literature discusses. It is possible that conditions of previous war, democracy–dictatorship divides, military escalation, and international coalitions are such overwhelming factors that any preventive action is likely to be "doomed"; the conflict-driving forces among the conflict parties are of such an overwhelming nature that preventive diplomacy seems like a lone person attempting to stop a train in full speed. The prevention literature may, on the whole, have another point of departure, however: all wars are human decisions, and the final decision is not taken until a very late moment in time. Thus, there is always scope for action. The train, instead, is about to start, and at that starting moment the engines can be turned off as well as turned up. Given what we know about systematic causes of war, it would, in other words, be interesting to find cases where the train seems to be at full speed as well as those where it is about to depart. That requires a different methodological approach.

In fact, it may suggest a typology of cases, differentiating between those at high, medium and low risk of escalation, based on such basic insights into the strength of conflict-driving and inhibiting factors. The chances of prevention success should then vary, depending on the group of situations. In a way, this would establish a tool also for decision-makers to allocate their efforts in a reasonable way.

Without, at this time, advocating a comprehensive prevention theory we have, at least, elements of hypotheses that then can be related to a set of data. That then leads us to discuss three different approaches for a study of prevention. Given time and resource constrains, some sharp decisions will have to be made on what is actually possible.

Promising approaches are (1) studies which work on the cases where prevention measures have been observed in reality (Approach 1 below), (2) large-N studies of cases including either wars and nonwars, in databases that already exist or developing a new database of serious disputes (Approach 2 below), or (3) diachronic studies, in which the same case (a dyad) is studied over time and there are experiences of crises that were averted as well as crises that escalated. This could be developed into small-*n* studies, in which cases that are intrinsically similar are paired and the outcome varies (escalation, no escalation, Approach 3 below).

Possibilities for a systematic study

Approach 1: Listing the disputes in which escalation did not take place

A way to start is to have a list of cases that, in the general and historical literature, are specified to contain elements of being high risk for military escalation, but in which this did not take place. Such situations might be locatable also in a computerized search.

Methodological issues

A first problem, then, is to find situations in which military escalation (etc.) was likely, but did not take place. A second problem is to define what this should be compared with: is it to be compared with those situations in which military escalation took place, and can that then be done in the same way, that is, finding situations that are said by observers to be likely cases of escalation and in which this also happened? What to do then with situations that went straight from nondisputes to armed conflict (coups, first strikes, etc.)? A third problem is to locate preventive actions that were taken in both these sets of situations (escalated and nonescalated) and a fourth is to determine if the preventive action actually helped cause the nonescalation, or if other, more traditional, explanations are more relevant. One should not exclude the possibility that preventive action actually helps escalate the conflict, although that may not be what is intended. A fifth, and final (?), task is to ask: if a conflict was prevented at one moment in time, did that conflict instead take place a certain amount of time later (i.e. the conflict was postponed) or in some other form (i.e. the conflict was deflected)?

In approaching these issues, there are a couple of important observations from the general literature, particularly that dealing with inter-state relations:

- Most disputes do not escalate into armed conflicts or wars (COW; see Fearon and Laitin 1996). A rule of thumb is that perhaps only one out of ten go from being small disputes to becoming wars. The road to war can often be long, in other words.
- In most disputes there are likely to be preventive actions taken, and the fact that disputes do not escalate may mean that such actions have been successful. Thus, it is hard to imagine that most disputes simply peter out. Some action is probably necessary, for instance, by one side withdrawing, by both sides finding face-saving measures or by other events reducing interest in the dispute.
- In most disputes, it could be that the parties themselves do not expect disputes to escalate. Much of what goes on is noise-making and posturing; thus, the parties do not intend to wage wars, and what is needed are only limited

actions to indicate that they get a certain level of attention. Prevention is, in those cases, easy.

Thus, conflicts in which real dangers of military escalation exist are a smaller number of disputes: those in which there are highly motivated actors and there is less prevention activity available. In fact, the findings from causes of war studies can be used. They point out that war is more likely if there is (a) an historical rivalry, (b) major power(s) involvement, (c) arms races or similar conditions, (d) one nondemocratic actor in the conflict dyad, or (e) regional instability or regional linkages. The list of high-risk cases could be narrowed down using such criteria. This works well for inter-state conflict; what, then, to do about intra-state conflict? If similar criteria can be developed a list would emerge from which larger-N studies may be conducted. It can also give information of use to other approaches (small-n and diachronic studies). In this way the first methodological problem could be solved.

The second problem follows from this: should it be all conflicts that escalated, or a particular subsection of these, namely those that also meet the five criteria?

The third problem is more straightforward: it is a matter of finding information on whether preventive actions were undertaken, but they have to come from both types of situations. The fourth problem (if preventive action actually helped) requires some theoretical way of approaching the data. The prevention theory is, for the time being, not well developed and we may have to rely on a more empirical approach. The fifth (long-term) problem can be discussed.

In summary, we conclude that Approach 1 is useful to demonstrate the utility and extent of preventive actions. However, there are a series of methodological problems that might be possible to handle through other approaches.

Approach 2: Locating "serious disputes": situations that indicate danger

In this approach one way is to translate the conflict data definition (developed by the Uppsala Conflict Data Program) into dispute data and, thus, develop a new dataset. A second route would be to use an existing data archive that has sufficient information for a particular category of conflicts. As a start this might be a promising beginning. In Magnus Öberg's dissertation (2002) such a database is provided for the onset of ethnic conflict. Thus, an economical project is to use this dataset for further study.[2]

Going back to the ambition of creating a new database the following considerations are pertinent. The elements in the definition of a "serious dispute" include, for instance, situations with a verbally high hostility level of interaction between the parties (ultimatum, one side complaining that the other is threatening with military action), a clear political incompatibility (government, territory), organized actors with military capacity (available or quickly mobilizable), and actions that are confidence-reducing (unilateral breaks of agreements, not ratifying agreements, slow implementation of what is agreed, production of biased history books, cancelled top-level visits, friendly reception of actors hostile to opposing side, etc., typical events data). This would generate a set of "serious dispute" data from a mixed bag of conflict situations. These could then, in turn, be categorized. It might give information from the same dyad over time as well as a number of dyads in which disputes actually escalated. In this way, a coherent database could be created from which prevention could be studied.

A problem with this approach is that many situations may not be picked up (too low levels of action, statements, etc.), which would in particular concern intra-state conflicts (for instance, where writers retrospectively determine that there were threats before a coup, but which threats were not captured by the local media owing to dictatorial concerns and which were not of concern to the international media because the country is not of strategic or commercial importance). A reverse problem is that too many situations may be included, particularly if there is a political culture with frequent use of accusations, etc.

Also, serious disputes are likely to exist as ingredients in the typical escalation of a conflict to war. Often there will be one, perhaps more, such disputes. It will raise the problem of how independent each dispute is from the next one. To categorize them all may generate a sequence of events that appears as escalation, and thus potential failures of preventive actions, although the action in one event (the last in a sequence) may be the one that terminates the chain, and the only one that would diplomatically be regarded as a "serious effort." Is this a problem that can be handled in the analysis?

In general, this will result in a major database, which can be used for large-N and small-n studies. It will be a large and costly undertaking, but could be seen as a complement to the conflict data that already exist. It can be reduced if the geographical scope is limited (the European space only, or even smaller geographical areas) or if the time-span is reduced (five or ten recent years, for instance).

In summary, this approach has a number of attractive features, particularly if it can be initiated from an already existing dataset. In that way also, experience can be gained for building an entirely new database.

Approach 3: Analyzing cases with repetitive experience of serious disputes

This approach would select carefully from a set of known situations, with and without war experience. By studying the same pair of actors over a period of time, it will be possible to see if there is an increased/reduced frequency of preventive actions and if they do have an impact, and thus minimize the impact of discussing very different and contrasting situations. If they were selected so as to be relationships which include the full conflict typology – (a) state–state conflicts, (b) internal conflicts, and (c) state formation conflicts – three important situations would be compared. It can be combined with Approach 2, by focusing on "serious disputes" in these relations. To improve relevance, one may require that there should at least be one war experience in the relation, in line with the finding reported above, that this increases the risk of war.

An obvious problem is that for (b) and (c) in the conflict typology the actors will change: governments shift, rebel organizations appear and disappear, contention continues over many years making surrounding actors also shift. The factors may make it hard to determine if it is the "same" actors that continue over the years. Still, the idea may work, as even under these circumstances actors are likely to learn from previous experiences, memories will be kept in various ways. The shorter the time-span, the more likely there will be such recollections, but also fewer changes.

As prevention has been more strongly on the agenda since the Cold War ended, the selection of cases could be restricted to this period.

Possible selection of situations

- State–state relations: Ethiopia–Eritrea, USA–Iraq
- For internal conflicts: Angola, Burundi, Rwanda, Colombia, Macedonia
- For state formation conflicts: Aceh, Burma, Kashmir, Palestine, Kosovo.

It can be valuable to illustrate the prevention problematique in these situations, beginning with the inter-state relationships.

On inter-state relations

The cases selected could be one of symmetry and one of asymmetry. The first should be rather clear and thus fit with the definitions of serious disputes. If a war criterion is added (there should have been a recent war experience), then the number of cases becomes manageable. Sequences could then be studied from an assumption that all actors should be aware of the potential danger of disputes escalation. The dispute would then be more readily attended to by the international community and open for third-party preventive action.

In the case of asymmetry matters may be more difficult. For instance, there are also sequences in which it may be difficult to judge whether what we observe can be seen as "escalation" from serious disputes to war, or more typical "interventions" in which decisions and time-table are already set, and actually not changed (at all, or not much) by the dominant actor.

A case in point is the US–Iraqi crisis and the war of 2003. It was clearly related to the war that took place in 1991 and the bombings of 1998. It was obvious that the dangers were great. Two days before the US strikes were initiated on Iraq in March 2003 an ultimatum was issued by the US president. That is certainly a serious dispute event, but it also gave very little room for any preventive action. Two days is too short a time. The demands on Iraq (stepping down of the government) were almost impossible to accommodate. All other avenues were by that time more or less exhausted and the decision to start the war was most likely already taken (military preparations were completed). Furthermore, the diplomacy that went on in the months before, beginning with Secretary of State Powell's presentation in January to the UN Security Council, was concerned more with the legitimization of the war than with constituting the actual decisions on the war. The objection to giving a UN mandate, in one way, was a preventive action, as it would possibly postpone US action, but also concerned the logic of the subject matters (time and mandate for inspectors, for instance). A study of the events from September 2002 to March 2003 will give a list of situations, some of which actually meet the criteria of a serious dispute. However, was there really any room for preventive action and were there actual measures taken by third parties that could be defined as such, particularly as the US war planning was proceeding unhampered by the diplomatic action pursued almost separately? The receptiveness to actions, other than those that meant the complete subjugation of the opponent, was probably minimal. The asymmetry of the situation may mean that fewer preventive actions will be taken by potential third parties. This suggests that the asymmetry aspect is important, but also that it may contain less that is of interest from the prevention methodology perspective. This case may also be an illustration of a crisis going at high speed, and where the stopping of the train became increasingly difficult (see "Searching for systematic approaches and independent variables" above).

On the two intra-state situations

All the examples given are well-known wars and crisis situations. The war experience has been repeated. International attention has been there at times, either through multilateral action (UN, regional organizations) or through bilateral relationships (USA on the parties over Kashmir or Palestine, for instance). The shifts in these conflicts should then, in principle, contain a number of serious disputes that can be studied at some length. However, there might be a difficulty in locating source materials.

This is to illustrate that the longitudinal case approach also has its merits and that it will be a useful addition to the other two. It may run the risk, however, of finding very few cases and also require access to information that is not yet available.

Conclusion (in 2011)

A decision on which approach to follow had to be taken, and there were numerous reactions to the three approaches. They were evaluated with respect to their ability to say something meaningful on conflict prevention, and help in the formulation of a possible prevention theory. Second, it had been asked if there are other known studies that could be relevant and helpful in furthering the design of the study. Third, there were considerations of resources and time. Bringing these factors together, we resolved on the second approach, beginning with an existing database, but planning to develop a new one, as an addition to the existing UCDP conflict database. Both these strands of action were possible to follow, and some advances can now be reported.

Funding was granted for collecting data on armed conflicts, with a focus on minor armed conflicts in the phase when they are minor, whether they escalated later or not. This information covers the years 1993–2004 and is now available for research. It means studying escalation from a lower level of violence, but when there has already been deadly violence in the conflict. This is late in the conflict dynamics but still provides a chance for some first understandings. For instance, for the full period from 1989 to 2009 UCDP has reported that there were eighty-four minor armed conflicts and forty-seven wars (Harbom and Wallensteen 2010). This may be read to mean that two-thirds of all conflicts did not escalate to war, and one-third did. This could be said to imply that, once disputes have become militarized to the level of at least twenty-five battle-related deaths (the UCDP threshold for inclusion), the chances of further escalation are high, but that there still is room for some preventive measures to succeed. It may, nevertheless, speak in favor of even earlier preventive actions. From the point of view of escalation twenty-five deaths may already be high.

The dataset on third-party action in intra-state conflicts demonstrates that there is considerable action taking place (Wallensteen and Möller 2008; Melander *et al.* 2009). Action also has a geographical focus; in particular, actions in the studied period were oriented toward crises in the Middle East and the Balkans. There were some results reported, which can be interpreted to mean that such action prevented full-scale conflicts. Still, for instance, the Palestinian conflict contained considerable violence (but not war, by the UCDP standard). Even if this suggests that preventive measures have an impact, this might rather be attributed to the fact that the actions express an international commitment, which in itself (rather than specific measures) is what has an impact on the parties. Even so, these studies point to a field that is now opened for additional research. Not least is it interesting to observe if combinations of measures, notably humanitarian relief combined with diplomacy (Öberg *et al.* 2009), provide for new inroads into measures that can effectively prevent escalation.

Somewhat pessimistically, Michael Lund has asked if conflict prevention is "an idea whose time has come and gone?" (Lund 2009). Certainly, the security agenda has shifted since the 1990s. The first decade of the twenty-first century has focused on terrorism, Afghanistan, and Iraq. However, surprisingly few armed conflicts have escalated into war. In 2009 there were six wars and thirty minor armed conflicts, that is, only one-sixth of the total were wars. This may imply that there is more preventive action going on that is commonly observed. It might even be that these are more routine operations than previously was the case. We may still be some way from a "responsibility to prevent" a dispute from escalating to armed conflict and war (Hampson 2008). However, it does not lead to pessimism. Rather, the new possibilities should spur research into an area where there are a multitude of approaches. This may only be the beginning of making the unknown knowable.

Notes

1   This chapter was presented to the Research Seminar of the Department of Peace and Conflict Research, Uppsala University, on October 9, 2003. Many useful comments,

not least by Dr. Magnus Öberg and Dr. Birger Heldt, have been incorporated. The authors remain solely responsible for the final content, however. This work is funded by a grant from the Swedish Emergency Management Agency. The original paper contained a list of conflicts with a potential of escalation. It has been left out from this version.

2   This project was carried out (see Öberg *et al.* 2009).

References

Ackerman, Alice. 2003. 'The Idea and Practice of Conflict Prevention', *Journal of Peace Research*, 40 (3): 339–347.

Annan, Kofi A. 1996. 'The Peace-Keeping Prescription', in Kevin M. Cahill (ed.), *Preventive Diplomacy: Stopping Wars before They Start*. New York: Basic Books.

Boutros-Ghali, Boutros. 1996. 'Challenges of Preventive Diplomacy: The Role of the United Nations and Its Secretary-General', in Kevin M. Cahill (ed.), *Preventive Diplomacy: Stopping Wars before They Start*. New York: Basic Books.

Box-Steffensmeier, Janet M. and Bradford S. Jones. 1997. 'Time Is of Essence: Event History Models in Political Science', *American Journal of Political Science*, 41 (4): 1414–1461.

Carment, David and Albrecht Schnabel. 2003. 'Introduction – Conflict Prevention: A Concept in Search of a Policy', in David Carment and Albrecht Schnabel (eds.), *Conflict Prevention: Path to Peace or Grand Illusion?* Tokyo: United Nations University Press.

Carnegie Commission on Preventing Deadly Conflict. 1997. *Preventing Deadly Conflict: Final Report*. Washington, DC: Carnegie Corporation of New York.

Eliasson, Jan. 1996. 'Establishing Trust in the Healer: Preventive Diplomacy and the Future of the United Nations', in Kevin M. Cahill (ed.), *Preventive Diplomacy: Stopping Wars before They Start*. New York: Basic Books.

Fearon, James D. and David D. Laitin. 1996. 'Explaining Interethnic Cooperation', *American Political Science Review*, 90 (4): 715–735.

Goertz, Gary and Patrick M. Regan. 1997. 'Conflict Management in Enduring Rivalries', *International Interaction*, 22 (4): 321–340.

Hampson, Fen Osler. 2002. 'Preventive Diplomacy at the United Nations and Beyond', in Fen Osler Hampson and David M. Malone (eds.), *From Reaction to Conflict Prevention: Opportunities for the UN System*. Boulder, CO: Lynne Rienner Publishers.

Hampson, Fen Osler. 2008. 'Responsibility to Prevent', in Anders Mellbourn and Peter Wallensteen (eds.), *Conflict Prevention and Third Parties*. Gidlunds: Hedemora.

Harbom, Lotta and Peter Wallensteen. 2010. 'Armed Conflicts, 1946–2009', *Journal of Peace Research*, 47 (4): 501–509.

Lund, Michael S. 1996. *Preventing Violent Conflicts: A Strategy for Preventive Diplomacy*. Washington, DC: United States Institute of Peace Press.

Lund, Michael S. 2002. 'Preventing Violent Intrastate Conflicts: Learning Lessons from Experience', in Paul van Tongeren, Hans van de Veen and Juliette Verhoeven (eds.), *Searching for Peace in Europe and Eurasia: An Overview of Conflict Prevention and Peacebuilding Activities*. London: Lynne Rienner Publishers.

Lund, Michael S. 2009. 'Conflict Prevention: Theory in Pursuit of Policy and Practice', in Jacob Bercovitch, Victor Kremenyuk and I. William Zartman (eds.), *The Sage Handbook on Conflict Resolution*. London: Sage.

Melander, Erik, Frida Möller and Magnus Öberg. 2009. 'Managing Intrastate Low-Intensity Armed Conflict 1993–2004: A New Dataset', *International Interactions*, 35 (2): 1–28.

Miall, Hugh, Oliver Ramsbotham and Tom Woodhouse. 1999. *Contemporary Conflict Resolution: The Prevention, Management and Transformation of Deadly Conflicts*. Cambridge: Polity Press.

Munuera, Gabriel. 1994. 'Preventing Armed Conflict in Europe: Lessons Learned from Recent Experience', *Chaillot Paper 15/16*. Paris: Institute for Security Studies, Western European Union.

Öberg, Magnus. 2002. *The Onset of Ethnic War as a Bargaining Process: Testing a Costly Signalling Model*. Uppsala: Department of Peace and Conflict Research.

Öberg, Magnus, Frida Möller and Peter Wallensteen. 2009. 'Early Conflict Prevention in Ethnic Crises, 1990–98: A New Dataset', *Conflict Management and Peace Science*, 26 (1): 67–91.

Rothchild, Donald. 2003. 'Third-Party Incentives and the Phases of Conflict Prevention', in Chandra Lekha Sriram and Karin Wermester (eds.), *From Promise to Practice: Strengthening UN Capacities for the Prevention of Violent Conflict*. Boulder, CO: Lynne Rienner Publishers.

Sriram, Chandra Lekha. 2003. 'Insights from the Cases: Opportunities and Challenges for Preventive Actors', in Chandra Lekha Sriram and Karin Wermester (eds.), *From Promise to Practice: Strengthening UN Capacities for the Prevention of Violent Conflict*. Boulder, CO: Lynne Rienner Publishers.

Sriram, Chandra Lekha and Karin Wermester. 2003. 'From Risk to Response: Phases of Conflict Prevention', in Chandra Lekha Sriram and Karin Wermester (eds.), *From Promise to Practice: Strengthening UN Capacities for the Prevention of Violent Conflict*. Boulder, CO: Lynne Rienner Publishers.

Talentino, Andrea Kathryn. 2003. 'Evaluating Success and Failure: Conflict Prevention in Cambodia and Bosnia', in David Carment and Albrecht Schnabel (eds.), *Conflict Prevention: Path to Peace or Grand Illusion?* Tokyo: United Nations University Press.

Väyrynen, Raimo. 2003. 'Challenges to Preventive Action: The Cases of Kosovo and Macedonia', in David Carment and Albrecht Schnabel (eds.), *Conflict Prevention: Path to Peace or Grand Illusion?* Tokyo: United Nations University Press.

Wallensteen, Peter. 1998. *Preventing Violent Conflict: Past Record and Future Challenges*. Uppsala: Department of Peace and Conflict Research.

Wallensteen, Peter, Birger Heldt, Mary B. Anderson, Steven J. Stedman and Leonard Wantchekon. 2001. *Conflict Prevention through Development Co-operation*. Uppsala: Department of Peace and Conflict Research.

Wallensteen, Peter. 2002, 2007, 2011. *Understanding Conflict Resolution: War, Peace and the Global System*. London: Sage (different editions).

Wallensteen, Peter and Frida Möller. 2008. 'Third Parties in Conflict Prevention: A Systematic Look', in Anders Mellbourn and Peter Wallensteen (eds.), *Conflict Prevention and Third Parties*. Gidlunds: Hedemora.

Yamaguchi, Kazuo. 1991. *Event History Analysis*, Applied Social Research Methods Series, Vol. 28, Newbury Park, CA: Sage.

11 Armed conflict and peace agreements[1]

with Lotta Harbom and Stina Högbladh

The year 2005

Since the end of World War II, there have been a total of 231 armed conflicts active in 151 locations throughout the world.[2] During the seventeen years since the end of the Cold War, the corresponding numbers are 121 conflicts in eighty-one locations. The annual numbers of conflicts in this period – by intensity and by type – are given in Tables 11.1 and 11.2 respectively. Figure 11.1 shows the trend in armed conflict by type back to 1946.

In 2005, there were thirty-one ongoing armed conflicts in twenty-two locations. The highest number of armed conflicts was recorded in 1991 and 1992, with fifty-one conflicts active. Thus, the overall trend since the early 1990s has been that of a marked, steep decline. However, this decline has not been constant: the number of conflicts increased marginally in 1996 and 1999, and again in 2004, when the number increased from thirty to thirty-two.

Notable for both 2004 and 2005 is that, while there were no major fluctuations in the number of conflicts, there were major changes when it comes to the conflicts listed. Ten of the conflicts that were recorded for 2004 were no longer active in 2005 and nine of the armed conflicts that were active in 2005 were not registered for 2004. One reason for these changes is that many ongoing conflicts are at fairly low intensities, some with a death toll hovering around the twenty-five battle-related deaths threshold. Thus, whereas some conflicts do end, for instance by the signing of a peace agreement, others simply drop below the twenty-five battle-related deaths threshold for a year and then reappear.

The number of wars remains lower than ever in the post-World War II period, except for some years in the 1950s (Gleditsch *et al.*, 2002: 621). In 2005 only five conflicts reached the intensity of war and the one with the most battle-related deaths was the internationalized internal conflict in Iraq.[3]

In all years since the end of World War II, a majority of conflicts have been fought within states. In 2005 all thirty-one conflicts were intra-state. Of these, six were internationalized: the conflict between the Ugandan government and the LRA (Lord's Resistance Army); between the Azerbaijan regime and the break-away republic of Nagorno-Karabakh; between the government of India and NSCN-K (National Socialist Council of Nagaland – Khaplang faction); between the Afghan government and the Taliban; between the numerous Iraqi insurgent groups and the Iraqi government; and between the USA and Al Qaeda.

Table 11.1 Armed conflicts and conflict locations, 1989–2005

Level of conflict	1989	1990	1991	1992	1993	1994	1995	1996	1997	1998	1999	2000	2001	2002	2003	2004	2005	1989–2005[a]
Minor	12	17	20	23	17	19	14	20	18	13	14	14	13	13	9	15	12	59
Intermediate	15	16	13	10	15	18	18	15	15	12	14	11	12	14	16	10	14	13
War	17	16	18	18	13	8	6	6	7	14	13	12	11	5	5	7	5	49
All conflicts	44	49	51	51	45	45	38	41	40	39	41	37	36	32	30	32	31	121
All locations	36	36	38	38	32	34	30	31	30	32	31	28	29	24	22	23	22	81

a At the highest level recorded.

Table 11.2 Inter-state and intra-state armed conflicts, 1989–2005[a]

Type of conflict	1989	1990	1991	1992	1993	1994	1995	1996	1997	1998	1999	2000	2001	2002	2003	2004	2005	2005
Intra-state	38	44	49	47	40	44	36	37	37	33	34	31	30	28	26	29	25	90
International-ized intra-state[b]	4	3	0	3	5	1	1	2	2	4	5	4	5	3	2	3	6	24
Inter-state	2	2	2	1	0	0	1	2	1	2	2	2	1	1	2	0	0	7
All conflicts	44	49	51	51	45	45	38	41	40	39	41	37	36	32	30	32	31	121

Notes

a For data back to 1946, see http://www.prio.no/cscw/ArmedConflict.

b The category "Internationalized intra-state" has been renamed and recoded (prior to 2002 it was called "Intra-state with foreign intervention" and included fewer conflicts) in order to be consistent with the terminology used in the database at http://www.prio.no/cscw/ArmedConflict/. In an internationalized intra-state armed conflict, the opposition or both sides receive military support from other governments.

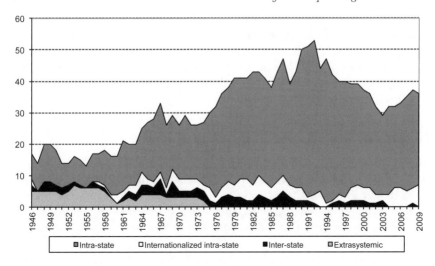

Figure 11.1 Armed conflicts by type, 1946–2009.

Conflicts restarted by new rebel organizations

During the year, four conflicts restarted with actions by new rebel organizations. In Chad numerous rebel groups have fought the government over the years. During 2005, the situation was very volatile, mainly on account of the continued fighting in the Darfur region in neighboring Sudan. In December a new rebel group, RDL (Rally for Democracy and Liberty), emerged in eastern Chad, calling for the overthrow of President Idriss Deby. On December 18 the group launched an attack on the border town of Adré from Darfur. The Deby government accused the Sudanese government of aiding the rebels, and relations between the two states became very tense.

In Iran a new rebel group became active in 2005. PJAK (The Free Life Party of Kurdistan) held its first congress in April 2004, aiming to replace the present regime in Iran with a democratic confederacy in which ethnic groups would have the right to self-governance. Although the group is of Kurdish origin and has ambitions to create a self-governing region for the Kurds in Iran, its goal is broader, concerning the change of the entire political system. In June 2005, a member of PJAK was killed by Iranian security forces, which for the first time sparked clashes between government forces and the rebel group.

In Turkey, a conflict over government was registered for the first time since 1992. There is a myriad of left-wing groups in the country, and in 2005 the MKP (Maoist Communist Party), fighting for a "Marxist–Leninist–Maoist state" in Turkey and a proletarian worldwide revolution, clashed repeatedly with government forces from January through June.

There has been on and off fighting in the north-eastern Indian state of Nagaland for decades, with the Naga tribes striving for independence. The group that became active in 2005, NSCN-K, was created by a split in the original NSCN in 1988. During the 1990s, this group fought occasionally, but other groups were more important. While negotiations have failed to lead to a political break-through, the government has concluded cease-fire agreements with several parties and the conflict was not active in 2000–2004. In 2005 the government together with Myanmar troops launched several attacks on NSCN-K bases in western Myanmar, attempting to shut them down.

Conflicts restarted by previously recorded actors

During the year, five conflicts were restarted by previously recorded actors. Three of Myanmar's territorial conflicts restarted in 2005. In the Karen conflict, the KNU (Karen National Union) and the government had announced a "gentle-men's agreement" cease-fire in 2003. After a year of relative calm, the government launched a large-scale offensive during the Karen New Year celebrations in mid-January 2005.

The conflict over the Karenni territory was coded as active in 2005 for the first time since 1996. One reason for this was the government's security considerations as part of moving the country's administrative capital to Pyinmana. Pyinmana is closer to Karenni state, where the KNPP (Karenni National Progressive Party) has launched occasional attacks in the past decade. The fighting continued to escalate through 2005.

In the conflict between Myanmar and SSA/s (Shan State Army – South Command) over the status of the Shan state almost no conflict activity was reported in 2003 and 2004. However, the fighting slowly increased and in April 2005 serious battles took place between the parties.

In 2005, the conflict between the LTTE (Liberation Tigers of Tamil Eelam) and the government of Sri Lanka became active after a year of relative calm. The situation deteriorated throughout the year as the impasse in the peace process could not be broken. The LTTE leadership accused the government of fueling infighting among the Tigers, but this claim was denied by Colombo. By the end of the year, Sri Lankan troops came under claymore mine attacks on a few occasions and the death toll mounted.

The conflict over the status of the Azerbaijan breakaway region Nagorno-Karabakh had been "frozen" since 1994 when it resumed in 2005. There had been breaches of the cease-fire during these years, but only in 2005 did they cause over twenty-five battle-related deaths.

Conflicts no longer active in 2005

As many as ten conflicts listed in 2004 were no longer active in 2005. The conflict between Georgia and the breakaway republic South Ossetia ceased once more, after a brief outbreak of fighting in August 2004. Negotiations failed to yield any progress and a long-term solution to the conflict is yet to be found.

The conflict registered in Uzbekistan in 2004 was no longer active in 2005. The rebel group JIG (Jihad Islamic Group) appears to have been defeated in late 2004, with at least 135 people arrested and convicted to prison.

In the Indian territory of Bodoland, the rebel group NDFB (National Democratic Front of Bodoland), demanding a Bodo homeland, declared a unilateral cease-fire in 2004, paving the way for negotiations. The truce held and was extended through the spring of 2005 and then again for another year.

In the conflict in the north-eastern Indian state of Tripura separatist rebel groups have fought the Indian government ever since the late 1970s. The violence de-escalated in 2005, and the death toll did not reach the twenty-five battle-deaths threshold.

No armed conflict was registered in Haiti in 2005. However, a year after the ousting of President Aristide, the situation remained volatile, with numerous actors attempting – and managing – to disrupt the political process and suspend the elections scheduled for the fall of 2005. The violent acts that did take place could not in most cases be clearly linked to specific groups.

For the first time since the conflict in Ivory Coast started in 2002 there was no fighting between the rebel group Forces Nouvelles and government troops. However, no substantial progress was made in implementing the 2003 and 2004 agreements and the Pretoria agreement of April 2005. Elections scheduled for October were postponed and for some weeks the country teetered on the brink of new violence before the parties in December could agree on a new transitional prime minister.

In the enclave of Cabinda, fighting between the FLEC (Frente da libertaçã do enclave de Cabinda: Front for the Liberation of the Enclave of Cabinda) rebels and Angolan government forces de-escalated once more in 2005, and the violence did not cause twenty-five battle-related deaths.

No fighting was reported in the conflict between the Ahlul Sunnah Jamaa, aiming to establish an Islamic state in a small part of northern Nigeria, and the Nigerian government. The rebels may have been defeated in October 2004, when government forces managed to drive them out into the swampy plain surrounding Lake Chad, killing and arresting numerous fighters.

The conflict registered in the Nigerian Niger delta in 2004 did not continue in 2005. The rebel group NDPVF (Niger Delta People's Volunteer Force), fighting for self-determination for the oil-rich delta, negotiated with the government in September 2004, and agreed on a cease-fire. One year later, in September 2005, NDPVF leader Mujahid Dokubo-Asari was arrested on charges of treason.

The protracted conflict between the government of Sudan and SPLM/A (Sudan People's Liberation Movement/Army), ongoing since 1983, came to a halt with the signing of the January 2005 Comprehensive Peace Agreement. The death of SPLM chairman John Garang, only weeks after he had been sworn in as first vice-president, was a blow to the peace process and sparked unrest in the capital. However, the SPLM/A leadership announced that his death had been an accident and called for calm.

Peace agreements 1989–2005

Sudan is only one of many well-known conflicts that have been terminated by a peace agreement in recent years. During 2005, peace agreements were concluded in four conflicts: Chad, Indonesia (Aceh), Ivory Coast, and Sudan (Southern Sudan). Studying the period after the Cold War we can identify 144 accords between warring parties covering one-third of the 121 armed conflicts active since 1989.[4] These are agreements solving, regulating, or deciding on a process to regulate the incompatibility.[5] UCDP has collected information and full-text versions on all these peace agreements for 1989–2005. Let us begin an analysis of one pertinent aspect of an armed conflict: the incompatibility (Wallensteen 2002). The central issues in a conflict are those that have to be dealt with explicitly for a conflict to be terminated.

There are three groups of agreements: full agreements, partial agreements, and peace process agreements. The most clear-cut of the accords are the full agreements, defined as an accord in which at least one dyad agrees to settle the whole incompatibility. For example, in the Democratic Republic of Congo, the government and all main rebel formations and civil society actors signed the Inter-Congolese Political Negotiations – The Final Act in 2003, ending the conflict, providing for elections, the interim governance, and a new constitution. There have been forty-three full agreements in the studied period.

A partial agreement is defined as an accord in which the parties in at least one dyad agree to settle part of the incompatibility. Some peace processes deal with one issue at the time in partial agreements, and the conflict is not regarded as solved until a final agreement has been signed. In Sudan partial treaties were signed over security issues, wealth sharing, power sharing, and the administration of certain areas, before a final agreement was concluded, formally ending the peace process. A partial agreement can also be one that notes outstanding issues to be solved in later negotiations. The San Andrés Accords in Mexico 1996 dealt with indigenous rights but did not address agrarian reforms or the conditions for ending hostilities. In partial agreements certain issues can also be delegated to a commission to work out the practical elements of implementation. In Georgia a committee was established chaired by the United Nations, with participation of representatives of the Conference for Security and Cooperation in Europe (CSCE) and the Russian Federation. It also included international experts. The aim was to reach a comprehensive settlement in the end. Some agreements regulate other political issues than the incompatibility. Therefore some agreements are treated as partial after comparing the outcome in the written agreement with the stated goal of the parties. For example the Donya agreement between Armed Forces of the Federal Republic (FARF) and the government of Chad provided for the transformation of FARF into a political party and the integration of FARF into the civil service. Since FARF was fighting for a referendum on the structure of the state and on bilingualism the agreement did not fully solve the incompatibility. There were seventy-nine partial agreements in the studied period.

A third group are the peace process agreements. These are accords in which at least one conflict dyad agrees to initiate a process to settle their incompatibility. A typical peace process agreement has a detailed agenda for talks, but in some the parties only agree to initiate negotiations on substantial issues, such as the territorial status of a region. In many high-profile peace processes, for instance the one in Guatemala 1990–1996, a number of agreements dealt with the agenda of the talks before approaching the conflict issues. The UCDP reports twenty-two peace process agreements for the period 1989–2005.

UCDP distinguishes between two independently defined types of incompatibility. Government conflicts deal with regime type and the composition of the government. In territorial conflicts the incompatibility concerns the status of a territory and may include demands for secession or autonomy (Wallensteen 2002; Harbom and Wallensteen 2005). The peace agreement data demonstrate the utility of this distinction. A majority of the peace agreements in 1989–2005, 70 percent, were signed in government conflicts,[6] whereas most conflicts were fought over territory.[7] It appears that conflicts over government are more prone to the making of peace agreements. This can be further illustrated. Figure 11.2 shows the number of peace processes and the number of conflicts with a peace agreement.[8] The figure illustrates that a higher number of peace agreements were signed per conflict and peace process in government conflicts. The peace process in such conflicts seems to have different characteristics from in territorial conflicts. A typical peace process in a conflict over government includes more partial agreements than a process in a conflict over territory. Follow-up agreements concluded after previous agreements have failed to be implemented are also more common in conflicts over government.

Features of the agreements

Table 11.3 gives data on the military provisions of peace agreements. A cease-fire between the warring parties is often regarded as a principal objective in a peace process. However, in some conflicts the parties had already agreed to end violence before starting negotiations on substantial issues. In other cases cessation of hostilities was only included in the final agreement. Either way, we can observe that formal cease-fires were included in 60 percent of the 144 peace agreements. Most of these, six out of ten, also provided for the demobilization of troops and for disarmament. Some agreements went even further and included the

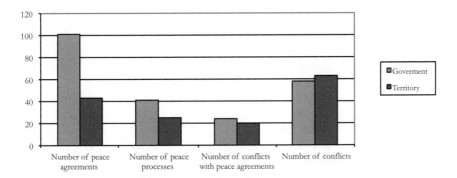

Figure 11.2 Peace agreements by incompatibility, 1989–2005.

Table 11.3 Military provisions in peace agreements, 1989–2005 (percent)

Military provisions	All	Intra-state: government	Intra-state: territory	Inter-state: territory[a]
Cease-fire	60	63	49	100
Disarmament	44	46	41	0
Integration in army	38	43	27	50
Amnesty	28	30	27	0
Deployment of PKO	23	25	20	0
Withdrawal of foreign forces	13	15	7	100
Any of the above	74	73	76	100
No. of agreements	144	101	41	2

a   All inter-state conflicts with peace agreements were fought over territory.

integration of former combatants into the national armed forces. It is interesting that 26 percent of the agreements did not include any military provisions at all.[9] Almost all were partial agreements signed in a peace process whereby cease-fire or other military provisions were found in separate arrangements. The San Andrés Accords in Mexico are exceptional as they included a list of issues to be dealt with in talks a month later but these talks stalled and the accord was never implemented. The parties never agreed on the cessation of hostilities but violence did not restart.

In Tables 11.4 and 11.5 the political provisions of peace agreements are categorized. Agreements in intra-state government conflicts often provide for elections and have provisions on the composition of an interim government. A number of the agreements grant the warring party a place in the government or the right to become a political party. These can be seen as elements of democratization, which thus is a feature in solving government conflicts. Researchers have emphasized that power-sharing is a logical solution to conflicts over government. Interestingly, this dataset shows that only 15 percent of the peace agreements in governmental conflicts included explicit power-sharing provisions. Even when considering only the full agreements, power-sharing provisions are not typical: they are found in 29 percent of the agreements. It suggests that power-sharing is used only in some conflicts, possibly in ethnically divided societies (Jarstad 2001).

Table 11.5 shows that the most common solution in intra-state conflicts over territory was to grant a disputed region local governance or autonomy. For full agreements the most common provisions were to grant extended cultural group rights or grant the region local governance. No agreement has granted the secessionists independence. However, some deals gave the right to vote for independence in a referendum, for example Papua New Guinea on Bougainville 2001 and Sudan for Southern Sudan 2005. Other typical features are contributions to regional development, local referenda, the creation of a federal state, and provisions of power sharing on the local level. The two agreements signed in inter-state armed conflicts were solved by demarcation of the borders.

Table 11.4 Political provisions in peace agreements in conflicts over government, 1989–2005 (percent)

Political provisions	Intra-state: all agreements	Intra-state: full agreements
Elections	48	68
Interim government	30	29
Integration into government/civil service	28	54
The right to become political party	26	54
Power-sharing	15	29
Any of the above[a]	70	93
No. of agreements	101	28

a The accords that do not include any political provisions are either peace process agreements or agreements reaffirming an earlier accord.

Table 11.5 Political provisions in peace agreements in conflicts over territory, 1989–2005 (percent)

Political provisions	Intra-state: all agreements	Intra-state: full agreements
Local government	39	57
Autonomy	37	43
Cultural freedoms	32	57
Regional development	27	36
Referendum on future status	22	36
Federalism	15	21
Local power-sharing	12	29
Independence	0	0
Any of the above	93	100

Tables 11.4 and 11.5 suggest that the distinction between conflicts dealing with government and territory is significant, particularly in the contexts of negotiations and conflict resolution. The two types of conflict will require different measures. In some cases, however, the issues can be intertwined, as has been the case in the Sudan conflict over Southern Sudan. In Sudan the peace process included both agreements stipulating power-sharing and agreements granting referendum on the future status of Southern Sudan.

Notes

1 This chapter reproduces 'Armed Conflict and Peace Agreements', *Journal of Peace Research*, 43 (5): 617–631, 2006. Some information has been deleted, notably Appendices I, II, and III. Figure 11.1 gives updated information on conflicts until 2009.

2 For more in-depth discussions on the terms, see http://www.pcr.uu.se/database/definitions_all.htm. Note that since 2002 the Uppsala Conflict Data Program (UCDP) has also collected data on two other categories of violence: nonstate conflicts and one-sided violence. This information is presented in the Human Security Report (Human Security Centre 2005) and can also be found at http://www.pcr.uu.se/research/UCDP/our_data1.htm. The one-sided category has recently been updated to include information from 1989. For a presentation of the new dataset, see Eck and Hultman (2007). For in-depth information on the conflicts active since 1989, visit the UCDP database at http://www.pcr.uu.se/database.

3 Note that the conflict in Iraq was classified as an inter-state war in 2003 (Eriksson and Wallensteen 2004).

4 A peace agreement has been signed in forty-six conflicts.

5 Data are available at www.pcr.uu.se/database. For a more comprehensive presentation of the new data, see Högbladh (2006).

6 One hundred and one agreements were signed in conflicts over government; forty-three agreements were signed in conflicts over territory. Of the latter, two agreements were signed in inter-state conflicts, in Ethiopia–Eritrea and Ecuador–Peru.

7 UCDP reports sixty-two conflicts fought over territory, fifty-eight that concerned government, and one conflict with a dual incompatibility over both government and territory in the studied period, the conflict in Southern Sudan. In this article the conflict, Sudan (Southern Sudan), is treated as a conflict over territory.

8 A peace process includes one or more peace agreements. Peace process is defined as a formal process in which either the warring parties have decided to settle the incompatibility in a process in which one issue at the time is regulated by an agreement, or an agreement that builds on a previous peace agreement is signed.

9 The thirty-seven agreements are found in the conflicts in Colombia, El Salvador, Guatemala, Mexico, Mozambique, Rwanda, Comoros (Anjouan), Israel (Palestine), and Sudan (Southern Sudan).

Sources and references

UCDP uses a variety of sources for the annual update of armed conflicts. Since 2003, the data collection for the armed conflict list has primarily been based on automatic scanning of the *Factiva* news database (http://www.factiva.com), which contains nearly 9,000 news sources from 118 countries. The automatic scanning procedure is complemented by material from a number of particularly useful sources: *Africa Confidential* (London), *Africa Research Bulletin* (Oxford), *Far Eastern Economic Review* (Hong Kong), *Horn of Africa Bulletin* (Uppsala), *International Crisis Group* (Brussels, various reports), *Jane's Intelligence Review* (Coulsdon, Surrey), *Journal of Palestine Studies*, Palestinian Central Bureau of Statistics (http://www.pcbs.gov.ps), Israeli Center for Human Rights in the Occupied Territories (http://www.btselem.org), *Keesing's Record of World Events* (Cambridge), *The Military Balance* (International Institute of Strategic Studies, London), and *South Asia Terrorism Portal* (New Delhi, http://www.satp.org).

Eck, Kristine and Lisa Hultman. 2007. 'One-Sided Violence against Civilians in War', *Journal of Peace Research*, 44 (2): 233–246.

Eriksson, Mikael and Peter Wallensteen. 2004. 'Armed Conflict, 1989–2003', *Journal of Peace Research*, 41 (5): 625–636.

Gleditsch, Nils Petter, Peter Wallensteen, Mikael Eriksson, Margareta Sollenberg and Håvard Strand. 2002. 'Armed Conflict 1946–2001: A New Dataset', *Journal of Peace Research*, 39 (5): 615–637.

Harbom, Lotta and Peter Wallensteen. 2005. 'Armed Conflict and Its International Dimensions, 1946–2004', *Journal of Peace Research*, 42 (5): 623–635.

Human Security Centre. 2005. *Human Security Report*. Oxford: Oxford University Press.

Högbladh, Stina. 2006. 'Patterns of Peace Agreements: Presenting New Data on Peace Processes and Peace Agreements', conference paper presented at the International Studies Association, San Diego.

Jarstad, Anna. 2001. *Changing the Game: Consociational Theory and Ethnic Quotas in Cyprus and New Zealand*. Doctoral dissertation, Department of Peace and Conflict Research, Uppsala University, Uppsala.

Wallensteen, Peter. 2002. *Understanding Conflict Resolution*. London: Sage Publications. Second edition 2007, third edition 2011.

12 Dag Hammarskjöld and the psychology of diplomacy

The relevance of Dag Hammarskjöld

UN Secretary-General Dag Hammarskjöld died in 1961. His achievements are still relevant in the field of international diplomacy. Perhaps even more so than when he was alive. The number of armed conflicts today is higher than in the 1950s, Hammarskjöld's time of operative practice. In the period 1989–1999 a total of 110 armed conflicts were waged around the world. By 1999 thirty-seven were active (Wallensteen and Sollenberg 2000). This is a higher number of conflicts than recorded for previous decades. At the same time, two-thirds of the recorded armed conflicts have been terminated, often through some form of negotiation. This is where issues of diplomacy enter. Hammarskjöld's diplomacy concerned the peaceful handling of armed conflicts. The 1990s have seen more peace agreements than any period in the entire twentieth century. This means that lessons drawn from Hammarskjöld's experience in the midst of the Cold War can be compared with those of the period after this major conflagration. Thus this chapter searches for lessons learned but it also focuses on Dag Hammarskjöld himself. What made him special? Did he have some traits that tell us something about the psychology of diplomacy?

Although there is a considerable literature on mediation, there has been little focus on particular individuals, and thus this study may add some further understandings (Bercovitch and Rubin 1992; Crocker *et al.* 1999; Keashly and Fisher 1990; Zartman 1989; Zartman and Berman 1982; Zartman and Rasmussen 1997).

When studying Hammarskjöld's involvement in conflict as a third-party UN official it is important to note that any conflict settlement moves through three phases.

There is an initial phase when the parties continue to give preference to war efforts, and when there is little room for peacemaking diplomacy by third parties. The warring party that has the upper hand will be reluctant to allow outsiders to get involved. For the outsiders it might be important to find ways to bring a particular conflict to the legitimate agenda of action for neighbors or international organizations. There is a phase of *agenda diplomacy*: getting the parties, as well as the international community, to focus on conflict resolution in the conflict.

A second phase enters when the parties are interested in finding an agreement, victory is seen as less likely, and, as a consequence, they are willing to enter into direct or indirect contact. This is the phase of *agreement diplomacy*. If it fails, the conflict may revert back to the battlefield, again bringing in the need for the first type of diplomacy.

If it succeeds, a third phase of *implementation diplomacy* enters. This includes the translation of an agreed text into reality, as well as making sure that the conditions are conducive for the implementation of the agreement. Diplomacy is needed along the whole process of peacemaking, but it will have different concerns.

Agreement diplomacy requires skills in making parties get to know each other, understand the positions of the opposite side, and find ways in which incompatibilities can be overcome or transcended. Agenda diplomacy precedes this event. It has an important element of secrecy, tacit understandings, and closed-door activities. It is no less dramatic, but less visible, and thus it receives less attention. Implementation diplomacy, on the other hand, takes place after the deal is made. It is open, observed, but less spectacular. It requires long-term commitment, intimate knowledge of the actors and their priorities, and attention to details and to matters and actors that may spoil an agreement. Thus, conflict resolution diplomacy deals with phases that have different priorities and concerns.

Needless to say, these conflict phases are not equally long, and they do not necessarily follow linearly, one after each other. Still the distinction is useful. They provide three different measures of "success." In the first phase, success is to get the conflict on the agenda; in the second, to arrive at an agreement; and in the third, to arrive at "normalization," whereby war is no longer the main concern.

Thus, understanding these three phases of diplomacy is highly relevant. Such insight can, of course, be generated in many ways, not least by closely analyzing ongoing peace processes. Knowledge may also be gained from looking at modern history and by following one single actor, representing a concerned international community. This is where the experiences of Dag Hammarskjöld enter. His way of dealing with crises as Secretary-General of the UN (1953–1961) may give us an understanding of the phases of diplomacy, the methods used, and the experiences of success and failure. Thus, this chapter is devoted to the operative practice of Dag Hammarskjöld and eventually asking if he carried any particular psychological attributes that could explain his achievements.

Hammarskjöld was involved in a number of conflicts. Many of these are customarily analyzed from the point of view of the parties. The third party is less often attended to and the work of such parties tends to be seen as secondary. The primary parties take most of any historian's attention, for instance, and many third parties prefer not to have too much light on their work. However, in the case of Dag Hammarskjöld, there is a thorough biography focusing on the Secretary-General as a third party in conflict resolution. The present analysis rests entirely on the work on Hammarskjöld done by a single person: Brian Urquhart's seminal biography, *Hammarskjold*, published in 1972 and reprinted in 1994 (Urquhart 1994). This work provides a balanced appreciation of the impact of Hammarskjöld as an actor. Thus, this chapter is not primarily a contribution to Hammarskjöld's life as a diplomat, but an attempt to understand psychological and contextual conditions that affect diplomacy in general.

It could be objected that the period in which Hammarskjöld acted was atypical. It was a time of very strong polarization between two seemingly coherent, united, and hierarchical blocs. There was, on the one hand, the West led by the United States in close alliance with Western European states, dominating South America and the rim of East Asia (South Korea, Japan, Taiwan, etc.). On the other hand was the Soviet Union, in strict control over Eastern Europe, closely allied to China and supporting, directly or indirectly, Communist rebellions in countries whose governments were closely tied to the West. The international system was uniquely bipolarized and hierarchical. It might make it difficult to generalize from the experiences of Hammarskjöld. At the same time these features makes this period even more interesting for an understanding of the social space that a polarized, conflict-prone relationship leaves for diplomacy. It can be debated whether such possibilities have been enlarged in the post-Cold War period. It is a world that on the one hand has several poles, more integration, and new challenges and on the other hand has one dominant pole from which more action is expected than it is willing to execute. Is the present world more or less hierarchical than the one in which Hammarskjöld found himself? Is the role of a third party more or less constrained? The answers are not obvious.

It could safely be stated that Hammarskjöld was the first expression of what we today, without much thought, label an international community. He was using the possibilities vested in his office and he wanted to act in a consistent manner in a series of crises. Accounts of diplomats and their actions have often dealt with actors rooted in their national foreign ministries. They have been pursuing national policies. They may still have achieved a lot in a number of crises (Metternich, Talleyrand, Disraeli, Lloyd George, to name a few) or in particular issues (Eleanor Roosevelt). The perspective and basis for action was different from the one Hammarskjöld had to apply as a chief executive of an unwieldy international system. There are other personalities that would constitute interesting comparisons. Ralph Bunche (Urquhart 1993) and Javier Pérez de Cuellar (1997) come to mind.

Before proceeding, the concepts in conflict diplomacy need some clarification. Then, crises in which Hammarskjöld were active will be presented, before proceeding to his way of acting.

Conflict diplomacy

Which are the traits to be expected in conflict diplomacy? The three phases suggest important differences. Theoretically, the following could be expected.

When analyzing *agenda setting*, a focus on the UN simplifies the job. There is a formal UN agenda, for the Secretary-General or the Security Council. There are rules for how an issue is brought up on the concrete agendas of these institutions. There has to be an appeal to "international peace and security," which often seems to mean that only inter-state conflicts that threaten to break out into war are to be considered. The perception of a distinction between internal and external violence predominates in international law. It is the external form of violence, sometimes described as "aggression," that determines if the conflict is moved to the agenda of international action. The way a particular conflict is described is important. For an "internal" conflict to enter the agenda, it has to be seen as endangering not only the inhabitants of a particular country, but also a region or the world as a whole.

Of course, agenda setting is linked to power. International dominant actors have a greater chance of defining conflicts as international issues or of preventing them from becoming such issues. The veto vested in the five permanent members of the Security Council gives them particular authority. At the same time, the Secretary-General has the mandate, if resorting to Article 99 of the UN Charter, to bring to the attention of the Security Council the issue "he" (gender according to the Charter) considers threatening. Ultimately, the resulting agenda will be decided by the permanent members: if they accept, a conflict is on the international agenda. In this way they can also instruct the Secretary-General to take (or not to take) action in particular questions. It is possible to imagine a situation when the Secretary-General does not want to bring matters to the agenda, as this may be disruptive for "his" position or affect quiet diplomacy. Agenda diplomacy is, as a consequence, highly intriguing and not as straightforward as might be imagined.

In *agreement diplomacy*, negotiations between the parties are central and the role of the outsider is to promote the success of such contacts in different ways. This involves meeting the parties face to face; bringing the parties to the same table, if possible; or finding ways in which agreement can be signed if no direct meetings are possible. In general, considerable attention has to be given to the creation of confidence between the warring sides, but also between them and the third party. Often the third party draws on the commitment of a broader grouping of states and actors interested in agreement. There may be a peace-supporting coalition, for which the third party is an expression or a spokesperson. Confidence building is key. In preventive diplomacy this is done before matters receive the attention of the Council or the world media. Thus, the dynamics of reaching agreement are different from those of bringing issues to the agenda of the international community. Among other matters, it involves working more directly with the parties in conflict, not with the UN structures as such.

Finally, turning to *implementation diplomacy*, it enters most dramatically where signed agreements are falling apart or threaten to do so. In this situation, the confidence between the parties may be eroding very quickly. The outside actor may be the only one who defends the agreement. It gives the third party a tricky role. For instance, should the outsider be the one upholding an agreement the signatories are no longer interested in? It may appear as an imposition. Alternatively, even more demandingly: what to do if only one side sticks to the agreement? Or if new parties with new concerns enter the situation? The diplomacy required when the de facto coalition that entered into an agreement is no longer holding together is very different from diplomacy in other phases. Implementation diplomacy becomes geared to the recreation of the coalition, but also has to take into account the changing circumstances. Compromises may have to be entertained, but they may contribute to the further erosion of this coalition. Implementation diplomacy may include taking the issue to the international community, but also entails keeping a low profile in order to act preventively. It is likely to be a matter of interpreting what has already been agreed and finding ways to work forward.

Hammarskjöld's record of conflict diplomacy

Table 12.1 lists the armed conflicts to which Dag Hammarskjöld devoted particular attention. The evaluation of success and failure follows those made by Urquhart (1994). Other evaluations may be made of Hammarskjöld's record. The one provided by Urquhart is insightful and balanced. It is also adapted to the type of crises Hammarskjöld faced. There may well be additional crises that should be included, although Table 12.1 is fairly exhaustive and covers those to which Urquhart gives considerable attention. The specific phases of crises may be divided differently. The delimitations in Table 12.1 are seen to correspond to an historian's understanding of the dynamics of particular crises.

Table 12.1 gives a quick overview of the turbulent times involving the personal diplomacy of Dag Hammarskjöld. It sometimes involved him in considerable risk-taking. He had a large measure of success: twelve outcomes are categorized in this way. There were six clear-cut failures and two issues left unsolved at the time of his death. There is no record to compare this with, but on the face of it it is impressive. There is a consistent pattern for the failures: these were crises in which Hammarskjöld encountered firm opposition by a determined major power (the USA in Guatemala and Laos, Britain in the Middle East, France in Bizerte, the Soviet Union in Hungary and Congo). Major power objection was not necessarily the end of crisis management, however. In several instances it was possible for the Secretary-General to overcome opposition from the majors, either by mustering the support of other permanent members or by drawing on a large following in the General Assembly. Hammarskjöld managed to build strong coalitions in particular issues. These coalitions shifted from one issue to another. It was a bridge-building effort that consumed much time, but for which his personal relations with key leaders, particularly among neutral and nonaligned states, were helpful. Also, he appears to have avoided antagonizing all permanent members at the same time.

Table 12.1 shows that some conflicts consumed more of Hammarskjöld's energy than others. It is notable that there were five almost consecutive crises in the Middle East (i.e., the Suez War of 1956 and its repercussions). Adding the conflicts over Lebanon and UK relations with Saudi Arabia, it means that one-third of his crisis diplomacy was devoted to this region alone. Another third of the crises dealt with Africa (mostly the Congo). The rest of the world, that is, Europe, the Americas, and much of Asia, received less of his diplomatic services. The Cold War was outside his range of action (e.g., conflicts over Germany, Cuba, Taiwan, Indochina).

As the overview makes clear, Hammarskjöld was not specializing in one type or pushed out of any particular field of diplomacy. This means he had to be knowledgeable and effective in handling varying circumstances. The fact that the Secretary-General was somewhat more engaged in agreement diplomacy, with

Table 12.1 Twenty crises: conflict diplomacy of UN Secretary-General Dag
Hammarskjöld, 1953–1961

Conflict	Type of diplomacy	Outcome of conflict	Outcome of DH diplomacy
1 Guatemala 1954	Agenda	Government overthrown	Failure
2 US pilots in China 1954–55	Agreement	Pilots freed	Success
3 Middle East 1956 I	Implementation	Cease-fire restored	Success
4 Middle East 1956 II (Canal crisis, Oct.)	Agreement	No agreement	Failure
5 Middle East 1956 III (Suez crisis, Oct. 29–Nov. 7)	Agreement	Cease-fire, withdrawal, PKO	Success
6 Middle East 1956 IV (UNEF in Egypt, Nov.)	Implementation	Peacekeeping	Success
7 Hungary 1956	Agenda	Invasion	Failure
8 Middle East 1957 (Israel leaving Sinai, Gaza)	Implementation	Withdrawal, peacekeeping	Success
9 Lebanon 1958 (infiltration and Western intervention)	Agreement	Observer group, withdrawal	Success
10 Cambodia–Thailand	Agreement	Relations restored	Success
11 UK–Saudi Arabia (Bureimi)	Agreement	Eventually solved	(After DH's death)
12 Laos 1959 I	Agenda	UN subcommittee	Failure
13 Laos 1959 II (UN Presence)	Agenda	UN presence, set up by SG	Success
14 Congo 1960 I	Agenda	Action by SC	Success
15 Congo 1960 II (Katanga)	Implementation	Removal of Belgian troops	Success
16 Congo 1960 III	Implementation	Congo aid through the UN	Success
17 Congo 1960 IV (Soviet attack on DH)	Agenda	Soviet critique, GA support	Success
18 Congo 1960–61 constitutional crisis	Implementation	Lumumba killed	Failure
19 Bizerte	Agreement	Not achieved	Failure
20 Congo 1961 (Katanga)	Agreement	Katanga secession	(DH killed)

Source: Urquhart (1994).

Abbreviations: DH, Dag Hammarskjöld; GA, General Assembly; PKO, peacekeeping operation; SC, Security Council; SG, Secretary-General; UNEF, UN Emergency Force.

conflicts that were already on the agenda, is difficult to interpret. In eight of the twenty crises he had this role. As there is, as of now, no other Secretary-General's record to compare, we do not know what is "normal."

It is more noteworthy that his success rate follows a particular pattern. He recorded the least success in agenda-setting (three out of six, i.e. 50 percent), the most success in implementation negotiations (five out of six, i.e. 83 percent). Statistically, the differences are too limited for generalizations about the office as such. Still, this particular profile suggests that the common remark "Leave it to Dag" had a particular ring. It often referred to cases of interpretation and implementation of agreements. Agenda setting and agreement making are likely to attract most attention in global policy circles. The complexities may be large, the fears higher, and the interests stronger. Once a settlement is concluded, such pressures subside, and the Secretary-General is given more room for maneuver. A holder of the office who has the confidence of the international community will be "left alone" to deal with the "technical" matters that seem to remain.

There is also a possible personality factor. Hammarskjöld's ability to interpret mandates and find ingenious solutions, principles for action, and practical courses of action may explain the profile. Thus, his intellectual capacity was geared to problem-solving. He understood very well that the survival of agreements depended on the ability to settle the first crises that follow the signing of an accord. The implementation of the agreement on peacekeeping troops in 1956 made the mission stick until 1967. His actions in the Congo crises draw on him finding principles that would last into the future, not just mere "fixes" for the day.

Agenda diplomacy

There were several instances of agenda-setting diplomacy, and success was recorded in three out of six cases. This is a reasonably satisfactory achievement, and it illustrates the conditions under which a Secretary-General has to operate. This is the category with the least success. Hammarskjöld's most notable accomplishments were scored in the Congo crisis in 1960, first by his action to bring the issue to the Security Council, where he explicitly used his rights under Article 99 in the Charter. He managed to get extraordinary media attention, in competition with a presidential nomination convention of one of the parties in the USA. The other situation refers to the crisis over his own post. He was able to prevent the Soviet Union from gaining support for the idea of a troika replacing him as the sole Secretary-General. Hammarskjöld saw that as a move to paralyze the UN in general, not only to impede his actions as a Secretary-General in a particular crisis.

The failures in agenda diplomacy were in cases that were close to the interest of a particular permanent member (for instance, the USA on Guatemala, the USSR on Hungary). In the case of Hungary, the new Hungarian government installed after the Soviet invasion of 1956 invited Hammarskjöld to discuss only humanitarian aid, not the political and military situation. The latter was seen as internal to the relations between Hungary and the Soviet Union. Thus, the

Soviet invasion could not be brought to a decision in the Security Council, and the actions decided on by the General Assembly could not be implemented. Agenda setting, in other words, is clearly in the purview of major powers. It is difficult for other actors to bring issues to the Security Council. When Hammarskjöld succeeded – as in the Congo – he had considerable support from a large coalition of African and Asian states. Their combined voting power in the UN as well as the attention to and optimism for decolonization made this "in line with the times." Furthermore, this crisis was initially seen to be outside the Cold War, and thus his actions were acceptable to the permanent members as well.

There are instances when Hammarskjöld refrained from bringing matters to the Council. One case is the war in Algeria. Already in 1955 African and Asian countries wanted him to take up the issue. It would have led to a confrontation with France. Hammarskjöld chose to define the conflict as an internal matter, and when the conflict continued to be debated he argued that France was attempting to negotiate a solution (Urquhart 1994: 309). His arguments do not appear convincing. It is more likely that he wanted to avoid a confrontation with a permanent member of the Council, particularly as the likelihood of his achieving a result beyond a demonstration effect was small.

There are examples of pre-agenda diplomacy, that is, situations in which Hammarskjöld acted before matters came to the Security Council or received wider international attention. In these circumstances, the parties may have accepted his good offices in order to prevent the dispute from reaching the agenda. Urquhart gives an example: the border dispute between Cambodia and Thailand in 1958–1959. There are also instances in which Hammarskjöld stalled Security Council action, although it could have had a preventive effect, as it did not have the full support of all sides in a particular conflict. A case is when the USA wanted a UN observer team sent to Laos in 1959. Hammarskjöld did not find enough support in the Security Council or among all concerned parties for this idea (Urquhart 1994: 338). He objected but was overruled. This also illustrates the limits of the office. The case still gave an interesting result. A subcommittee was set up and reported on the situation. Hammarskjöld then appointed his own *personal* representative, an innovation comparable to the existing Special Representatives (which were approved by the General Assembly or the Security Council). It appears that this novel channel became a useful way of keeping the Secretary-General informed and it also contributed – in the case of Laos – to a stabilization of the internal situation. Hammarskjöld turned a defeat into a constructive move.

Agreement diplomacy

In the eight cases of agreement diplomacy, there is an interesting mixture of success and failure. The Secretary-General was the architect of a number of agreements. There are even examples of near-agreements that potentially solved the issues of conflict. This is most evident in the Canal crisis that preceded the Suez invasion in 1956. By mid-October 1956 Hammarskjöld had secured the support from Egypt for principles that largely met the conditions laid out by the users of the Suez

Canal that had been unilaterally nationalized by Egypt. Nevertheless, Britain and France moved on with their war preparations. In November they launched an intervention, coordinated with Israel. Their UN diplomacy aimed at obstructing agreement by pressing particular points, so as to show that the issues could not be solved by diplomacy. Hammarskjöld's actions threatened this strategy (Urquhart 1994: 167–169). This illustrates a basic truth, close to a truism, in negotiations and diplomacy: if key parties do not want negotiations to succeed, agreements are unlikely.

Again this applies to parties that are strong enough to prevent agreement. For other actors, agreement, through the Secretary-General, may have been a preferred alternative to dealing directly with the adversary. Hammarskjöld's diplomatic breakthrough came in such a crisis, involving two of the strongest powers of the time, the USA and China. There were no diplomatic relations between the two. The issue of US pilots held in China created tensions. It may also have been in the interest of China to use these pilots to improve its international relations. The contacts established by Hammarskjöld led to the release of the pilots in an extraordinary gesture. Later, direct contacts were also established between Beijing and Washington, through their embassies in Warsaw. The key decisions were taken in the two capitals. To allow the Secretary-General to succeed was part of a de facto understanding between the major powers. Hammarskjöld could use this to build up his position. The reverse can be seen in other situations. In the case of the Bizerte crisis between France and Tunisia, France was determined not to let Hammarskjöld have a success. This could have served to strengthen the role of an actor France was not willing to strengthen at the time.

Implementation diplomacy

Hammarskjöld became involved in implementation diplomacy, that is, keeping the peace that has been created through agreement, primarily through UN peacekeeping operations. The conditions agreed on for UNEF in Egypt became guiding principles for all peacekeeping operations during the Cold War. The withdrawal of Israeli troops from Sinai in 1957 included considerable negotiations and delicate arrangements. In both these cases, successes were recorded. It should be noted, however, that the UN was not the only actor in bringing this about. In both cases, the role of the USA was highly important. Also in the Congo, Hammarskjöld had to solve problems of implementation of the Council's resolution. This resulted in severe crises primarily around the secession attempts of Katanga, supported by Belgian interests. Hammarskjöld's implementation diplomacy became highly transcontinental. It involved meeting the demands of actors in the Congo, handling questions with Belgium, and finding workable formulas in New York to keep the Security Council on board. In such complicated situations, Hammarskjöld was a master, able to keep the positions of all parties in mind at the same time. Some of his collaborators only saw one of the three arenas. The intellect of Hammarskjöld may have been well suited for such complex relationships, finding their practical application in very concrete matters. It is interesting that there is only one failure on the part of Hammarskjöld in implementation diplomacy. The issue has been very much debated. The assassination of the first prime minister of independent Congo, Patrice Lumumba, in early 1960 was upsetting in its brutality. Could the UN have intervened more effectively in this crisis? It would have been a heavy involvement in internal affairs of an independent country, but it might also have served to direct the country's development in a different direction.

In all, the Hammarskjöld record of success is strong, although we have no comparable data to draw on. Thus, this judgment is based on what we see in Table 12.1 as well as on the conditions that Hammarskjöld was operating under. It was a period of shifting tensions in major power relations. The UN was able to be a world center in diplomacy.

Success and diplomatic psychology

How can we explain the record of Hammarskjöld? Would any Secretary-General have acted as he did? Did his action demonstrate particular traits? Could they be related to his personality? We have already alluded to an important structural element: the interest of major powers and the relationship between them. This is often a determining factor and something all actors in global affairs are acutely aware of. Hammarskjöld's background made him well suited to understand the significance of the power dimension. His father was prime minister of Sweden at a trying moment in the country's history (World War I). Dag Hammarskjöld worked closely with one of the most influential men in Swedish politics in the first part of the twentieth century, Ernst Wigfors. Later, Hammarskjöld himself was a cabinet minister. Thus, he was not new to power. He could appreciate its limits and read the signals when he was going too far in a particular direction.

At the same time he was neither an admirer of power nor its humble servant. On the contrary, he knew its mechanisms and had seen how power could be used to serve the needs of the one who wanted to achieve something. It meant knowing the direction of change and finding ways to promote your goals, without provoking unnecessary resistance. Such a reformist approach can be detected in his way of approaching international conflicts. His personality and experience made him adept at the power dimension of UN diplomacy.

It is important to note that when categorizing diplomacy as a "success" this does not mean success only for Hammarskjöld. Others have been pushing the parties in a similar direction. In the same vein, "failure" does not mean failure only for Hammarskjöld's efforts. In some instances, Hammarskjöld was the chief negotiator, but he might not have been able to succeed, unless there had been strong support from others (e.g., the USA, Canada, African and Asian countries). Thus "success" is success for a constellation of forces interested in agreement, "failure" is failure for a similar constellation. Similarly, failure may not mean failure for diplomacy as such. Other considerations may have been given more weight by primary parties. Coalition-building, in other words, was – and is – integral to the operation of the UN system. A successful Secretary-General has to be an expert at this. Swedish politics may have provided some training, as governments often relied on coalitions or a minority. It gave insight in a negotiation culture for creating majorities.

Central to Hammarskjöld's coalition-building was his ability to work, at the same time, with the strongest state in the UN system, the USA, and the weakest ones, the newly independent states. This is the more remarkable as the latter often were highly critical of the USA and the West in general. Noteworthy is that Hammarskjöld repeatedly ran into conflict with the American administration (in Guatemala 1954 and Laos in 1959) and still worked in parallel with it in other cases (the pilots in China 1954–1955, Suez 1956, Congo 1960–1961). Thus, there was flexibility on both sides, which made the relationship complex and difficult to untangle. It contrasts with the relationship with the Soviet Union, which was positive in 1956 (Suez in spite of the Hungary crisis) and went very sour in 1960 (Congo), when the USSR wanted to undermine the entire structure of the UN. There seems to have been a trend of growing tensions. With France, the relationship appeared negative throughout the period (Suez 1956, Bizerte 1961), although Hammarskjöld's style should have intrigued the French leadership. These relations are in contrast to the closeness Hammarskjöld had with many Third World leaders throughout his period. India's Prime Minister Jawaharlal Nehru was significant in many crises. The relationship was strong, but not without disagreement. The implicit coalition that maintained the UN operation in the Congo was not easy to manage. Hammarskjöld was able to maintain it in spite of setbacks and turbulence.

There are also short-term and long-term aspects of success. For instance, Hammarskjöld may have scored some success in his work toward a broad coalition government for Laos for a period of time (November 1959 to June 1960), all being undone by a series of military coups, civil wars, and harsh, right-wing government after August 1960. Hammarskjöld could promote agreement, but not maintain it for a longer period of time, when facing increasing Cold War rivalry over Laos. Thus, short-term success could not always be translated into long-term processes. The power of his position was limited. Elegant and reasonable solutions were not necessarily in the interests of those with more power. Table 12.1 shows both the potentials and the limits of third-party diplomacy. This may have been a more frustrating aspect of international diplomacy than would normally be encountered in domestic affairs, particularly Swedish affairs. The Swedish model of welfare-building was a construction project in which one block was added to the previous one. In international affairs, the first block could suddenly be removed. The cumulative nature of domestic affairs was not translatable to the bewildering reality of conflicts the UN encountered.

Thus, the success record of Hammarskjöld can largely be attributed to the international circumstances of the time, and Hammarskjöld's ability to understand and exploit them for the benefit of the UN. Still, we may ask, if there were any special techniques that he employed. Was there a psychology of diplomacy?

Special features of Hammarskjöld's diplomacy

There are some features that may have been peculiar to Hammarskjöld. Certain traits stand out. It can be discussed whether they were unique or not. They seem to have been associated with his successes. The following are worth recording.

a *Travel diplomacy: going to the area of conflict.* The breakthrough for Hammarskjöld's diplomacy came with his visit to China in 1954. Meeting the Chinese leader Chou En-Lai paved the way for the later release of the American pilots held by the People's Republic. This created tremendous attention and general applause, particularly in the United States. In most of the subsequent crises listed in Table 12.1 Hammarskjöld went to the scene and personally conducted negotiations. This was the case for the Middle East conflicts in 1956–1957, where Hammarskjöld's first visit in April 1956 laid the foundation of good relations with leading personalities in the region (Ben Gurion and Nasser, to name two). He wanted to go to Hungary, but was denied that possibility. In the Lebanon crisis of June 1958, Hammarskjöld presided over the first meeting of the UN Observation Group in Lebanon (UNOGIL), in Beirut. Hammarskjöld's diplomacy in the crisis in the Congo initially took place in New York. Thanks to his Africa tour half a year earlier, he had gained personal insights and connections, which were highly useful as the Congo crises unfolded. The first UN troops to go to Katanga in August 1960 were led by Hammarskjöld personally. His aircraft was circulating around the airfield in Elisabethville while he was negotiating the landing of the UN troops with the Katangese leader, a daring case of diplomacy, not repeated by many world leaders. Indeed, it was on a trip of personal diplomacy that Hammarskjöld died.

This form of personal diplomacy became Hammarskjöld's trademark. It was more effective at the time than it might be today. It was not easy to travel as much as Hammarskjöld did, and leaders were not used to as many meetings as they are today. One visit then might be what ten visits are today. To make an agreement was an opportunity that might not come back again. Also, Hammarskjöld's travels were very closely associated with particular crises, which were, thus, elevated to central concern. In today's world with more routine traveling such personal diplomacy may no longer be as effective.

b *Build on mutual and personal trust.* Egypt's President Nasser had never "gone back on anything he said to me personally" Hammarskjöld said when others complained about Nasser's action (Urquhart 1994: 269). He trusted that promises made to him would be kept, but it also made him convey promises to others. Thus, deals could hinge on the ability of others to fulfill their pledges. The least that was required was that everybody understood the promises in a reasonably similar way. By establishing trustful relations, partly through travel diplomacy, partly while in New York, Hammarskjöld could be a channel of contact, but also a spider in a web. He was often the only one that maintained relationships with opposite sides, and could communicate messages from one to the other. He was able to deliver correct messages with the necessary interpretation, and with added-on proposals for ways out.

In the end the trust in Hammarskjöld depended on an agreement being carried out as intended. Nasser responded to Hammarskjöld's comment: "I wish to maintain that record" (Urquhart 1994: 269). Thus, a promise made to Hammarskjöld was a promise not broken. In an international system often described as "anarchical" with actions only guided by "national interest" it is refreshing to find that a promise is a promise, even though the actor to which it is given does not command an army or even represent a state. Hammarskjöld obviously established such relations with many political leaders, e.g. Jawaharlal Nehru, Chou-En Lai, many leaders in the Middle East, and the King of Laos (Urquhart 1994: 148, 355). In the Lebanon crisis of 1958, Nasser made some commitments to Hammarskjöld and US intelligence confirmed that Nasser carried them out (Urquhart 1994: 275). The strategy worked with the leaders Hammarskjöld encountered. It was less successful in the turbulent Congo crisis.

c *Creating diplomatic leverage.* Hammarskjöld had little traditional power. There were no forces under his command, no economic resources that could be used as leverage (but the prospect of economic assistance could be raised, as a carrot). Thus, his power had its bases in civilian, nonmilitary resources. Legally it rested with the UN Charter, of course, but the practical implication came from Hammarskjöld's strong position in the UN itself. By threatening to bring a conflict to the agenda, he could gain leverage. By having them on the agenda, he could convince parties by explaining possible outcomes of votes in the Security Council or General Assembly. With the peacekeeping troops as an instrument, even more leverage could be gained. The UN arena was, so to say, Hammarskjöld's home turf. With strong support from the African, Asian, and some other countries, he wielded remarkable influence.

The requirement for this strategy was that issues came to the UN. Thus, on matters kept off the UN agenda he had no real significance. The Soviet invasion of Hungary illustrated this, as did the US actions in Guatemala. In neither case could he affect the issues. The same is true, of course, for the German and Berlin questions, the crises over Cuba in 1959–1961 and other questions strongly related to Cold War dynamics.

Clearly, Hammarskjöld was well aware of this global dichotomy. His actions in the Congo aimed at preventing the Cold War from spreading to this country as well. In that ambition he was, no doubt, successful. Congo was not divided between east and west, nor was it divided between north and south. The peacekeeping operation gave Hammarskjöld leverage; in fact it was an army, under UN command. Also, international economic assistance was to be channeled through the UN, an additional factor that increased the significance of the UN, and of Hammarskjöld, in this particular crisis. The problem faced by the UN later, that countries gained influence over the peacekeeping operation by threatening to bring their contingents home, was not something encountered by Hammarskjöld. This also meant that Hammarskjöld's future position depended strongly on the outcome of the Congo crisis. It was a risky operation also from the point of view of the international standing of the Secretary-General.

d *"Act early, when possible!"* Hammarskjöld's actions in Guatemala, the Middle East (1956 I and II), and Lebanon all aimed at preventing conflicts from escalating. In two cases there was (Middle East I and Lebanon) some element of success in this, at least for the immediate time period. In two others,

Hammarskjöld was effectively blocked by permanent members (the USA in Guatemala, Britain and France in Middle East II). The term "preventive diplomacy" was coined by Hammarskjöld, and again achieved prominence in the 1990s. The assumption is that, in an earlier phase of a conflict, the positions of the parties have not hardened and thus there is more room to find a conflict-solving formula. Once conflict action has set in, violence has taken place, and troops are in battle, the options quickly narrow. The mixed record in preventive diplomacy also indicates some of the difficulties encountered. It may sometimes simply be too early to act and parties may not see the necessity of outsiders contributing to a peaceful settlement. When Hammarskjöld discussed the situation in Guinea (Conacry) with French President de Gaulle in July 1959, arguing that the economic decline of Guinea – as predicted by de Gaulle – should be prevented through assistance, de Gaulle responded that he was "complètement désintéressé" (Urquhart 1994: 379). Many of the possibilities for such early action were nevertheless used in other conflicts. Hammarskjöld's successful engagement in Lebanon built on the establishment of UNOGIL, a fact-finding mission, which credibly could show that the allegations of "infiltration" were exaggerated. The risk of conflict escalation was reduced.

e   *Coalition building* was, as already noted, as an important element in Hammarskjöld's way of operating. This means having all parties agree on the procedure that he wanted to follow, and for him to object if "wrong" procedures were applied (as happened in Laos 1959, according to Hammarskjöld). To be efficient, coalition-building requires that the Secretary-General not only can operate with the member-states through their representatives, but also can go directly to the real decision-makers in international security affairs, that is, the political leaders. His intensive traveling gave him such access, and this in turn gave him further access to others. Hammarskjöld could often operate in a spiral of positive expectations. Others thought that he had leverage, his opinions mattered, and thus new coalitions could continuously be molded for the issues that arose, and leverage created. The coalitions shifted over time, from the success in the case of the American pilots in 1954–1955, to the support of most member-states in the Suez crisis in 1956 and to the split in the Security Council in the Congo conflict.

f   *Protect the integrity of the office of the Secretary-General.* The standing Hammarskjöld acquired for himself and the UN at times seems to have tempted him to think of the institutions and his office as a force above the politics of others. It might be turned into an independent actor in international affairs (Urquhart 1994: 258–259). This would be unacceptable to the majority of the member-states. In fact, Hammarskjöld was coming close to such a position in international affairs. The hot debate between him and the Soviet leader, Nikita Khrushchev, in the autumn of 1960 on the role of the Secretary-General had such undercurrents. The Soviet proposal for a troika replacing the Secretary-General reflected dissatisfaction with the independence of the office. This is also what Hammarskjöld saw and, thus, he defended his position vigorously in a remarkable and defiant speech to the General Assembly in October 1960 (Urquhart 1994: 456–472). The role of the Secretary-General was also extended through Hammarskjöld's uses of the positions of Special Representatives (SRSGs). It was a way to enlarge the commitment of the Secretary-General, not a way of keeping the office from being involved. Hammarskjöld used it as an extension of his own prestige. The representatives were to sense that they also worked from that position. In line with this was the creation of the new posts of Personal Representatives, with even closer links to the Secretary-General.

g   *Multi-arena diplomacy.* A trait of significance is to manage what today sometimes is described as two-level games (Putnam 1988), that is, to be able to work in several different arenas (international as well as domestic). As mentioned, Hammarskjöld operated in three arenas in the Congo crisis: in Congo itself, in Belgium, and in the UN. These were different dynamics and only he had full insights and understanding of what went on. The interplay between what one actor did in one arena to what another did thousands of kilometers away may not have been apparent to each of the separate actors. Hammarskjöld saw the entire picture. It certainly made operations highly fragile and difficult to maintain. It required an ability to assimilate considerable amounts of information, weigh it, and find imaginative ways of moving forward. In the 1950s it was probably novel to operate in this way. The term "two-level games" suggests that political leaders in international affairs consider both their country in relation to other countries and their own standing in domestic affairs. In UN politics and much of international diplomacy, this is too limited a perspective. There are constantly more levels and actors to consider. There are the internal dynamics of a great number of states (not only the major powers, for instance), and the special politics of UN policy-making, but also the international relations entangling major powers in difficult webs of linkages and conflicts.

The way leaders handle these complexities is an increasingly urgent research task. On the one hand, there is the Hammarskjöld approach of trying to anticipate what will happen in this entire web, and thus take actions that may prevent the worst scenarios from materializing. This is an anticipatory and preventive strategy, which relies on information and political intuition. There is another strategy, which is trial and error. Leaders may try a particular course of action, to see what will result. The approach seems to be "if it works, it works; if it doesn't, find an excuse and still claim victory." The strategy is convenient, but assumes authoritarian control over a society. It is not likely to work for a UN Secretary-General.

The features a–g are special, action-oriented, and general traits. They are available to any third party or Secretary-General. They do not necessarily reflect any personal traits of Hammarskjöld's, except for his skill in using them. There were, however, two noteworthy factors that may have been particular to Hammarskjöld himself: risk-taking and stamina.

h *Hammarskjöld's risk-taking* could be see in many instances. There was considerable risk in going to Beijing in 1954 without any guarantees of a successful
outcome. The risks were increased by the media coverage and by the difficulties in estimating what the leaders of the People's Republic of China would
think of a representative from an organization to which they did not have
access. By involving himself personally, and, thus, his office, in negotiations,
visits, and proposals there was also a possibility of undermining whatever
position he had. Failure may lead to further failure, as success may stimulate further success. He was well aware that he took a "calculated risk," for
example in Laos 1959, and in the Congo, where he was also concerned by
the consequences of not acting (Urquhart 1994: 353, 389). He also admitted,
speaking of Congo, that "I am not optimistic" (Urquhart 1994: 394). Still he
took the risks, as he said in a reply to King Baudouin of Belgium, after bal-
ancing all the factors. Certainly, entering Katanga with UN troops in August
1960 was a daring move, as was his last flight to Ndola in September 1961
(Urquhart 1994: 414, 416–427).

This was not bravery for the sake of bravery, however. It was the result of
calculations. In a way it may reflect his earlier career as an economist, giving
training in weighing plus and minus. He was, in a sense, an early user of game
theory, estimating the utilities of different moves. The record, furthermore,
suggests that he often made the correct estimates.

i *Stamina and simplicity.* There is considerable testimony to Hammarskjöld's ability to work. The breakthrough visit to Beijing took place in January 1955 (after
a flight from New York via London, Paris, Delhi, Canton, and Hankow to
Beijing), when the weather was very cold. Hammarskjöld still walked around
in the city without a hat and "at a terrific pace." His visit to the Middle East
in April 1956 is described as a "diplomatic marathon." His brisk walking
was also commented on by Lebanese security guards, who had difficulties in
keeping up with the Secretary-General. In June 1958, he flew to Beirut, and
immediately set out to work until 2:30 the following morning having had only
a meal consisting of mangos and whisky. Another example is his tour through
Africa in December 1959 and January 1960, when he visited twenty-four
countries and territories in less than a month and a half, consistently full of
enthusiasm (Urquhart 1994: 104, 141, 144, 266, 381).

Clearly, Hammarskjöld was not fussy about living conditions. When visiting the Congo in July 1960, he shared meals with the entire staff in the simple
apartment building housing the UN mission, combining eating with work
(Urquhart 1994: 410). The informal work-style appealed to Hammarskjöld.
The many long-distance flights in an age without the relative comfort of
present-day travel, improvisations for work, food, and housing, late working
hours and early-morning sessions, all could have served to wear down any
persons in this position. This is without accounting for all the problems of
diplomacy, economy, and politics that had to be tackled with a sharp intellect.
The explanation for Hammarskjöld's ability may be found in a comment
made already on his visit to Beijing in 1955. Ahmed Bokhari, from Pakistan,

commented on the Swedes, which included Dag Hammarskjöld's nephew Peder Hammarskjöld and the Swedish Ambassador: "I was the only person in the party that was used to a reasonable climate. Everybody else in his weaker moments had been an Alpine climber" (Urquhart 1994: 104). Clearly, Hammarskjöld was an outdoor person as often as he could get time for it. His physical strength must have interacted strongly with his ability to withstand long travel, work late, and still keep his mind fresh. Indeed, he was also the Vice-President of the Swedish Tourist Association, the Swedish counterpart of the National Geographic Society. He went on long hikes into the wilderness, writing articles about it in the Association magazine.

These particular traits of Hammarskjöld were part of his success. Particularly important was his ability to forge coalitions that supported his actions but also expressed the interests of the coalition. These are political skills. The UN Secretary-General is, of course, a political actor, and Hammarskjöld turned acting into an art.

We have also noted that he was willing to take risks. These were risks for peace, not for his country, God, or any other general matters. The risk-taking aspect is somewhat of a surprise. At his election, he was expected to be more of a "secretary" and officer, not an agenda setter and promoter of a UN perspective of conflict resolution. The transformation is challenging and worthy of consideration. Was this a feature of Hammarskjöld himself, his perception of the duties the office required of him, or a result of the particular circumstances? It points to the interplay between personal psychology and international society.

Conclusions for diplomacy

The three types of diplomacy identified – agenda, agreement, and implementation diplomacy – suggest three different tasks for international diplomacy as well as for research. As we have seen, Hammarskjöld, in a remarkable way, mastered them all.

To get an issue to the agenda requires that it is presented in a way that makes it relevant for the international community, thus possibly leading to concerted action. In the 1950s, this was largely possible only in inter-state conflicts. The Congo crisis was an internal issue, with huge potential international implications, and Hammarskjöld was able to generate international action. It is now safe to say that the UN action prevented the country from falling apart, although it is hard to project what would have happened without UN action. Today, more issues are on the agenda of international diplomacy, and humanitarian concerns provide new inroads to such diplomacy. Still, it remains a puzzle what determines the agenda. Is it possible for a strong-willed political leader to bring any matter to the agenda? Are there special features explaining how a conflict is "detected"? The media often appear to set the agenda, but it will give attention to matters believed to concern international power. This interplay requires closer scrutiny.

In agreement diplomacy, Hammarskjöld's strategy emphasized the ability to actually solve the issue at hand. He was more successful than he expected, for instance, in the Suez crisis in 1956. He was about to deprive two major powers, Britain and France, of their main argument for a secretly planned military intervention. It suggests that issues actually can be settled, if parties want to have them settled. Why would they not want them to be settled? Hammarskjöld's experience suggests that this is not necessarily so, even among leading states and top decision-makers. Is there a particular attraction in actually fighting? Where does it come from: a gender factor? Hammarskjöld's final tour was planned for a meeting where he would negotiate with an actor who was not known for his credibility. Previous negotiations had rested on the assumption that a promise is a promise. Was it likely that the leader of Katanga would be willing and able to honor an agreement? Hammarskjöld took a gamble. Perhaps there are certain leaders with whom one should not make deals?

In implementation diplomacy, Hammarskjöld scored the most successes. It required ingenuity as well as authority. The authority came from the mandate and the accords made previously. Ingenuity was Hammarskjöld's particular contribution. The 1990s have been an era of peace agreement making. It has stopped some wars; it has postponed some others. It has focused on the difficulty of implementation of agreements. At the time of signing it may seem easy; in reality it is more difficult. Little research has focused on such transitions. The realities faced by Hammarskjöld are present today as well. The international system may have changed, but no change is total. It is now more urgent than ever to face the challenges of psychology and diplomacy.

References

Bercovitch, Jacob and Jeffrey Z. Rubin (eds.). 1992. *Mediation in International Relations*. New York: St. Martin's Press.

Crocker, Chester A., Fen Osler Hampson and Pamela Aall (eds.). 1999. *Herding Cats: Multiparty Mediation in a Complex World*. Washington, DC: United States Institute of Peace.

Keashly, Loraleigh and Ronald J. Fisher. 1990. 'Towards a Contingency Approach to Third-Party Intervention in Regional Conflict: A Cyprus Illustration', *International Journal*, 45: 425–453.

Pérez de Cuéllar, Javier. 1997. *Pilgrimage for Peace*. New York: St. Martin's Press.

Putnam, Robert D. 1988. 'Diplomacy and Domestic Politics: The Logic of Two-Level Games', *International Organization*, 42 (3): 427–460.

Urquhart, Brian. 1993. *Ralf Bunche: An American Odyssey*. New York: Norton (paperback 1998).

Urquhart, Brian. 1994. *Hammarskjold*. New York: Norton (first published 1972).

Wallensteen, Peter and Margareta Sollenberg. 2000. 'Armed Conflict, 1989–99', *Journal of Peace Research*, 37 (5): 635–649.

Zartman, I. William and Maureen R. Berman. 1982. *The Practical Negotiator*. New Haven, CT: Yale University Press.

Zartman, I. William. 1989. *Ripe for Resolution: Conflict and Intervention in Africa*, updated edition. New York: Oxford University Press.

Zartman, I. William and J. Lewis Rasmussen (eds.). 1997. *Peacemaking in International Conflict: Methods and Techniques*. Washington, DC: United States Institute of Peace Press.

Part IV

Sanctions and peace research

13 Sanctions and peace research

The role of sanctions in peace research

For a whole generation, the question of minority rule in Southern Africa in the 1960s was a formative experience. Its question was: How could a world concerned about racism, apartheid, discrimination, and domination actually assist in bringing about change? The discussion posed violence against non-violence. The more repression increased in South Africa, the more many seemed to favor liberation struggles of the type just initiated in Angola, Mozambique, Guinea-Bissau, and Cape Verde. However, the white settler-dominated societies of South Africa, South West Africa (today Namibia), and Southern Rhodesia (today Zimbabwe) seemed to defy such challenges. Confronting a weak Portuguese empire was one thing; doing the same to entrenched, well-funded, and elaborate systems of white minority rule seemed another. In reality, neither challenge turned out to be simple. For many concerned about South Africa the choice was to work for international sanctions by governments, in addition to the consumer boycotts that emerged against South African products such as wine and oranges. Economic sanctions were seen as a reasonable choice. However, when the British government in 1965 and 1966 imposed wide-ranging sanctions on the regime of Rhodesia that declared unilateral independence, the debate shifted. Why did not the UK intervene militarily against this particular rebellion? Sanctions became debated in a new way. They came to be seen as an instrument of choice, when a political actor did not want to engage fully.

It also sparked an interest in research on sanctions. The question on how they actually affect a population can be studied and sanctions effectiveness estimated. The use of sanctions was not just a matter of policy; it was also a matter of research. For peace research it had particular salience. Sanction measures appeared to be a means of influence in situations that might otherwise turn into wars. As an alternative instrument, providing options to decision-makers, this could be valuable. A leading peace researcher, Johan Galtung, went to Rhodesia to find out in 1966. He came back with a report that changed sanctions research (Galtung 1967) and he invited the present author (who had been writing his first academic studies on the Rhodesia question) to come to the Peace Research Institute, Oslo (PRIO), to do a larger study. It resulted in a list of ten comparable cases of sanctions, which could be handily analyzed. The result was published in the *Journal of Peace Research*

(Wallensteen 1968). With the accompanying dissertation this work demonstrated that sanctions were not instrumental in changing governments unless there was a viable opposition that politically could use sanctions-induced hardship in its campaign against the government. Without this factor, however, international pressure led powerful groups to line up behind the government, as Galtung had demonstrated in his work. Instead of weakening a regime, the sanctions could strengthen it (Wallensteen 1971; Nincic and Wallensteen 1983). It was not to say that military interventions would have been easier or more successful. Nor did the result say that a war of liberation was the only way out. Rather, it meant that the opposition was key to change and that the international task could be to support it.

Research for smarter sanctions

The unfolding debate on economic sanctions is captured in Chapter 14, demonstrating how sanctions have been seen in different light at different junctures. It also includes Table 14.2, which has updated the UN (United Nations) sanctions record to the end of 2010. Each debate has led to a refinement of this tool.[1] It has turned into more sophisticated, less costly measures for sender and target alike. In media the new types have become known as smart sanctions.[2] Key developments are the following.

The tools of sanctions have gone

* from being comprehensive to becoming targeted,
* from isolating a whole country to zooming in on particular decision-makers, and
* from including all types of trade to dealing with particular commodities.

The expected impact has developed

* from paralyzing an entire economy to affecting particular sectors,
* from creating revolt-inducing hardships to a concern for humanitarian effects, and
* from targeting any "suspect" individual to maintaining higher standards of human rights.

In short, the study and practice of sanctions have both become more complex.

An element in this refinement was the sanctions reform process that was initiated in the late 1990s, largely initiated in dialogue with the Sanctions Branch of the UN Secretariat. It involved three processes that built on a similar idea: focus on "new" sanctions; involve key governments in official capacity; bring in expertise in fields of banking, customs, air traffic, etc.; have non-governmental participation; and, in particular, rely on academics for setting the agenda. These efforts were termed after the main places of meeting, thus the first ones were labeled the Interlaken Process (financed by Switzerland and dealing with financial sanctions, Biersteker *et al.* 2001) and the Bonn–Berlin process (sponsored by

Germany, dealing with arms embargoes and other measures, Brzoska 2001). Both presented their findings to the UN Security Council in 2001. The present author coordinated the subsequent efforts, the Stockholm Process on the Implementation of Targeted Sanctions (SPITS) at Uppsala University 2001–2003 (Wallensteen *et al.* 2003; Wallensteen and Staibano 2005), presented to the Security Council in February 2003.

These reports had an impact on the way sanctions have been conducted, primarily by the UN, but later also by the European Union (EU) and African Union (AU). Thus, researchers have continued to improve the instrument (Cortright 2009; Cortright *et al.* 2010; Eriksson 2010). However, there were also basic questions on the research agenda. For instance, could sanctions have different impact depending on the aims? Could the sanctions play a greater role in preventing a conflict from escalating (very much an original sanctions idea, hoping to stop war and aggression) and have less impact in others (e.g., preventing terrorism or nuclear proliferation)? Could they have a role in peacebuilding, after a war? Chapters 14 and 15 demonstrate that there are several types of sanctions. They could also be positive, adding or promising to add something to parties if they comply. This opens up for the possibility of mixing positive and negative. This could mean keeping sanctions even after compliance for a period of time in order to induce parties to carry out additional changes that might stabilize a new situation. As the sanctions will ultimately be lifted, the targeted actors have an incentive to shorten the period and the imposer could possibly couple this to additional rewards. Sanctions for peacebuilding is a theme in the study reproduced in Chapter 15.

Different sanctions could also be expected to have varied impact. Thus, arms embargoes may be particularly well suited for ending ongoing wars. In work with the Stockholm International Peace Research Institute (SIPRI), SPITS could show that this may actually be the case. It seemed that parties in a war became more interested in discussing peace proposals after the imposition of an arms embargo (Fruchart *et al.* 2007). This makes perfect sense, as war efforts in poor countries build on a continuous supply of armaments and munitions. If this is not secured and there are no alternative sources (such as having one's own production facilities, which however also would be easy military targets) the war effort is affected. Further studies show that international arms embargoes reduce the likelihood of a conflict ending in victory (Escribà-Folch 2010). However, the same measure may not in the same way affect countries engaged in nuclear development programs with potential military application. It may not make terrorists change their mind. Thus, sanctions could be designed more properly with respect to the effects envisioned, and perhaps also those not expected, such as an escalation into armed action.[3]

In recent work the reactions of the targeted individuals are taken into account. The idea of targeting particular personalities starts from the theory that they actually will have the will and power to change national policies. Studying eight cases of UN sanctions dealing with non-terrorist situations, the authors find remarkably little impact on the targeted individuals, both in terms of economic losses and in their will to affect policies (Wallensteen and Grusell 2011).

The challenge of positive sanctions

This means there is also reason to consider other ways of influencing governments. One is to use positive sanctions, alone or in combination with negative sanctions. The negative sanctions discussed so far mean an outside actor's deliberate disruption of another actor's external connections, with the explicit purpose of achieving a specified change by the targeted actor, be it a government or a non-governmental group. Positive sanctions, then, refers to the reverse, the initiation of new connections to stimulate or reward changes in the targeted actors (Wallensteen 2005). There are no systematic records available of positive sanctions, which makes a more general study difficult. There are some difficulties in delimiting negative from positive sanctions (Lawson 1983; Newnham 2000; Griffiths and Barnes 2008). This may hamper the interest in compiling necessary data. Still, some relevant collections exist, particularly in the field of conflict prevention measures. This has shown that positive sanctions may be more useful in earlier stages of conflict, as was mentioned in Chapter 10 (also by Lund 1996). Some authors give a large role to positive actions as political instruments (Newnham 2000; Nye 2004) and, during the Cold War, they were sometimes seen as a way to reduce tensions (Osgood 1962).

A central consideration is that positive measures are coupled to policy changes. Lawson gives an example: the Gulf countries offered a large-scale economic compensation scheme in exchange for a cease-fire agreement in the Iran–Iraq War (Lawson 1983). Although the proposal was rejected, it still is interesting to understand. Crumm's (1995) work included forty cases of Soviet influence attempts toward India during a thirty-year period from 1953 to 1983. Twenty-two were classified as at least moderately successful. Interestingly, Crumm observed that, when the Soviet Union was trying to change India's behavior in areas where India strongly held a different view, the success rate was lower. Crumm also reported a declining utility in the incentives, concluding that they may be more effective if used sporadically. Drezner (1999) compared "carrots" and "sticks" in US policy on nuclear programs in South and North Korea in the 1990s. He finds that the use of negative sanctions was more effective against an allied country (South Korea), and positive use of "carrots" worked in the case of hostile North Korea. Newnham compared negative and positive sanctions, in an analysis of thirty-two sanctions used by Germany on Russia/the Soviet Union and Poland over a century. Remarkably the study reports eight negative and unsuccessful cases and twenty-two successful positive sanctions, out of a total of twenty-four. A successful case, according to Newnham, was the historical deal leading Germany's reunification in 1990.

Many of the studies have seen positive sanctions in the context of inter-state relations. Applying sanctions in intra-state situations may lead to ethical and political problems. For instance, if an outside actor offers military cooperation, security guarantees, or diplomatic support to the targeted actor it also means supporting a particular side in an internal dispute. At least, that could easily be the perception on the other side of a conflict divide. Trying to achieve a change of regime with the help of positive measures may include paying leading personalities to leave the country (such proposals were significant in Haiti in the 1980s, in Angola in the 1990s, and in Liberia in 2003). This could mean an end to a war, but also that war crimes are not pursued.

These cases were the result of crisis-related action. However, positive sanctions could have more long-term aims, for instance attempting to stimulate or support domestic opposition or other non-governmental actors, thus contributing to a more plural political life in a particular country. This would mean for the outside actor to have access to a set of measures whereby targeting the government and/ or the opposing community can be differentiated, for instance negative sanctions on the former and positive ones on the latter.

This would then mean developing a sanctions strategy that consists of both positive and negative sanctions. For instance, negative measures could be targeted on individuals and organizations supporting the incumbents. If these measures are parallel to positive sanctions, the recipients of which are the civil forces opposing the government, there will be additional reasons for a government to reconsider its policies. Clearly, positive sanctions require further development as a non-violent policy tool. In that process it is important to consider how they can be related to a skillful application of negative sanctions.

Sanctions for the future

Sanctions constitute an important measure. They have been practiced by the UN in about twenty conflicts since 1990, and the records for the EU and AU are also becoming impressive, in some way complementing those of the UN. For instance, the EU has imposed sanctions on Zimbabwe and Burma/Myanmar, which has not been the case for the UN. The AU has a record of imposing sanctions to prevent unconstitutional change in Africa, in matters on which the UN and EU have been more reluctant to act (Eriksson 2009). Thus, there is international complementarity among international bodies.

However, this can also be seen in a different light. Since the end of the Cold War there have been 130 armed conflicts (1989–2009, UCDP conflict database). Sanctions have been used in fewer than 10 percent of these situations. The sanctions instrument is not used for every war situation and not all UN sanctions relate to ongoing wars. There are also cases of terrorism and fear of nuclear proliferation that stimulate UN sanctions. In fact, there is a selection effect. When the nuclear proliferation issue is a concern, sanctions are more likely. The same goes for countries that are seen to cooperate with terrorist groups. Whether sanctions will be used to prevent war is uncertain. However, if these are the cases with the highest success rate, this is perhaps the situation for which this instrument should be refined. It would mean thinking about monitoring, implementation and mediation to solve the conflicts. The two cases in Chapter 15 deal with such situations. They point to possible new avenues for the use of this tool.

In cases of a regime's violating basic norms of conduct, the efficacy of sanctions can be questioned. As sanctions now consist of different types, the efficacy of each should be an important field of scrutiny. Arms embargoes have been more analyzed than many others. The new use of sanctions on banks and banking transaction is also worth closer scrutiny. Again there may be unintended harmful effects, for instance making remittance from the diaspora difficult and thus in effect hampering the work of those who may otherwise be in favor of change. The impact of the freezing of assets and travel bans needs also to be assessed more carefully.

The targeting of individuals is interesting, in particular if the focus is on the top leaders. It is worth remembering that countries and leaders do not like to find themselves exposed to sanctions. To them it means to be excluded by the outside world, implying a loss of power (as the sanctions cannot be prevented) and humiliating (as the country and the leaders are lumped together with other "shady" characters). Even if a country might prefer to develop a policy of self-reliance and minimize its relations with the outside world, many leaders would want that to be *their* choice, not the result of imposition from the outside. Once in the situation, however, leaders and followers are quick to adapt to the new conditions and make the most of them, for their particular purposes.

However, it is not only leaders who are targeted, which has raised serious human rights concerns (Cameron 2003). Legal challenges in Europe as well as a change of administration in the United States led the UN to make it possible to appeal against the procedures through which individuals are listed and removed (delisted) from UN sanctions.

Interestingly, in a globalized world, new forms of negative and positive sanctions are evolving. Popular campaigns have an impact in particular situations, much as the consumer boycotts hoped to achieve in the early 1960s. To see a reduction in the flow of tourism is negative for a leadership. The loss of markets for a country's produce is not what decision-makers relish. Furthermore, the involvement of the International Criminal Court results in additional lack of comfort. To be indicted also means that travel is restricted as countries that have ratified the convention are under an obligation to apprehend those listed and hand them over to the Court. The ICC practice of secret indictment – as seen in the case of the senator and former Vice President of the Democratic Republic of Congo Jean-Pierre Bemba, who was captured in Europe and turned over to the Court – creates unpredictability and fear.

Together such sanctions will have an impact, but compliance may not come when the outside world wants. It is more likely to be associated with internal upheaval and change may not be complete. Sanctions have demonstrably been part of dramatic shifts in a number of countries. This ranges from democratization in South Africa (where sanctions may have been one of three or four determining factors) to the closing down of the nuclear programs in Libya (again one of a few factors that influenced this decision) and possibly ending or at least preventing a recurrence of war in Liberia (making it impossible for the warlord Charles Taylor to challenge the peace established after the 2003 peace treaty).

As these cases suggest, sanctions cannot be expected to work alone. This measure is part of a larger package, which together can bring about the desired development or, more likely, prevent a particular outcome from happening. In a study of the civil war in Côte d'Ivoire, it was concluded that the confluence of international peacekeeping (UN and West African forces), sanctions (partially monitored by the peacekeepers), and peacemaking efforts (primarily by African countries) contributed to preventing an escalation to genocide in the early 2000s (Wallensteen *et al.* 2011). A promising direction for future research is to study such strategies. How can different elements of international peaceful action together provide for peaceful outcomes of international crisis? How can they in particular stimulate outcomes that allow for the necessary changes away from the conditions that created the crisis in the first place? There are, indeed, more challenges to sanctions research.

Notes

1   The debate was both normative – "is this human sacrifice acceptable?" – and empirical – "do they accomplish their goals?" On the latter see for instance Pape (1998).
2   The origin of this term is difficult to establish. In the late 1990s German scholars discussed "intelligent sanctions." It has been associated with David Cortright and George A. Lopez, whose many books on the subject at that time were important for the field (Cortright and Lopez 2000). They do not claim the term, however. The website www. smartsanctions.se is a useful resource on UN sanctions.
3   An alternative is, of course, that the sanctions may signal an interest from the sender of sanctions to actually become involved, also militarily. Lektzian and Sprecher (2007) note that many sanctions cases, particularly with democracies as senders, have actually been involved in a militarized dispute after using sanctions. This, of course, runs counter to the original peace research idea of sanctions as a credible *alternative* to military action, not a step toward such measures.

References

Biersteker, Tom J., Sue E. Eckert, Peter Romaniuk, Aaron Halegua and N. Reid. 2001. *Targeted Financial Sanctions: A Manual for Design and Implementation.* Report from the Interlaken Process. Providence, RI: Brown University.

Brzoska, M. (ed.). 2001. *Design and Implementation of Arms Embargoes and Travel and Aviation Related Sanctions: Results of the 'Bonn–Berlin Process'.* Report from the Bonn–Berlin Process. Bonn: BICC.

Cameron, Iain. 2003. 'UN Targeted Sanctions, Legal Safeguards and the European Convention on Human Rights', *Nordic Journal of International Law,* 72 (2): 159–214.

Cortright, David. 2009. *Patterns Implementation: Do the Listing Practices Impede Compliance with UN Sanctions?* Notre Dame, IN: Sanctions and Security Research Program, University of Notre Dame.

Cortright, David and George A. Lopez. 2000. *The Sanctions Decade: Assessing UN Strategies in the 1990s.* Boulder, CO: Lynne Rienner.

Cortright, David, George A. Lopez and Linda Gerber-Stellingwerf. 2010. *Integrating UN Sanctions for Peace and Security.* Notre Dame, IN: Sanctions and Security Research Program, University of Notre Dame.

Crumm, Eileen M. 1995. 'The Value of Economic Incentives in International Relations', *Journal of Peace Research,* 32: 313–330.

Drezner, Daniel W. 1999. *The Sanctions Paradox: Economic Statecraft and International Relations.* Cambridge: Cambridge University Press.

Eriksson, Mikael. 2009. *Rethinking Targeted Sanctions.* PhD dissertation, European University Institute, Florence.

Eriksson, Mikael. 2010. *Supporting Democracy in Africa: African Union's Use of Targeted Sanctions to Deal with Unconstitutional Changes of Government.* Stockholm: Swedish Defence Research Agency.

Escribà-Folch, Abel. 2010. 'Economic Sanctions and the Duration of Civil Conflicts', *Journal of Peace Research,* 47 (2): 129–141.

Fruchart, Damien, Paul Holtom, Siemon T. Wezeman, Daniel Strandow and Peter Wallensteen. 2007. *United Nations Arms Embargoes: Their Impact on Arms Flows and Target Behaviour.* Stockholm: SIPRI.

Galtung, Johan. 1967. 'On the Effects of International Economic Sanctions, with Examples from the Case of Rhodesia', *World Politics,* 19 (3): 378–416.

Griffiths, Aaron and Catherine Barnes. 2008. *Powers of Persuasion: Incentives, Sanctions and Conditionality in Peacemaking.* Accord 19. London: Conciliation Resources.

Lawson, Fred H. 1983. 'Using Positive Sanctions to End International Conflicts: Iran and the Arab Gulf Countries', *Journal of Peace Research,* 20: 311–328.

Lektzian, David J. and Christopher M. Sprecher. 2007. 'Sanctions, Signals and Militarized Conflict', *American Journal of Political Science,* 51 (2): 415–431.

Lund, Michael. 1996. *Preventing Violent Conflicts: A Strategy for Preventive Diplomacy.* Washington, DC: U.S. Institute of Peace Press.

Newnham, Randall E. 2000. 'More Flies with Honey: Positive Economic Linkage in German *Ostpolitik* from Bismarck to Kohl', *International Studies Quarterly,* 44: 73–96.

Nincic, Miroslav and Peter Wallensteen (eds.). 1983. *Dilemmas of Economic Coercion: Sanctions in World Politics.* New York: Praeger Special Studies.

Nye, Joseph S., Jr. 2004. *Soft Power: The Means of Success in World Politics.* New York: Public Affairs.

Osgood, Charles E. 1962. *An Alternative to War or Surrender.* Urbana, IL: Illini Books.

Pape, R.A. 1998. 'Why Economic Sanctions Still Do Not Work', *International Security,* 23 (1): 66–77.

Wallensteen, Peter. 1968. 'Characteristics of Economic Sanctions', *Journal of Peace Research,* 5 (3): 248–267.

Wallensteen, Peter. 1971. *Ekonomiska Sanktioner.* Stockholm: Prisma.

Wallensteen, Peter. 2005. 'Positive Sanctions: On the Potential of Rewards and Targeting Differentiation', in Peter Wallensteen and Carina Staibano (eds.), *International Sanctions: Between Words and Wars in the Global System.* London: Frank Cass.

Wallensteen, Peter and Helena Grusell. 2011. *Targeting the Right Targets? The UN Use of Individual Sanctions* (forthcoming).

Wallensteen, Peter and Carina Staibano (eds.). 2005. *International Sanctions: Between Words and Wars in the Global System.* London: Frank Cass.

Wallensteen, Peter, Carina Staibano and Mikael Eriksson. 2003. *Making Targeted Sanctions Effective: Guidelines for the Implementation of UN Policy Options.* Uppsala: Department of Peace and Conflict Research, Uppsala University.

Wallensteen, Peter, Erik Melander and Frida Möller. 2011. 'Preventing Genocide: The International Response', in Mark Anstey, Paul Meerts and I. William Zartman (eds.), *To Block the Slippery Slope: Reducing Identity Conflicts and Preventing Genocide.* New York: Oxford University Press (forthcoming).

14 A century of economic sanctions
A field revisited

A thirty-year cycle?

Economic sanctions have many names: blockades, boycotts, embargoes, sometimes even described as quarantine or economic coercion. These concepts are almost synonymous. Under such headings the issue of sanctions was of concern through-out the twentieth century. In the early years "tariff wars" were on the agenda (Nicholson 1967). The continental blockade of the Napoleonic wars was on the mind of decision-makers. World War I saw the application of sanctions against the allied countries of the continent. Following the war debates on sanctions have been intense at times. In retrospect, it appears to be a matter of thirty-year inter-vals. Sanction policy was a major issue of discussion in the 1930s. In the 1960s a new intensive debate emerged and in the 1990s there was a repeated interest in sanctions issues. These three big debates on the topic of the uses and misuses of sanctions are interesting in themselves as a part of the ongoing evolution of peace thinking. They also show important shifts in the foci of concern, changes in related studies, and the creation of new political practices. Let me quickly review the debates and then make some comparisons, which will help to put the present debate in perspective.

The first sanctions debate: sanctions against aggression

In the 1930s the discussion concerned the question of aggression. The issue was clear-cut: what was the international community to do in face of major powers attacking another country with the intent of occupying it? One of the conclusions from World War I was a belief that the economic blockade of Germany had been effective. The German imperial armies were not militarily defeated, it was argued, but it was the "home front" that succumbed, owing to the economic strains put on the Wilhelminian regime. As a consequence, economic sanctions acquired an important role in the Covenant of the League of Nations (Walters 1965; Mitrany 1925; Clark 1932; Taubenfeld 1958).

The first challenge was Japan's attack in 1931 on China and the ensuing occu-pation of Manchuria. According to the legal framework of the League of Nations, this should have been a simple case of aggression and the clause on economic sanctions should have been activated. It was not. When Italy some years later, in a similar fashion, initiated a war against Ethiopia, using a border incident as justification, there was more resolve. Sanctions were initiated, failed miserably, and were declared ineffective by the League of Nations and removed, nine months after their imposition (Taubenfeld 1958; Walters 1965; Baer 1967). The debate around this failure was more intense than over the inability to initiate actions against Japan. The consequences of the nonperformance of the sanctions were far-reaching. It resulted in the demise of the League.

The second sanctions debate: sanctions for decolonization

The experience of sanctions against Italy did not, however, end sanctions policy. The UN Charter retained sanctions, "the economic weapon," as an option (Taubenfeld and Taubenfeld 1964). In the 1960s a whole set of sanctions were initiated, mostly by major powers and outside the framework of the UN. Examples include sanctions on Cuba and the Dominican Republic (by the USA), on Albania and China (by the USSR), and on Portugal, South Africa, and Rhodesia (by Afro-Asian states) (Wallensteen 1968). In the 1960s also a vigorous debate raged on the possible UN sanctions on South Africa and Rhodesia (Segal 1964; Leiss 1965; Taubenfeld and Taubenfeld 1964). In none of these cases, however, was the old form of territorial aggression the key issue. Instead, the concern was with regimes and their treatment of their populations, the foreign policies they pursued (notably the alliances the governments were part of), or the threats they may have posed to neighboring countries.

The unilateral declaration of independence (UDI) by the Smith regime in Southern Rhodesia in 1965 resulted in the first UN application of mandatory sanctions as a main tool of the world body. The sanctions, first initiated immediately after UDI by the colonial power, Great Britain, then recommended by the UN Security Council, became mandatory in 1966 and remained in force until the end of 1979. After the Lancaster House agreement on the future of Rhodesia the sanctions were finally removed. The sanctions on Rhodesia were, by that time, the most comprehensive ones imposed by a world body. Sanctions on South Africa were instituted as well, first in the form of an arms embargo, and in the 1980s also in the form of investment restrictions. The second sanctions debate, in other words, was concerned with issues of decolonization, discrimination, and democratic rule – very different indeed from the first debate. In fact, the relationship between the two debates was rarely observed in the second. The sanctions against Italy appeared to belong to an entirely different era and few wanted to point to this as a relevant experience.[1]

The third sanctions debate: sanctions and the new wars

The third debate can be dated to the decision by the UN Security Council to impose sanctions on Iraq. The purpose was to end Iraq's occupation of Kuwait. The sanctions were instituted immediately after the invasion in August 1990. They remained in force until the US invasion of Iraq in 2003, when they were changed to targeted sanctions on the deposed leadership. In a way, this application of sanctions was more like the first debate and its focus on territorial aggression. The Security Council defined Iraq as the country that had broken the peace and, thus, measures under Chapter VII could be taken.[2] In effect, Iraq was branded as an aggressor, although this language was avoided. A military build-up followed and a short, intensive war in January and February 1991 resulted in the forceful eviction of Iraqi troops from Kuwait. Sanctions remained in place, however, but now for the purpose of forcing Iraq to agree with the inspection provisions imposed after the Gulf War. As this short description makes clear, sanctions were not the only instrument. In both the first and the second debates, sanctions were seen as *the* option for achieving desired change, to be kept separate from military action. In the Gulf crisis it was one of the instruments. After the Gulf War pressure was also kept up on Iraq with repeated air raids on Iraqi installations.

Since the Gulf War the UN Security Council (Table 14.1) has initiated eighteen new cases of economic sanctions, sometimes as the only action, sometimes in combination with other measures. Thus, the debate has had a rich array of cases for discussion (Hufbauer *et al.* 1990; Martin 1992; Cortright and Lopez 1995; Stremlau 1996; Pape 1997, 1998a,b; Baldwin 1998; Elliot 1998 belong to this debate)

This means that the 1990s show a record number of sanctions applications by the United Nations. This is remarkable, not least since the experiences of the earlier sanction periods have been mixed, to say the least. This record once again makes sanctions a pertinent topic for research and discussion. The situation is now improved by the fact that there are several more systematic studies on which to base conclusions (Galtung 1967; Wallensteen 1968, 1971, 1983; Doxey 1980; Hufbauer *et al.* 1990; Martin 1992) and some more penetrating discussions (Baldwin 1985; Pape 1997). To what extent such studies have had an impact on policy-making is a different question, however. A mark of the sanctions of the 1990s, as compared with previous periods, is their link to internal war situations. This is clear-cut in the cases of Somalia, Liberia, Angola, Rwanda, Sierra Leone, and the former republic of Yugoslavia (Kosovo). The break-up of Yugoslavia could be seen as a special case of internal war becoming international. Haiti was a case of pre-empting an internal war by international pressure. Two cases are related to the phenomenon of terrorism (Libya and Sudan). In the first and second sanction debates, such motivations would not have been acceptable. The sanctions on Rhodesia and South Africa, although concerning internal affairs, were internationally legitimate as they connected to the decolonization process. This process was supported by the two alliances of the Cold War and belonged to the few agreements between these two sides. The sanctions directed against internal rule, such as those against Cuba and Albania, were not accepted in international organizations outside the domination of sanctions-imposing major powers.

The three major sanctions debates reflect not only different concerns but also different expectations. In the 1930s, sanctions were expected to be powerful enough to prevent major powers from unleashing war. The deterring effects turned out to

Table 14.1 UN economic sanctions, conflicts and peace, by 2010: UN sanctions started
after 1990

Country or actor targeted	Status (2010)	Armed conflict	Peace agreement	Measures included (at minimum)
Afghan, Al Qaida, Taliban	Ongoing	Yes	No	Arms, assets, travel
Angola	Ended	Yes	Yes	Diamonds, arms, assets, travel
Côte d'Ivoire	Ongoing	Yes	Yes	Arms, assets, travel
Dem. Rep. Congo	Ongoing	Yes	Yes	Arms, assets, travel
Eritrea vs. Ethiopia	Ended	Yes	Yes	Arms
Eritrea	Ongoing	Yes	No	Arms, assets
Former Yugoslavia	*Ongoing*	*Yes*	*Yes*	*Assets, travel*
Haiti	*Ended*	*Yes*	*Yes*	*Oil*
Iran	Ongoing	No	No	Arms, finances, assets, travel
Iraq	*Ended*	*Yes*	*No*	*Oil vs. food, arms, assets, travel*
Lebanon	Ongoing	Yes	No	Arms, threat of other
Liberia	Ongoing	Yes	Yes	Diamonds, timber, arms, assets
Libya	Ended	No	No	Aviation, spare parts
North Korea	Ongoing	No	No	Arms, finances, goods
Rwanda	Ended	Yes	No	Arms
Sierra Leone	Ongoing	Yes	Yes	Diamonds, arms, assets, travel
Somalia	Ongoing	Yes	No	Arms, assets, travel
Sudan	Ongoing	Yes	Yes	Arms, assets, travel

Notes
Sanctions in italics are those that might correspond to the definition of comprehensive sanctions,
as applied in Table 14.2. There are also a number of sanction-type actions pursued by parties in
violent conflict, for instance in the conflicts over Cyprus, Nagorno Karabakh, and Somaliland. For a
period African states had sanctions against Burundi, to promote the peace process. Peace agreements
referred to are those in sanctions cases that were signed, or reactivated, and became durable.
In the cases of the former Yugoslavia and Iraq there are actually two separate sets of sanctions,
relating to different conflicts (Bosnia and Kosovo, the wars in 1990–1991 and 2003, respectively). For
Liberia there are in fact three different sanctions regimes.

be weak, however, and a similar use of sanctions was not seen after World War
II. In the 1960s, UN sanctions were part of a decolonization strategy, a goal that
was widely shared. Countries that "normally" would have rejected interference in
internal affairs had a different perspective on South Africa and Rhodesia. The use
of sanctions against a major power, such as those against Italy, was ruled out by the
veto in the Security Council.[3] Consequently, UN sanctions could be used against

smaller countries only in cases when the permanent members of the Security Council could agree. This was rare, and many sanctions were instead imposed outside the framework of the UN. The comprehensive US-led strategic embargo on the Soviet Union was initiated as early as in 1947 but was never legalized through the UN (instead a special organization, the Coordinating Committee or CoCom, connected to NATO, was used; Adler-Karlsson 1968). The Arab League and its special Sanctions Bureau in Damascus ran the Arab boycott of Israel. Still other sanctions were administered through superpower-dependent organizations such as the Organization of African States (OAS), Council for Mutual Economic Assistance (CMEA), or other regional organizations.

Here there is a difference from the 1990s, when sanctions were carried out more consistently within the framework of the United Nations. They have been able to build on a broader consensus among the major powers, including opposition not only to territorial aggression and decolonization, but also to the break-up of states, ethnic division, terrorism, and opposition to the rule of legal authority. Thus, more situations have become eligible for UN action. The agenda of the UN has been enlarged, and, in the general search for options, sanctions have again come to the forefront.[4]

Still, the possibility of acting outside the UN has not been abandoned. There are old and new sanctions outside the UN framework. Table 14.2 includes some examples. Others are the cases of US sanctions on China and Vietnam (ended during the 1990s), Cuba, North Korea, and Iran (continued), India and Pakistan (on missile technology, and with international support on nuclear weapons development), sanctions imposed by Greece on Macedonia, African states' actions on Burundi and Liberia, EU sanctions on Nigeria (diplomatic links), and some Arab

Table 14.2 Ten comprehensive economic sanctions, 1932–1966

Sender	Target	Type	Start	End
UK	USSR	Trade	1933	1933
League of Nations	Italy	Trade	1935	1936
Arab states	Israel	Trade	1945	Ongoing
USSR	Yugoslavia	Trade	1948	1955
African states	South Africa	Trade	1960	1994
(UN	South Africa	Arms	1977	1994)
USA	Dominican Republic	Trade	1960	1962
USA	Cuba	Trade	1960	Ongoing
USSR	Albania	Trade	1960	1989
African states	Portugal	Trade	1963	1975
UN	Rhodesia	Trade	1965	1979

Notes
This builds on Wallensteen (1968, 1971, 1983).
South Africa: UN action was limited, others were broader.

states' continued sanctions on Israel. The war between Armenia and Azerbaijan has also resulted in curtailment of economic relations between the two nations.

It should be noted that most of new sanctions are fairly limited in scope. The sanctions on Rhodesia contained an almost complete ban of export and import. Oil was specifically targeted, as were arms, travel arrangements, air connections, financial operations, and diplomatic relations. Table 14.2 gives a list of comprehensive sanctions that were the chief instrument of the sender against the target. Only two other UN sanctions have been this comprehensive: the sanctions on the former Yugoslavia and Iraq, both in the 1990s. The non-UN sanctions are often even more limited, possibly with the exception of the African embargo on Burundi.

The three sanctions debates are, thus, instructive to compare. We may ask whether there is a cycle in the use of sanctions by global organizations. The sanctions debates have evolved. Perhaps it is a coincidence or an exaggeration that they appear to come in thirty-year cycles. However, it could also be an accurate observation. The experiences may be lost between generations. What were important lessons from the 1930s were not seen as relevant for the generations in power in the 1960s. Equally, the conditions of the 1990s may have appeared to be so different that whatever was learnt from the previous debates no longer appeared relevant. Thus, sanctions were thought to be more effective than before. The constraints of inter-war or Cold War politics were not longer relevant for the 1990s. So it could legitimately be asked if sanctions could be used in a new way, and with more effect. This also shows that some issues remain the same. The first and foremost is the issue of success. Are sanctions today more successful than they were in the first and second periods? Have conditions for success changed? If so, why? If not, why not? The answers involve the issue of what is meant by success and its measurement, as well as the causal mechanisms.[5] This study deals with the success and failure of sanctions. After establishing the record in this regard, three clusters of explanations are related to the experiences of the 1990s.[6]

Success and failure: the rate of success remains low

Economic sanctions, whether operated within the UN or outside, have never had a high record of success. A study of ten cases in which comprehensive trade sanctions were instituted found that only two were successful, that is, the changes advocated by the sender, the initiator, were also carried out by the receiver, the target country (Wallensteen 1968, 1971; Nincic and Wallensteen 1983). In a study of a much larger set of sanctions, with considerable variation in scope and content, success was recorded in one-third of the cases (Hufbauer *et al.* 1990). In a recent reevaluation of this work it was found that only 5 percent were actually successful (Pape 1997). In his seminal work of the American strategic embargo on the Soviet bloc, Adler-Karlsson found that the embargo may have slowed Soviet development by half a year, but not more (Adler-Karlsson 1968). The historical record is one of caution as to the ability of making sanctions effective.

The definition of success is, of course, crucial and can be part of longer discussion. In military strategy it is often two outcomes that matter: victory or defeat.

Thus, success and failure of sanctions could be a parallel: either the sender gets the receiver to change goals as desired by the sender (success) or not (failure). It is possible to make a closer grading of this, particularly if there are many cases to review. Baldwin (1985, 1998) has tried to capture this by introducing a greater variety of impacts and, creatively, wants to replace economic sanctions with the concept of economic statecraft. However, the credibility of the instrument of economic sanctions will depend on its ability to deliver at least some clear results (i.e., changes in behavior) at reasonable costs, within a reasonable time limit, and where it is reasonable to conclude that the results are related to the effects of the sanctions. This speaks in favor of a rather sharp and dichotomous definition of sanctions.

This requires some further elaboration. First, economic sanctions have strong dislocating effects on any economy. It could mean that, the longer they are in operation, the stronger this effect will be, thus ultimately resulting in the inability of a state's economy to operate properly. This is one argument for the continuation of sanctions, for instance by the USA against Cuba (in operation since 1959, i.e. for forty years, probably the longest sanction effort to run without any interruption in the twentieth century). However, the purpose of sanctions is often more precise and the time limits much shorter. The British prime minister Harold Wilson in 1965 said that it was a matter of "weeks" before Rhodesia would capitulate. The Rhodesian leader, Ian Smith, did not step down until fourteen years later, long after Wilson had left politics. Thus, the expectation that sanctions will be more effective the longer they continue simply is not true. As students of economy could testify, the economy will adapt to the new circumstances, and in fact gradually loses its dependence on the sender. This is an argument in favor of asking for a definition of sanction success that expects changes in a short period of time. Second, it is interesting to see that a sender often makes the goals clear at the outset of the sanctions operation. Thus, there is a criterion by which the sanctions can be judged, a criterion that is independent of the economic effects of the sanctions. There are particular reasons why sanctions are imposed, and only when these have been fulfilled will the sanctions be lifted. These reasons are often straightforward. In the case of Cuba, it was the end of the Castro regime that was expected. In other cases the sender demanded, for instance, access rights for international arms inspections (Iraq), return to democratic rule, or an end to a war.

These are all political demands and specific changes are to be undertaken by the target government. The economic effects, in other words, are means to achieve ends, not ends in themselves. This is often made clear by the sender government, which sometimes even apologizes for the hardships created for the public at large. It is regarded as a necessary sacrifice for a higher cause, however. Success is different from the economic dislocation; the dislocations are means to reach the goals. As a second-level defense of economic sanctions, governments and observers alike will often resort to pointing out the successful imposition of the sanctions, rather than their ability to accomplish the changes demanded. Thus, meeting the initial goals will be crucial for the judgment of success. If they have been met, to the satisfaction of the initiator, then the sanctions are successful. This can be judged by observing statements of the sender government.

Third, relating to the second, if the sanctions have achieved the goal, it is logical that the sanctions also should be terminated, preferably with some declaration indicating the sender's satisfaction with the outcome. That will also make clear that the sender believes the changes have been induced by the sanctions.[7] Operationally this means that we should look for successful sanctions among those cases where sanctions have ceased. Where they continue, clearly they have not met the conditions for success. If this is an acceptable procedure, we can note that in only two of the eleven sanctions cases initiated by the UN during the 1990s had the sanctions been lifted by the end of the decade (i.e., December 31, 1999), the initiator having stated that the target country changed behavior and it being possible to argue that there was a connection between sanctions and the behavioral change. These are former Yugoslavia, following the Dayton Accords, and Haiti, following the resignation of the military junta and the reinstatement of the democratically elected government.[8] This would give a success rate close to 20 percent, well in line with previous experiences. As mentioned, in the study of ten cases there was a success rate at this level for sanctions that were wider in scope than those imposed during the 1990s. As mentioned, in the Hufbauer *et al.* study the success rate was given as 34 percent, a comparatively high number.[9] It is safe to conclude, however, that the 1990s, in this regard, do not show a record of more successful economic sanctions than any previous experience.

Even so there is a need for closer scrutiny. The sanctions on the former Yugoslavia (1992–1996) followed a war with Croatia in 1991 and again in 1995, a devastating air campaign, and considerable military setbacks for the Belgrade-supported government in Bosnia. The sanctions had economically weakened the regime, and it was in need of access to international markets and so on. The military efforts certainly also contributed to the country's general economic crisis. All these elements, most likely, contributed to its agreeing to the Dayton Accords in November 1995. However, we should also note that the agreement did not, as such, pose a threat to the regime in Yugoslavia. The agreements regulated the situation in Bosnia, not elsewhere. In fact, almost the reverse is true: the agreements made the Milosevic regime a partner in peace and reduced the external threats to its survival.

The intention of the sanctions was simply to separate Yugoslavia from Bosnia, not to change the regime in Belgrade or affect its behavior in general. There was no connection to a general democratization of Yugoslavia. Nor did the Belgrade regime change its way of operation. By 1998 it was again engaged in a war, in Kosovo, using very similar tactics to those that had been applied in the wars in Bosnia and Croatia. At least, we have to conclude that the effects of the economic sanctions were only one part of the equation explaining Yugoslavia's acceptance of the Dayton Accords. It is, nevertheless, reasonable to conclude that the sanctions had an impact on the political calculations of the regime's policy with respect to Bosnia.

Haiti is a more obvious case of success. It is reminiscent of previous removals of juntas and ruling dynasties in the Caribbean. One successful case of sanctions reported earlier is the US-led embargo on the Dominican Republic in 1960–1962, ending the Trujillo regime (Wallensteen 1968, 1971). The overwhelming power of the US has often prevailed. In this case, the threat of an imminent US invasion, as well as persuasion by a US delegation, led by former President Carter, contributed to the peaceful ending of the situation.

As mentioned above, very few of the new UN sanctions have been comprehensive. They have often included a limited range of goods. Most comparable to sanctions on Rhodesia are the cases of Yugoslavia and Iraq. In both cases, the effects were influenced by the target's involvement in war, or, in the case of Iraq, the experience of repeated air attacks. Either way, the same regimes remained in power, and their modus operandi did not change under the impact of the sanctions and other international pressure. It could legitimately be argued that the success of sanctions should not be understood only in terms of the submission of the target nation to the wishes of the sender. Sanctions might also be important for other reasons (Baldwin 1985). They show that the international community takes certain norms seriously, such as democratic government (e.g., sanctions against military coups; see Haiti) or the fight against terrorism (e.g., sanctions against countries suspected to harbor terrorists; see Libya, Sudan). Also, the resort to arms is such a norm, and the invasion of Kuwait fits that pattern. It is more debatable if there are such international norms prohibiting the internal uses of force by governments or rebels, as the cases of sanctions against Somalia, Liberia, Sierra Leone, Angola, Rwanda, and the former republic of Yugoslavia (Kosovo) would suggest. In all these cases, arms exports were prohibited to the country as a whole, or to certain actors. There are also situations of indiscriminate use of weapons and force against civilians. As genocide is an international norm, sanctions could be related to this in the case of Rwanda. Thus, it appears fruitful to relate some sanctions to a wish to maintain or develop particular norms in the international community. As there are more such references in the sanctions debates and practice in the 1990s, there could today be a broader consensus on such international norms than previously. This would explain the more frequent use of sanctions by global organizations. It might not make sanctions more successful, however, if such norms are seen to be repeatedly violated even after the use of sanctions. An alternative interpretation is that sanctions are expected to reduce fighting and lead to the support of particular peacemaking efforts. In the case of Angola, there was a peace agreement to uphold. In the cases of Liberia and Sierra Leone, such efforts were emerging. Most notable is that there are five such situations in the continent of Africa. With the use of sanctions, the international community could show its concern for the situation and its commitment not to make the situations worse. It also says that it could not find other ways of dealing with the internal wars. This illustrates that the norm-promoting aspect of sanctions is not easily interpreted. Which norms are actually intended to be promoted and what is the effect to be expected? Success would have to be judged by the ability of sanctions to deter repetitions of norm breaking. On this score, there is little evidence of success.

What happened in one part of Africa or even in a neighboring country did not deter leaders in other parts, such as in Liberia or Sierra Leone, from pursuing their goals. Arms embargoes had little deterring effect. In the end, the credibility of any sanction will depend on the success in the narrower sense. The conclusion is that only if the instrumental application, to arrive at the requested change in the target's behavior, has a good track record will sanctions work as a deterrent for other actors and become a credible demonstration of international commitment.

The arms embargo and the pressure on Yugoslavia in the Kosovo crisis relates to another and more recent norm change: the ambition to act early in conflict. The scenarios triggering Western action in this conflict are obvious. They all involved the danger of a conflict spreading from Kosovo into Albania (which had remained tense since the 1997 crisis), Macedonia (which had a preventive deployment already), and from there on to Greece (with which Macedonia had had a serious conflict recently) and connecting to the protracted Turkish–Greek confrontation. The Kosovo conflict had not reached the magnitude of other conflicts, but the requirements of preventive diplomacy seem to spur the actions of Western countries in the war that began in 1998. Sanctions were a part of the measures, but not a strong element.

Thus, it is clear that in the 1990s the world had arrived at a situation where the UN sanctions had not become more effective, although they had been put to a wider use for a wider set of purposes. Looking at the cases outside the UN framework, we have to draw the same conclusion. The US sanctions during the 1990s against North Korea, Iran, China, India, and Pakistan do not seem to have changed the behavior of these states or their leaders in the direction demanded. The EU diplomatic action against Nigeria did not result in changes. In this case, however, a new leader took over in 1998 displaying a different attitude to democratization. Here it can legitimately be asked if this can be attributed to the sanctions policy or, at least, if there is an important combination effect.

Against this background we see that sanctions rarely bring about the dramatic shifts in policy demanded by the sender.[10] As already made clear, this does not exclude the fact that economic sanctions have economic effects and, thus, become serious concerns for leaders. The leaders have to handle difficult problems, and sometimes have gained considerable experience in dealing with difficult situations. All the cases of UN sanctions during the 1990s were directed against authoritarian or totalitarian regimes, which can command the country's resources almost without opposition in dealing with the effects. In addition, they are able to hide the sender's purposes in imposing the sanctions. Certainly, the leaders desire a situation in which the sanctions are lifted, but that is not the same as stating that the sanctions have the political effects intended. Often the demands from outside mean that a regime will have to step down or that it has to abandon a central element of its internal or international policy. Such shifts are more difficult to contemplate, and the economic costs to the country may appear, to the leaders, as smaller than the changes in a central policy concern would be. The trade-off too often speaks in favor of defiance.

The continued low rate of success needs a pause for reflection. The sanctions debate has, in the 1990s, been able to learn a little more from systematic research than previous debates. However, the record of the actual application of this knowledge at the moment of decision-making appears equally poor. This is notable, as the record of failure in sanctions could most effectively be rectified if the policymaker's selection of cases for sanction use was done so as to ensure success. This would mean that sanctions would not be used as often. Also it might be discovered that sanctions are more successful when applied to targets against which they are not at all used today. If such a perspective gained ground, the use of sanctions would not be different from the application of any other instrument: the chances of success and failure should be assessed before the strategy is being used. It would improve the reputation of the sanctions and it would give the world an effective nonviolent instrument.

Sender perspectives

Throughout their modern use, sanctions have been tied to international organizations. They have remained part of the statutes of leading organs. During the Cold War, however, it appears that more sanctions were applied outside such frameworks, whereas in the 1990s they were clearly more frequent inside international organizations. By their very nature, sanctions will require international support, as their technique is to reduce availability of external goods to a particular country and its regime. Thus, bilateral sanctions will seldom be effective in achieving the necessary isolation.

The significance of major powers in making sanctions was evident also in the 1990s: the USA, UK, and France have been important in bringing about sanctions on Yugoslavia (two instances), Iraq, and Haiti. There are still examples of smaller countries inflicting sanctions on other small countries, notably the African states on Burundi. However, the fact that major powers lead sanctions does not in itself determine whether or not sanctions will succeed. Perhaps it is fairer to say that sanctions imposed by major powers will receive more attention than those carried out by other actors. Media coverage is not related to success, however.

The role of media in the 1990s appears more complex than in previous periods. In particular, the ability of media to release support for humanitarian concerns has become a new factor. There was such concern behind the sanctions on South Africa and Rhodesia, but this cannot be compared to the remarkable coverage of Somalia or the international interest in the humanitarian effects of sanctions in Iraq.

The media interest suggests a continuous shift in sanctions motives. In the 1930s the debate was focused on the action of states, in particular major states, and their aggressive actions. In the 1960s, debate, and actions, had a broader concern, but dealt with conflicts such as white–black, colonialism–liberation, racism–democracy, in other words an aggregate level. In the 1990s, however, the individual suffering of women and children has become apparent. The tendency is one of increasingly reducing the sphere of state sovereignty and replacing it with a concern for human beings. The repressive nature of Italy's Fascist regime was part of the consideration, but the major power relations paid less regard to this. The repression of South Africa and Rhodesia's minority regimes was important.

In the internal wars of the 1990s the motives of the different parties appeared secondary to the sufferings inflicted.

In the earlier debates, there was an important *left–right distinction*. Sanctions on Italy, South Africa, and Rhodesia were more likely to be supported by the left than by the right in the Western political spectrum. In the 1990s the patterns have been more complex. Sanctions on Iraq was seen as an adequate reaction by the left, but not by the right. In the crisis over Yugoslavia the left–right continuum was blurred, as happened in Somalia and other African cases. In internal political affairs, left–right considerations have not ceased to be important, but as a guide to international actions they have become less useful. The issues of states, nationality, and territory were more difficult to fit with the established pattern. There might today be a tendency for the right to be more in favor of sanctions than the left: sanctions on Yugoslavia had strong support from conservative regimes in Western Europe, as did sanctions on Libya and Sudan (views of the terrorism issue may follow a left–right continuum). In several of these cases, the "left" may not have been able to suggest a more coherent alternative strategy.

Were there new *internal political constellations* that made sanctions an attractive alternative to leaders in the Western countries? In an innovative analysis, Hoffmann suggested that sanctions were pursued in order to handle domestic cleavages. If this is applied in particular to leading countries, it makes sense, as Hoffmann shows with the cases of Italy and Rhodesia (Hoffmann 1967; Wallensteen 1971). The use of military actions against Yugoslavia or the Serb Republic of Bosnia-Herzegovina was not convincing to leaders and public in Western Europe. The suffering of the populations in Bosnia was apparent, however. The use of peacekeeping troops was seen as a way to protect international humanitarian relief efforts. Sanctions also gained support as a way of reducing fighting. It was possible for leaders in Western countries to show concern, maintain parliamentary and popular support, and not take risks. Unfortunately, it all had little impact on the course of the conflict. Thus, domestic politics may have played an important role in the choice of the strategy. In the sanctions debate, the realization that sanctions are made with a close eye to the national political scene has seldom gained a prominent role, however. It is not difficult to realize that leaders are more concerned about ruling their own country than one far away, where there are no votes to be gained.

There were some changes during the 1990s in motives but, as before, the explanations for success and failure are to be located elsewhere. Major powers or international organizations are not more successful today than they were before.

Target perspectives

Smart sanctions

Much of the focus in the three debates is on the sender, the initiator, of sanctions. The motives are of course important: which goals are to be accomplished and why sanctions are used for this. However, the question of success and failure is more determined by the effects in the recipient country, the target, which suffers the economic onslaught that economic sanctions constitute. The ability of targeted economies to adapt to the new circumstances still tends to be underestimated in the debate. The question of failures of sanctions, thus, reverts to the sender: which groups are, actually, the targets of the sanctions? Here some interesting changes can be observed in the debate as well as in practice. Not only is it true that the targets have shifted from aggressive actors in international affairs to internally repressive actors. Now there are also targets *inside* countries.

The following are some examples. The Security Council actions on Angola have included the targeting of one particular actor, UNITA (National Union for the Total Independence of Angola), as the party not following the internationally recognized agreements (decisions were taken in 1993, 1997, and 1998). The sanctions were targeted on oil and arms deliveries to UNITA, then came to include travel and funds for UNITA officials and their families. In 1998 it also included freezing of funds and trade in diamonds. In the sanctions on former Yugoslavia instituted after the onset of the war in Bosnia in 1992, specific sanctions were imposed on Bosnian Serb areas in 1994. The case of Haiti not only included oil and arms, but the sanctions also aimed at junta members directly, and included the freezing of their bank accounts. In this case, the sanctions were also turned on and off: they were imposed first in June 1993 and were suspended in August the same year, as events were seen to be favorable. However, by October 1993 they were reinstituted and by May 1994 included further categories. In this way, the Haiti case is one of fine-tuning sanctions as well as applying them instrumentally as punishments and rewards for "bad and good behavior" of the junta. A new way of doing the same is to impose sanctions, and then exclude the government the Security Council wants to support. This has been done against Rwanda (arms embargo imposed 1994, government of Rwanda excluded in 1995) and Sierra Leone (oil and arms embargo 1997, ECOWAS [Economic Community of West African States] excluded and since 1998 also the government. In this case, the entry of members of RUF [Revolutionary United Front] is specifically mentioned). These sanctions operate on a level of interference in internal affairs that was unheard of in the previous debates and in the traditional experiences of the UN system. Thoughts of "smarter sanctions" are parallel to the development of smart weapons: more precision, less collateral damage, and thus more efficacy.[11]

There is even a paradox. Whereas such smarter sanctions previously would have been seen as too soft, they are now viewed as the most hard-hitting. Humanitarian concerns have clearly had an effect in the debate. This has to do most closely with the reported effects of sanctions on Iraq (see more below).[12] These concerns are new developments and have considerable attraction. The use of smart sanctions would be ideal. These would include travel restrictions for particular persons and their families, visa requirements, preventing sale of tickets, loss of diplomatic immunity for certain officials, prevention of monetary transactions for particular individuals, withdrawal of scholarships for family members, prevention of normal medical treatment for identified persons, and so on. The list of possible sanctions can be made longer.

Politically, smart sanctions assume that the leaders can be separated from their populations in a simple way. It may have been possible in the case of Haiti, where the members of the military junta were identifiable. The same may have been true for the sanctions against the Dominican Republic thirty years earlier, when the Trujillo family was well known. In these cases the rulers built on a legitimacy that separated them from the rest of the population. In other cases, however, regime leaders may be seen as representatives of entire groups (Smith of the whites in Rhodesia, Milosevic for the Serb nationalist parties, etc.). Sanctions are there not only to remove a particular leader, which smart sanctions seem to imply, but to change the thinking of an entire social group. Otherwise a consequence may be that identified leaders who are undermined by new sanctions are replaceable by other, even "harder," representatives of the group in question. The utility of smart sanctions requires a closer analysis of the target country and the strength of the representatives of the incumbent regime.

It should also be observed that the "smart" approach functions only if the leaders are dependent on international relations. Historically, it can be seen that financial operators are those who are most immediately hit by international sanctions. Thus, if traders, investors, and other commercial interests control the powers of a society, they are likely to be vulnerable to sanctions. They have a strong interest in accommodating the wishes of the sender. The prohibition of travel documents and flight connections as well as financial movements are "smart" sanctions in this case. However, what is to be done in case the regime shows little interest in such operations and is not sensitive to disruption in international relations?

In the case of Rhodesia, the group most directly affected by the sanctions were those who were most dependent on and loyal to Britain. The unilateral declaration of independence was made by other whites who sustained themselves on agriculture and thus were less dependent on international commerce. The sanctions had the effect that, in a short time, the liberal whites were forced to leave the country or find means of living that meant that they contributed to the defense against the sanctions. It is likely that the same has happened with sanctions on Iraq, Sudan, and Libya. Furthermore, these countries have enough resources and regional connections to maintain their economies without facing mass starvation. The example of Haiti tells us that, in cases of close dependence, sanctions are likely to have more devastating effects than in other contexts. It appears that Saddam Hussein, Colonel Khadaffi, and General Bashir are neither interested in visiting Western countries nor dependent for their political survival on the links with these countries. The opposite is actually true: they are sustaining themselves in power partly on the fact that they are anti-Western. The sanctions, paradoxically, serve their political purpose! Their opposition to the West is made more visible to the public.

The bank account sanctions also require a high integration into the international economy. Such sanctions have been instituted on Libya, UNITA in Angola, and Haiti. They are likely to be effective on very corrupt regimes, which constitute a part of the international economy, have resources that are attractive to the outside world, and thus are sensitive to disruptions in financial flows. Such sanctions may be more effective against a Zaire under Mobutu, or an Indonesia under Suharto. They might in fact be so effective that a discreet threat may be sufficient for them to submit to external demands.

Smart sanctions have to face a special challenge. It becomes a way of singling out individuals. They will have vested interests of their own in the outcomes. Thus, settlements of sanctions situations might include a factor of personal fear that has not been the case before. The leaders will ask themselves "will the sanctions against me actually cease or will I face renewed troubles?" Whether such fears help to bring out a readiness to agree or rather result in increased defiance needs to be sorted out. As has been observed in the case of the war crimes tribunals, it might provide an extra incentive for leaders not to submit to the opponent. Such sanctions do open up new possibilities and would be interesting to explore further.

Comprehensive sanctions

Among the new, comprehensive sanctions, the former Yugoslavia is an interesting case. The economies of the different Yugoslav republics were interlinked and the violent break-up also meant that the economies of the new units were grinding to a halt. The war efforts added to this. The sanctions contributed to reduce the economic dynamics. Instead a culture of smuggling emerged, and Mafia networks were created throughout the neighboring countries.[13] The sanctions resulted in a perverse economy, which served to cement the existing regime. The former republic of Yugoslavia became a center for organized crime operating clandestinely all over Europe. The regime was not shaken, however. Instead, sanctions have become a part of Serb mythology as propagated by the official media. The targets of the UN economic sanctions display one consistent pattern: they are all authoritarian regimes or groupings which rely strongly on the use of police and military for maintaining control. This is an important observation affecting the outcome of sanctions, particularly in the case of comprehensive sanctions. The regimes have often had power instruments under their control already before the sanctions were imposed. This means that they have been able to project their view of the issues of contention and the reasons from sanctions.[14] The complaints by the initiators of sanctions have been a consistent one: the targets do not understand why the sanctions are imposed. The ability of the targets to see themselves as victims is not surprising and should be expected. Authoritarian regimes are likely to be able to fight sanctions with whatever means are at their disposal, including their control over media. Thus, we find in all cases of sanctions smuggling, shady deals, strange transaction, shipments that have gone "astray," falsification of documents, and so on.

Still, economic sanctions do have economic effects. Governments often will admit that and may, on many occasions, blame more on sanctions than is warranted. The sanctions may provide a convenient scapegoat for mismanagement or incompetence on the part of the target government. Sanctions can also stimulate economic investment in areas that previously depended on imports. In such cases the sanctions actually function as tariffs, with the advantage of being imposed from the outside.[15]

Clearly, a new element in the sanctions debate is the question of *humanitarian effects* of sanctions. This has been given particular significance in the case of

sanctions against Iraq. It is surprising that the same aspect has not received prominence in the sanctions against former Yugoslavia. The basis for the claim of the
particular humanitarian effects of the sanctions against Iraq is an article published
in *The Lancet* (Zaidi and Fawzi 1995). The calculations made by the Food and
Agriculture Organization of the United Nations on the basis of this study suggested that up to 560,000 Iraqi children may have died as result of UN economic
sanctions. However, few observers seem to have taken note of the subsequent letter
to the editor by one of the authors, reporting that the results from the 1995 survey
could not be verified in follow-ups for 1996 and 1997. Clearly, the death rates of
children were much lower and consequently the effects of sanctions less dramatic,
to the extent that there is a direct link between the sanctions and the suffering
(Zaidi 1997).[16] The humanitarian concern is new. There were reports suggesting
that sanctions on South Africa would in fact hurt the black African population
more, but these were often dismissed as part of South African propaganda. In the
case of Iraq, which is not likely to meet human standards of honesty, the impact
discussion has been different. It is interesting to ask why.

There are two plausible explanations, which do not exclude each other. The
first is that, in general, humanitarian concern has become greater. The reactions
to many of the crises facing the world in the post-Cold War period has had a
humanitarian root. The conflicts have been seen primarily as humanitarian disasters, and thus prompted humanitarian support. It is a sign of the times that
the UN created a Department of Humanitarian Affairs only in 1992, following
a General Assembly resolution in 1991. The interventions in the wars in Bosnia
and Somali were undertaken as ways of protecting humanitarian deliveries. In the
Cold War period, humanitarian concerns were, in the dominant discourse, made
dependent on whether it benefited one or the other side in the Cold War. Wars
since the early 1990s may be seen more realistically as the human suffering they
actually always have been.

The second explanation is that the sanctions on South Africa and Rhodesia had
strong support from the opposition movements. Solidarity groups carried the sanctions efforts in public opinion, particularly in the West.[17] The opposition in these
countries expected to benefit from the weakening of the regime that the sanctions
were expected to inflict. It was part of a strategy to bring down the government.
In the case of Iraq, the opposition groups had little role in forming Western public
opinion. They may not even have had influence on Western decision-makers'
policy. Their popular support in Iraq is debatable. Clearly, they were not the source
of alternative information or alternative interpretations. They were not the ones to
explain whether or not the suffering of the Iraqis was going to result in a political
change. This is to suggest that sanctions require an opposition for success. This can
be seen as a causal mechanism for sanctions success: the double grip.

The "double grip"

A key finding for success of sanctions is what could be termed the double grip
theory.[18] The economic sanctions will create political problems for the incumbent

government in the target country. It will use the instruments available to maintain itself in power. If there is a strong opposition, which is in agreement with the externally imposed sanctions, it can use this situation in order to bring pressure from inside on the government. The government will, thus, face a two-way struggle: to reduce the sanctions from abroad and to handle the opposition at home. If the sanctions are maintained and the opposition is acting internally, the government will find itself squeezed from two sides, a double grip. This may explain why sanctions succeed in some instances in bringing down a government. This was the pressure that operated on the Dominican Republic in the early 1960s. It was also the situation in which the apartheid regime found itself in the late 1980s (its lack of military success added to this). It can be debated if the same arguments also apply in other instances of (limited) sanction successes. The Milosevic regime may have been under more domestic pressure in 1995 than is readily admitted. The large mobilization against the government a year later (against the fraudulent elections, 1996–1997) suggests this. In the case of Haiti, there was considerable public discontent with the military junta and it must have realized that it had little staying power in face of continued sanctions or a military invasion. Let us return to this theme shortly.

International system perspectives

Major powers and sanctions

The reactions of the international community are obviously important for the success of sanctions. The political and economic isolation of the target country is a prerequisite for success. This is a reason why international organizations are used for sanctions, as this will generate more international support for the sender and more isolation for the target. Most important are the reactions among major powers and the target's neighbors.

The most obvious change between the three sanctions debates is the difference in the major power configurations. This is captured by the commonly used labels: "inter-war," "Cold War," and "post-Cold War" periods. The world has moved from a system of five or six major powers via bipolarization to the present situation with one superpower. Sanctions against Italy between the wars were abandoned as several major powers were not supportive (in particular the USA and Germany). In the period of the second debate, sanctions were mostly made outside the UN framework and often became part of the Cold War dynamics. The two UN-imposed sanctions in this period had significant support from major powers. Even that proved not sufficient to achieve the isolation desired by the sanctions initiators.

It is noteworthy that, in the third debate, the isolation issue has not been as prominent. Instead impatience with the sanctions record has resulted in a strategic discussion about military action. In the cases of Iraq and Sudan such measures were actually taken. The bombings were repeated against Iraq, reaching a peak with the heavy bombardments in December 1998. The actions were done outside the framework of the UN. This is a clear indication that, first of all, the sanctions had not achieved the desired goals and, second, that the UN is increasingly seen as an obstacle for US policy. The sanctions against Sudan were supplemented in 1998 with the bombings in Khartoum, following the attacks on the US embassies in Dar-es-Salaam and Nairobi. Even before this the United States was supporting a military strategy against Sudan. The various movements resisting the National Islamic Front regime in Khartoum were brought together in a broad alliance. A new military front was opened in 1997. The military actions have so far not brought about the desired changes.

Military action was in 1998 repeatedly threatened against Yugoslavia, in connection with the Kosovo conflict. In this case, the United States acted in concert with leading allies in NATO. The option of renewed sanctions, apart from the arms embargo imposed in 1998, against Yugoslavia seemed to be less important, perhaps indicating dissatisfaction with their impact in the previous period.

In the case of Haiti, a military invasion was very close when the military junta agreed to step down. In some of the remaining cases, the threat of military action has been less important or nonexistent (Angola, Liberia, Somalia, Rwanda, Sierra Leone, perhaps Libya).

The threat of escalating sanctions into military action by major powers is a new feature in the debate. It can be linked to the changed international scene. In the Cold War years, there was always a danger of military measures bringing a conflict into the Cold War followed by nuclear escalation. In some instances, military actions were taken (e.g. Czechoslovakia, Afghanistan, Granada, Panama) without considerations of sanctions. In these cases the danger of escalation was low as the interventions occurred in areas that were part of the "sphere of interest" of either side. In the post-Cold War period there are fewer constraints of this sort. The military intervention option gains ground. For the future this might be a more ominous development. If a relatively peaceful option, such as sanctions, is seen as unsuccessful, the temptation to instigate military action may increase as the "only alternative" available.

Neighbors and sanctions

Isolation with the help of other major powers is not the only international system aspect of sanctions. A consistent concern in the sanctions debate has been the significance of neighboring countries. In the case of Italy, neighbors such as Switzerland were neutral, which meant that trade could continue as before. Other neighbors suffered considerably when trying to follow the sanctions. In the case of Rhodesia the trade could continue through South Africa and Portuguese-controlled territories. A neighbor faithful to the sanctions was Zambia, thus being exposed to severe economic strains and receiving little understanding internationally. In the cases of the 1990s the lack of cooperation of neighbors such as Iran in the case of Iraq, or many of the weak neighbors around Yugoslavia, has been important for breaking the sanctions. The issue is a consistent one and no ways of carrying the sanctions to a complete implementation have been devised.[19]

All cases, whether successful or not, point to the difficulties in isolating a particular country or, even more so, a part of a country. The target regime will have strong incentives to evade the sanctions and will use available resources to make a flow of crucial goods coming through, be it oil, spare parts for military equipment, machinery, or other important items. It can build on the fact that no government is strong enough, and government control over the economy is globally receding. It can also take advantage of an increasingly globalized world where the market is more supreme than ever and purchasing power matters more than political affiliations. Isolation strategies are likely to become even more difficult for the future.

Isolation, opposition and the double grip

How, then, can sanctions be successful at all? The theory of double grip points to the need for political isolation. There has to be a certain economic effect, but not having political allies in the international system may be more important for a regime. Such allies can be instrumental in helping to break sanctions. However, they may be most important in bolstering the will to fight back. The Iraqi regime has not been that isolated. On the contrary, the highly publicized actions against Iraq have consistently generated support for Iraq throughout the Arab world, although not among other Arab regimes. This may have helped the regime's morale. The same is not true of the Serb nationalist regime in Belgrade. It has found little appeal globally outside Serb nationalist circles. Russia has acquired a political significance for Belgrade beyond its economic or military role in the world. Thus, Milosevic would have been more willing to adapt Yugoslavia's policies if this had been a request from Russia. It would probably be able to withstand sanctions longer, but not without that crucial support. It appears safe to conclude that Russia's policies may have been more important in making Yugoslavia obey the Dayton Accords or come to the negotiations in Rambouillet on Kosovo. The internal weaknesses combined with the strength of international political isolation is what provides the success of the sanctions, that is, the regime in the target country is exposed to a double grip.

Organizations and sanctions

Sanctions policies have been important for organizational identity. Had the League of Nations' sanctions against Italy resulted in the withdrawal of Italian troops from Abyssinia in the 1930s it would have been a boost to the organization. In a way, the architects behind the League's sanctions policy gambled and lost not only the sanctions but the entire international organization. In the second debate, sanctions issues have been important to particular organizations (e.g., CoCom, OAS, OAU [Organization of African Unity], CMEA, The League of Arab States). They served to give them a role. The same is true for the UN sanctions. However, it means that the future of such organizations may hinge on the success of sanctions. The sanctions undertaken during the 1990s, if not successful, could affect the legitimacy of the UN. However, the organization has also been involved in other actions, notably a large number of peacekeeping operations and peace treaties, which probably have a more lasting impact on the credibility of the organization. It is not likely that the reputation of the UN today rests only on the sanctions issue. It has more diversified functions than did the League of Nations.

It is interesting to see that the sanctions policy, in some cases, served to unite countries which otherwise might have been at loggerheads. There is a tendency for regional organizations to have particular enemies as focal points for internal cohesion. This is clear in the case of the Arab League and its boycott against Israel. Also a similar significance could be seen in the sanctions against Portuguese colonialism, Southern Rhodesia, and South Africa. As decolonization now is over as a major process, the OAU today is finding a new role as an instrument for conflict resolution in African states. The repeated crises over Bosnia and Kosovo, which both position NATO countries against the government in Belgrade, may have similar functions in consolidating a new role for NATO in the post-Cold War period. This is particular true if the outcome is a semi-permanent stationing of NATO forces in Southeast Europe.

General conclusions

UN sanctions are today more often resorted to than before. In the three sanctions debates, those of the 1930s, the 1960s, and the present day, there are some consistent patterns. There continues to be a preoccupation with the motives of the initiator, but they have less to do with the outcome than the countermeasures of the receiver, the target of the sanctions. A new concern is the one of humanitarian considerations. They did not play much role in previous debates, partly because they were dismissed as unimportant, partly because the sanctions were having less such impact. It also seems that the humanitarian effects in the sanctions against Iraq have been exaggerated. Little suggests that sanctions today are more effective than they were before. The conditions for successful sanctions, the double grip, are often lacking and sanctions are brought about less as an effective, nonviolent tool for the solution of a problem. More often the choice of sanction is conditioned by a need to appear to be "taking action," particularly to the domestic audience. The continued globalization makes it less likely that sanctions will become more successful in the future. Reduced control by governments means that it will be more difficult to enforce sanctions and the increasingly unfettered markets will provide more opportunities for sanction breakers. The interest in smart sanctions is one way out of the present sanctions dilemma. However, smart sanctions may in fact tilt the use of sanctions even more to become an instrument only of rich actors against poor ones. Already, there is a tendency for sanctions to be one instrument – among many – for major powers. In a world of only one superpower, it becomes an instrument to be used with others, in a huge arsenal. Thus, it remains important to insist that sanctions be carried out through the framework of the UN to keep them as a less frequently used, better targeted, and more legitimate measure for the world community. A more optimistic but long-term approach is to support the development of a global civil society consisting of nongovernmental organizations, action groups, and transnational linkages, thus building up internal peaceful opposition in potential problem countries. This would enable earlier reaction to threatening developments, create channels for communication in crisis, and be a resource in post-crisis developments. In this way the sanctions debate of this century might find inputs for a fresher start.

Notes

1 As is the case in any summary, this is too sharp a conclusion. For instance, the Taubenfelds consistently pointed to the Italian experience, as did others with a background in international law. The proponents of sanctions, however, seldom made such linkages.

2 It is noteworthy that the concept of "aggression" was not used in the formal documents, although the concept was very much part of the debate (Christer Ahlström, Uppsala, has pointed this out).

3 Sanctions were actually imposed on the People's Republic of China in the Korean war, but this was possible only through the absence of the Soviet Union at the meeting. In this conflict, furthermore, the armed intervention was the chief instrument.

4 The author is presently conducting a study on this theme.

5 The answer to the question why is not clearly responded to in the latest round of the debate (Pape 1998a,b; Elliot 1998).

6 It should be made clear that this chapter builds on thorough research into the previous periods of sanctions and that reflections on the 1990s are more intuitive.

7 There are cases in which changes took place, and sanctions were ended, but the senders did not attribute the changes to the sanctions, notably the ending of African states' sanctions against Portugal after the May 1974 revolution. The revolution set in motion the liberation of the territories of Angola, Guinea (Bissau), Cape Verde islands, and Mozambique. Only East Timor saw a different development.

8 One more case may be in the making as Libya agreed in 2000 to a trial of the men accused of the Lockerbie bombings.

9 Pape (1997, 1998a,b) argues that is should rather be 5 percent.

10 There is a slight shift in the argumentation pointing to the role of sanctions in a package of measures. The contribution of sanctions specifically is then even more difficult to entangle, but the trend is interesting (see Elliot 1998).

11 The concept of "smart sanctions" was used in the conference in London, December 1998. The word captures well the new intentions in the modern sanctions debate.

12 Pape (1998b: 197), who argues very strongly against sanctions, claims that the sanctions on Iraq have inflicted "incredible human costs (including the deaths of more than 500 000 children)." Paradoxically, if the numbers were to be true the sanctions must be economically very efficient.

13 In Albania this resulted in an artificial "economic growth" and the ending of the sanctions by 1996 resulted in a complete economic collapse in 1997, leading to a Western peace operation to help stabilize the country. By 1998 Albania had become a supporter of the Kosovar Albanian uprising against the former republic of Yugoslavia.

14 Galtung (1967) gives the first analysis of the dynamic effects of sanctions on the target country and it remains valid as a study not only of Rhodesia but of sanctions in general.

15 This was an important finding in Wallensteen (1968, 1971, 1983) and was seen in a number of the cases of comprehensive sanctions (listed in Table 14.2).

16 I am grateful to Johan von Schreeb for this reference. For arguments pointing to the inadequacy of the Iraqi government in making sure humanitarian assistance reaches the needy, see Stremlau (1996: 44–45).

17 Sellström (1999) shows this for the case of Sweden.

18   Wallensteen (1968, 1971, 1983), but this term was not used in those texts.
19   An interesting surveillance scheme was instituted for the sanctions that were aimed at the Bosnian Serb Republic on the border to Yugoslavia (see Pellnäs 1996).

References

Adler-Karlsson, G. 1968. *Western Economic Warfare, 1947–1997*. Stockholm: Almquist & Wiksell.

Baer, G.W. 1967. *The Coming of the Italian–Ethiopian War*. Cambridge, MA: Harvard University Press.

Baldwin, David A. 1985. *Economic Statecraft*. Princeton, NJ: Princeton University Press.

Baldwin, David A. 1998. 'Evaluating Economic Sanctions', *International Security*, 23 (2): 189–195.

Clark, E. (ed.). 1932. *Boycotts and Peace*. A Report by the Committee on Economic Sanctions, New York.

Cortright, D. and G.A. Lopez (eds.). 1995. *Economic Sanctions: Panacea or Peacebuilding in a Post-Cold War World?* Boulder, CO: Lynne Rienner.

Doxey, M. 1980. *Economic Sanctions and International Enforcement*. London: Macmillan.

Elliott, Kimberly Ann. 1998. 'The Sanctions Glass', *International Security*, 23 (1): 50–65.

Galtung, J. 1967. 'On the Effects of International Economic Sanctions: With Examples from the Case of Rhodesia', *World Politics*, 19 (3): 378–416, also in M. Nincic and P. Wallensteen (eds.), *Dilemmas of Economic Coercion*. New York: Praeger.

Hoffmann, F. 1967. 'The Functions of Economic Sanctions', *Journal of Peace Research*, 4: 140–160.

Hufbauer, Gary Clyde, Jeffrey J. Schott and Kimberly Ann Elliot. 1990. *Economic Sanctions Reconsidered*, 2nd ed., 2 vols. Washington, DC: Institute for International Economics.

Leiss, A.C. (ed.). 1965. *Apartheid and United Nations Collective Measures: An Analysis*. Carnegie Endowment for International Peace (mimeo).

Martin, L. 1992. *Coercive Cooperation: Explaining Multilateral Economic Sanctions*. Princeton, NJ: Princeton University Press.

Mitrany, O. 1925. *The Problem of International Sanctions*. New York: Oxford University Press.

Nicholson, M. 1967. 'Tariff Wars and a Model of Conflict', *Journal of Peace Research*, 3 (1): 26–38.

Nincic, M. and P. Wallensteen (eds.). 1983. *Dilemmas of Economic Coercion*. New York: Praeger.

Pape, R.A. 1997. 'Why Economic Sanctions Do Not Work', *International Security*, 22 (2): 90–136.

Pape, R.A. 1998a. 'Why Economic Sanctions Still Do Not Work', *International Security*, 23 (1): 66–77.

Pape, R.A. 1998b. 'Evaluating Economic Sanctions', *International Security*, 23 (2): 195–198.

Pellnäs, B. 1996. *De hundra dagarna*. Stockholm: Bonniers.

Segal, R. (ed.). 1964. *Sanctions against South Africa*. London: Penguin.

Sellström, T. 1999. *Sweden and National Liberation in Southern Africa*, Vol. 1. Uppsala: Nordiska Afrikainstitutet.

Stremlau, J. 1996. *Sharpening International Sanctions: Towards a Stronger Role for the United Nations*. A Report to the Carnegie Commission on Preventing Deadly Conflict, New York.

Taubenfeld, H.J. 1958. *Economic Sanctions: An Appraisal and Case Study*. Columbia University, New York (mimeo).

Taubenfeld, H.J. and Taubenfeld, R. 1964. 'The Economic Weapon: The League and the United Nations', *Proceedings of the American Society of International Law*, 1964: 183–205.

Wallensteen, P. 1968. 'Characteristics of Economic Sanctions', *Journal of Peace Research*, 5 (3): 247–266.

Wallensteen, P. 1983. 'Economic Sanctions: Ten Modern Cases and Three Important Lessons', in M. Nincic and P. Wallensteen (eds.), *Dilemmas of Economic Coercion*. New York: Praeger.

Wallensteen, P. 1971. *Ekonomiska sanktioner*. Stockholm: Prisma.

Walters, F.P. 1965. *A History of the League of Nations*. London: Oxford University Press.

Zaidi, S. 1997. 'Child Mortality in Iraq', *The Lancet*, 350: 1105.

Zaidi, S. and Fawzi, M.C. 1995. 'Health of Baghdad's Children', *The Lancet*, 346: 1485.

15 Sanctions and peacebuilding

Lessons from Africa[1]

Sanctions in Africa

What are the lessons that can be drawn from cases of sanctions dealing with the end of wars and pertaining to supporting peacebuilding efforts after war? This chapter reports on two such situations, which can help generate lessons of value for the use of sanctions with such ambitions. In all, eight countries in sub-Saharan Africa have been exposed to United Nations (UN) sanctions since the end of the Cold War (Wallensteen 2011). All but one has dealt with civil war situations, the eighth case being South Africa, where the sanctions were targeted on ending the apartheid regime in the country. This field study was carried out in 2006 in two cases in Western Africa. They were selected as both found themselves in fragile, ongoing post-conflict experiences. They are neighbors and the events in one country affect those in the other. Both had been prosperous, building on mineral exports in one case and on cocoa in the other. Sanctions were used to influence the development. In one of the cases, Liberia, a peace agreement in 2003 aimed at ending fourteen years of war. A successful election in 2005 helped to stabilize the situation and the elected candidate, Mrs. Ellen Johnson Sirleaf, was installed as president. A UN operation, UNMIL, was in place. In the other case, Côte d'Ivoire, the country was in an uneasy post-conflict situation without a comprehensive agreement having been implemented and the country was territorially divided between North and South, each with its army, in a cease-fire supervised by a UN peacekeeping operation (UNOCI) which incorporated forces from the Economic Community of West African States (ECOWAS), the West African regional organization. France also had forces in the country. Thus, sanctions had different ambitions: peacebuilding in the case of Liberia, preventing a return to war in Côte d'Ivoire.

The war in Liberia was initiated in 1989 and continued until 2003, whereas the armed conflict in Côte d'Ivoire began in September 2002, and lingered on until 2005. There is not only a temporal sequence pointing to connections. Arms flows and soldiers could easily go from one country to the other, and the UN was running parallel peacekeeping missions in the two countries.

Sanctions were imposed by the UN Security Council at various junctures of the political developments, beginning with measures on Liberia in 1992 and then on Côte d'Ivoire in 2004. The sanctions have included arms embargoes, sanctions on particular commodities, and measures targeting particular individuals (freezing of assets and travel bans). The UN has combined its sanctions efforts with other engagements, notably peacekeeping missions, Special Representatives as mediators, and development programs by different UN agencies. In addition, the European Union (EU) has been present. Major powers paid attention to the two countries, notably France, with its own forces stationed in Côte d'Ivoire; the USA, with a particular concern for Liberia; and the UK, with its forces intervening in neighboring Sierra Leone in 2001.

The aim of the sanctions on Côte d'Ivoire was to stimulate the peace process, following the success of the cease-fire in ending actual fighting between the two sides. The government controlled the south of the country, and the opposition forces were merged into one army, the New Forces (Forces Nouvelles, FN). The opposition demanded a more correct process of deciding on citizenship, making issues of ID cards and identification central in the peace process. There were serious disagreements over who would be regarded as a citizen, and many in the North felt that that they were excluded from national politics. The war erupted following contested elections in 2001. Coupled to this was the question of disarming the opposing forces to prevent intimidation in the planned elections. Both sides saw free, fair, democratic elections (particularly to the presidency) as the most reasonable way of ending the military stalemate.

The aim of the UN sanctions in Liberia was partly also to prevent the return of war but largely through supporting the efforts of peacebuilding undertaken after the war. This meant a concern not only for elections and democracy but also for economic revenue for a more representative state. Thus, sanctions on diamonds and timber were kept long after the war had ended and a peace agreement had been signed.

The possible effects of these sanctions have to be measured in relation to all other international activities as well as to the general political and military dynamics of war and peace locally, regionally and globally. This chapter discusses the ability of sanctions to bring about the changes demanded by the UN in two fragile states. The chapter incorporates the report that the present author did together with colleagues Mikael Eriksson and Daniel Strandow in 2006. It was written for the attention of the Swedish Ministry for Foreign Affairs, the UN Secretariat, and the concerned public at the time. Thus, the text in the next three sections is kept in its original time reference, supplemented with postscripts updating the situation to the end of 2010.

Sanctions on Côte d'Ivoire: a report from 2006

Challenges to the UN

The general atmosphere which the UN encounters in Côte d'Ivoire is one of considerable tension underneath a surface of cordiality and calm. There is an alarming negative spiral of events marked by a lack of a serious understanding of the dangers possibly facing the country in a short period of time. For instance, President Laurent Gbagbo referred at the UN Peacekeeping Day on May 29, 2006, to the situation in Côte d'Ivoire as a "small crisis." Moreover, an attitude of continuing "politics as usual" prevailed in the interviews we conducted with political leaderships, in spite of very clear warning signals of what could come if the political situation does not improve. It was remarkable to find media coverage of peace efforts and the UN to be unfriendly. On July 17, the President was quoted as saying in a radio broadcast that the UN peacekeepers were biased in favor of rebels and that they "should understand that they are here because we want them." On July 26, the UN Security Council issued a statement calling on all parties to "play their parts to implement commitments."[2] In short, the presence of the UN appears respected and effective but not liked or loved, and the situation requires close observation.

Given experience in West Africa of many "small crises" having developed into major wars and state failure, this attitude of normal politics is remarkable, not to say disturbing. After all, a large part of the country is outside government control; the economy is gradually slowing down and unemployment increasing. All these are signs which responsible leaders would consider worrisome and lead to quick and creative solutions. Rather than displaying such concern, the UN processes of disarmament, demobilization, and reintegration (DDR) and identification of citizenship have been – deliberately by the parties, it seems – slowed in some parts of the country. This is bothersome and the process might have serious difficulties reaching the necessary completion, to make elections scheduled for October 2006 free and fair. For the UN this is a challenge to deal with, without sounding too alarmist.[3]

More specifically, we could observe that the UN and its peacekeeping mission in the country faced unique experiences. One was the organized, hostile but not armed, demonstrations directed at the UNOCI headquarters in January 2006, which created security concerns for the peacekeepers and UNOCI staff. The political leadership finally got together and paid respects to the UN, thus reducing antagonism. This illustrated both how closely related violence is to the political developments and inadequacies in the composition of the UN force, particularly its lack of a robust force (such as the Quick Reaction Force, QRF, with UNMIL in Liberia, anti-riot police and helicopters).

Thus, the UN-arranged Peacekeeping Day of May 29, 2006, was a timely event and a success as it may have helped to strengthen the attitudes of the importance of UN presence. However, only two days later one of the newspapers warned of another Rwanda in Côte d'Ivoire, suggesting that the fate of the people of the South lay in the hands of those of the North just as the fate of the Tutsis of Rwanda lay in the hands of the Hutus. The message was also reinforced by pictures of slaughtered people from the Rwanda genocide (*Le Temps*, May 31, 2006). This was inflammatory and not likely to facilitate the creation of a reasonable climate for future negotiations. This is the more noteworthy as the media are directly connected to leading personalities in the South. There are strong reasons for the UN Security Council and/or the EU to consider whether such media coverage is reconcilable with the demands of Resolutions 1572:6, 1609:2(v), and 1633:16 or with the EU requirements indicated in the Cotonou Partnership Agreement (covering the principles of Good Governance, Human Rights and Democracy). EU sanctions might be a possible addition or supplement to those of the UN in this regard.

UN Secretary-General Kofi Annan visited Yamoussoukro on July 5, convening a mini-summit including the presidents of Côte d'Ivoire, Nigeria, and South Africa. Speaking to the press he said that the participants agreed that they were "going to do their maximum to ensure that the calendar is respected."[4] This way of highlighting the significance is very much in line with our conclusions.

The UN arms embargo

All sides appear to agree that the arms embargo has been useful. There was little publicly stated interest in removing this measure. However, there were considerable complaints about possible violations. Interviewees gave few specifications, but there was communality in views that the national borders are porous and that neighboring countries (particularly those where there is no UN peacekeeping presence) are not properly monitored, and that both parties were not complying fully. For instance, it was reported that small arms were brought from Liberia toward the separation zone in Côte d'Ivoire (without the control of the government). Such reports have also come from the UN Expert Panels, UNOCI, and French sources. This suggests a need for a more robust presence of the UN, especially a significant deployment during the upcoming elections, so as to prevent the accumulation of weapons for use in the event of an "undesirable" electoral outcome.[5]

Patrolling of borders with helicopters and cooperation with UNMIL are additional measures, but also agreements with neighboring countries, notably Burkina Faso and Guinea-Conakry, should be contemplated, even allowing for the stationing of UN monitoring missions in these countries. Patrols should be made both of the long forest borders and of the sea coast (the last point stems from our hearing unspecified reports of clandestine deliveries of cargo from boats along the coast). Such measures should be seen as only temporary and preventive in nature, so as to ensure a peaceful outcome after the ending of the UNOCI mandate period. The promise of lifting these measures after the formation of a democratically elected government would provide the parties with an incentive to find a mutually satisfactory solution.

Furthermore, in order to target the flow of arms as accurately as possible and to prevent smuggling through the borders, regional assessments are needed. In-depth scrutiny could be made by well-trained, local researchers. Researchers expressed willingness to take on such tasks, given some basic resources. Another possibility is to engage local communities, clans, and ethnic groups, particularly at crucial transit spots, to act like watchdogs of smuggling routes. They are most knowledgeable about ongoing border trade.

Individual sanctions

Three persons were listed by the UN Sanctions Committee in February 2006. The selection of these individuals has created some consternation and a bit of ridicule.

This was true both among those targeted (for instance, one of the targets "threw a large party to celebrate his listing") and among independent observers who saw little point in the present selection of targets. In many interviews and discussions it came out that at least two of the three targeted individuals were not seen as "big fish."

Given the long period with a threat of sanctions, the actual use of them was now seen as something "to scare children" with, nothing more. It was often pointed out that the use of UN sanctions was not consistent with the four Council resolution criteria. Instead, the present targeting appeared to stem from the threats to the UN itself, and not to the peace process as such. Hence, the signals were not clear to the audience in Côte d'Ivoire. Furthermore, targeting these three persons has not been adequate to drive home the need for fair elections and the importance of preventing renewed fighting. However, when asked to come up with suggestions on "bigger fish" to be targeted, most interviewees were not forthcoming. Some pointed to the existence of a list from 2004 of some ninety persons suspected of involvement in a massacre. Clearly, UNOCI had not specified these three particular targets to be those for targeted sanctions. There is an urgent need to improve on the UN record on this score and consider a wider application of sanctions, so as to ensure the orderly continuation of the present electoral, identification, and disarmament processes, and the overall peace process.

Throughout our mission we heard about the slow pace of this process, and that more urgency was needed. To move these efforts forward, sanctions could contribute with a more complex use of targeting. For instance, adding more significant individuals such as owners of some of the most troublesome media would make the message clearer. Also this would have to include people acting irresponsibly on both sides.

By stating explicitly why particular individuals have been selected and by specifying a first time period of application, the aims of listing become more obvious. Those listed would know what they need to do to be removed from the list. Such a vigorous use of individually targeted sanctions against more significant individuals is likely to increase personal impact (as they are traveling and/or have resources abroad). Clearer explanations of who is on the UN sanctions list would also improve the significance and credibility of UN sanctions. Such flexible usage has been a common conclusion from the three formative international processes on targeted sanctions (the Interlaken, Bonn–Berlin, and Stockholm processes: Biersteker *et al.* 2001; Brzoska 2001; Wallensteen *et al.* 2003).

A particular element in this conflict is the presence of UN personnel in the country. There might be retaliation against UN personnel if such measures affect significant individuals. Some precautionary measures might, thus, be needed to protect staff and peacekeepers, when the Council takes sanctions decisions.

Sanctions on natural resources: diamonds

A diamond embargo was imposed on Côte d'Ivoire in December 2005 through UN Security Council Resolution 1643 (2005). Since it was so recently imposed it has been difficult to get clear-cut opinions regarding its effect. The diamond production areas are located in the north of the country and are mainly controlled by the New Forces, the rebel group challenging the government at the time, and now, in principle, part of the national government. According to the Panel of Experts for Côte d'Ivoire, a source of income for New Forces is "taxes" from the production and export of diamonds to neighboring countries. The greater part of their income is, however, estimated to be based on timber and, possibly, gold. With New Forces militarily holding most of the north and since UNOCI cannot control all border regions, diamonds may exit Côte d'Ivoire fairly easy. The diamond embargo does, most likely, have the effect of preventing a return to pre-war production levels of 200,000 carats per year (Expert Panel Report, S/2006/204, 10).

DDR, the identification process and the upcoming elections

Almost all current political energy appeared concentrated on the upcoming elections. They are to take place by the end of October 2006. Sticking to the time lines, however, requires an acceleration of processes of citizen identification (the ID cards are needed for voter registration) and for disarming forces (DDR). This is why the July 5 mini-summit was significant. Political leaders have indicated that dates may be changed by "a day or two," particularly "if we are not ready." This opens the way for manipulation. If this is the preference of leaders on all sides, it, of course, has to be respected as a matter of internal affairs. Nevertheless, as soon as a date is specified, that should be adhered to and in that situation there is not much to be gained from a delay. To the contrary, the only result is likely to be growing suspicion of manipulation. The time frame is tight, as identification has to be done in a way that gives rise to general satisfaction and as some progress in disarmament has to be demonstrated, for both North and South.[6] It seems that assistance could be contemplated in helping this process, through technical means as well as other expertise. However, there are also other important measures. Further imposition of targeted sanctions might be an alternative if elections are not conducted properly. The understanding in this report is that sanctions can be used to accelerate the peace process. The process has made considerable advances, by having a new government led by prime minister Charles Konnan Banny, who has a record of responsible actions. From those concerned with the peace process he gets considerable credit for being effective. However, there is a sentiment that, for instance, civil society is not involved in the process; that peacemaking becomes the exclusive concern of conventional political actors and takes on a technical character (on identification, on disarmament). Thus, the peace process risks becoming one that does not involve significant sectors of society, notably women, nongovernmental organizations (NGOs), and others concerned. An idea is that there should be a National Dialogue Forum on Peace, where all actors could be participating and be helpful in generating ideas. To avoid polarization and societal tensions in connection with the elections this should be considered as a useful means.

Côte d'Ivoire is facing a tough near future. Only visionary thinking based on a realistic understanding of the dangers can help guide the country to reunification, democracy, and a return to economic growth. The experience of neighboring countries should be constantly in focus. For instance, another high-level visit by the UN Secretary-General, by a team from the Security Council (P5), and from the EU (Solana) as well as from the AU mediation team led by South Africa's President Tabo Mbeki might help to direct serious attention to the conflict and support the preventive peace efforts. The UN must also signal that it is committed to stay as long as it takes for the situation to transform. Setting up the July 5 mini-summit was in line with these considerations, and might be a useful device to repeat, for instance by September. At his press conference on July 5 the UN Secretary-General mentioned that such a meeting might be scheduled at the beginning of the new session of the General Assembly. Since external forces had a crucial role in stopping the fighting they should not leave without being certain that the armed conflict will not start again.

Finally, we are concerned that there is a high risk of electoral violence: intimidation and harassment may well color the elections and affect the credibility of the outcome.[7] Thus, a temporary strengthening of the UN forces and additions of international observers by the EU, AU, and others (such as NGOs) will be required (North and South). This is also a point in time when the threat of individual sanctions could be emphasized. It is, however, important that the threats have backing and that there is a real willingness to add more individuals who obstruct the advance of the elections and peace processes. A plausible scenario in case the elections are not respected is, no doubt, the resumption of the war efforts. One should remember that the war started in 2002 very much as a result of (perceived) manipulations in the previous elections. A repetition now, in spite of considerable efforts to achieve a fair result, is likely to generate lasting conditions of suspicion, frustration, and aggression.

The armed conflict has already had an impact on people's mindset and there is no "return" to pre-war days. Matters have changed and irreversible actions have been taken. Thus, there is a need to investigate war crimes. That might be a matter for the International Criminal Court in The Hague to consider. As part of a reconciliation process, following fair elections, this is a natural next step.

Postscript December 2010: was prevention achieved?

The central concern in the conflict in Côte d'Ivoire was the issue of identity: who was actually a citizen of the country? The opposition did not want the North to break away, but demanded a fair chance to be represented properly in the national government. For instance, in late 1994 an electoral code had been passed for the presidential elections in 1995 requiring that only candidates whose parents were Ivorian were eligible to run. This was based on an exclusive ideology of "ivoirité," "Ivorian-ness," reserving the country for some of its inhabitants. One effect was to prevent a strong candidate from the North, previous Prime Minister Allasane Outtara, from running (Akindès 2004: 36–40; Wallensteen 2011). In 2000 such regulations were part of the explanation for Mr. Laurent Gbagbo's victory.

Thus, what we observed in 2006 concerned the manipulation and delay of the process of giving ID cards to the inhabitants in a correct fashion, where there also were substantive problems in terms of documentation, for instance. The elections were still scheduled for the autumn. However, most remarkably President Gbagbo announced his own peace plan, late in 2006 initiating direct negotiations with the leader of the New Forces, Guillaume Soro. Elections were postponed. Even more remarkable was that President Compaoré of Burkina Faso (also chairing the West African organization ECOWAS) served as the facilitator. He had previously been accused of undue interference. Importantly, the negotiations resulted in the Ouagadougou Political Agreement of March 2007 and a series of other accords. The direct involvement of outside actors was limited, although they continued to provide basic security for the country and for the peace process. The agreements included a way of settling the identity issue through an open identification and registration process using mobile courts. The need for documentation was relaxed. Mr. Soro became prime minister. The first round of presidential elections was finally undertaken in November 2010. The Security Council followed the development closely and issued a warning in October 2010 of the possibility of targeted sanctions on particular individuals if there were violations of the peaceful process (Security Council Resolution 1946). It also made it possible to move peacekeepers from Liberia to Côte d'Ivoire.

Predictably, no candidate won a majority the first round of presidential elections and a runoff was held on November 28, 2010, with Gbagbo and Outtara as the two opponents. The outcome would be the real test of whether this process had managed to establish conditions for a peaceful management to antagonisms that had polarized the country for two decades. UN sanctions and peacekeeping operations were kept in place throughout this process. From a conflict resolution perspective, direct negotiations between the primary parties are always preferable as this means they take responsibility for what is agreed. The international presence, including the sanction, may have helped to handle tensions and provided a potential for reaction if needed.

Sanctions on Liberia: a report from 2006

The challenge to the UN

In general, there is a great appreciation of the UN and UNMIL in Liberia, even accepting the fact the UN is a serious source of authority in the country. War-weariness and realism pervade, people are concerned, tired, and hopeful, particularly after the election of the new president, Ellen Johnson Sirleaf, representing a new departure for Liberian politics. This means that the UN can operate in a remarkable climate of goodwill and hope. Sanctions are part of that, generally appreciated and well known (sanctions issues are recurrent topics in national newspapers).

The inauguration of Mrs. Sirleaf as the first elected woman president in Liberia (and in Africa) has created a unique chance for reconstruction and constitutes a potentially decisive break with a past which has been marked by continuous violence, economic stagnation, and poverty. The support of the international community is strong and the expectations are realistic. It is also clear that

Mrs. Sirleaf has a period of six years for achieving significant change. All cannot be achieved even in such a period, but the directions generate hope for all concerned: fighting corruption and restoring basic services of health, infrastructure, education, and economic development. The issue is what role the UN sanctions can play in this regard, particularly to what extent they should be maintained, given positive developments, and what the conditions are for their termination. This confronts the international community with unusual choices, whose task is not one of crisis management but helping in societal reconstruction. Liberia may provide lessons for the newly established UN Peacebuilding Commission as well as the hope of finding ways to merge development cooperation with conflict prevention.[8]

Typical is that Secretary-General Kofi Annan on his visit to Liberia on July 4, 2006, was received by a joint session in the parliament as a tribute to the UN efforts. His press conference included many sanctions-related questions. Relevant responses will be referred to below.

The UN arms embargo

The first arms embargo on Liberia was imposed in 1992 and terminated in March 2001 (UN Security Council Resolution 1343). With this resolution a second arms embargo was established to end Liberian support to RUF (the Revolutionary United Front, an armed grouping in Sierra Leone). In December 2003, Resolution 1521 dissolved this Sanctions Committee and created a third round of sanctions. The new goal was to have the cease-fire respected, the DDR process and the Security Sector Restructuring (SSR) completed, the Comprehensive Peace Agreement fully implemented, and significant progress made in establishing and maintaining stability in Liberia and the subregion. In total, an arms embargo against Liberia has now been in place for fourteen years, one of the longer in UN experience.

A common belief is that in order to really prevent the flow of arms more countries in the region should have been targeted with arms embargo measures. Although the borders are leaky, the arms embargo did, according to our interviewees, have a positive impact on the situation in Liberia. The impact was partly symbolic (a political cost) since the Liberian government under Charles Taylor was clearly named and shamed, and partly substantial (economic cost) since the embargo made the purchase of new weapons more difficult and expensive while delivery became more unpredictable.

The latest arms embargo, established in December 2003, is also generally assessed to have had a constructive effect. Even if the borders are difficult to control and some small arms may have entered, the obstacles to importing major arms or larger quantities of small arms have increased. It is difficult to undertake major shipments without detection. This was already the case during the second arms embargo, when heavier equipment which could affect the military situation on the ground, such as attack helicopters, could be imported only with great difficulty. For instance in February and March 2001 two helicopters destined for Liberia were stopped by Slovak and Moldovan customs and security services (Expert Panel Report, S/2001/1015: 53–54).

Judging from an analysis of battlefield developments the arms embargo had a stabilizing effect since the actors know that they, as well as their opponents, could only with difficulty acquire material that could rapidly change the situation on the ground (see Strandow 2006). With these considerations in mind, we observed unanimity of views on maintaining the arms embargo.[9]

One observation is that the international community might need to consider types of arms that are used on the ground in an open conflict and concentrate its attention on this. Instead of preventing large amounts of some arms reaching the country, a focus might be laid on the kind of arms which are most likely to be used for restarting a war. However, UN conferences have emphasized small arms in general, and a more targeted approach may be difficult to implement. Moreover, arms are now in Liberia seen as symbols of an evil past as well as carriers of illegitimate power. The question that faces the new government as well as the international community is how to refurbish the new army and the new police force. Recruitment is under way and Liberian police so far remain unarmed. This means that the UN has constituted the country's only source of coercive authority, undisputed at that, a quite unique situation. A criterion for lifting of the embargo might be based on a review of the new army and police in terms of meeting modern demands, for example human rights, gender mainstreaming, conflict resolution skills, and nonviolent techniques.

From a gender perspective, more female police officers could set a good precedent. UNMIL might be a good training ground for this, for instance by having international female police officers patrolling together with Liberians (especially higher rankings). The new police commissioner is a woman, also providing a possible avenue into new thinking. This is actually an area where countries with influential female police may have a significant role in shaping the future of Liberia. Here Sweden has experiences to provide.

When it comes to equipping the Liberian Army, sooner or later some import of arms to the government will be necessary, as UNMIL cannot be maintained at present force levels, perhaps beyond the second half of President Sirleaf's term of office. The process has to be done with great care, and a gradual lifting with evaluation on the ability of the army and police to control its weaponry will be crucial. All this is likely to be part of the SSR programs now in place. This cautionary approach seems to be the one taken by the UN Security Council. In Resolution 1683, adopted on 13 June 2006, it was decided that weapons needed for training the security forces are exempted from the embargo and limited supplies of weapons and ammunition can be supplied if approved in advance on a case-by-case basis by the Sanctions Committee. It is important that every measure be taken to ensure the trustworthiness of the security forces, for instance by continuing the close cooperation between UNMIL and the Liberian Police. As the Sanctions Committee is to be responsible for monitoring this gradual increase of import of arms, a close and effective dialogue between New York and Monrovia is needed.

Individually targeted measures

The targeting of individuals was included in the March 2001 decision (Resolution 1343) and the measure was imposed after a two-month delay. The sanctions were intended to pressure the Taylor government to end its support for RUF. As that war ended and a peace process was under way in Liberia, sanctions were revised in December 2003 through Resolution 1521. The new, individual sanctions were explicitly aimed at strengthening the peace process in Liberia and not concerned primarily with Liberia's role in the security of the region, as had been the case with the earlier measures. Individuals already listed remained subject to sanctions. The updating of sanctions was generally perceived to lead to a tighter enforcement of the travel bans. Asset freezes were also instituted on the same individuals. Initially it appeared that the effects of the bans were mostly symbolic, but as the implementation has improved the sanctions have meant tangible restrictions on the behavior of targeted individuals. It is difficult to distinguish substantial effects during the period when the conflict was raging. Nevertheless, we conclude that the UN sanctions are one of the factors that contribute to keeping the post-war situation calm.

The individual sanctions are also generally supported among the many interviewees in this study. A problem frequently mentioned was that the sanctions were not properly applied on the domestic level. In Liberia, no freezing of individual assets was made, although measures could have been taken. For instance, some of the actors receive salaries and have invested in large companies. Although sanctions were not implemented domestically, it was known that the USA had been instrumental in freezing assets in that country. This caused some interviewees to express gratitude to the USA. At the same time others remarked that targeted individuals still held untouched accounts in that country.[10] US action notwithstanding, there is a discrepancy between UN expectations and Liberia's behavior. Asked about Liberia's performance, Kofi Annan – while acknowledging not having the details on this – said at his press conference on July 4 that the "resolution was passed under Chapter VII and each government has an obligation to implement it, including the Liberian government."[11]

Although there is a call for freezing of assets domestically, little political energy has been used to enforce this (despite the existence of local commercial banks and some financial infrastructure). There are legal and political reasons for this. However, it also means that a UN member-state benefiting most from international UN measures is not applying them itself. The issue needs to be kept on the agenda. Liberia has to be reminded of its duties under the UN Charter. Obviously, the government's fear is that a necessary sanctions law could be blocked by the parliament as some of the listed individuals have now been elected and hold seats in this body. In addition, there is said to be a problem with retrospective legislation. There is, for the time being, no indication that these individuals are engaged in armed activities in the country or among neighbors, although they are still on the sanctions list for this as an ultimate reason. This sends mixed signals to the electorate, and can be used for propaganda by those who are on the sanctions list. Still, many observe a sobering of behavior of the individuals who are under targeted sanctions. This suggests that being listed has a disciplining effect, even on those who were previously on the list. The threat of Liberian action on this account may serve to reinforce this effect.

Many of the issues raised by those under personal sanctions dealt with delisting. Obviously, many listed people want to get off the list; some that we interviewed indicated that they do not "understand" why they are targeted or what they need to do to be removed. Hence, there could be reasons to consider a UN policy for informing on how a sanctions listing is made and on the procedure for delisting. There is, no doubt, a degree of "suffering" for some individuals, but for most interviewees this "hardship" is hardly comparable to what the entire nation has gone through. There is little to gain from a blanket lifting of individual sanctions. As times passes and "new" behavior appears sustained, there might be reasons for a more generous exemption policy. It is important to note that the current sanctions list needs to be constantly updated, which is not necessarily the case for the latest versions.

The political landscape changes, and actors who were directly engaged in war efforts are now incorporated into functions of society. This needs to be reflected in revised sanctions lists. One way to do this is to update the sanctions lists as soon as there are changes on the ground, for example after elections. Adopting such a procedure makes the entire listing more fit to unfolding realities and turns it into a dynamic tool that can change with the political conditions. The incentive/ disincentive aspects become clearer.

Sanctions on natural resources: diamonds

The decision to impose a diamond embargo was taken in March 2001, in Security Council Resolution 1343, and was, as part of the package, imposed with a two-month delay. In May 2003 the commodity embargo was extended to include timber (Resolution 1478). The Council cited Liberia's active support of RUF in Sierra Leone and the government's lack of compliance with Resolution 1343 (2001) as reasons for the extension of the sanctions. About six months later, with Resolution 1521 (December 2003), the goals of the commodity and the other sanctions were revised, as mentioned earlier, to include supporting the implementation of the peace agreements. A specific goal before lifting of the sanctions on diamond exports was that Liberia must join the Kimberley certification scheme. The idea behind this is to allow the government to control the country's foreign trade and generate needed tax revenue for state operations.

There is a debate on the future of the diamond sanctions. A common argument in favor of lifting these measures is that there are many local producers who are dependent on diamond exports, and, thus, trade would generate local income and contribute to alleviating poverty. Although the requirements for Liberia's compliance with the Kimberley scheme had not yet been met, at the time of our visit, it was obviously progressing and is likely to soon be finalized. On the other hand, there are valid arguments against lifting the sanctions, notably that middlemen and international interests are likely to wade in, and take control of the trade. These are often closed networks operating with little transparency. The aims of the government in generating revenue may then be difficult to accomplish, once controls are relaxed. Thus, we conclude that a prudent course is to find a way to ensure that the established control system actually functions. This could be done by lifting sanctions for a short period and having international and national experts closely monitor subsequent events. The aim would be to ensure competent operation of a prospectively lucrative source of income. In that regard, we also find it important to connect licensing of production and trade to environmental restoration requirements.

As this author understands it, the diamond sanctions have been important in many regards, not the least reducing government income (during the Taylor regime), thus contributing to ending the war. It is, nevertheless, important to state that they did not succeed in stopping illegal extraction of diamonds. In fact, an estimated 50,000 individuals are currently engaged in this work. Many of these are ex-combatants. Illegal mining is made possible through agreements between mining companies and local tribes whereby the former are able to utilize property belong to the latter.

In addition, we find it important to establish clearer Liberian ownership and responsibility of the diamond production, trade, and income, not least through increased transparency. This means that there is a need for increased efforts from the international community to support the Liberian government to control this resource for the Liberian people as a whole. Several experiences and much knowledge can be gained through NGOs involved in this issue, not least local ones.

Finally, we are aware that incomes from diamonds are not enough to make Liberia rich. As there are many other valuable resources such as iron, gold, rubies, offshore oil, and timber, the way diamonds are handled may set a precedent. With the Kimberley process a new school of thought is emerging in responsible international trading. It provides standards for other precious resources.

Sanctions on natural resources: timber

Liberia's forests are an important asset for the country's future development. For instance, logs are now needed for the country's reconstruction. The UN sanctions are directed toward export, meaning that logging can take place for internal purposes. Again, a policy such as the one outlined for diamond mining is important, particularly with ways to evaluate necessary control mechanisms, in matters such as taxation, labor conditions, and environmental concerns. Preferably such government regulations should be in place before permanently lifting the prohibition on international trade. The idea is that these resources should come to benefit the local producers, local communities, and national economy as well as the international investors, without having significant sources ending up in the pockets of shady interests. Historical experience makes it clear that transparency is a must.

The Security Council decided on June 20, 2006, in Resolution 1689 (2006), that the timber sanctions are not to be renewed. They will instead be reviewed after ninety days and reinstated if the new Liberian forestry legislation has not been approved by that time. The easing of the timber sanctions is from a technical viewpoint peculiar since the Forest Development Authority has not yet developed a full capacity to control all aspects of logging. Thus, it is significant that the resolution contains a threat that sanctions could be reinstated. This provides an incentive for the concerned interests to keep up the much-needed restructuring of Liberia's logging industry.

A particular issue is that some forest companies have employed their own security guards. We heard reports that some are former ex-combatants who have dropped out of the SSR program. Hence, there is also a security concern with the timber trade that has to be dealt with by the government and has to be attended to by international organs.

Liberia in a post-sanctions era

Liberia now finds itself at a juncture. The outcomes of the national elections and the sympathy of the international community provide an unusual window of opportunity. It is our conclusion that international efforts have been an important factor in achieving this, through peacekeeping, sanctions, negotiations, and development cooperation. Liberia is a sovereign country and there is a limit to how much international involvement is effective. Gradually lifting sanctions, in close cooperation with the present government, is a way to strengthen a peaceful future.

Among the sanctions, it appears that the arms embargo is the one to be maintained the longest, as the conditions for lifting should be such that a return to civil war is unlikely. This means a new army and a new police force need to be operative, professional, and closely adhering to the constitution as well as to democratic principles of governance.

A question that will need to be faced is the one of war crimes. With former ruler Charles Taylor at the Sierra Leone tribunal (in the premises of the International Criminal Court in The Hague), a most urgent issue has been solved. Soon, however, attention will focus on other events in the country's recent history, notably a series of political murders that will have to be prosecuted locally. This is perhaps of particular concern to the EU, in much the same way it has acted on the Balkan countries (with an emphasis on war crime issues in return for negotiations, aid and possible future membership). In the case of Liberia, however, the entire judiciary needs an overhaul (courts, police, lawyers, prosecutors) and credible trials are still far off. A tribunal of truth and reconciliation has been created and is now being trained. It might be the most appropriate transition measure that can be conceived and is thus worthy of determined international support. To support Liberians building a new Liberia should be something of specific concern for the EU, which has otherwise been slow in living up to its responsibility for Africa.

Postscript: Liberia at the end of 2010

Liberia faces new elections in 2011. The present post-peace agreement period has been one of the least conflictual in Liberia's recent history. It has also been coupled to a reform process, in terms of democracy, rule of law, and civil society involvement.

The improvement can be seen in the 2010 Ibrahim Index of African governance, in which Liberia is mentioned as one of the three countries in Africa showing most improvement, measured in scores on this index (Mo Ibrahim Foundation 2010). The score rose from 32 in 2004/05 to 43 in 2008/09, thus approaching the average for Africa, which is 49. It can be compared with Côte d'Ivoire, which received a score of 36 for 2004/05 and 37 for 2008/09. At the same time, neighboring Ghana, which has been spared from wars, rose from 60 to 65. The same picture of Liberia passing Côte d'Ivoire emerges from the parallel index published by the World Peace Foundation (Rotberg and Gisselquist 2009), in which Liberia goes from 40.7 (in 2000) to 50.0 (2007) compared with Côte d'Ivoire's decrease from 44.7 to 42.7 (in the same period Ghana goes from 63.7 to 70.8). The Human Development Index also shows an improved situation (from an index value of 0.259 in 2006 to 0.300 in 2010; http://hdrstats.undp.org/en/countries/profiles/LBR.html). Still Liberia is below the average for sub-Saharan Africa countries. This should also be compared with the value for 1980, when Liberia was on the same level as other African countries. It is one among many measures of what fourteen years of civil war has meant to the country. The value in 2010 means its now back to a level of human development that parallels the one recorded for 1980. After thirty years the country is now where it was before the wars. The combined effects of domestic measures and international support clearly have helped to lift the country out of the dynamics of war. However, preventive actions, such as the ones undertaken in Côte d'Ivoire, may be a more effective way, particularly if they succeed in sparing the country decades of lost development potential.

The international development in Liberia includes some novel elements. The use of sanctions to pressure the government and parliament for reform is one. It may have helped the country to run its economy properly. The Security Council has only gradually removed sanctions and kept reviewing developments with an eye to eventually instituting them again. Sanctions on particular individuals have been maintained. Over the years since the peace agreement Liberia has run a cash-based budget, meaning it has not taken up new loans and has successfully negotiated the reduction or canceling of some of its outstanding debts. The government's revenue from export commodities is important and the global financial crisis affects the government's possibilities to pursue long-term development policies.

An innovation that has captured the imagination is the deployment of an all-female international peacekeeping operation. It responds to some of the issues mentioned in the 2006 report above. It provides some assurance to women that their security concerns are also being attended to. The test of Liberia's return to peaceful politics will be the elections in 2011.

Sanctions in Africa: implications for UN policy

The UN is a global actor that often sets the norms for other international organizations, including the EU, including in the field of sanctions policies. Thus, the way the UN utilizes the sanctions instrument requires careful consideration in choice of situations for sanctions, goals, targeting, composition of measures, implementation, and duration of the measures.

With the advent of individually targeted sanctions there are increasing concerns with respect to the situations, the persons, and the procedures for selection, the reasons for listing, and ways of delisting. A set of general conclusions can be drawn from the two cases described in this report.

Implication 1: on monitoring of sanctions

The experiences from Liberia and Côte d'Ivoire illustrate the importance for the UN to be in place on the local scene, so as to monitor actual developments. The combination of global sanctions and local verification schemes has been illustrated in other instances to be an effective tool, notably in the ambitions to achieve the elimination of Iraq's capacity to develop weapons of mass destruction (see Wallensteen *et al.* 2005). This suggests that it is not realistic to expect governments that themselves are targets for sanctions (or have targeted individuals in their legislature) to carry out all necessary actions. The monitoring by Expert Panels can only be a complement to a more regular monitoring. It is simply not enough to have random visits, even though they may function as surprise inspections and thus be a control of the systems set up. If the warring parties are less cooperative (such as in Côte d'Ivoire, where the DDR process was to start already in 2003 according to the Linas–Marcoussis agreement) or do not have the political or administrative means (such as in Liberia, where the government is just being organized according to international standards) UN schemes take on a particular significance. Thus, the seemingly randomized arrivals of Expert Panels serve a significant function. However, actors on the ground are likely to learn quickly. One way to strengthen the implementation and the enforcement of targeted sanctions is to provide UN peacekeepers with a better mandate for implementation.

Of the two cases, clearly Liberia has benefited the more from the presence of a robust UN force in a situation where there was also a determined program of DDR. In the case of Ivory Coast, the UNOCI had considerable difficulties in getting a corresponding role. Its requests to UN headquarters even for police to deal with demonstrations outside its offices took long to be supported, making it difficult for the peacekeepers to maintain their own security. This is not acceptable and the credibility of sanctions will also depend on the credibility of the peacekeeping mission. In the case of Liberia the QRF has been significant in that regard, whereas the robust French presence in Côte d'Ivoire has a mixed record: providing useful assistance in some monitoring, but also being a complicating factor, owing to the link between France and Côte d'Ivoire.

Our conclusion is that, whenever there are UN missions in place and the Security Council imposes sanctions, it is important to strengthen these missions to also have a role in sanctions monitoring, in addition to the Expert Panels.

Implication 2: on arms embargoes, more global scrutiny required

The Liberia case points to the significance of connecting the removal of sanctions with DDR and SSR requirements. The advances in building of a new army and police force are also highly relevant criteria for a discussion on the termination of sanctions. The recent easing of the arms embargo seems cautious and leaves control in the hands of the Sanctions Committee. It is our conclusion that deliveries of new weapons for Liberia's police and military should be done when they are meeting such criteria. Also, producers and exporters should adhere to export restrictions, such as the Wasenaar arrangements. Arms embargoes activate a series of connections from the producer (often far away from the conflict scene, located in more affluent societies), through the middlemen (often shady figures), to the users (be they legitimate governments or warlords). Such connections require a closer scrutiny that goes beyond the individual cases, as many of the same networks reproduce themselves from one conflict to the next. A global study in this field would be welcome.

Implication 3: on individual sanctions, the need for more elaborate procedures

This study indicates that targeted sanctions have had a sobering effect on the targeted individuals. Their basic beliefs are not likely to change, nor are their political convictions. However, there might be a discernible pattern of more restraint in agitation and more responsibility in carrying out civic duties. Thus, there might be a behavioral change, for instance individuals not sabotaging peace efforts as they did before. This raises the issue of what type of change is expected, by the UN and by the targeting of individuals.

There are different considerations. For many advocating individually targeted sanctions this is also a way of administering punishment, helping to generate compassion for victims of the condemned policies and even leading to repentance. Our interviews do not suggest that such reconsiderations are typical. On the contrary, individuals exhibit a basic lack of understanding of why they have been selected. There is a tendency to claim innocence, victimization, and martyrdom (even using the sanctions as an illustration of justice in their "struggle" and making themselves into "heroes"). Typically, the individuals will claim that they had "no idea" that their names were contemplated and that the listing was known "only from the Internet." This should not necessarily be taken at face value. Many of the individuals in fact understand very well why they are listed, as they often are experienced political operators. The sanctions are used by them to further their own goals. There is no change of heart, but there is a discernible pattern of changed ways of operation. There might, however, also be cases in which listing is unwarranted. It suggests that there is a need to reform the procedure of providing information on listing and delisting by the UN Sanctions Committees. This relates to what kind of change one is expecting.

Some ideas are the following:

•   The goal of targeting particular individuals needs to be clearer. We observe a sobering effect, but is this what is intended? In that case, sanctions are quite successful. This, however, is no guarantee of what will happen once sanctions have been lifted.

- Furthermore, as many interviewees noted: one cannot undo one's deeds. If repentance is required, that needs to be spelled out. If there is an element of the UN administering justice, that is also a different matter. If the hope is that the persons should somehow disappear from the political scene, that is a third type of ambition.
- These goals, furthermore, will raise the question of whether the "right" person is targeted: the one who has the most to repent, the one who has committed the worst crimes, or the one who is key for political change. The goals and the selection of target are closely connected, of course, and it is important to explain this in a way that is consistent to the victims, to the general public, and to the UN decision-makers themselves.
- Several of those who are being targeted express a desire to face their accusers. Although this is not always possible or necessary, the Sanctions Committees need clear policies and guidelines for this. This will help the target, the mission, as well as those working in the Committee. Informing the individuals directly, with the notification of rights of reply and ways of response, the possibilities for delisting (different procedures seem to have been used), and transparency on the removal of individuals (to avoid rumors about unequal treatment that now can be heard) would improve the system significantly. Human rights claims of these individuals need to be given serious consideration. The improvements in procedures that have been seen since the 2003 Stockholm Process are still not convincing and not obvious to the targeted personalities.
- Several targeted individuals testify to considerable personal impact of the sanctions, for instance difficulties in getting medical treatment or family exemptions. The reluctance to grant exemptions is mostly a realistic attitude of the Sanctions Committees, as there are likely to be hidden assets abroad and as telecommunications still provide for interactions across borders. However, if a more generous exemption policy were to be implemented it might be combined with a closer reporting by the person on matters such as travel destinations, meetings, and other activities, possibly to the point of being accompanied by UN staff.
- Also there is a specific UN need: what should be the UN policy for contacts with targeted individuals? Peacekeepers need guidelines; practice seems to vary (which was obvious when comparing Côte d'Ivoire with Liberia). In general we recommend that contacts could be established, kept, and maintained, as part of maintaining options for peaceful solutions to a crisis. This can only be maintained through impartiality and trust. However, in order to avoid accusation of double standards, official high-level interactions should be minimized and remain invisible.
- A related question is what guidelines Expert Panels and Chairs of Sanctions Committees should follow once they are out in the field. For instance, should a chairperson be allowed to meet with targeted actors? It was noted in our interviews that listed persons were aware when the committee chair was around, and saw it as a missed opportunity not to have had the possibility to meet to get first-hand information on delisting, for instance.

- An important aspect of individually targeted sanctions is whether those who are being targeted should be allowed to run for public office. We have noted that individuals seemed to have entered into election campaigns for the sake of getting immunity, so to say taking cover under the country's constitution (it should be noted, though, that many constitutions do not provide immunity if their elected officials constitute a threat to peace and security). When it comes to travel bans it was noted that – with some effort – fake passports could be obtained on the black market (also false ID cards). This is a delicate problem the international community is already trying to tackle. We suggest that an additional way is to make sure that travel agencies are not allowed to issue tickets to those who are on UN sanctions lists.
- Another issue the international community needs to come to terms with is how the sanctions list is established in the first place. Throughout our interviews with inside and outside actors, nobody really knew how the sanctions were conceived. To make the listing more credible, the Sanctions Committee might have to inform the individuals which governments or organizations suggested their names. In fact, in some Committee guidelines, it is stated that the targeted actor needs to turn to such a "designated" state in case he or she wants to be taken off the list.

Implication 4: on sanctions on natural resources: what is the purpose?

Both timber and diamond sanctions have had a discernible effects on the conflicts. The selection of these resources was well conceived and very much a result of alert civil society organizations, such as Global Witness. At least in the case of diamonds the sanctions on Liberia, Sierra Leone, and Angola have contributed to international efforts and certification of diamonds, to reduce their utility as a source of conflict financing. Corresponding efforts have not had the same effect with timber or other crucial resources, which also appear as possible sanctions commodities. To undertake such efforts will require additional action beyond the sanctions decisions, however.

A difficulty is often to establish, on a global level, the origins of the commodities in question. However, in the cases we studied, the issue appeared simpler as it was quite possible to decide in which fields mining was going on and institute local or nearby controlling measures. Furthermore, it might not be necessary to stop all trade, only enough to reduce the flow of goods in a reasonable way. This, we believe, seems to have taken place in the cases where the international community has considerable oversight, such as Liberia today. However, the trade going on through northern parts of Côte d'Ivoire is presently beyond the scope of international sustained monitoring. Thus, further use of this instrument of sanctions will have to require accompanying permanent monitoring measures.

The idea behind sanctions on commodities such as diamonds and timber is basically to reduce income to the government or to an organized opposition in order to reduce its capacity to purchase arms for war and/or repression. Targeted actors may instead shift to other commodities, which indeed is what happened in the case of the Taylor regime in Liberia. A reduction in revenue seems to have been accomplished, nevertheless. At this point, one may ask if untargeted financial sanctions could have accomplished the same goal, that is by preventing international borrowing or freezing of assets in national bank accounts, as accompanying measures. There has been little discussion of such sanctions, and it may be time to bring them to the agenda. A vigorous use of financial sanctions, in other words, may create difficulties for governments and organized opponents. The drawback is that it might endanger the economy of a whole country or region, and thus go beyond the idea with targeted sanctions.

However, the cases of Liberia and Côte d'Ivoire demonstrate that actors can shift from one commodity to another, and that the international control measures will be late in following such changes. Indeed, for many commodities there are no certification schemes at all to draw on. To build up dynamics corresponding to the Kimberley process for all commodities seems impracticable and will, in any case, take considerable time. It will also have to be generated from other concerns, such as labor conditions or environmental considerations. Thus, there is a need to stimulate a debate on alternative means of targeted sanctions. The experiences from Liberia and Côte d'Ivoire generate new lessons for UN sanctions and for international involvement in conflict prevention and peacebuilding. This chapter contains some such observations. It is hoped that it serves to bring forward these lessons and stimulate analysis of others. There is more to be learned from the UN sanctions history.

Postscript: UN sanctions at the end of 2010

The issues of listing and delisting, as exemplified by the cases of Liberia and Cote d'Ivoire, continued to be problems for the Security Council. Only with the advent of the Obama administration in the United States, however, were actions taken. The Security Council Resolution 1904 of December 2009 included decisions that improved transparency in listing as well as in delisting of individuals, even creating a special Ombudsperson for these matters. To date this is the largest reform in the Security Council's operation of targeted sanctions and meets some of the human rights objections that the listing/delisting procedures have faced.

Although new measures have been instituted on already ongoing cases, such as the nonproliferation disputes with Iran and North Korea, as well as on terrorism, it appears that the Council has been reluctant to expose new countries to sanctions. Eritrea was added in 2009 on account of its actions in the conflict in Somalia, but no individuals were listed at the time. The debate on the human rights issue, as well as difficulties in seeing obvious impacts in nonwar cases, may have made the Council reluctant to add new cases. Obviously, the conflict between Russia and Georgia over South Ossetia and Abkhazia did not lead to Council action; neither did issues concerning Tibet or Burma/Myanmar. In terms of conflict prevention, however, the Council expressed concern on the implementation of the Comprehensive Peace Agreement for Sudan.

The issues covered in this chapter suggest that sanctions have many more functions than often attended to in the scholarly literature. The use of sanctions for prevention needs further exploration. The combination of strategies applied in the case of Côte d'Ivoire is instructive and the interactions between different components worth considering. It could well be that the international actions in effect forced the parties to negotiate directly with each other, as the possibility of restarting the war was blocked by these efforts. Also, keeping pressure by possibly withdrawing international measures after the parties managed to run elections in a proper way indicates other types of commitments.

Clearly, the peacebuilding efforts in Liberia were stimulated by international action. Again, this is a type of situation that has not been discussed much in the sanctions literature. The use of sanctions, in particular, constrained the leaders in their choice of actions. It may have reduced the country's sovereignty, but the options were not many. Obviously, the war experiences contributed to a general acceptance of this as well. The advances, as documented for instance in comparative indices, show that the country has reformed itself and that it gradually will be able to reemerge as a credible actor in the political and economic arena.

The war in Côte d'Ivoire was curtailed by international action, but this may have given the leadership a belief that war could still have been beneficial to them. Thus, the achievement in reconstructing Liberia based on its own resources and appropriate international support provides an example of how much is required to return to pre-war conditions. The unique support for Liberia is not likely to be easy to replicate elsewhere. Also, it demonstrates how much a post-war situation constrains a leadership and reduces its independence of action. A successful conflict prevention scenario in Côte d'Ivoire could instead be an effective way of communicating to leaders that war is not an option and that much can be achieved through a peaceful course of action.

Sanctions, in other words, are also ways to communicate to leadership what real constraints there are on independence. The message could be: wars tend to result in dependence; only through peaceful action is it possible to sustain sovereignty.

Notes

1   This chapter reproduces large parts of Wallensteen *et al.* (2006). The introduction and the three postscripts are written separately for this volume by Wallensteen. The study builds partly on interviews conducted in the region May 27–June 16, 2006. Full references are found in the 2006 report, available at www.smartsanctions.se. The field work segment of the report was made possible by the support of the UN Secretary-General Special Representative of UNOCI, Ivory Coast; the AME University, Liberia; UNMIL Civil Affairs, Liberia; and researchers at the University of Freetown, Sierra Leone. The work was entirely financed by the Swedish Ministry for Foreign Affairs. The authors remain solely responsible for the text and the propositions.

2   See BBC News, http://news.bbc.co.uk/go/pr/fr/-/2/hi/africa/5187210.stm, and UN News Service, July 27, 2006.

3 It was pointed out to us that the Côte d'Ivoire military receives extra payment to be prepared for war, an ominous sign and certainly not a monetary incentive for peace.

4 For a report see UNDPI, July 6, 2006, SG/T/2500; for a transcript of the press conference, see www.un.org/apps/sg/offthecuff.asp?nid=900. On July 26, 2006, the Security Council reminded the parties of their obligations under this agreement (UN News Service, July 27, 2006).

5 In fact, on June 2 the Security Council authorized an additional 1,500 personnel for UNOCI to cover this crucial period (UNSCR 1682).

6 Progress was reported. On July 27, 150 militiamen in a government-controlled area did hand in weapons, in return for a sum corresponding to US$240 and free return to their villages of origin (UN OCHA, reported in IRINnews.org, August 4, 2006).

7 An indication is that the violent incidents during July 2006 were all related to the process of identifying eligible carriers of ID cards. It resulted in at least two deaths in two separate incidents (UN Integrated Regional Information Networks [IRIN], July 26, 2006).

8 The Peacebuilding Commission selected its first countries to work with in June 2006: Burundi and Sierra Leone. Liberia has also been mentioned as a candidate country, for instance, together with Haiti and Timor-Leste.

9 Typical is that this issue was not raised at all during Kofi Annan's press conference in Monrovia on July 4, 2006, although it covered a range of sanctions issues.

10 On July 18, 2006, the US President decided on a one-year continuation of American special measures on Charles Taylor and other persons (White House Press Release, July 18, 2006).

11 Monrovia, Liberia July 4, 2006, Secretary-General's press conference (unofficial transcript), UN SG website, www.un.org/apps/sg/offthecuff.asp?nid=899.

References

Akindès, Francis 2004. *The Roots of the Military–Political Crisis in Côte d'Ivoire*. Research Report 128. Uppsala: Nordiska Afrikainstitutet.

Biersteker, Tom J., Sue E. Eckert, Peter Romaniuk, Aaron Halegua, and N. Reid, 2001. *Targeted Financial Sanctions: A Manual for the Design and Implementation*. Report from the Interlaken Process. Providence, RI: Watson Institute for International Studies, Brown University.

Brzoska, M. (ed.). 2001. *Design and Implementation of Arms Embargoes and Travel and Aviation Related Sanctions: Results of the 'Bonn–Berlin Process'*. Bonn: International Center for Conversion. Report from the Bonn–Berlin Process.

Mo Ibrahim Foundation. 2010. *2010 Ibrahim Index of African Governance*. Summary. Revised edition (http://www.moibrahimfoundation.org/en/media/get/20101108_eng-summary-iiag2010-rev-web-2.pdf)

Rotberg, Robert I. and Rachel M. Gisselquist. 2009. *Strengthening African Governance: Index of African Governance, Results and Rankings 2009*. Cambridge, MA: World Peace Foundation.

Strandow, Daniel. 2006. *Sanctions and Civil War: Targeted Measures for Conflict Resolution*. Uppsala: Department of Peace and Conflict Research, Uppsala University.

United Nations, Expert Panel Reports. n.d. (http://www.un.org/Docs/sc/committees)

Wallensteen, Peter, Carina Staibano and Mikael Eriksson. 2003. *Making Targeted Sanctions Effective: Report from the Stockholm Process*. Uppsala: Department of Peace and Conflict Research, Uppsala University.

Wallensteen, Peter, Carina Staibano and Mikael Eriksson. 2005. *The 2004 Roundtable on UN Sanctions against Iraq: Lessons Learned*. Uppsala: Department of Peace and Conflict Research, Uppsala University.

Wallensteen, Peter. 2011. 'Sanctions in Africa: International Resolve and Prevention of Conflict Escalation', in Thomas Ohlson (ed.), *From Intra-State War to Durable Peace: Conflict and Its Resolution in Africa after the Cold War*. Dordrecht: Republic of Letters Publishing.

Wallensteen, Peter, Mikael Eriksson and Daniel Strandow. 2006. *Sanctions for Conflict Prevention and Peace Building: Lessons Learned from Côte d'Ivoire and Liberia*. Uppsala: SPITS, Department of Peace and Conflict Research, Uppsala University.

Part V
Academics in peacemaking

16 Academics in peacemaking

Applied peace research

An ambition in early peace research was to also contribute directly to actions for peace. Knowledge that is generated through research also has to be brought to the public and have an impact on policy. This is, in some sense, what the taxpayers or donors are expecting from their funding, although what the impact could be cannot be predicted. This means that this volume now has come full circle. In Chapters 1 and 2 we discussed how to prevent research from being misused for purposes not consonant with the individual researcher's own convictions, for instance research results being used for war or repression. The Uppsala Code of Ethics was designed to provide guidance for this. However, in this part we need to discuss if and how a more positive approach can be developed. Research is not just for the academic community; it is also there to be applied. However, applied peace research is a topic on which very little has been written and there is a lack of empirical insights. In Chapters 17 and 18 two cases are presented by a researcher in the situation of armed conflict. Obviously, research can be applied in many other ways. Let us consider some roles that the researcher can take up, and point to their advantages and disadvantages.

Applying research to actual conditions is not a simple matter. We have already encountered this in Chapter 3, in which the popularity in political circles of "democratic peace" was noted. To many researchers this resulted in a simplification of the notions implied. There are several concepts stemming from peace research concerns that have traveled into the arena of politics. Karl W. Deutsch developed the notion of a "security community," which also has acquired popularity. In Part IV of this volume the notion of "smart sanctions" was mentioned. The term was used by US Secretary of State Colin Powell in 2002, when presenting new sanctions measures against Iraq. It made the term controversial in the Arab world. "Preventive diplomacy," "conflict prevention," "track II diplomacy," "peace process," and "peacebuilding" are terms that also move between academia and politics. Findings and terms have their own life and it is hard to make them keep the qualities the researcher may want. Let us, however, also consider a situation in which it is not only the intellectual properties that are transiting from academia to actual decision making but also the researcher. Adding such assignments to the role of a researcher creates additional dilemmas.

Obviously, there are many possible ways for researchers to have a role in policy-making for peace. One is to be an *advisor* to decision-makers with the same ambition, for instance as part of their office, such as the UN Secretary-General. This could also be the mandate, for instance, of a mediation- or disarmament-oriented Minister for Foreign Affairs. It puts the peace researcher close to the political action and may give an opportunity to have direct impact on policies. The advantage is the access to decisions and having action taken. Perhaps it is also comforting that responsibility for action rests elsewhere. It is likely that a number of peace researchers have found themselves in such advisory roles, as part of a political or expert appointment. Normally, such arrangements last for a specific period of time. The impact is dependent on the impact the political leader can have. It may also, however, tarnish the reputation of the researcher. He/she may find himself/herself involved in decisions where the peace perspective may be diluted or even contradicted. There are very few accounts of such experiences. It is as story that needs to be written. There are even fewer cases of a peace researcher actually entirely moving into the political field and becoming a decision-maker. It is more common to find the researcher's students in such a role.

A position in government or an international organization may be the most common role of a peace researcher, but, with the strength of civil society, a corresponding role may also be found in organizations such as advocacy movements, for instance. The value to the movements is the researchers' general insights, but also their methodological competence, which can be applied to a number of issues and fields. As in the previous case, the integrity of the researcher is central, and it has to be protected for the sake of the researcher as well as for the organization.

An alternative is to be involved in peacemaking through *independent projects*. An example is the one mentioned in Chapter 13, the Stockholm Process on the Implementation of Targeted Sanctions (SPITS). It was designed to provide input to the UN reform process on sanctions. The Swedish Ministry for Foreign Affairs financed the process. It was carried out at the Department of Peace and Conflict Research at Uppsala University. The integrity of the researcher was never questioned or challenged. On the contrary, it was an advantage to the Ministry that the task was done independently, thus making it possible for the Ministry, if necessary, to put some distance between itself and the conclusions of the researchers. The integrity of both sides was preserved. The process clearly had on impact on improving targeting of sanctions. It was a short-term commitment that generated many important lessons, some of which have been conveyed in Chapters 13–15. There are likely to be many more experiences of this nature.

This points to a slightly different role that peace researchers can take, notably through writing of the *report of a top-level commission* that will, it is hoped, impact on international policies and which can be largely based on ongoing research. In this case there is a commission that takes the responsibility for the report to be done, but the actual work is done by academics. It is, for instance, noteworthy that researchers were greatly involved in the High-Level Panel on Threats, Challenges and Changes that the UN Secretary-General appointed in 2003. For instance, its executive director was Professor Stephen J. Stedman, a well-known and respected researcher in the field of peace and security. This panel presented a host of suggestions for UN reforms. Many of them were part of the UN General Assembly agenda in 2005/06 and several were implemented, notably on peacebuilding, human rights, terrorism, and other concerns.

Another role – which builds on the competence of peace researchers as researchers –is the more traditional one: *commentary* in, for instance, the media, lecturing, or giving seminars to government and nongovernment organizations (NGOs). It is a matter of communicating research to the general public. These are efforts that are normally seen as university outreach. A quick glance suggests that, among scholars involved in the media, peace researchers take a larger role than their small number would suggest. In these cases, however, the distinction between research and advocacy is clear. The researcher normally builds his/her participation on published reports or accumulated knowledge, and the division of roles is quite clear.

A more complicated relationship emerges when researchers start their own *advocacy* NGOs and in effect become advocates of particular positions in a public debate. It may originate in research but the dynamics of NGO action and general politics may soon make the researcher appear like any other movement representative. In such cases, the researcher has to give due consideration to how to structure a balance between engagement in particular issues and the role of a neutral teacher and researcher.

A particular situation is to become involved as a researcher in an exercise that builds on research insights but posits the researcher in the role of *a third party*. This is what is here referred to as academic diplomacy: the use of academics in diplomacy for peace. Chapters 17 and 18 reproduce two such experiences of this author. The basis for involvement is the integrity of the researcher as a researcher. The researcher brings along insights, but also an approach that the warring parties may appreciate. The researcher is not siding with any of the parties and acts in a way that is parallel to both of them (and in some way reflects the teacher's impartiality in evaluating students). Let us consider this particular role somewhat further.

The peace researcher as a third party

Early on in peace research there were ambitions to have an impact on conflicts. The first approach seems to have been the one of creating seminars with the conflict parties present. These became known as *problem-solving workshops* (Mitchell and Banks 1996). The meetings organized by the diplomat and conflict researcher John Burton are often described as the first ones (Fisher 1997). This may be true if one takes a narrow definition of what such a seminar does. The Pugwash conferences, which began in 1957, did the same, but their concern was with nuclear disarmament and East–West relations. The first conference was convened in a small place in Nova Scotia in Canada – which gave its name to the whole movement – as there was a need for an inconspicuous venue in one of the few countries where nuclear scientists from the Soviet Union, UK, and USA could meet (Rotblat 1972). The importance of the Pugwash movement clearly surpasses many other attempts at focused exchanges and dialogue. It was the origin, for instance, of the Stockholm International Peace Research Institute (SIPRI), in 1966, but Pugwash participants also had important roles as advisors to significant decision-makers in the three nuclear powers at the time. Their scientific expertise gave them remarkable influence on arms control and disarmament treaties. The movement received the Nobel Peace Prize in 1995 in recognition of its achievements.

This is to say that researchers can contribute through workshops to connect different parties. This should also apply to conflict situations that involve ongoing or recently stalemated conflicts. Such workshops have been documented for some conflicts such as Cyprus, Lebanon, and Palestine. Fisher (1997: 187–212) estimated that at least seventy-six such workshops were conducted in the period 1969–1995, led by respected researchers, notably John Burton, Hal Saunders, and Herbert Kelman. Adding to the history of such meetings, arranged under the auspices of an academic institution and with the use of academic practices, the present author recounts the academic seminar convened outside Uppsala, Sweden, in June 1990 (Chapter 18).

However, what happened in June 1990 built on what had gone on before, which is presented in Chapter 17: *the researcher as an academic mediator*. Here is an area with even fewer accounts. Some are known for this, notably Professors John Paul Lederach and John Darby of the Kroc Institute, University of Notre Dame (see, for instance, Lederach and Wehr 1996). For confidentiality reasons many are unwilling to tell of their experiences. A predecessor was Adam Curle, a professor of education at Harvard. Curle and a colleague were involved in secret diplomacy in the Nigeria–Biafra war in the period 1967–1969 (Princen 1992: 186–214; Wallensteen 2011a). There are academic institutions that have been involved in such work, in addition to their regular tasks. The list includes not only the Department at Uppsala University or the International Peace Research Institute, Oslo (PRIO), but also the University of Notre Dame's Kroc Institute, George Mason University's Institute of Conflict Analysis and Resolution (ICAR), and activities based at Johns Hopkins University. In other words, there is more material on this than presently known and the topic is worth further study.

The particular contribution of such an academic mediator can be discussed. Academic skills can be useful in mediation situations. Such skills include an ability to listen and to distill points, as well as giving persuasive presentations, bringing attention to other relevant experiences, and drawing conclusions from theoretical insights. However, these are also qualities that others can exhibit. Svensson and Wallensteen (2010) studied the same mediator in six different situations over a thirty-year period to get closer to the craft of mediation. They found that the style of a mediator has an effect on process and outcome. The academic style may be closer to the seasoned diplomat of trying to persuade rather than forcing actors to agree, for instance. The problem-solving workshops seem also have had that as an ambition, stimulating communication among the participants. This is probably an important new challenge to mediation research (Lindgren *et al.* 2010). In political life, however, the use of force may be more common, and many agreements may in fact be the result of persuasion techniques far from the academic intellectual exercise.

Research on the researcher in peacemaking

Thus, we have pointed to two roles in peacemaking for academics: the use of the seminar to bring parties together and the use of the academics as mediators. There is some writing on the former, as has been indicated. There is much less on the latter. Whether this reflects the paucity of such involvements (which would be a sad state of affairs) or an unwillingness to give accounts (which in some instances clearly is the case, and is plausible) remains to be considered. However, as peace research comes of age, such experiences are probably also accumulating, and thus should now be increasingly possible to account for. The two situations described in Chapters 17 and 18 are now twenty years old and, thus, much of what happened can be explained without jeopardizing confidentiality, or creating peril for particular actors. It is only to be hoped that there will be more such accounts forthcoming.

What, then, is the impact that could be expected? Can the academic diplomat contribute something another could not? Certainly that is an overarching question and difficult to respond to. For a start it will require a typology over possible ways for an outside actor or third party to have an impact on a conflict (Wallensteen 2011a).

First, the third party can take a quiet or assertive approach, in consonance with "quiet diplomacy" (such as has been the approach of Curle and Lederach, as far as we know) or be more pushing for particular solutions the third party believes the parties can agree to (see the account in Chapter 17). This corresponds to a style of mediation that emphasizes a fostering or forcing approach (Svensson and Wallensteen 2010).

Then there are three elements in a conflict that need to be addressed: the parties, incompatibility, and the actions (Wallensteen 2011b). This element can be combined with the style dimension. This gives six possibilities:

1   *An assertive approach to the parties.* This involves the intricate question of which parties should be invited to the negotiations. A dilemma is how this can be done in such a way that one invitation does not mean another party will not attend. The academic mediator could take the initiative and invite parties to a particular event, trying to get them to connect, possibly outside formal negotiations, but as a complementary approach, and without making this a secret channel. The academic form can be convincing and make parties attend. An additional typical approach is for the third party to suggest an agenda for meetings and thus bring the parties to discuss the central issues in an academic setting.

2   *An assertive approach to the incompatibility.* This is a situation in which the third party specifies for the warring actors what an outcome could look like. The

example in Chapter 17 is the autonomy solution. Presenting this to the parties involves a risk. They may come to identify a particular mediator with a particular solution. It may also be the matter that moves the negotiations forward. The independence of the academic third party may here be an asset: he/she is not necessarily tied to the situation, but can take the risk of being excluded in later phases. Diplomatic negotiators may be more constrained by national considerations.

3   *An assertive approach to building confidence.* This would be when the mediator pushes for restrictions on the use of weapons, for instance, or a fully fledged cease-fire agreement, even helping the parties to work out the issues of monitoring.

4   *A quiet approach to the parties.* This means that the mediator is offering himself/ herself as an indirect channel of communication between significant parties, letting the parties control the flow of interactions, only making sure there is a flow. This is the facilitative approach that is often mentioned in the literature on mediation.

5   *A quiet approach to the incompatibility.* The academic mediator takes the role of a teacher or trainer, organizing seminars on particular solutions to the basic disagreement, thus hoping to enrich the parties on the possible options. Such workshops could be conducted in university settings away from the scene of conflict in order to give the participants a necessary detachment to explore particular options. It could be connected to a form of problem-solving workshop.

6   *A quiet approach to the actions.* This involves making the parties exchange information whereby they can explain their particular actions. The primary purpose may be to reassure the other side that specific measures are not meant to escalate a conflict. An example is to find ways in which the parties can reduce hostile propaganda.

Obviously each of these approaches involves decisions by the mediator. Where should a particular mediator put most of his/her efforts? It will depend on an assessment of the parties' willingness to engage. In the study of the six cases of mediation, it could be seen that one of the first tasks for a go-between when going in to mediation is to make just such an assessment. The mediator needs to ask himself/herself questions such as "What can I reasonably achieve during the time I am involved?" and "Do I know at the outset if there are areas of possible agreement among the parties?" The approach a mediator takes will be significant for the continuation of the efforts (Svensson and Wallensteen 2010). There is a need for more investigation in this field as well as in many of the others that we have dealt with in this volume.

References

Fisher, Ronald J. 1997. *Interactive Conflict Resolution.* Syracuse, NY: Syracuse University Press.
Lederach, John Paul and Paul Wehr. 1996. 'Mediating Conflict in Central America', in Jacob Bercovitch (ed.), *Resolving International Conflict: The Theory and Practice of Mediation.* Boulder, CO: Lynne Rienner Publishers.

Lindgren, Mathilda, Peter Wallensteen and Helena Grusell. 2010. *Meeting the Challenges to International Mediation*. UCDP Report 7. Uppsala University: Department of Peace and Conflict Research.

Mitchell, Christopher and Michael Banks. 1996. *Handbook of Conflict Resolution: The Analytical Problem-Solving Approach*. London: Pinter.

Princen, Thomas. 1992. *Intermediaries in International Conflict*. Princeton, NJ: Princeton University Press.

Rotblat, Joseph. 1972. *Scientists in the Quest for Peace: A History of the Pugwash Conferences*. Cambridge, MA: MIT Press.

Svensson, Isak and Peter Wallensteen. 2010. *The Go-Between: Ambassador Jan Eliason and Styles of Mediation*. Washington, DC: USIP Press.

Wallensteen, Peter. 2011a. 'Academic Diplomacy: The Role of Non-Decision Makers in Peacemaking', in Zachariah Mampilly, Susan Allen Nan and Andrea Bartoli (eds.), *Peacemaking: A Comprehensive Theory and Practice Reference*. Praeger Security International.

Wallensteen, Peter. 2011b. *Understanding Conflict Resolution*, third edition. London: Sage.

17 The strengths and limits of academic diplomacy

The case of Bougainville

The phone call in mid-January 1990 from the Bougainville branch of the University of Papua New Guinea (PNG) is short and crisp:

> Is this Professor Wallensteen? It is Graeme Kemelfield calling.
>
> Yes, that is me.
>
> We have read your article!
>
> Yes. . .
>
> We find it relevant!
>
> Oh!
>
> Can you come?

This unexpected call became the starting point of an intense involvement in a conflict in the South Pacific. It also sparked an interest in the use of peace research for practical diplomacy, with the advantage of a base in the academic community. It was an exercise in academic diplomacy for peace and security. The story that unfolded also illustrated a series of key concerns in mediation theory: the entry of the third party (who is inviting whom at what moment in time for what particular function), the process of third-party actions (what to do, when, how, and with what results), and the exit of the third party (when to end, how, and what happens then).

All these questions are challenging, and systematic information to answer them is only slowly being gathered. In 1990 the literature was highly limited (e.g. Touval and Zartman 1985; Azar and Burton 1986). There are now an increasing number of case studies, particularly on the Palestine conflict (e.g. Corbin 1994; Makovsky 1996; Kelman 1997; Bercovitch 1997; Zartman 1997; Aggestam 1999) and Sri Lanka (e.g. Höglund and Svensson 2002), and reports from participants in various peace processes (Bildt 1998; Savir 1998; Holbrooke 1999; Mitchell 1999; Egeland 2008). There are several volumes with comparative case studies (e.g., Zartman and Richardson 1997; Stern and Druckman 2000) and some systematic collections of data with analysis (Bercovitch 1996; Greig 2001; Harbom et al. 2006; Nilsson 2006, 2008; Svensson 2006, 2007).

Still, an eyewitness/participant account of a phase of academic diplomacy in Bougainville may have its particular value. The peacemaking in this conflict has attracted increasing attention, particularly following the peace agreement in 2001 (Rolfe 2001; Regan 2002; Boege 2006; among many others). The events of 1990, however, have not gained the same attention (Carl and Garasu 2002; Wallensteen 2005 has a little on this). Now, for the first time, I am providing a detailed account as such an invited third party, close to twenty years later, when some of the tensions may have subsided. It will draw some conclusions for mediation theory and ask whether such academic diplomacy does have a role to play: what are its strengths and weaknesses?

Entering the conflict

Through the work of the conflict data project in the Department of Peace and Conflict Research, I was aware of the land conflict in Bougainville. From a distance it seemed peculiar: the landowners were rebelling! Our thinking was normally geared to tenants and small farmers reacting against major landowners. In Bougainville it was landowners who took up arms against a major international corporation, Bougainville Copper Limited, a subsidiary of an Australian company, and against the government defending its mining operation. Bougainville was not only a beautiful island in the western waters of the South Pacific. It was also built on a geological formation rich in high-quality copper ore. Its beauty, I soon witnessed, was tarnished by tailings from the open pit mining that had gone on for fifteen years. It was one of the most lucrative mining operations in the world. Indeed, the mine was said to have earned back its initial investment in the very first year of production. However, there was a price: rivers and waters outside the river mouth were polluted, the fish had disappeared, and the mine was literally eating up the ground that had provided the income for the landowners.

The landowners had been paid by the early representatives of the company, but it was mostly men who had signed the deals, taken the money, and wasted it in the nearest bar. They did not mind, as they knew it was their wives, not they, who were the true owners. Bougainville has a strong matriarchal tradition and land was passed down from mother to daughter, while the boys, as one mother told me, "were married away in the next village." Thus, according to custom, the agreement had no value. However, PNG was applying Western laws and the PNG government – in distant Port Moresby on the main island – received its share of the copper income. Many in Bougainville felt cheated. The association of landowners had made specific but expensive demands, which went unheeded. This led some members to encourage the taking up of arms. An armed movement developed its own explosives by using some of the remnants from the major battle that went on between the Americans and Japanese in Bougainville, almost fifty years earlier, during World War II.

By January 1990 the conflict had escalated. There had been an attempt at indirect negotiations, but to no avail. The PNG government under Prime Minister Rabbie Namaliu was a coalition of several parties with different agendas. The balance had shifted toward a military solution and the government initiated a new offensive to crush the rebels once and for all. The rebels, now organized as the

Bougainville Revolutionary Army (BRA), were led by the mysterious and reclusive Francis Ona, who seldom participated in public functions, and his commander, Samuel Kauona, who was trained in Australia and had the bomb-making skills that BRA needed.

Thus, by January 1990, the conditions on the island had deteriorated considerably. The copper mine had ceased to function in May 1989. Many of the workers and others attracted by the strong economy of the island began to leave. To some extent they were pushed out by the Bougainvilleans, a form of "ethnic cleansing" clearly taking place, although the term had not yet gained currency. The government's campaign, however, misfired: the locals, whether supportive or not of BRA, felt harassed and abused by the PNG forces, who largely came from other parts of the ethnically diverse state. BRA gained new recruits, but was also pushed into the forests of the island. BRA began to argue for secession, developing plans to make the island an independent republic. This, in turn, made the national government even more determined to end the rebellion, fearing other parts of the culturally diverse state could follow suit.

In this situation, the local administration of the province, the North Solomons, found itself squeezed between the national government and the rebels. To find a way out, it formed a "think-tank" led by a university teacher, Graeme Kemelfield, originally from Australia, but married to a Bougainvillean. The think-tank had come across an article I had written on the conditions of conflict resolution. It got it from a former participant in a Sida (Swedish International Development Agency)-sponsored program at Uppsala University. They contacted International Alert, a nongovernmental organization (NGO) in London led by Martin Ennals, formerly Secretary-General of Amnesty International, who in turn gave them my telephone number.

Of course, it was a challenge to become a third-party actor in a difficult conflict. The think-tank had no money, but the Director General of Sida, Carl Tham, was willing to give me SEK 50,000 (about US$7,000) to go. I canceled my lectures in Uppsala and flew to the capital of PNG, where I arrived on February 10. It resulted in three weeks of very intensive diplomacy. The fact that an academic professor in peace from the other side of the planet unexpectedly had a key role drew attention, not least as some results were achieved. It gave me some insights into the strengths and limits of academic diplomacy.

The parties

The way I entered the conflict, as a complete outsider, with no experience in the area, from a neutral country that also had no record or particular interest in the region, and from a university which was respected and seen as a civil, nongovernmental institution, constituted three significant assets. Professors earned respect for impartiality but also for creativity and knowledge. A lack of national or business interest added to my credibility. A first question skeptics asked me was: Who is paying you? To be able to answer truthfully – that this was Sida – improved my standing, not the least since development aid carried high regard at this time, to some even implying the promise of future support. Thus, there was no suspicion among the parties in PNG against either me or my role, as far as I could determine.

The same day I landed in Port Moresby I was taken to the prime minister's office in one of the tallest buildings in the city. In fact, from the office, one could only see one taller building in the neighborhood. "That is the Australian High Commission," I was told, with an undertone of bitterness.

Prime Minister Namaliu outlined his and the cabinet's views of the Bougainville conflict. In condensed form this is what he told me:

> We want to end this conflict peacefully. We do not like seeing our own citizens killed. We do not like the bad publicity our country is receiving in the international media. We are a peaceful and diverse country. We want to open the copper mine again. The incomes are needed for Bougainville and for the country. Please, explain this to the rebels when you meet them. Everything can be discussed. But we cannot accept secession. That has to be clear. I inherited Papua New Guinea as a country of many peoples united as one state. That is the way I am going to hand over this state to my successor one day. I am not going to see a dismantling of the state.

In short, Prime Minister Namaliu outlined the principle of territorial integrity. It was not possible for him and his government to operate differently, he made clear. PNG, I was informed, consists of peoples with more than 700 different languages. If one area were to secede, others might want to do the same, particularly those with resources, leaving all the others in poverty. He could illustrate the point with recent riots in some gold-mining areas. To my direct question of whether some form of autonomy were possible, he did not rule that out. In fact, the constitution allowed for self-rule for different provinces. Bougainville, being the main part of the North Solomons province, already had considerable autonomy. "It even has its own Premier," he said. Certainly this was true; the decentralization that had been offered had been particularly well received in Bougainville. This, in turn, was the result of a short-lived declaration of independence that island representatives had made in 1975, when PNG became independent. A delegation had actually gone to the UN to demand recognition. A leader of that movement was now a representative of the province and had a seat in the government.

The issues were clearly stated by the government: end to the violence, a discussion on the opening of the mine, but also a discussion on the status of the island within PNG.

With this in the back of my mind, I flew to Bougainville, which was under a state of emergency. Nobody was allowed to visit without special permission of the government. This was all arranged. The think-tank, indeed, had prepared for this mission properly. It became very significant for what was to follow. The idea was originally that we were to be three, but the two others withdrew for various reasons. That left me as the lone outsider.

On arrival at the airport I was met by Graeme Kemelfield. When we set out for the university branch, we were stopped at a PNG roadblock. I began to understand the harassment to which ordinary people were exposed. The soldiers were arrogant, nervous, and not willing to accept the papers I had from their own government. Grim-looking, armed soldiers climbed into our car and we were driven off to the military headquarters. My luggage was searched and some papers on the Bougainville conflict were confiscated. It was not a promising start to a peace mission!

However, the security officer in charge was better informed. He apologized and listened to Kemelfield's explanation of our mission. Finally, he assured us that the Toyota Land Cruiser with the University of PNG emblem on its doors was allowed to pass through the lines, as far as the government side was concerned. However, some of the papers were not returned.

Thus, we arrived safely at the meeting of the think-tank, which consisted of some four additional persons with vast contacts across the island. Through informal channels they had already arranged a visit with BRA leader Samuel Kauona.

A day later, February 15, we set out to visit BRA-held territory. The PNG soldiers around the airport now made no difficulties; the university car could pass. We entered abandoned territory, passing an empty schoolhouse, and continued on the main road, where there was no other traffic but our vehicle.

Suddenly, we were stopped by a group of men with odd-looking weapons, including some old rifles. Most of them had no shoes, and they were wearing shorts and T-shirts (I recall one with the inscription "I love New York"). This was the BRA roadblock. The BRA soldiers were indeed a different crowd from the PNG forces. They were distinctly less well equipped, even demonstrating the slingshot as their "best" weapon. They were more black (it turned out they subscribed to the notion of "Black is Beautiful" and in fact called the PNG forces, which were drawn from other islands, "Redskins"). They were in a happier mood and welcomed us to their area. They climbed onto the car and gave directions to the drivers. We veered off onto smaller and smaller roads, until the road turned into a path. The car was hidden under the thick coverage of trees and brushes. "We are worried about the government's attack helicopters," they explained. From there on, we progressed by foot. My think-tank colleagues did not look worried, but I reflected on whether I would ever return to Uppsala.

The walk was not too long and we arrived at a camp, where the meeting was to take place. The military leader of the BRA, Samuel Kauona, appeared, smiling happily, offered a drink of coconut milk as a welcome, and we sat down for a conversation. It lasted for about four hours. He outlined his view of the conflict. In summary form, the following was his perspective:

> We do not want to fight this war. But we have no choice. The copper mine had destroyed our land, our waters, and our fish. The environment was deteriorating. By stopping the production, we have also stopped pollution. The fish are now recovering. We have ruled ourselves for 40,000 years. We have survived on our lands; we can continue to live by ourselves. We do not need the mining; we do not need the PNG government. The government only wants to destroy us.

He turned to me and asked a pointed question: "We hear on the BBC that Lithuania has declared itself independent. We understand that. Tell me, Professor, why do we have to be with this country [he meant PNG] which we have never asked to be with? Is that democracy?"

The position was very clear. He and the BRA did not want violence, they did not want the mine, and they did not want to be ruled by the PNG government.

Except for the desire to stop the violence, there was nothing on which he and the government agreed. The parties were in a situation where they had positions that entirely contradicted each other. The elements of conflict were obvious: there was fear on each side of what the other wanted to do, there were actions that underscored this, and the key issues seemed to be incompatible. Indeed, there was a need for a third party to look at the situation.

A third-party perspective

After his initial explanation of the BRA position, the conversation with Sam Kauona turned into a serious discussion on self-rule and independence. I told him of the Åland Islands, located between Sweden and Finland. It made him interested, not only because these were also islands, albeit distant. What interested him were the demilitarization and the autonomy of the islands. "We do not want armies in our land," he explained, although he had a military background himself in the PNG Defence Forces. Formally, he had actually deserted the national force to join the rebel movement: "We want to rule ourselves, but we are not interested in embassies in other countries or in the UN." I understood this to mean that, to him at least, island self-rule was the most important, not necessarily statehood as an independent republic. Much of what one could have as an independent state would actually be acquired with a sufficiently strong autonomy.

However, he was not interested in opening the mine again. Others around him were less resolute on this issue. Some actually indicated to me that they could accept mining production from the present mine (but no new mines) if it were under "responsible management." To them that meant it could not be under an Australian company. Other companies could be possible, one person confided to me, even hinting at the possibility of a Swedish one.

From my conversations with Kauona, it emerged that he could imagine a discussion on the key issues with the government. He even said "the sooner, the better." In his view, however, a third party had to be present. He would not trust the government. That had to do with the fighting: "There can be no talks as long as the government wants to wipe us out. The government has proclaimed a 'total war' against us. That has to stop!" In other words, a credible cease-fire was a first step.

Much peace research literature discusses the significance of cease-fires. There are too many examples of failed cease-fires. Either they are extremely short-lived (violations can occur easily, conditions can be unclear, and fears can linger) or they are very long-lasting (thus, in effect freezing a situation along military lines, as seen in the cases of the divided Korea and divided Cyprus). A cease-fire arrangement, in other words, has to be strongly coupled to a peace process, not a measure on its own.

However, Kauona was more concerned with the modalities of a cease-fire. It would have to include the withdrawal of the PNG Defence Forces from the island. He had no problem with the simultaneous disarming of the BRA forces. However, the cease-fire had to be supervised by the UN. The government, he made clear, could not be trusted. The idea of involving the UN, thus, was not to have inter-national recognition of the BRA, but to have someone observing the government. For me, it was not difficult to anticipate the government's objections to a UN presence: the conflict was a domestic matter, and the government was opposed to any internationalization of the issue. This was the common view in 1990, and few countries had yet accepted international involvement in domestic affairs. However, I explained to Kauona that the UN does not have its own forces, but has to call on countries to supply them. Which countries that would be acceptable then became an issue. In the end, the reply from the BRA side was "no countries in the region and only countries with a good record of human rights, such as Sweden, Norway, Denmark, and Canada." For some reasons BRA also wanted to include an African country; in the end, that became Ghana. Indeed, New Guinea was actually given the name by a European explorer who also had been in the Bay of Guinea in West Africa and saw a similarity between the inhabitants. However, in this context, Ghana was a symbol as it was the first black African country to gain independence from colonial rule.

The think-tank was pleased with the discussions and we set out to work on a cease-fire within a broader framework. I flew back to Port Moresby and explained what Kauona had told me. Prime Minister Namaliu was satisfied: autonomy could be discussed, as well as the mining operations. The cease-fire conditions, however, were more difficult: it would require making an agreement with "rebels" who actually had been breaking PNG law by taking up arms. The prime minister was willing to accept this, to improve the chances of peace, but other coalition partners were not. The government would have to have a special cabinet meeting. It was definitely not an easy decision.

A particular stumbling block was, not unexpectedly, the international observ-ers. The government did not want that, and during the discussions I could point to the situation in Nicaragua as an interesting "model." Certainly, the peace process in Nicaragua was not high on the minds of the PNG politicians, but the conflict was still well known. The Sandinista government had agreed to international observer missions of its national elections in early 1990, as part of a process of ending the civil war with the US-sponsored rebels, the so-called Contras. The formula was that the government invited the outsiders to observe the elections. Thus, I suggested, if the PNG government invites some countries to observe the cease-fire, this means the government using its sovereignty to do what it chooses to do. It is not an arrangement imposed from the outside. This formula was accepted, but the fact that there was a precedent was particularly convincing. The PNG foreign ministry was assigned the task of formulating the invitations to the governments that were agreed between the government and the BRA. Thus, two Swedish diplomats ended up in Bougainville in March 1990, in a mission led by a diplomat from Ghana.

From this experience I concluded that academic insights were useful and, in particular, could help to strengthen the role of a third party. By following different conflicts, ideas could be identified and their use in particular settings could be reviewed. Ideas are not tied to contexts. They are transferable, even globally. Ideas from the Åland Islands and Nicaragua were applicable in the South Pacific. Thus, academics not only served as impartial listeners, but could also inject proposals into a process. In this case, a central element was the autonomy idea. As the conflict continued, this element became controversial in its own right. I became identified with the autonomy proposal. As this was closer to some parts of BRA, BRA wanted me to continue as a third party. I had been useful also for Prime Minister Namaliu, who may have seen it the same way. To others, however, this became too active a role. They preferred, in later rounds of negotiations, to have third parties who were only observing, not suggesting. That, in my view, meant that the parties could not benefit from the value-added of a third party.

Secondary parties

Australia was the closest major country to Papua New Guinea. It had held control over the entire territory since World War I, when it took over the parts that had belonged to Germany (which included Bougainville, by the way). It was, however, not a regular part of Australia, but a mandate under the League of Nations (later a trust territory under the UN). That is why it was natural that a group went from Bougainville to the UN at the independence of PNG in 1975. It was the UN that "supervised" the trusteeship. Thus, it was to the UN that one could turn in times of crisis. However, the UN did not pay attention to the Bougainville situation until the mid-1990s. Australia may have had something to do with that. In 1990 UN action was still a farfetched idea.

Australia was the central secondary party to the conflict. It was the main provider of assistance to the PNG government. It was an Australian company and Australian management that ran the copper mine in Bougainville. It was Australia that had provided helicopters for the PNG Defence Forces (ostensibly not for aggressive purposes, but it was not difficult to use them to track down people on the ground). Thus, BRA saw Australia as a hostile actor. Also, the PNG government wanted to demonstrate its distance from the Australians. However, the reality was that Australia could not be ignored. It had to be on board. Thus, I went to Canberra to inform the Swedish embassy and it, in turn, told the Australians.

The ones most concerned about my mission and my doings in PNG, even baffled, were no doubt members of the Australian foreign service. One of them later said, in the blunt style that is typical: "We were really laughing when we heard the idea of a peace professor from Sweden coming to Bougainville. Now we have stopped laughing." I take that as praise. There was, however, no intention of having Australia directly involved in my and the think-tank's approach to the mediation. The idea that emerged was a different one that turned out to be fruitful: the Commonwealth.

The British Commonwealth had transformed itself into an international organization, the Commonwealth of Nations. PNG was a member, as well as some fifty other countries, many of which were smaller than PNG in terms of population. A Commonwealth member-state, Grenada, had been invaded by US forces in 1983. This had upset the leading member of the organization, the UK, and by 1985 a report on security assistance to small states had been worked out. It was accepted by the Commonwealth meeting in Nassau the same year. It meant that PNG could ask for assistance from the Commonwealth Secretariat for the crisis in Bougainville. This is what now happened, apparently one of the first times this mechanism was put into practice. The idea was that the Commonwealth would participate in the observation of the cease-fire. This, it was hoped, would make the Australians more comfortable with the development.

Thus, the contours of an ad hoc peace mission were gradually taking shape. It was to consist of a set of countries, as agreed by the primary parties, and the Commonwealth. It would be recruited primarily from the diplomatic corps in Canberra, as most relevant countries did not have a representative stationed in PNG itself. The mission was to go to the island to watch the withdrawal of the PNG forces and the disarming of the BRA.

Thus, the way the talks evolved in the Bougainville conflict made international participation inevitable. The BRA – like most other rebel groups around the world – could not trust the government. Indeed, that was the basic reason why they had taken up arms. The government, on its side, would not trust the rebels, as they were breaking the laws of the country. Thus, it seems quite obvious that an international participation in any agreement is the logical answer to the dilemma. The ad hoc arrangement for Bougainville nevertheless was one of the first of its kind. Both sides were nervous about the outcome and international presence helped to reassure them about what the opponent would be able to do. Thus, having secondary parties supporting the peace efforts was crucial for ending violence in March 1990.

The agreement

On my return to Port Moresby, I noticed that the communications between the government and BRA were about to break down. The think-tank members were traveling across the roadblocks with a tape recorder. Sam Kauona recorded his message; the officer responsible for the PNG forces on the island, Colonel Leo Nuia, responded. The idea was that the two would meet and sort out the many details of making a cease-fire. That turned out to be impossible. Neither side would be secure or could guarantee that their side could be prevented from attacking the other. My suggestion that they use new things called mobile phones (I even indicated the name of a leading Swedish producer that might be happy to supply the equipment) was turned down: "I can be tracked," Kauona claimed. Thus, the tape recordings were an appropriate solution. However, the two military leaders began gradually to shout at each other. The situation seemed critical. If there were no agreement on the cease-fire, there would be no continuation of the peace process. It now seemed crucial to find a way to connect the two sides directly. The prime minister wanted me to talk to Kauona. I suggested that he should also send a leading envoy. He agreed. The idea was transmitted to Kauona, who responded quickly and positively. On February 24, the think-tank members, the prime minister's special envoy, and I met with Kauona on the island.

The rain was pouring down and we were crammed into a small traditional house. The atmosphere was very tense. The BRA leaders were suspicious of having the "enemy" among them; the envoy was worried but brave. He said he had a message from the prime minister and he pulled out the tape. It was inserted into the recorder, but the machine refused to start. The batteries were dead. It was blamed on the rain. Frantic actions ensued. Soldiers and assistants were sent out in all directions to find batteries. The tension in the small house was almost palpable. Not having a functioning recorder was a failure for BRA. After some time, batteries started to come in. In the end we had a bag full of batteries. The tape recorder began to function and was switched on: only classical music! The BRA leaders stared at the special envoy: was this a joke? He tried to calm them: the message is hidden in the tape. Clearly, the government was worried about the tape falling into the wrong hands and wanted to conceal the message. The "fast forward" button brought us further into the tape. Suddenly, there was the message from the prime minister! The rain continued; all other movements ceased completely. The prime minister explained the role of the special envoy and of me. He went on to say that he had not proclaimed a "total war" on the rebels. They were all citizens of the same country. There had been a tradition of living in peace among the inhabitants on Bougainville and on PNG. He wanted to restore that. He was willing to discuss any grievances the listeners might have, and he wanted to conclude a cease-fire as a first step. To this end, his special envoy was authorized to cooperate with Professor Wallensteen and the think-tank to conclude an agreement. The prime minister also mentioned the need for a special peace ceremony to seal the deal. His voice disappeared and the music began again. There was a moment of complete silence. How were the guerrillas going to respond? In an instant, everything changed. They began to cheer and applaud. There were big smiles on all faces. Kauona ordered food to celebrate! The envoy looked relieved. Certainly I was. I had watched the men in the house as they listened attentively. They showed no reactions while the prime minister spoke. Now, the meeting turned into a major feast. Traditional foods were combined with more Western dishes. Drinks, yes, but no alcohol. The discussions continued. Darkness fell. But an agreement was worked out on when to start the cease-fire and how it was to be understood. The basics of a text were there, to be refined over the following days with the help of the think-tank and its computer. The cease-fire was to start at 6 a.m. on Friday, March 2, 1990. The PNG forces were to be withdrawn by March 16. BRA weapons were to be assembled in three places. Neutral international observers were to supervise the process. Following implementation of the cease-fire, negotiations were to start on the issues of the status of Bougainville and on the mining operations. The agreement was to be signed by the two military commanders, Colonel Nuia for the PNG and Samuel Kauona for the BRA.

Thus, we could leave the meeting in a good mood. We drew back toward the government lines. It was late. Actually, it was well past the start of the curfew. Thus, the fact that a car was approaching from the rebel side toward the government outpost drew considerable attention from the PNG soldiers. Our car was surrounded by a rowdy crowd of soldiers who spent the evening drinking and shooting their guns into the darkness. The prime minister's envoy introduced himself and explained to the commanding officer who he was. The officer just stared back and laughed: "Yes, sure, and I am Colonel Nuia!" The others around laughed and one soldier began to pull one of the think-tank members from the car. We held him back. The soldiers grabbed his glasses and took them. This was about to get out of hand. It was quite a contrast to the happy meeting with the BRA that had finished less than an hour before! Could the government really control its own forces? After further discussions a more senior officer appeared, noted our names and let us through. The special envoy was steaming, and I would later hear him report to the prime minister. He was shouting so that nobody around could miss a word.

There were probably more phone calls that evening, as we received an apology the next morning and even the glasses were brought back. But it was not a good sign. For me, however, it had been an unforgettable experience. It was also my twenty-second wedding anniversary!

The agreement was turned into an official document. The first version covered two pages, but that was too long. One of the parties insisted that it should be on one page: "If one page is covered by another, there might also be other hidden pages." The computer provided the technological ability to adjust the margins and font size, but some lengthy sections still had to be deleted. The government wanted the emblem of PNG to be on the document. I worried what the BRA would say, but the response was: "That is fine, it means the government has to implement it if it is on PNG letterhead." The agreement was completed, the commanders signed and Kauona spent some time walking around to his troops to explain what was now expected of them.

The impact of the cease-fire was immediate. Even before it was in place, the soldiers in the roadblocks began to relax. One told me that he now wished to go home as soon as possible: "We have no business here, they are very different from us, why should we be here?" The market opened up. Youngsters began to play football on the beautiful beaches that previously had stood empty. War and the fear of war have tremendous psychological impacts on all concerned. It is not a natural state of affairs for human life.

Exit of a third party

A day after the cease-fire I went back to Sweden. The government and the BRA expected me to return when negotiations on the real issues were to start. However, on the eve of my departure, an envoy from New Zealand came up to me in the bar of the hotel in Port Moresby. He said that the PNG security services were looking for me and that there were grumblings among the military about the cease-fire. It was probably wise for me to leave the scene, he indicated. He certainly was well informed. Also, he was to play a crucial role some seven years later. I was not too worried, however, as I had the support of the prime minister.

But soon some unexpected events happened. The PNG forces suddenly withdrew from Bougainville, before the international observers had arrived. Some remaining issues, notably on the stationing of PNG police on the island, had not yet been worked out. Deliberately, the head of the PNG military forces created a new situation. By mid-March the troops were assembled outside Port Moresby. There was considerable irritation among them about the withdrawal. After some drinking an unorganized military group set out toward the residence of the prime minister. They wanted to "talk" to him or, possibly, arrest him. Was it a military coup? It is hard to know. The responsible officer resigned the following day but, as is often the case in PNG politics, returned to power a year later, openly proclaiming his opposition to the 1990 cease-fire agreement.

The international inspectors noted that the Bougainville cease-fire had been implemented by the parties, although its report also remarked on the premature departure of the PNG forces. A strange situation now prevailed on the island. Instead of tension as a result of armed action, there rapidly developed a void of any authority at all. This was not what the peacemaking had been all about. Furthermore, the government was unclear how it should proceed. The problems with its own military were one part of it. Presumably there were also issues within the coalition and with parliamentarians. I was constantly adjusting my reservation for a return flight. But I was only asked to wait for the right moment. It never came.

BRA also felt that the situation was unclear. Why was the government stalling the start of the talks? Was it planning some drastic move? Increasingly concerned, but also realizing that the withdrawal of the PNG forces had provided it with an unprecedented opportunity, it moved. On May 17, 1990, it proclaimed the independence of Bougainville, formed a coalition "government" of its own and broke into the sealed storages to retrieve its weapons. The conflict took an entirely new turn. The government responded by cutting off all transportation, trade, and interactions with the island, in fact imposing its own sanctions and isolating Bougainville. No country ever recognized the new state. Smugglers appeared, coming to the islands, for instance from the nearby Solomon Islands. The isolation created hardships on the islands. Particularly devastating was the lack of medical supplies. Gradually the conflict returned to armed action, with the government landing troops and supporting splinter groups. There were repeated attempts to restart negotiations, but really significant efforts were only those that New Zealand organized in 1997 and led to the peace agreement in 2001. A basic trait of the agreement was a referendum on regional autonomy, within a ten- to fifteen-year timespan.

Lessons for mediation

In retrospect, one might say that the opportunity for negotiations was "ripe" in January and February 1990. The government had tried a military solution without success; the rebels had lost and were pushed back, but they were not defeated. It dawned on the opponents that the armed confrontation could go on for a long time. So there was an interest in negotiations. However, there were many similar situations in the following years that did *not* lead to negotiations. Furthermore, the think-tank that took the initiative started its work because the situation was deteriorating and it wanted to do something about it. It saw how the society around it was beginning to fall apart. It established the necessary relations, but without regard to the "ripeness" of the situation. The prime minister's perspective was probably similar. Thus, the offer of a third-party action provided an opportunity to pursue a different course of action, for a time.

For the members of the think-tank it was close to an existential issue to stop the war; for the government it was one of its options. The failure of this first peace effort also had a price. Many of the members of the think-tank had to leave the island. Graeme Kemelfield took his family to Australia, where he died some years later. He had tried to avert the danger, but the conflict unleashed a dynamic he could not withstand. It was symbolic that the only car that could pass the battle lines was torched and burned. The prime minister also had to leave office, but short tenures were the rule in PNG politics.

Thus, from this experience it is hard to say that a particular "hurting stalemate" either produces peace initiatives or is a necessary precondition for them (see the works of Zartman). It is more typical that peace initiatives always are needed, and that it is difficult to determine if the time is "ripe." It is to the credit of the think-tank that it was persistent and took the initiative. Indeed, the opportunity might not have arisen had Sida not been willing to support the endeavor.

Furthermore, in conflicts many issues are obscure and many actions difficult to understand, no less to control. As a third party I had some insight into the interactions between the two sides, but it was hard to know what was going on within each. For the different sides, their internal dynamics were probably highly significant. The prime minister had to keep his cabinet intact and survive challenges in the parliament. He also had to deal with a host of other pressing government matters. The relations between Sam Kauona and Francis Ona were elusive, not to say mysterious. The prime minister had a diverse coalition to manage, but the BRA also had many and undefined tensions: some wanted independence, others not; some wanted the mine to start, others not; some may have been in the war for family honor, others for loot and personal gain. Leaders on both sides feared being undermined by opposition from within. These are dynamics into which the outside third party enters: peace proposals, actions, and statements are evaluated by different factions in their particular light. However, the third party is not likely to have access to these deliberations. Both sides prefer to present a unified position to the outsider and to the opponent. The reality may never be entirely clear to any of those involved. What matters are the decisions that can be derived from the messiness of the situation. On March 1, 1990, there was agreement on some measures with clear real-world implications. In 1997 another truce was concluded. It still took another four years to advance from that shared decision to a peace agreement.

In the February 1990 discussions the idea was to couple the cease-fire to a sustained peace process. There was agreement on this. However, that could not be written into the cease-fire document. It dealt strictly with the conditions for ending hostilities. This fact may have indicated that there was opposition to a continuation of peacemaking within either or both sides. It was defended, however, with the argument that this was not a "political" document, only a military one, and thus to be signed by the military commanders, not the political leaders. It was presented as a technical document, which, of course, it was not. It meant that the two sides at least identified whom they were fighting and that they thought it would be possible to discuss issues with the other.

It was a most public process. To me, it is obvious that the agreement carried the support of the population at large on Bougainville. There was joy about the end of fighting. However, there were no spokespersons who pushed for continuation of the process. The think-tank and the North Solomons provincial government did, but there was a lack of popular manifestations. In Port Moresby, there was even less public support. The conflict seemed to concern only those displaced by the conflict and they were, understandably, hostile to the BRA. The government was more troubled by the fiscal implications of the conflict: to sustain a military force in Bougainville was costly and at the same time the copper incomes were lacking. The government had in fact appointed a "razor gang" to make deep cuts in government spending. If the fighting ceased, that saved money and, as a new mine was about to open up elsewhere in PNG, money would start coming in. Thus, a thorough peace agreement had few supporters in the capital. The peace process was left to a small group of concerned leaders and citizens. It is interesting to observe that by the end of the 1990s the situation had changed, not the least through the emergence of women's groups that pressed strongly for an end to the conflict. Peace processes without manifest popular support are likely to be more fragile and be more exposed to the wishes, hopes, and even whims of particular decision-makers who may act without accountability.

This means that individual third parties are not involved in a conflict for a long period of time. They are probably more useful under particular conditions, when there are possibilities of agreement. The very moment the opposing sides agree to receive a third party may be the optimal one. There is curiosity about what will now happen; the third party may bring in some fresh perspectives and thus bring about some changes in the dynamics. If it is successful, an agreement can be concluded. As time passes, however, conditions also change (new issues, new power constellations, new events on the battlefield, new policies among secondary parties, new economic developments). It is likely that a third party or third parties are most effective if he/she/they can ride on an initial momentum and thus bring about a movement in the conflict in a peaceful direction. After a while, that momentum is likely to be lost, and new injections may be needed.

Certainly, this is true when the third parties come from small countries, from NGOs, or from universities. The picture may be different if the mediator also has a vested interest in the situation and can bring power to bear. The line between a mediating third party and a self-motivated power-broker may then be blurred or even eradicated. Certainly, the USA took over a "mediating" role from Norway when the first agreement was signed between Israel and the PLO on the White House lawn in September 1993. The issue of peace became vital foreign policy for the Clinton administration. However, that turned into another type of peacemaking than the one that took place on the island of Bougainville in 1990. There are limits to academic diplomacy, but it also has its strengths. Some of those were demonstrated during some hectic weeks in February 1990.

A general note

This account is largely based on my own notes, memos, and recollections. Considerable information on the background of the conflict was available at the time from many researchers at the University of Papua New Guinea in Port Moresby. They were helpful in briefing me and sharing published and unpublished papers. The entire endeavor benefited from the tireless efforts of the members of the think-tank. They have not been consulted for this account. I remain entirely responsible for this text. Many thanks to Bill Montross for repeatedly reading this chapter and contributing to a more precise narrative.

References

Aggestam, Karin. 1999. *Reframing and Resolving Conflict: Israeli–Palestinian Negotiations 1988–1998*. Lund Political Studies 108. Lund: Lund University.

Azar, Edward E. and John W. Burton (eds.). 1986. *International Conflict Resolution: Theory and Practice*. Brighton: Wheatsheaf.

Bercovitch, Jacob (ed.). 1996. *Resolving International Conflicts: The Theory and Practice of Mediation*. Boulder, CO: Lynne Rienner.

Bercovitch Jacob. 1997. 'Conflict Management and the Oslo Experience: Assessing the Success of Israeli–Palestinian Peacemaking', *International Negotiation*, 2: 217–235.

Bildt, Carl. 1998. *Peace Journey: The Struggle for Peace in Bosnia*. London: Weidenfeld & Nicolson.

Boege, Volker. 2006. *Bougainville and the Discovery of Slowness: An Unhurried Approach to State-Building in the Pacific*. Occasional Papers Series 2006:3. Brisbane: The Australian Centre for Peace and Conflict Studies.

Carl, Andy and Sr. Lorraine Garasu (eds.). 2002. *Weaving Consensus: The Papua New Guinea–Bougainville Peace Process*. London: Conciliation Resources.

Corbin, Jane. 1994. *Gaza First: The Secret Norway Channel to Peace between Israel and the PLO*. London: Bloomsbury.

Egeland, Jan. 2008. *A Billion Lives. An Eyewitness Report from the Frontlines of Humanity*. New York: HarperCollins.

Greig, J. Michael. 2001. 'Moments of Opportunity: Recognizing Conditions of Ripeness for International Mediation between Enduring Rivals', *Journal of Conflict Resolution*, 45 (6): 691–718.

Harbom, Lotta, Stina Högbladh and Peter Wallensteen. 2006. 'Armed Conflict and Peace Agreements', *Journal of Peace Research*, 43 (5): 617–631.

Höglund, Kristine and Isak Svensson. 2002. 'The Peace Process in Sri Lanka', *Civil Wars*, 5 (4): 103–118.

Holbrooke, Richard. 1999. *To End a War*. New York: The Modern Library.

Kelman, Herbert C. 1997. 'Some Determinants of the Oslo Breakthrough', *International Negotiation*, 2: 183–194.

Makovsky, David. 1996. *Making Peace with the PLO: The Rabin Government's Road to the Oslo Accord*. Boulder, CO: Westview Press.

Mitchell, George J. 1999. *Making Peace*. New York: Alfred Knopf.

Nilsson, Desiree. 2006. *In the Shadow of Settlement: Multiple Rebel Groups and Precarious Peace*. Uppsala: Department of Peace and Conflict Research, Uppsala University.

Nilsson, Desiree. 2008. 'Partial Peace: Rebel Groups Inside and Outside of Civil War Settlements', *Journal of Peace Research*, 45 (4): 479–495.

Regan, Anthony J. 2002. 'The Bougainville Political Settlement and the Prospects for Sustainable Peace', *Pacific Economic Bulletin*, 17 (1): 114–129.

Rolfe, Jim. 2001. 'Peacekeeping the Pacific Way in Bougainville', *International Peacekeeping*, 8 (4): 38–55.

Savir, Uri. 1998. *The Process: 1,100 Days that Changed the Middle East*. New York: Random House.

Stern, Paul and Daniel Druckman (eds.). 2000. *International Conflict Resolution after the Cold War*. Washington, DC: National Academies Press.

Svensson, Isak. 2006. *Elusive Peace: A Bargaining Perspective on Mediation in Internal Armed Conflict*. Uppsala: Department of Peace and Conflict Research, Uppsala University.

Svensson, Isak. 2007. 'Bias, Bargaining and Peace Brokers: How Rebels Commit to Peace', *Journal of Peace Research*, 44 (2): 177–194.

Touval, Saadia and I. William Zartman (eds.). 1985. *International Mediation in Theory and Practice*. Boulder, CO: Westview Press.

Wallensteen, Peter. 2005. 'Conflict Prevention and the South Pacific', in John Henderson and G. Watson (eds.), *Securing a Peaceful Pacific*. Christchurch: Canterbury University Press.

Zartman, I. William. 1997. 'Explaining Oslo', *International Negotiation*, 2: 195–215.

Zartman, I. William and J. Lewis Richardson (eds.). 1997. *Peacemaking in International Conflict: Methods and Techniques*. Washington, DC: US Institute of Peace.

18 An experiment in academic diplomacy

The Middle East seminar 1990

The invitation

On June 27–29, 1990, a group of Israelis and Palestinians met under top-secret circumstances at the remote conference facility outside Stockholm. Although planned to be clandestine, the meeting created major headlines in Swedish and international media. In fact, the meeting was part of Swedish "quiet" diplomacy for a peace dialogue in the Middle East. It was probably the first time a Swedish academic department demonstrated its value in a sensitive diplomatic operation. It could have resulted in a sustained peace process, well before the Oslo Process became the designated main track in Israeli–Palestinian diplomacy during the 1990s. This is the first time that this episode has been described in English and thus available for a larger audience.

It was an experiment on many counts. Could "peace researchers" based in a solid university atmosphere really be useful for peace? Early on in peace research history, Johan Galtung had maintained that possibility, even at times arguing for "peace specialists" in the proximity of government. Was that just another Utopian idea? The "academic" connotations of a department for peace and conflict research made many practitioners uneasy: was there anything of practical use to come from such endeavors?

It was also an experiment for the researchers. Could it really be that they had something to tell people who know their own conflict from the inside out? Was it hubris to be involved? Was it stretching academic insights too far; should researchers really be involved in what might emerge from "cooptation" into political games they would have little chance of mastering?

And, for peace researchers, was there really the option of declining an invitation to contribute to peace, however elusive, in a conflict that had an impact not only on a region but on world affairs, being the world's most well-known crisis?

To me, having received the approach from the Swedish Ministry for Foreign Affairs, there was no option: we simply had to engage in this experiment and try to make sure of the best outcome, for peace, Swedish diplomacy, and academic integrity. Thus, this was a first experiment in academic diplomacy, trying to make the optimal outcome for all three considerations: peace, diplomacy, and integrity. The challenge was accepted and this is the story of what happened.

The setting

In December 1988, Yassir Arafat, Chairman of the Palestine Liberation Organization (PLO), made a path-breaking statement at a well-attended press conference in Geneva. This followed a turbulent United Nations (UN) General Assembly session. Because of his presence, the entire session had been moved out of New York as he had been refused a visa to visit the United States. Media interest was at its peak, making this Assembly session a significant occasion for a major announcement. The PLO, Mr. Arafat made clear in English, "rejects all forms of terrorism."

That was all; it took only a couple of seconds. A short sentence of historical significance for the conflict between Israel and the Palestinians. Still, it was the result of months of Swedish diplomacy. The statement had been carefully drafted. Once made, direct relations could be established between the US administration and the PLO leadership in Tunis, Tunisia. Within hours, the US responded favorably. In the Swedish strategy for a peaceful, negotiated settlement of the Palestinian question, this was the first step, to create a channel between the United States and the PLO. The issue of terrorism was central: if the general black mark on the PLO for being involved in terrorism could be removed, the US administration was willing to engage. Furthermore, the Swedish government maintained closed contacts with Jewish groups in the United States. Being well represented in Washington and in Israel, such groups were crucial. Also, Swedish foreign policy and social democracy were close to the Israeli Labor Party, a formative force in Israeli society. Thus, a set of interactions had been established where Arafat's statement was a key element.

The breakthrough in Geneva created expectations for continuation. Indeed, that was a reason for the PLO's willingness to entertain the idea of a statement. Secretary of State George Shultz was, however, on his way out, soon to be replaced with James Baker. That was not a problem, however. More problematic was that Israel was led by a Likud government, highly opposed to the idea of talking even to "former" terrorists. Swedish diplomacy persisted and that is why, in its plan, a peace research department could be a significant actor.

Let me give a bit of the peace research background. In 1985, I was appointed as the first professor of peace and conflict research at Uppsala University, a chair named after the late Dag Hammarskjöld. Through the department's conflict data project, which mapped all ongoing conflicts around the world, and through its educational program in conflict resolution, which made our work known in the region, I was called in as a third party to a conflict in Bougainville, Papua New Guinea (see Chapter 17 in this volume). This resulted in a cease-fire in March 1990. To my surprise, it created attention in Sweden, very distant from Papua New Guinea, of which Bougainville was a part. I was called to meet the foreign minister, Sten Andersson. To him and his Middle East team, the department turned out to be of value.

Creating the academic seminar for conflict resolution

I was approached by the top diplomats of the Middle East team, Mathias Mossberg and Anders Bjurner. Swedish diplomacy hoped to create a link between Palestinians and Israelis on a high level. Clearly, after the breakthrough in Geneva, there was disappointment with the lack of progress. I could surmise that this was also the PLO's position. Furthermore, Swedish relations with Likud were, to say the least, not intimate. In fact, Israeli prime minister Yitzhak Shamir had been part of the group that assassinated the Swedish Count Bernadotte, the UN mediator, in 1948 for the same conflict the world was still facing. The foreign minister was willing to make an attempt, however.

Our conversations resulted in agreement on an approach whereby an academic seminar was to be held on the situation in the Middle East with participation from the different sides. Israeli legislation at this time prohibited direct contacts between Israeli citizens and the PLO and, despite Arafat's actions more than a year before, Israeli law still branded the PLO as a terrorist organization. However, Israel encouraged its citizens to participate in international scientific conferences. Thus, having the department and Uppsala University as credible organizers of a scientific seminar would make possible Israeli participation. The strength of the department's research and its recent diplomatic experience demonstrated that it could perform a competent role in this situation. The foreign ministry was willing to undertake the experiment, and so was I, being at the same time the only professor and head of department.

However, to me it was important that the event be an academic seminar and that participants had academic credentials. This was a necessary element in our academic credibility and integrity. The seminar was not to be a public affair, but kept as a low-key, ordinary academic activity. It was also important to have a balanced composition. The seminar, thus, was to include three groups: Palestinians from the occupied territories as well as from the diaspora, including those in Tunisia; Israelis with political as well as academic backgrounds; and a group of "neutrals," that is, Swedish and American academics, including Jewish personalities who had been important for the breakthrough in 1988. From the department was also included PhD candidate Kjell-Åke Nordquist. I was the chair of the seminar. There was also a significant issue of the costs. Security provisions and the conference were paid for directly by the ministry, but all transactions relating to seminar activities and the participants were handled by the department and by Uppsala University. Certainly, this was based on a grant provided by the ministry, but invitations, communications, and scheduling were done by the university. The participants could demonstrate that they were participating in an academic seminar under the auspices of a leading university. Indeed, all procedures were conducted in the same way as any other scholarly conference.

There was, however, one disturbing factor outside the typical academic arrangement: the need for secrecy. There were security provisions, as the whole event or some of the participants could be targeted for attack. Media attention could either increase expectations or make some participants withdraw. Thus, I could not inform the university leadership too early. Neither my nor Norquist's family was informed where we were. In that way, when media learned of the meeting, family members could all truthfully say that they did not know. Strangely enough, the media never located the conference premises.

Conducting the academic seminar

Invitations were sent out in May 1990. At the end of the month a strange terror attack was carried out on a beach outside Tel Aviv. It was carried out by an Iraqi-based group, called PLF. Arafat delayed his condemnation. Sweden tried to influence Arafat by sending Mossberg to see him. When Arafat finally released a statement, it was general and bland. The United States was not satisfied. It wanted clear proof that the PLO really had renounced terrorism and violence against Israel. PLF was part of the PLO and Arafat's vagueness led President George Bush (Sr.) to break off contacts with the PLO on June 20, just a week before our seminar! The Swedish initiative found itself in a political twilight zone: if the United States did not have contacts, why would Israel? Fortunately, many of those invited did not reason that way. Rather, they reversed the argument: it was now even more important for some space to connect. This contributed to making the seminar a particular surprise, as President Bush was thought to have stopped all contacts.

On June 27, participants arrived at the Arlanda airport and were brought to the conference center. On arrival, the atmosphere was tense. All realized that the meeting had to be secret as there were security concerns. The most acute problems rested with the Israelis. Upon his departure from Israel, Knesset member Dedi Zucker had told the media that he was going to a seminar where Palestinians would also be present and that this was legal since it was in an academic setting. A spokesperson for the Israeli Embassy in Stockholm commented that his assertion would have to be assessed after the event. Thus, there were real uncertainties as to what would happen to the Israelis when they returned home, something that initially affected their posture. Other Israelis at the meeting were General Avraham Tamir, Ari Rath, the former editor-in-chief of the *Jerusalem Post*, and Professor Yohanan Peres from the University of Tel Aviv. All were at some risk but, at the same time, they were sufficiently prominent to be able to count on support from groups back home. However, the uncertainty added to the tension in the seminar.

The Palestinian side was in a happier mood. This was an important event to them. Many had been at official or private meetings in Europe but those often were arranged by various solidarity movements. This was a seminar on a high level at a crucial time. Two professors were among the Palestinians: Hanan Ashrawi and Sari Nusseibeh, both from the Bir Zeit University in Ramallah. The group also included Faisal Husseini (from a well-known Palestinian family) and editor Ziad Abu Ziad. Two persons were, so to say, official representatives of the PLO: Afif Safieh and Nabil Sha'ath. The "neutrals" consisted of Kjell-Åke Nordquist, Americans Drora Kass and Stanley Sheinbaum, and me. The Swedish diplomats kept a low profile and were seated not around the table but in the back of the conference room.

Thus, the composition of the meeting was balanced and had a clear academic profile. The delegates displayed strong intellectual capacities, spoke good English, and had considerable polemical capabilities, something the chair was to experience several times during the deliberations.

The seminar started immediately in the afternoon. A number of special measures were instituted to ensure that the Israeli participants would not have problems with their authorities upon their return. All delegates had special seats at the table. No Israeli was placed next to someone connected to the PLO office in Tunis or in any other way being an official representative of the PLO. To avoid the creation of camps, all participants were seated in alphabetical order, as far as it was possible. The idea was that the seminar would lead to an open discussion among all participants, not a negotiation between two "sides." The "neutral" participants were distributed strategically so as to make the mix complete.

Being chair, I declared that everybody was present in a private capacity and that nobody could be quoted outside the conference without permission. I emphasized that this was an academic seminar, which meant that the right to try ideas freely and to exchange proposals without necessarily being tied to them was both cherished and protected. The purpose of the seminar was to present possible visions for a solution to the Palestinian conflict and suggest concrete steps for the immediate future. A particular instruction was that participants not address themselves directly or explicitly to the PLO. Again, this was a measure to protect the Israeli participants. If someone wanted to convey a message to the PLO, the person was to address the chair. This instruction had the effect of making everyone quiet each time an Israeli participant said "Mr. Chairman" as it might imply a message to the PLO!

To improve the atmosphere and create some personal connections, I suggested that the participants introduce not themselves but rather their neighbor to the left: "The solution is about getting to know your neighbor." This message created some confusion in a group of strong personalities accustomed to presenting themselves eloquently. However, they followed the instructions, which resulted in intensive discussions from the outset of the meeting. Some were more ambitious than others and carefully noted personal facts about their neighbor, which they could spring on the audience when their turn came up. In fact, the presentations came to include surprising information and led to a lot of laughter around the table.

General Tamir sat next to Faisal Husseini. I cannot recall how this happened, as it broke the alphabetical order. Husseini was not a member of the PLO so there was no potential legal problem on that account. The two talked intensively and for a long time. Faisal had already been in Israeli prisons twenty-seven times and had used the time to learn Hebrew. Tamir, customarily called "Avracha," was very engaged in their dialogue and he made a short, memorable statement instead of introducing his neighbor: "I took part in the planning of the occupation of the West Bank in 1967. I remember why we were doing this: to exchange land for peace. I do not understand why we don't do that." With military precision he had identified the central question and opened it up for a discussion.

One of the key contributions was by the political scientist Yohanan Peres. He had investigated changes in public opinion in Israel during the Intifada. The Palestinian uprising had started in December 1988 and surprised both Israel and the PLO in Tunis. With graphs and tables Peres demonstrated that the largely peaceful revolt had strongly affected opinion toward seeing Palestinians as a national grouping and someone to negotiate with. His presentation gave rise to a host of comments. The other Israelis concurred in his conclusions. The Intifada had given Palestinians a new identity in the eyes of Israelis. They were no longer seen as either weak and subdued or highly dangerous airplane hijackers. To many Palestinian participants this was hopeful as they previously thought the Intifada had achieved nothing, particularly as the links to the United States had just been suspended.

The impact of the Intifada, several of the delegates suggested, was that the "demonization" of Palestinians had given way. Palestinians were seen more as "ordinary human beings." This turned into one of the strongest experiences during the seminar. To maintain such a more nuanced Israeli view of Palestinians, many felt, would be important for peace negotiations.

The data also suggested that the Israeli public distinguished between Palestinians on the West Bank and those in Tunis. It was interesting to see this difference also appearing during the seminar. Those who had daily encounters with the Israeli occupation had different experiences of Israel. They were more knowledgeable about the Israeli political landscape and were not dismissive of differences between Israeli political parties. They could see divergences on the opposite side and understood the value of it from their point of view.

However, the seminar also made clear that there were limits. Palestinian demands that peace-oriented Israelis reject soldiers serving in the occupied areas received strong protests. "This is interference in our internal affairs!" one Israeli shouted. "If you come with such demands, we have no chance to carry them out, but if *we* raise them by ourselves they have a greater chance," said another, once the situation had calmed down. There were political dynamics on each side that the outsiders had to understand in order to avoid hurting the prospects for peace.

The Swedish foreign minister, Sten Andersson, visited the seminar in the evenings. What was discussed, I do not know. There were long, nightly calls to Tunis, where the PLO leadership was informed by Palestinian participants on our deliberations. Was this possibly the beginning of a "Stockholm channel" directly connecting Israeli citizens and Palestinian citizens, without US involvement? The boat excursion that was arranged in the pleasant Swedish summer night gave additional space for confidential conversations. In fact, few participants seemed to notice the beautiful archipelago they traveled through!

The seminar ended with a whiteboard full of ideas on ways forward. Economic visions played a major role. The idea was that the economic integration would yield benefit, not least to the Israeli side, and thus make it more willing to accept a two-state solution. The costs of occupation would be replaced by the gains of economic cooperation. The income gap between the two populations would be reduced, and so would political tensions. Thus, the seminar discussed the opening of transportation routes, harbors, airports, shared free trade zones, and so on. At the core was a mutual recognition of Israel's existence and the Palestinian people as legitimate parties. The Intifada appeared to have created a basis for mutual acceptance. The Palestinians were prouder, Israelis were more uncomfortable in their role as occupiers. The enthusiasm at the end of the seminar was remarkable and contrasted dramatically with the initial hesitation. There were expectations of additional meetings. Many issues had been discussed, which was important in itself, but no solutions had been worked out. Confidence had been created and telephone numbers exchanged.

The end of one beginning

During the month of July we learned how the participants were in touch with each other and how the circles of involved people had widened. There seemed to be a momentum. The Israelis were exposed to questioning by the police on their return, but nobody faced legal consequences. The political situation in Israel remained a stalemate. The government was dissolved, but the Labor party could not form a government on its own.

Iraq's occupation of Kuwait in August 1990 was a political disaster also for continued contacts. Kuwait was integrated into Iraq and Saddam Hussein declared that this was the beginning of the liberation of Palestine. To the consternation of many seminar participants, young Palestinians were celebrating. Many of the young seemed to miss the lack of logic, or the dangers in Saddam's action. The Iraqi leader had not only acted like Israel, but even gone one step further by annexing the territory of another country. How could this be described as the beginning of the liberation of Palestine?

The PLO found itself in a political dilemma. Arafat spent considerable time in Baghdad. He was obviously close to Saddam and seems to have believed in Saddam's interest in a negotiated solution to the Kuwait crisis. The PLO decided to remain "neutral" in the conflict. As most of the Arab world was against Iraq, the PLO found itself in a small pro-Iraqi camp. It lost support, economically as well as politically. The PLO was weakened by its own actions.

The negative image of Palestinians gained in Israeli public opinion. A new "demonization" gripped the Israelis. Young Palestinians celebrating when Iraqi missiles hit Israeli cities in 1991 contributed to the image. The PLO lost its space for negotiations; its options were shrinking. However, the American–Soviet conference that was convened in Madrid in 1991 had an impact. Many of those who had been at the academic seminar now appeared as articulate spokespersons. Hanan Ashrawi and Faisal Husseini were part of a Jordanian–Palestinian delegation and could give media a new picture of responsible and responsive Palestinians. There was a de-demonization among international and American media, if not among the Israeli public. The Swedish efforts may have helped to convey such a more nuanced picture to some American decision-makers.

The change of government in Sweden in September 1991, secret meetings in Oslo from late 1992, and the first agreement between Israel and the PLO in September 1993 changed the dynamics of the conflict. There was no direct follow-up from the academic seminar, even if there were initiatives and attempts. The Oslo Process became the main track for peace in the Middle East for the remainder of the 1990s.

The experiment and its limits

The academic seminar proved to be a useful umbrella for direct talks. It served as a way to enhance confidence among the parties. It gave a chance for free and safe interaction. This is a lasting positive experience. In fact, the Oslo Process also used an academic setting for its initial efforts, ostensibly as part of an academic project on living conditions on the West Bank.

However, for a protracted conflict with many interlocking and interblocking interests, academic input is not sufficient. There has to be an interest among the major actors to move in the same direction. Mediators cannot get warring parties to make concessions beyond their own set parameters. The mediator, as well as the academic seminar, can shed new light on known situations. Comparisons with other peace processes can stimulate the primary actors to think differently. In the end, however, they are the ones that have to bear the responsibility for making peace.

The academic seminar as well as the Oslo Process began at an appropriate moment. There was a window of opportunity created by the first Intifada. The second Intifada that broke out in October 2000 did not have the same impact as its less violent predecessor. The second Intifada was more bloody and more polarizing. It actually divided the Palestinians more than it did the Israelis. The Israeli wall separated Palestinian areas, made negotiations more complicated, and resulted in greater hopelessness on the Palestinian side. The Palestinian elections of 2006 were carried out in a remarkably democratic fashion during conditions of occupation, but the results provided further complications. Hamas had been outside all peace processes during the 1990s. Its short-lived Palestinian government found itself in the same situation as the PLO before 1988. Hamas now had to respond to the same questions that the PLO struggled with twenty years earlier. Hamas today finds itself in the same unsatisfactory position of vague statements that previously were the hallmark of the PLO. Controlling Gaza since 2007 has not given Hamas an easier relationship, either with the PLO or with Israel. The Israeli attack on Gaza around New Year 2009 appears not to have strengthened Hamas's long-term standing among Palestinians in general but made it more important for Hamas to maintain control over Gaza. The gap between the two Palestinian factions has widened, rather than been bridged.

Furthermore, the Oslo Process did not involve Hamas and was, in fact, run along almost entirely secular lines. The outcomes were difficult to explain to rabbis, clergy, and imams. Such a primarily secular approach may not be possible today. Even if the issues remain the same, the rise of religious political actors on both sides makes the issues change as well. Framing has changed, and the peace process has to be pursued in a different way.

The experiment with the academic seminar in 1990 gave many lessons, and brought the Department of Peace and Conflict Research at Uppsala University into a new reality. It became involved in a number of peacemaking efforts during the following years. Thus, it made its brand of peace research become a form of peace activity, in which academic insights proved to be useful for decision-makers, whether in government or in nongovernmental organizations.

The experiment combined peace, diplomacy, and integrity. Indeed, the academic integrity was intact and was a basis for the entire experiment. If anything it was strengthened. Diplomacy was difficult, but the academics could do well on that score too. However, academics cannot be full-time diplomats. Peace was more elusive. It is in the hands of the primary parties, who are likely to pursue more narrow concerns: their own power, prestige, and personal survival. Peace is a "good" but not always sufficiently "good" to rally all parties to do the utmost to resolve the conflict. Short-term political consideration are often the priority, but this is serious when a vision for a settlement is needed the most. In 2017 the conflict will have continued a full century. It is time to replace the Balfour Declaration with a real peace agreement. The academic seminar can – and should – help to address some of these concerns even if the ultimate power lies elsewhere. Academics cannot – and should not – say "no" when an opportunity emerges to try to do something that may improve the chances of peace for all.

Selected bibliography for further reading

Evolution of peace research

Höglund, Kristine and Magnus Öberg (eds.). 2011. *Understanding Peace Research*. London: Routledge.

Galtung, Johan. 1996. *Peace by Peaceful Means: Peace and Conflict, Development and Civilization*. London: Sage.

Machiavelli, Niccolo. 1975. *The Prince*. Translated by George Bull. Rev. ed. Harmondsworth: Penguin Books.

More, Thomas. [1516] 1997. *Utopia*. Mineola, NY: Dover Publications.

Singer, J. David. 1989. 'The Making of a Peace Researcher', in James Rosenau and Joseph Kruzel (eds.), *Journeys through World Politics*. Lexington, MA: Lexington Books.

Tickner, J. Ann. 1992. *Gender in International Relations: A Feminist Perspective on Achieving Global Security*. New York: Columbia University Press.

Wallensteen, Peter (ed.). 1988. *Peace Research: Achievements and Challenges*. Boulder, CO: Westview.

Causes of war and global governance

Brown, Michael E., Owen R. Coté, Jr. Sean M. Lynn-Jones and Steven E. Miller. 1998. *Theories of War and Peace*. Cambridge, MA: The MIT Press.

Geller, Dan and J. David Singer. 1998. *Nations at War: A Scientific Study of International Conflict*. Cambridge: Cambridge University Press.

Malone, David. 2004. *The UN Security Council: From the Cold War to the 21st Century*. Boulder, CO: Lynne Rienner Publishers.

Melander, Erik. 1999. *Anarchy Within: The Security Dilemma between Ethnic Groups in Emerging Anarchy*. Uppsala: Department of Peace and Conflict Research, Uppsala University.

A More Secure World: Our Shared Responsibility. The Secretary-General's High-Level Panel Report on Threats, Challenges and Change. 2004. New York: The United Nations.

Morgan, Patrick M. 2006. *International Security: Problems and Solutions*. Washington, DC: Quarterly Press.

Ohlson, Thomas. 1998. *Power Politics and Peace Policies: Intra-State Conflict Resolution in Southern Africa*. Uppsala: Department of Peace and Conflict Research, Uppsala University.

Rittberger, Volker, Bernhard Zangl and Matthias Staisch. 2006. *International Organization: Polity, Politics and Policies*. New York: Palgrave Macmillan.

Russett, Bruce M. 1993. *Grasping the Democratic Peace: Principles for a Post-Cold War World*. Princeton, NJ: Princeton University Press.

Russett, Bruce M. (ed.). 1997. *The Once and Future Security Council*. London: Macmillan.

Russett, Bruce M. and Oneal, John R. 2001. *Triangulating Peace: Democracy, Interdependence, and International Organizations*. New York: W.W. Norton.

Sarkees, Meredith Reid and Frank Wayman. 2010. *Resort to War 1816–2007*. Washington, DC: CQ Press.

Senese, Paul D. and John A. Vasquez. 2008. *The Steps to War: An Empirical Study*. Princeton, NJ: Princeton University Press.

Singer, J. David (ed.). 1979. *The Correlates of War, vol. I: Research Origins and Rationale*. New York: Free Press.

Sorokin, Pitirim A. 1937. *Social and Cultural Dynamics, vol. 3*. New York: American Book Company.

Vasquez, John A. (ed.). 2000. *What Do We Know about War?* Lanham, MD: Rowman & Littlefield.

Wright, Quincy. 1942. *A Study of War*. Chicago: University of Chicago Press. Second edition 1965.

Conflicts and conflict resolution

Ballantine, Karen and J. Sherman. 2003. *The Political Economy of Armed Conflict: Beyond Greed and Grievance*. Boulder, CO: Lynne Rienner.

Bercovitch, Jacob and R. Jackson. 1997. *International Conflict: A Chronological Encyclopedia of Conflicts and Their Management*. Washington, DC: Congressional Quarterly.

Bercovitch, Jacob, Victor Kremenyuk and I. William Zartman. 2009. *The Sage Handbook on Conflict Resolution*. London: Sage Publications.

Berdal, Mats and David M. Malone. 2000. *Greed and Grievance: Economic Agendas in Civil Wars*. Boulder, CO: Lynne Rienner.

Collier, Paul. 2009. *Wars, Guns and Votes: Democracy in Dangerous Places*. London: HarperCollins.

Collier, Paul, Lani Elliott, Håvard Hegre, Anke Hoeffler, Marta Reynal-Querol and Nicholas Sambanis. 2003. *Breaking the Conflict Trap: Civil War and Development Policy*. Washington, DC: World Bank.

Crocker, Chester A., Pamela R. Aal and Fen Osler Hampson. 2001. *Turbulent Peace: The Challenges of Managing International Conflict*. Washington, DC: USIP Press.

Darby, John and Roger MacGinty. 2003. *Contemporary Peacemaking: Conflict, Violence and Peace Processes*. Basingstoke: Palgrave.

Fortna, Virginia Page. 2004. *Peace Time: Cease-Fire Agreements and the Durability of Peace*. Princeton, NJ: Princeton University Press.

Gurr, Ted R. 2000. *Peoples versus States: Minorities at Risk in the New Century*. Washington, DC: United States Institute of Peace.

Hampson, Fen Osler. 1996. *Nurturing Peace: Why Peace Settlements Succeed or Fail*. Washington, DC: United States Institute of Peace.

Höglund, Kristine. 2008. *Peace Negotiations in the Shadow of Violence*. Leiden: Brill Academic Publishers.

Kaldor, Mary. 1999. *New and Old Wars*. Stanford, CA: Stanford University Press.

Kostic, Roland. 2007. *Ambivalent Peace: External Peace-Building Threatened Identity and Reconciliation in Bosnia and Herzegovina*. Uppsala: Department of Peace and Conflict Research, Uppsala University.

Miall, Hugh, Oliver Ramsbotham and Tom Woodhouse. 2005. *Contemporary Conflict Resolution*, 2nd edition. Cambridge: Polity Press.

Mitchell, Christopher R. 1981. *The Structure of International Conflict*. New York: St. Martin's Press.

Olsson, Louise. 2009. *Gender Equality and United Nations Peace Operations in Timor Leste*. Leiden, Netherlands: Martinus Nijhoff.

The Responsibility to Protect. Report of the International Commission on Intervention and State Sovereignty. 2001. Ottawa: International Development Research Centre.

Stedman, Stephen John, Donald Rothchild and Elizabeth M. Cousens. 2002. *Ending Civil Wars: The Implementation of Peace Agreements*. Boulder, CO: Lynne Rienner.

Touval, Saadia and I. William Zartman (eds.). 1985. *International Mediation: Theory and Practice*. Boulder, CO: Westview.

Wallensteen, Peter. 2011. *Understanding Conflict Resolution: War, Peace and the Global System*, 3rd edition. London: Sage.

Walter, Barbara. 2001. *Committing to Peace: The Successful Settlement of Civil Wars*. Princeton, NJ: Princeton University Press.

Conflict prevention and international sanctions

Ackermann, A. 2000. *Making Peace Prevail: Preventing Violent Conflict in Macedonia*. Syracuse, NY: Syracuse University Press.

Carment, D. and A. Schnabel. 2003. *Conflict Prevention: Paths to Peace or Grand Illusion?* Tokyo: United Nations University Press.

Carnegie Commission. 1997. *Preventing Deadly Conflict*. Final Report. Washington, DC: Carnegie Commission on Preventing Deadly Conflict.

Cortright, David and George Lopez. 2000. *The Sanctions Decade: Assessing UN Strategies in the 1990s*. New York: International Peace Academy.

Hamburg, David. 2002. *No More Killing Fields: Preventing Deadly Conflict*. Lanham, MD: Rowman & Littlefield.

Jentleson, B.W. 2000. *Opportunities Missed, Opportunities Seized: Preventive Diplomacy in the Post-Cold War World*. Lanham, MD: Rowman & Littlefield.

Lund, Michael S. 1996. *Preventing Violent Conflicts: A Strategy for Preventive Diplomacy*. Washington, DC: United States Institute of Peace Press.

Malone, David and Fen Osler Hampson. 2001. *From Reaction to Conflict Prevention: Opportunities for the UN System*. New York: The International Peace Academy.

Wallensteen, Peter (ed.). 1998. *Preventing Violent Conflicts: Past Record and Future Challenges*. Uppsala: Department of Peace and Conflict Research, Uppsala University.

Wallensteen, Peter and Carina Staibano. 2005. *International Sanctions: Between Words and Wars in the Global System*. London: Frank Cass.

Mediation, academic diplomacy and peacebuilding

Doyle, Michael and Nicholas Sambanis. 2006. *Making War and Building Peace*. Princeton, NJ: Princeton University Press.

Holbrooke, Richard. 1999. *To End a War*. New York: Modern Library.

Lederach, John Paul. 1997. *Building Peace: Sustainable Reconciliation in Divided Societies*. Washington, DC: United States Institute of Peace.

Mitchell, George J. 1999. *Making Peace*. New York: Knopf.

Paris, Roland. 2004. *At War's End: Building Peace after Civil Conflict*. Cambridge: Cambridge University Press.

Philpott, Daniel and Gerard F. Powers (eds.). 2010. *Strategies of Peace*. Oxford: Oxford University Press.

Svensson, Isak and Peter Wallensteen. 2010. *The Go-Between: Jan Eliasson and the Styles of Mediation*. Washington, DC: US Institute of Peace Press.

Index